RED LIGHT

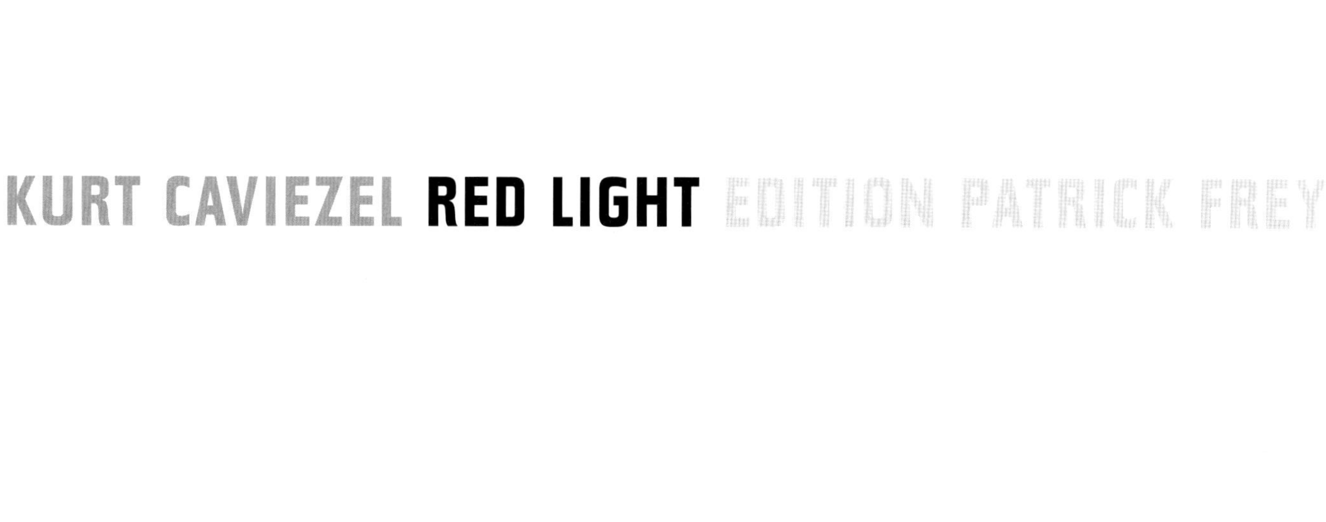

KURT CAVIEZEL **RED LIGHT** EDITION PATRICK FREY

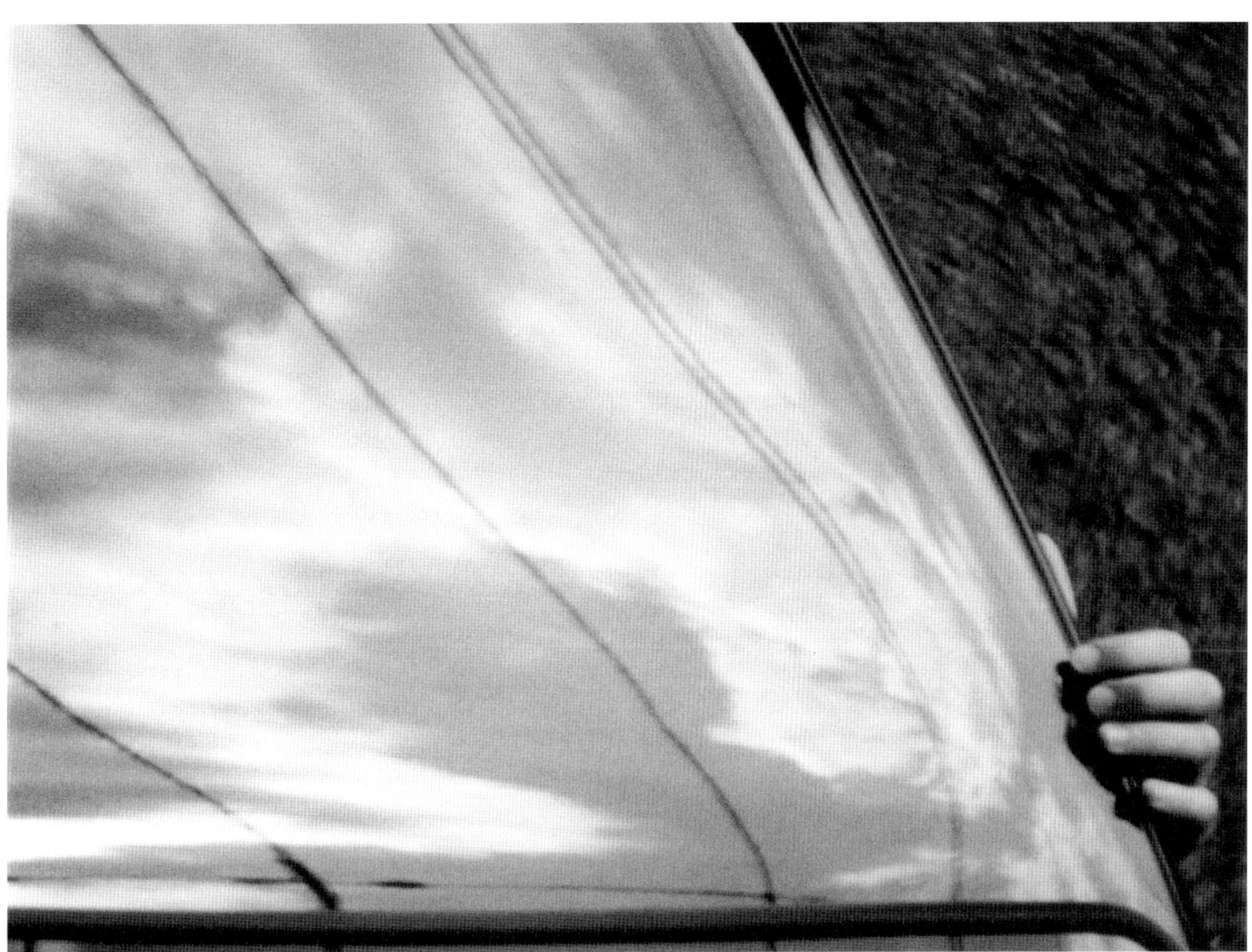

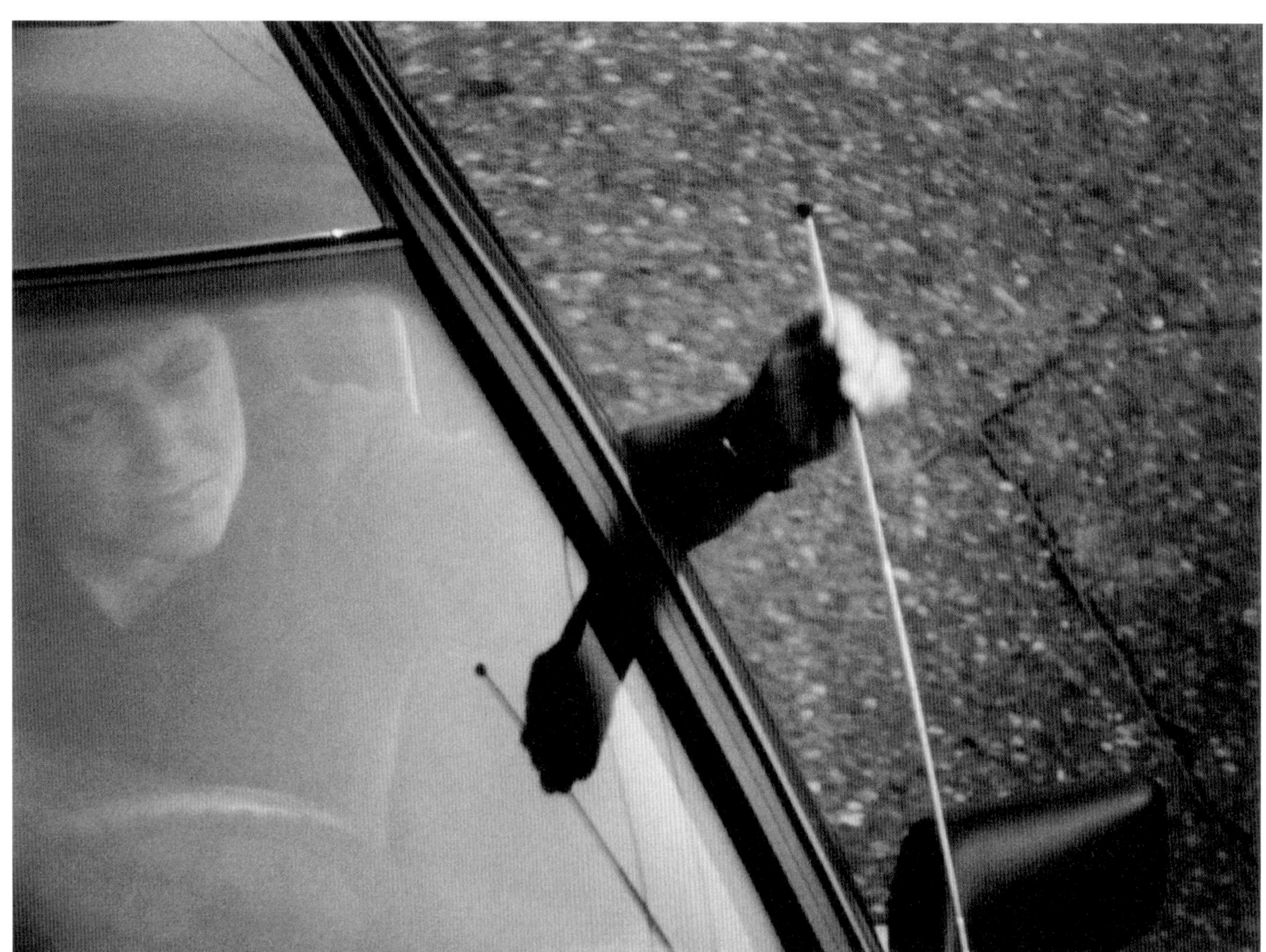

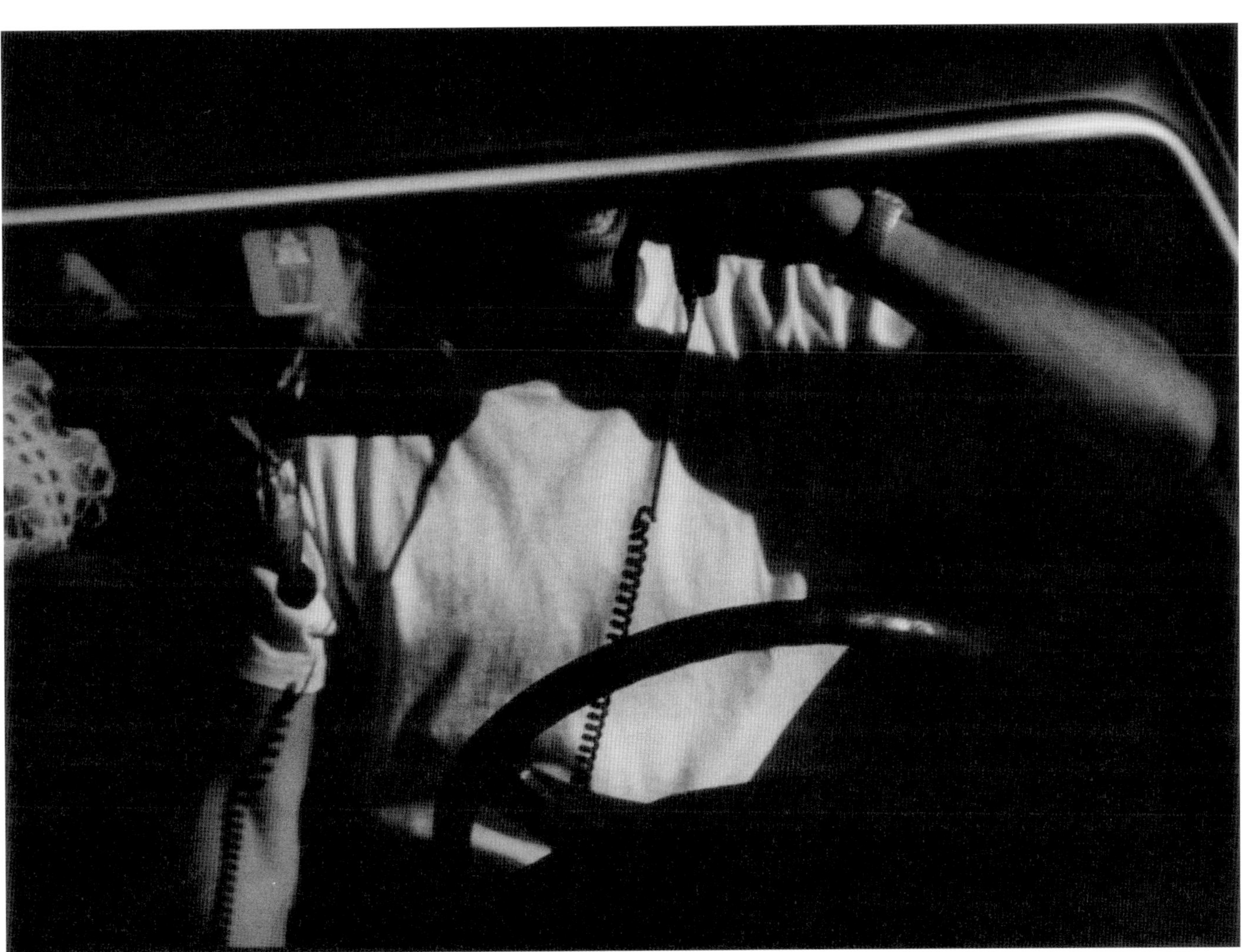

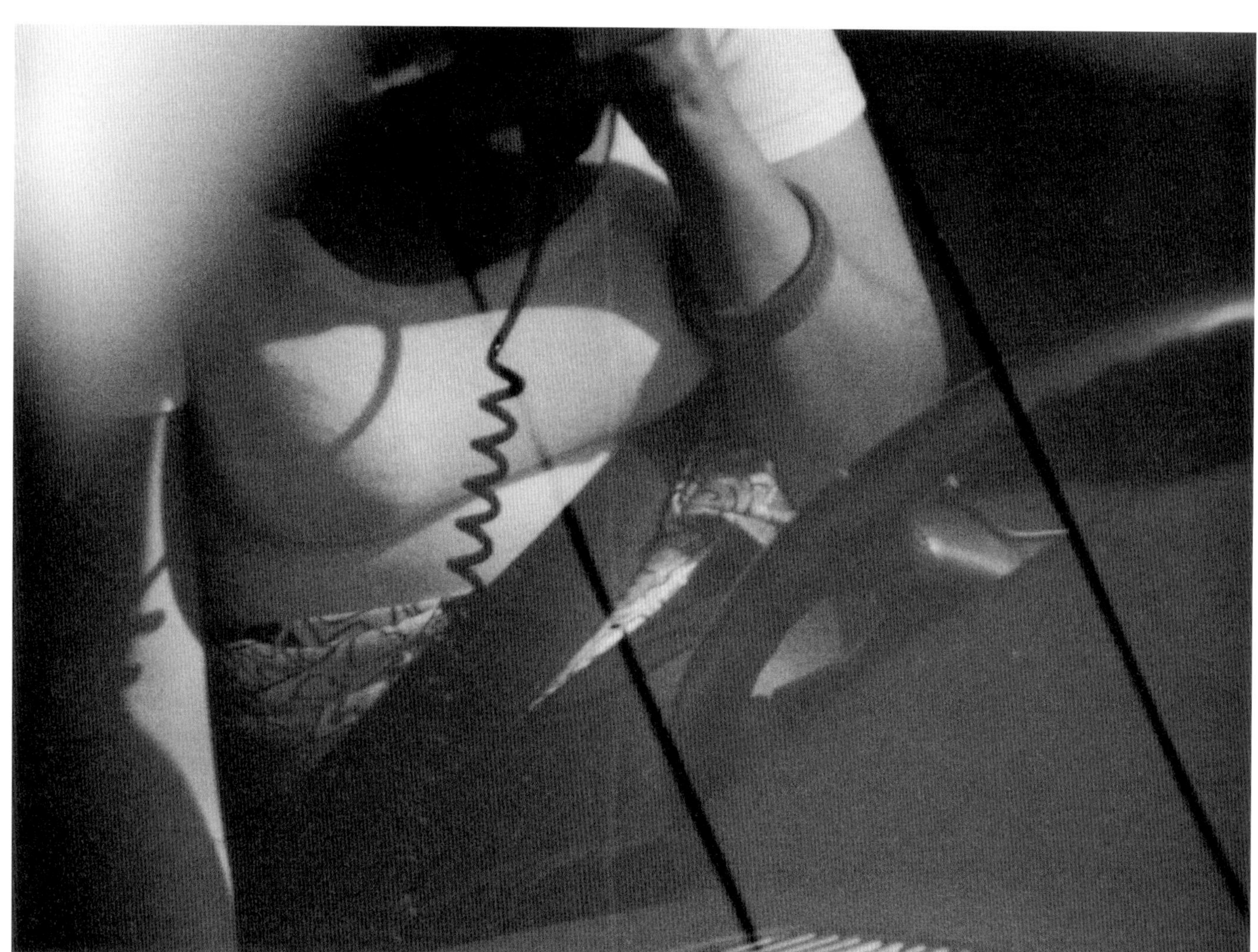

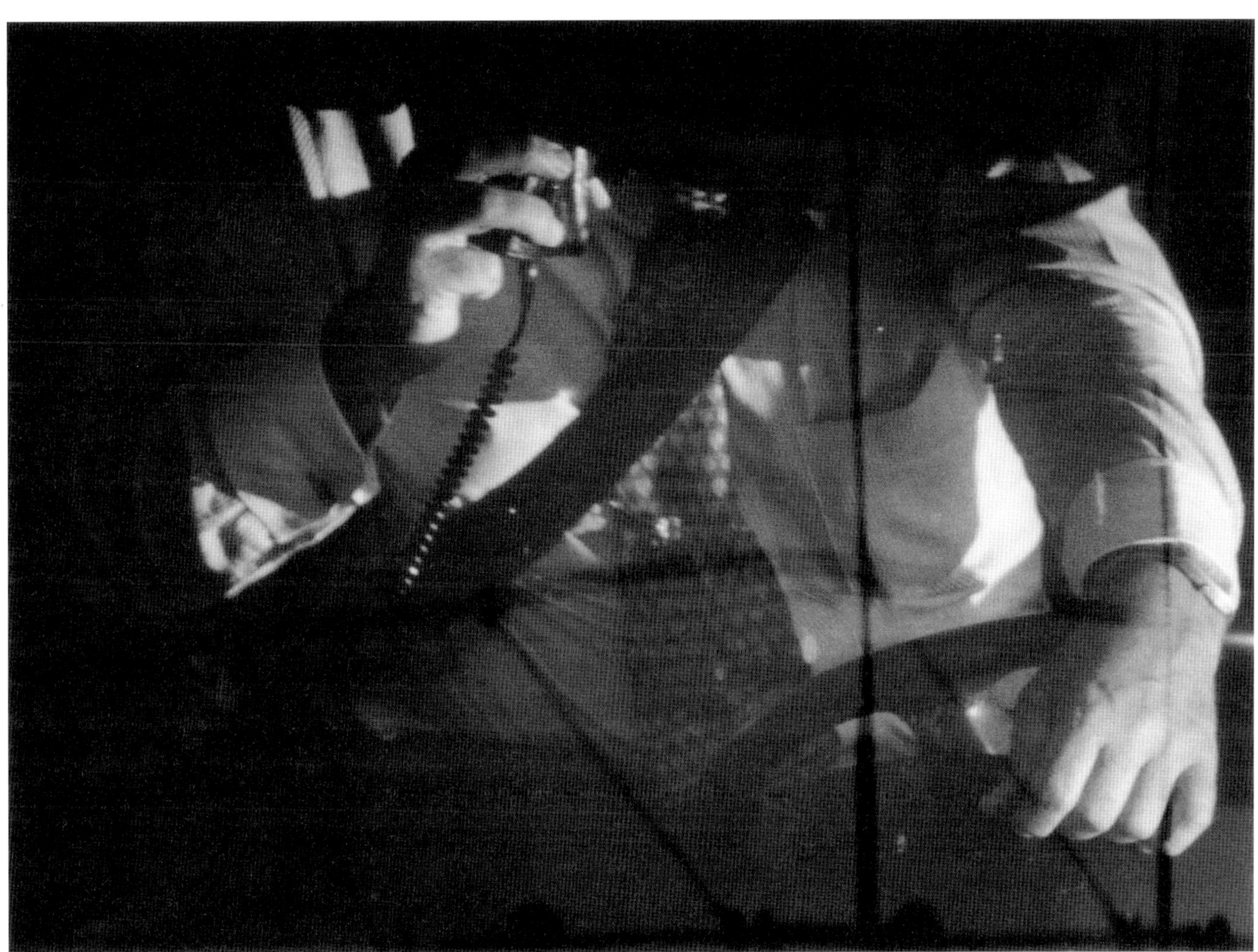

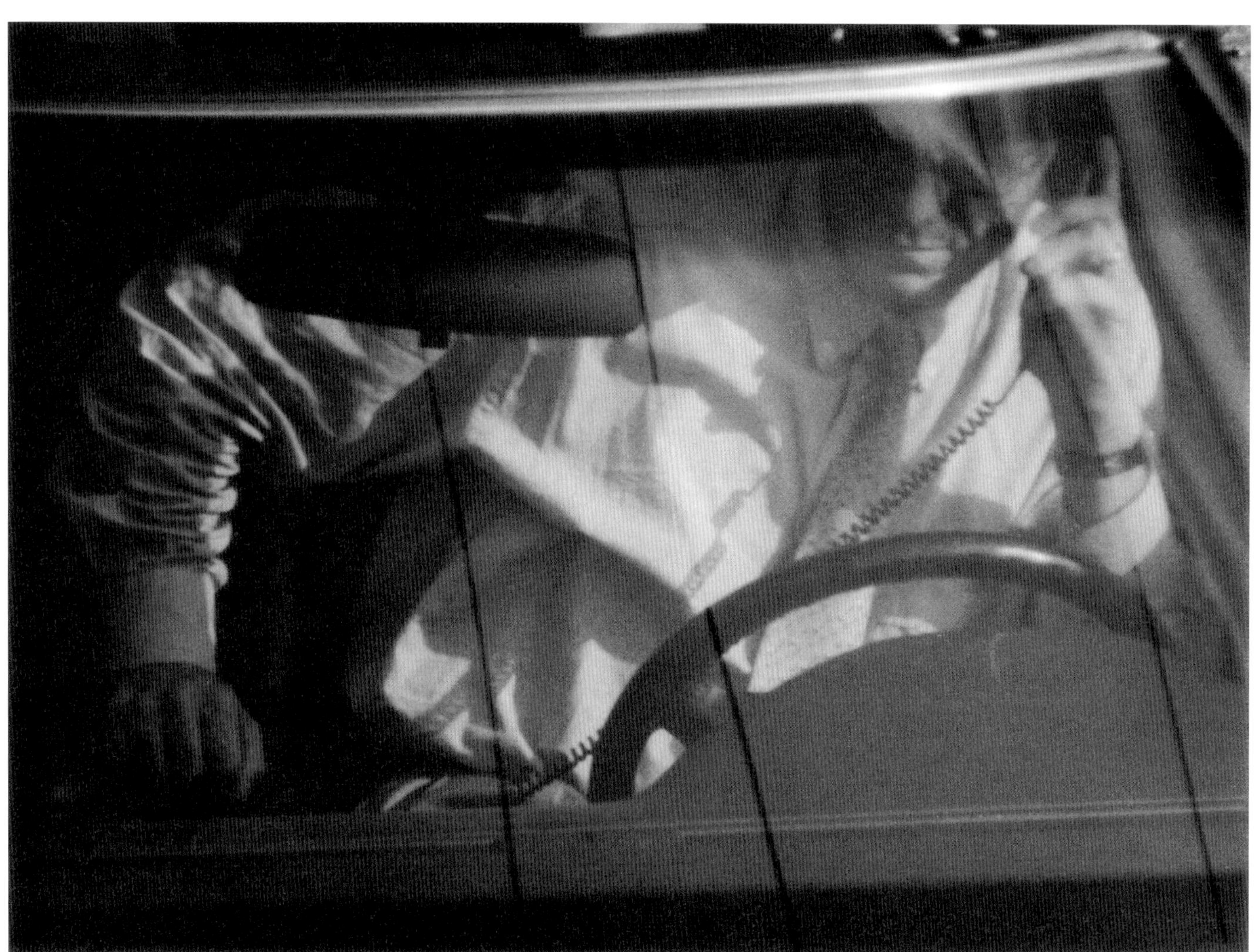

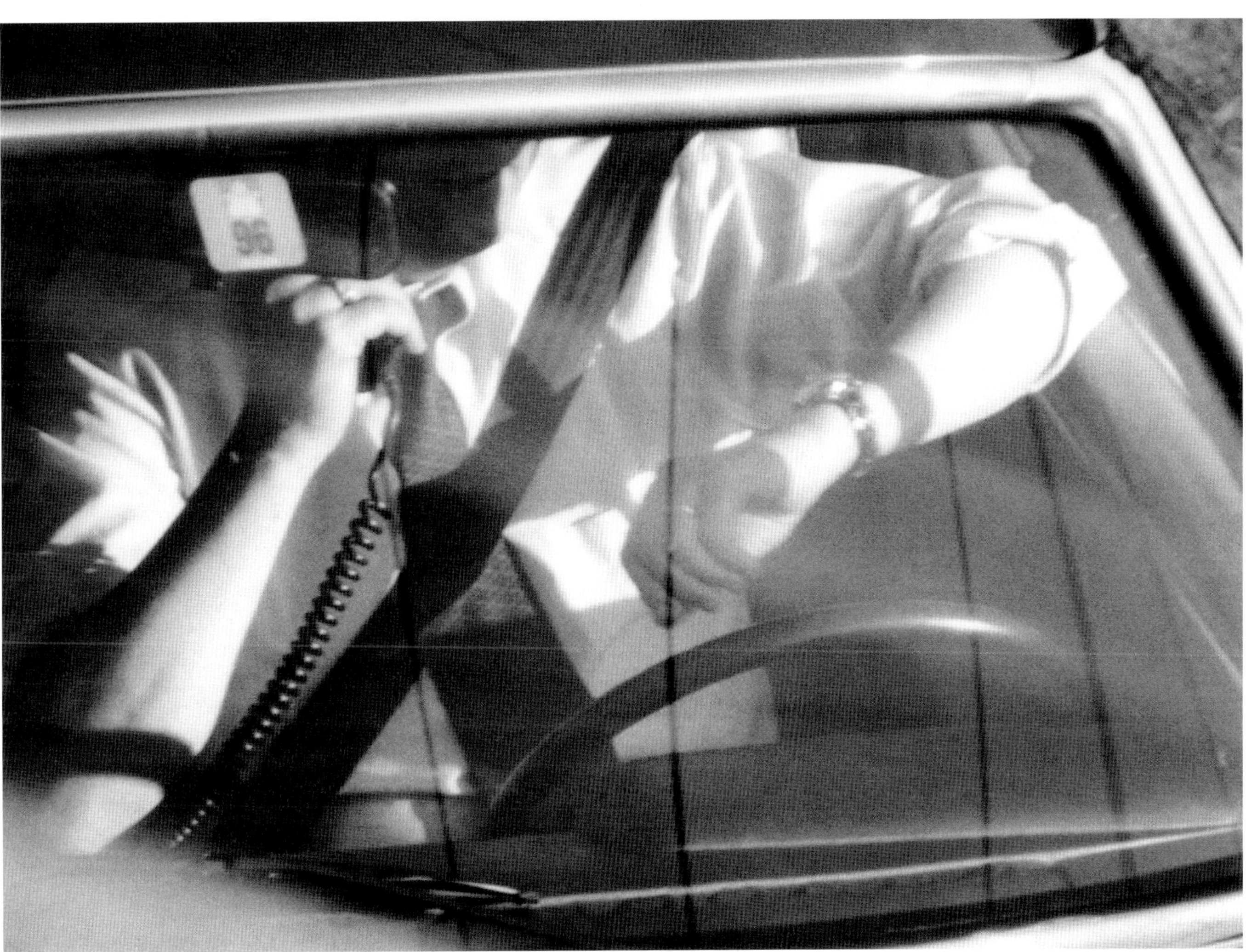

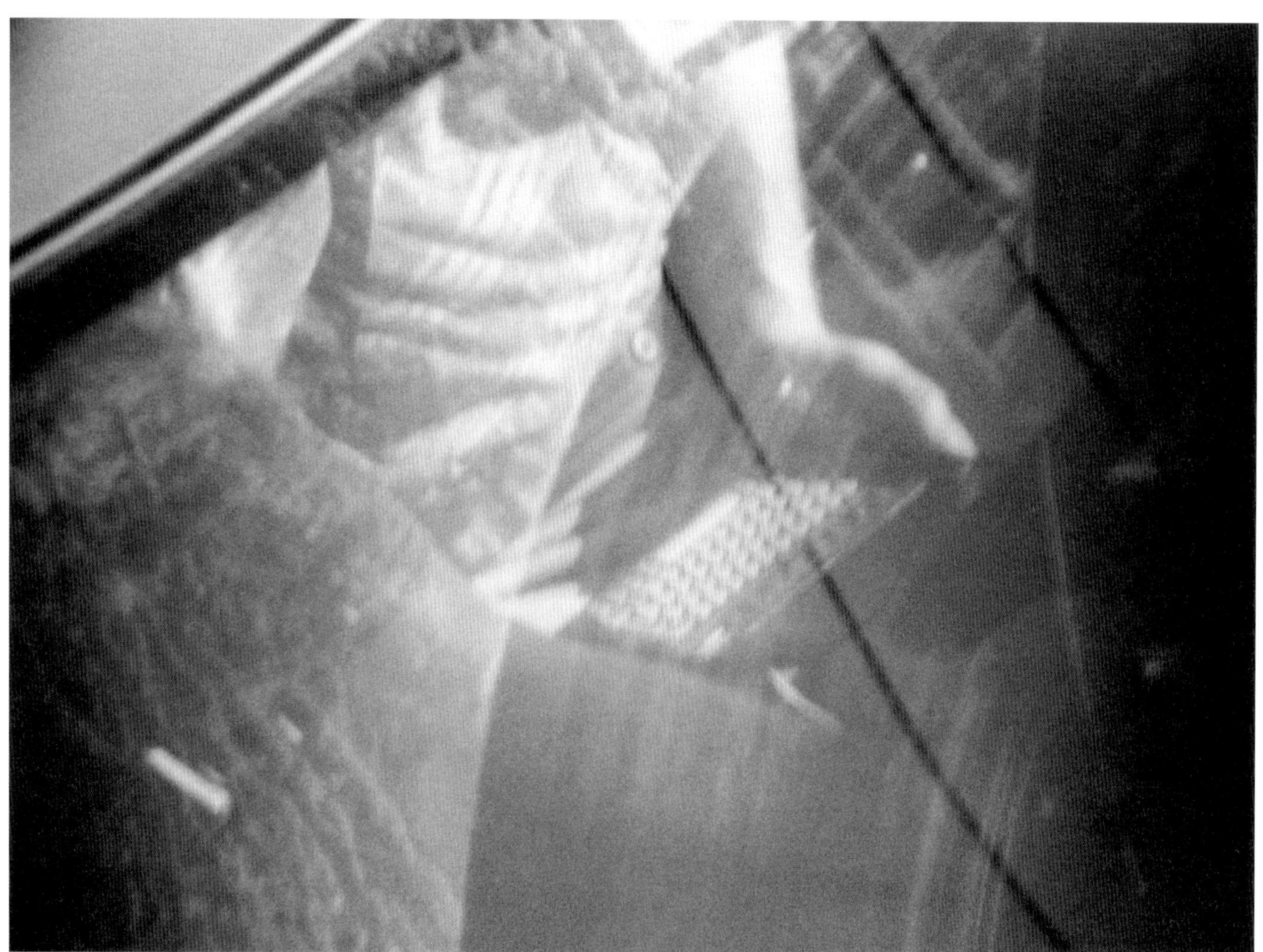

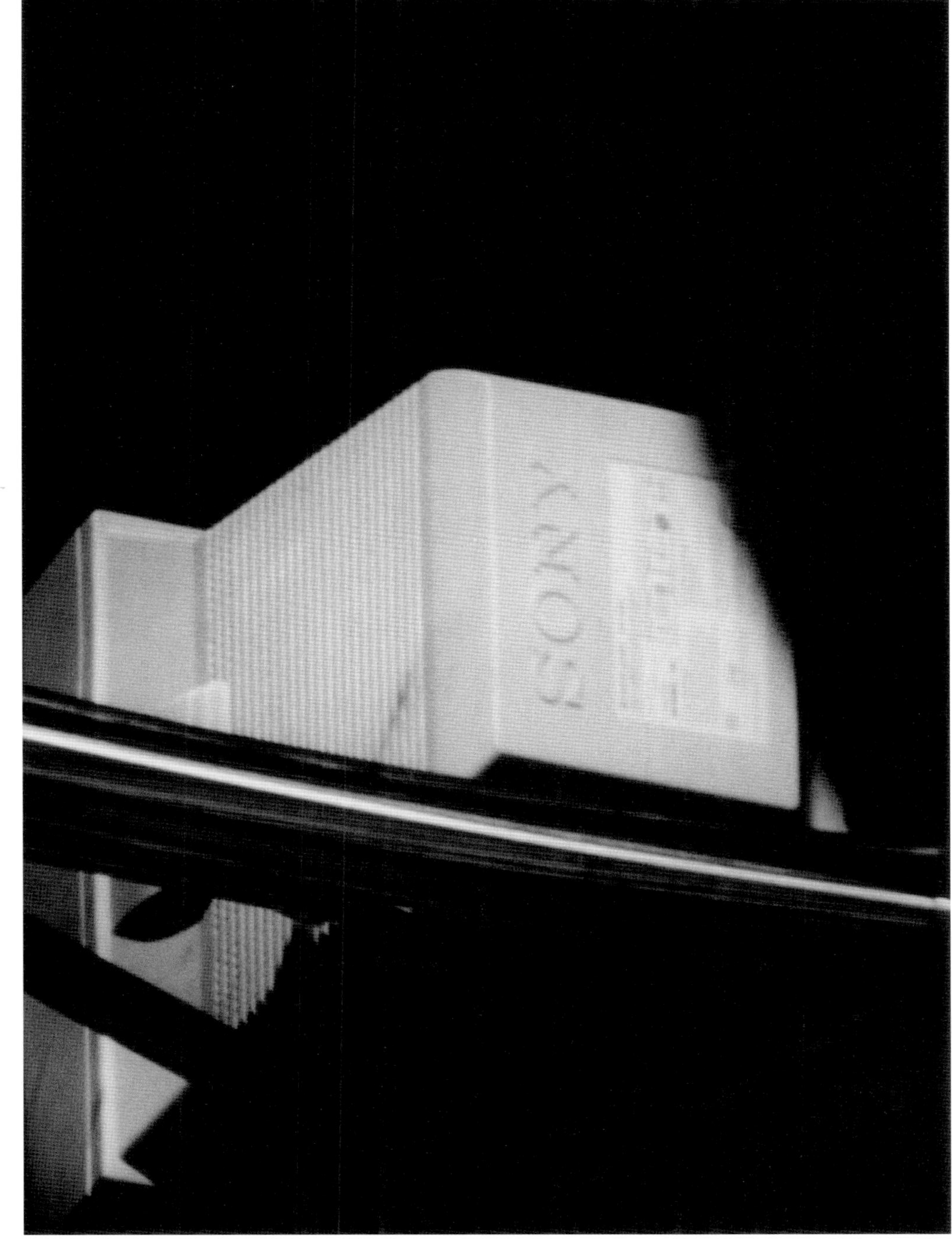
SONY

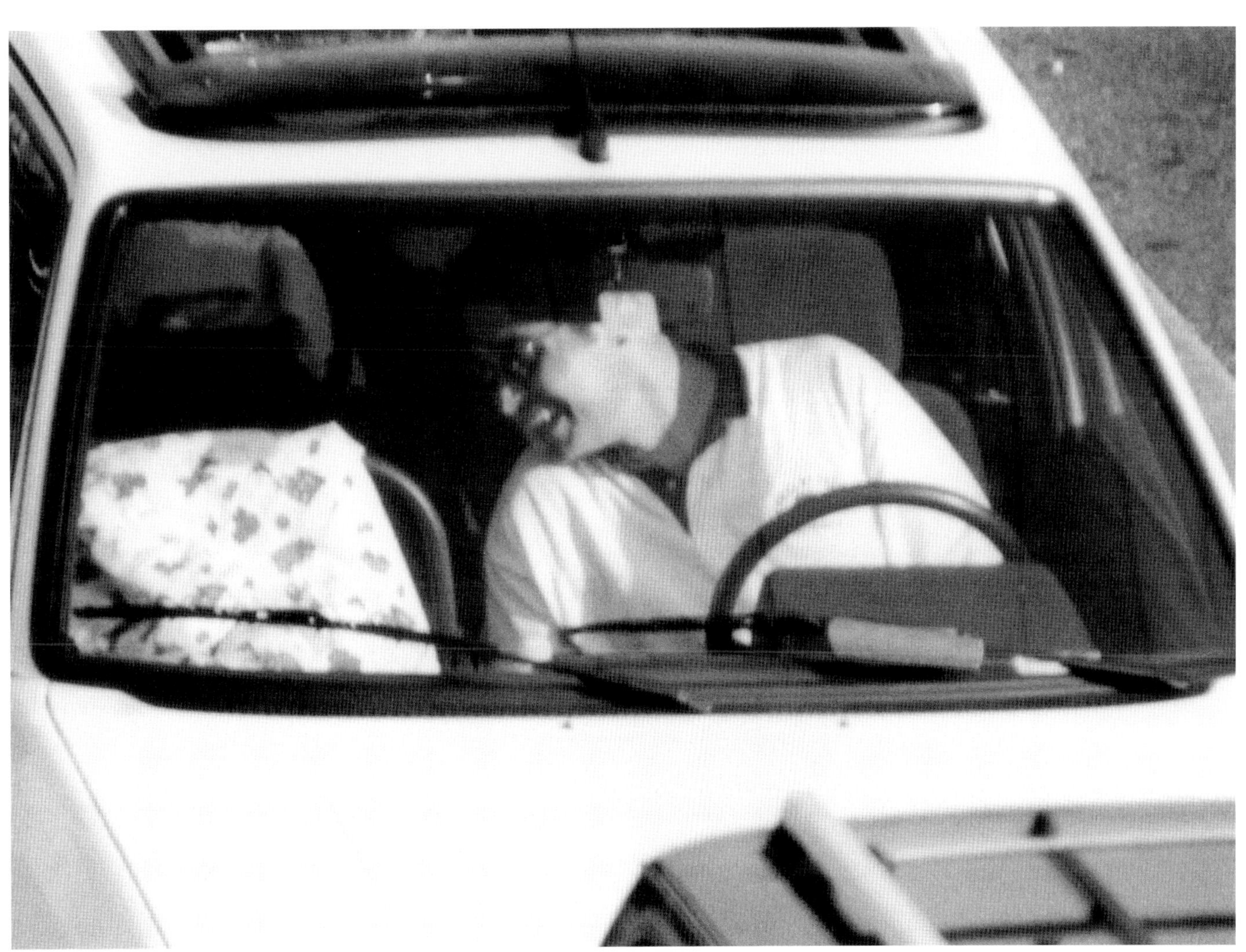

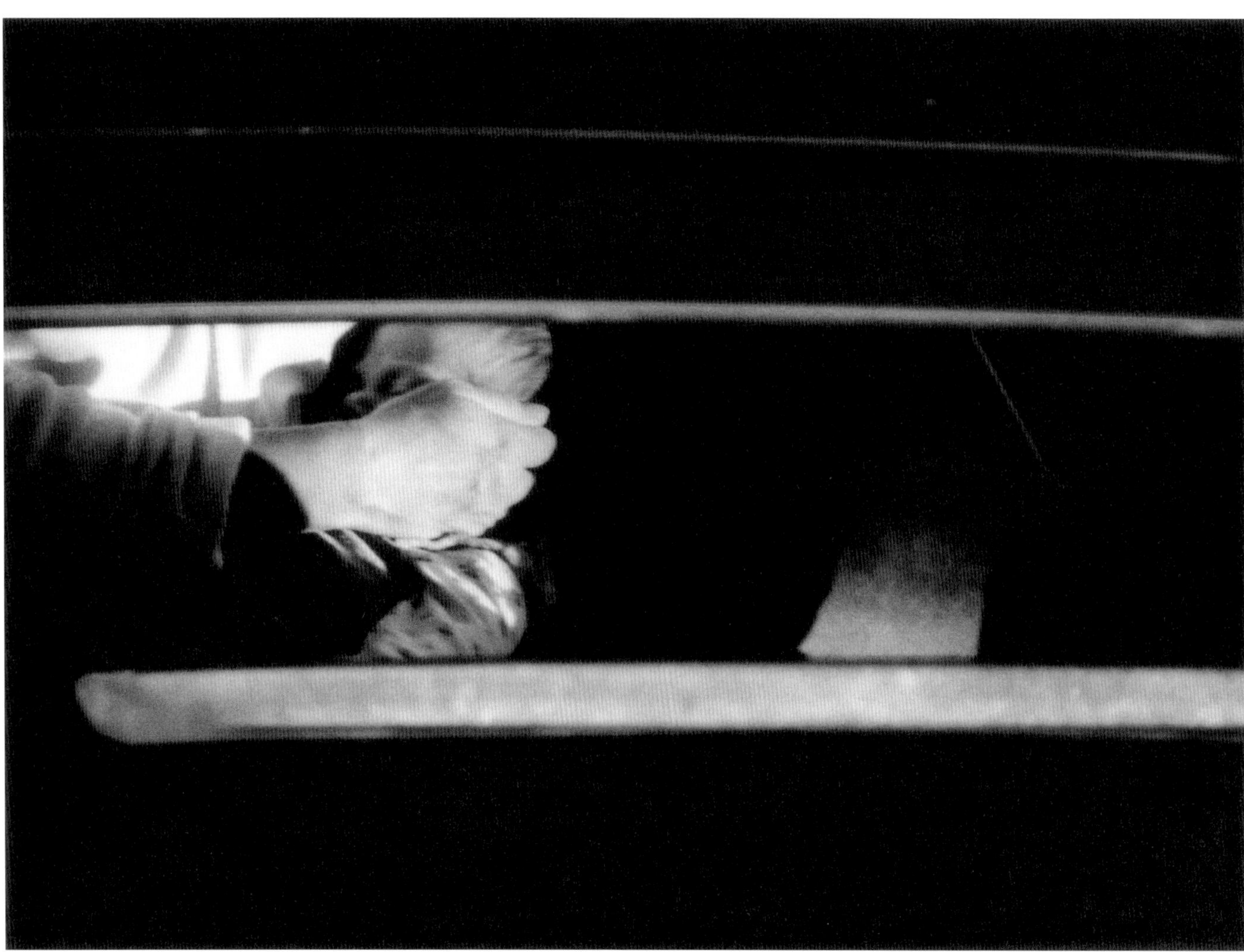

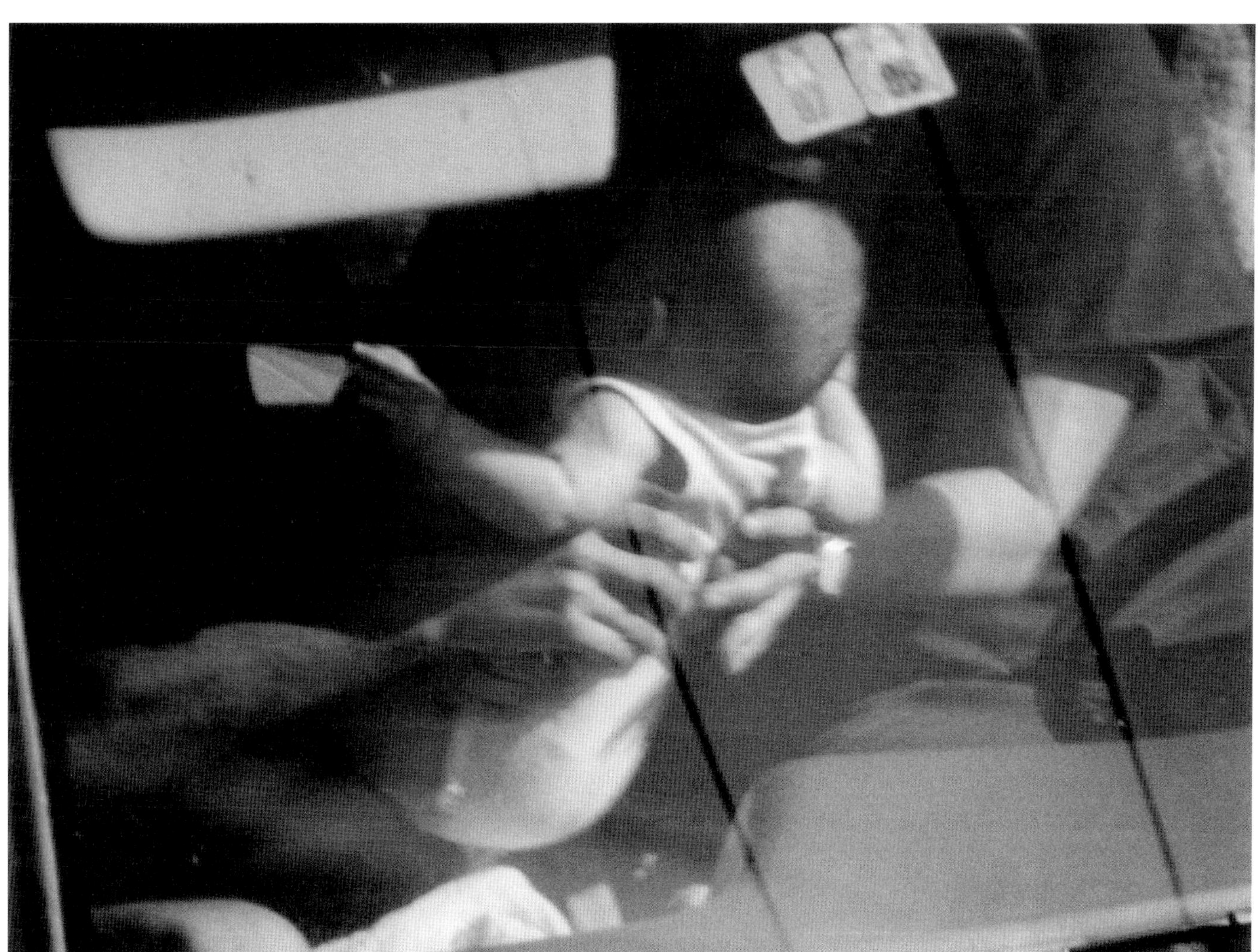

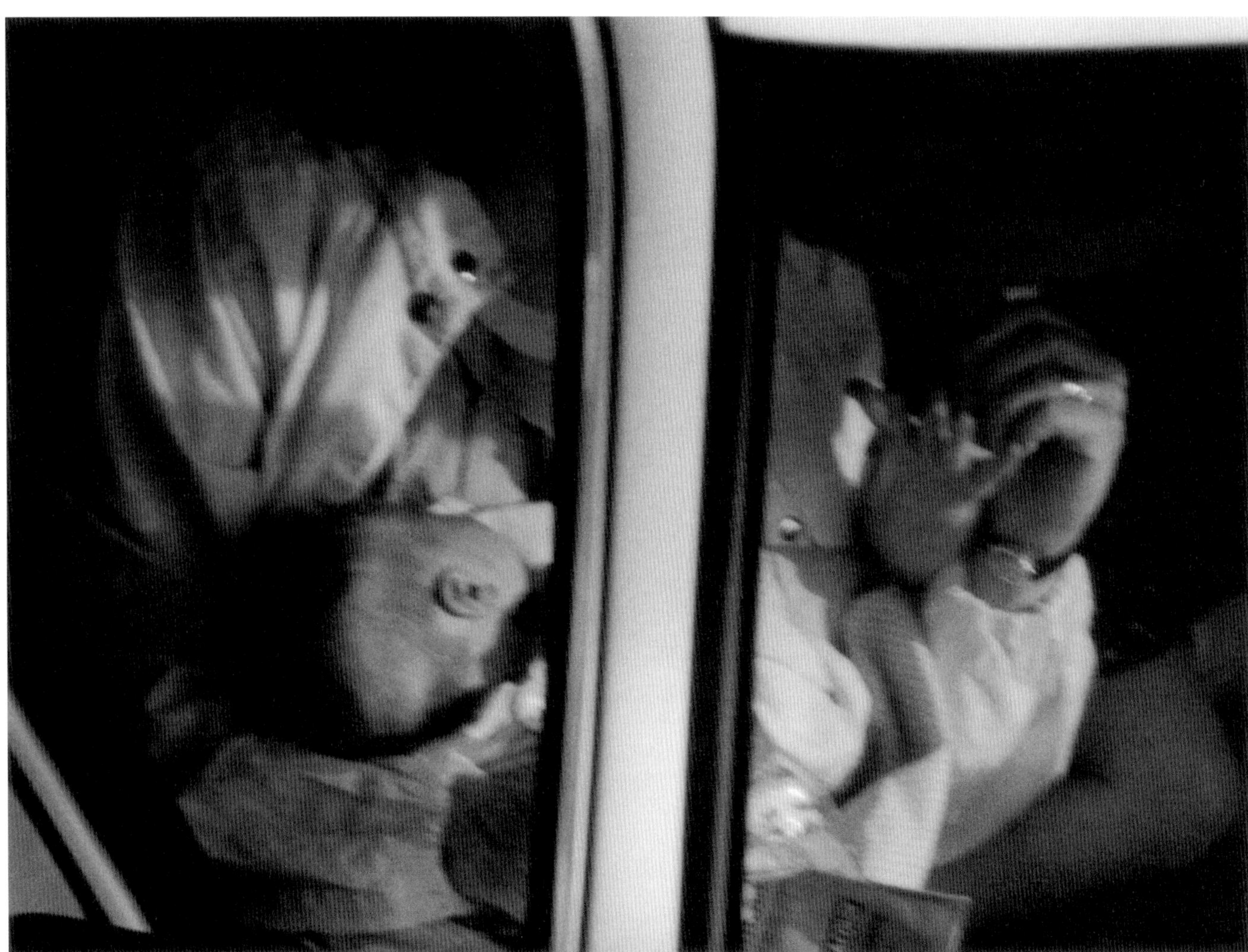

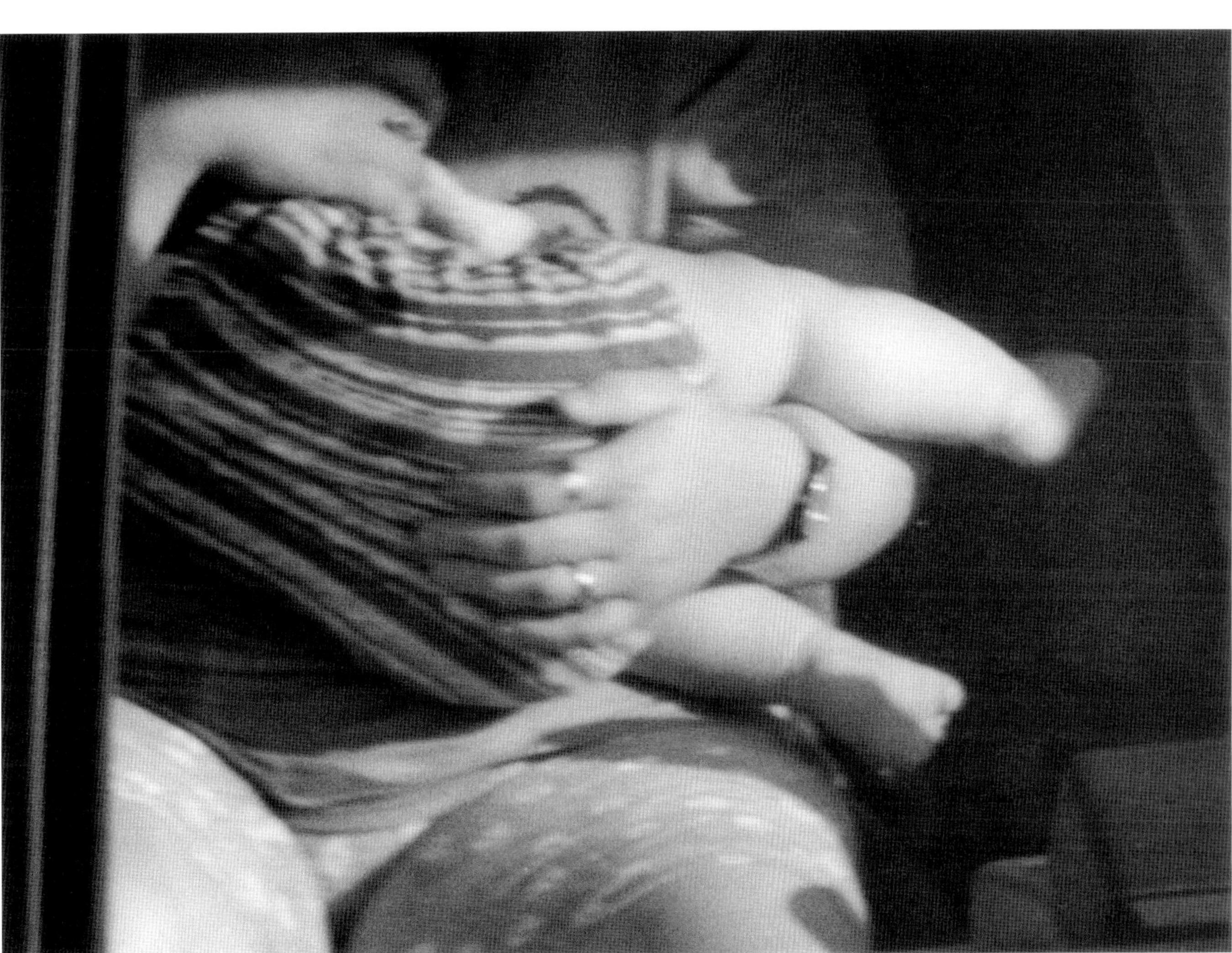

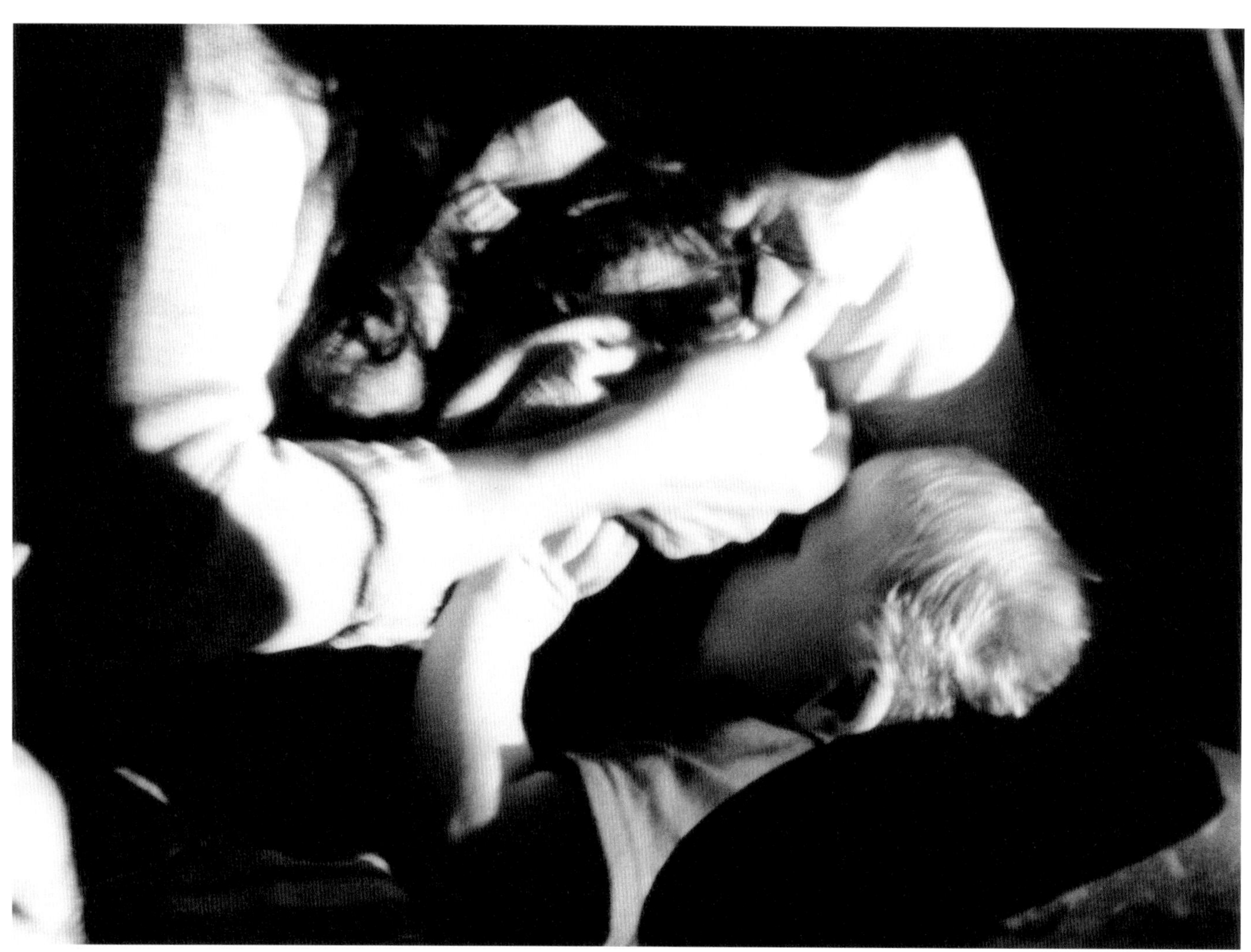

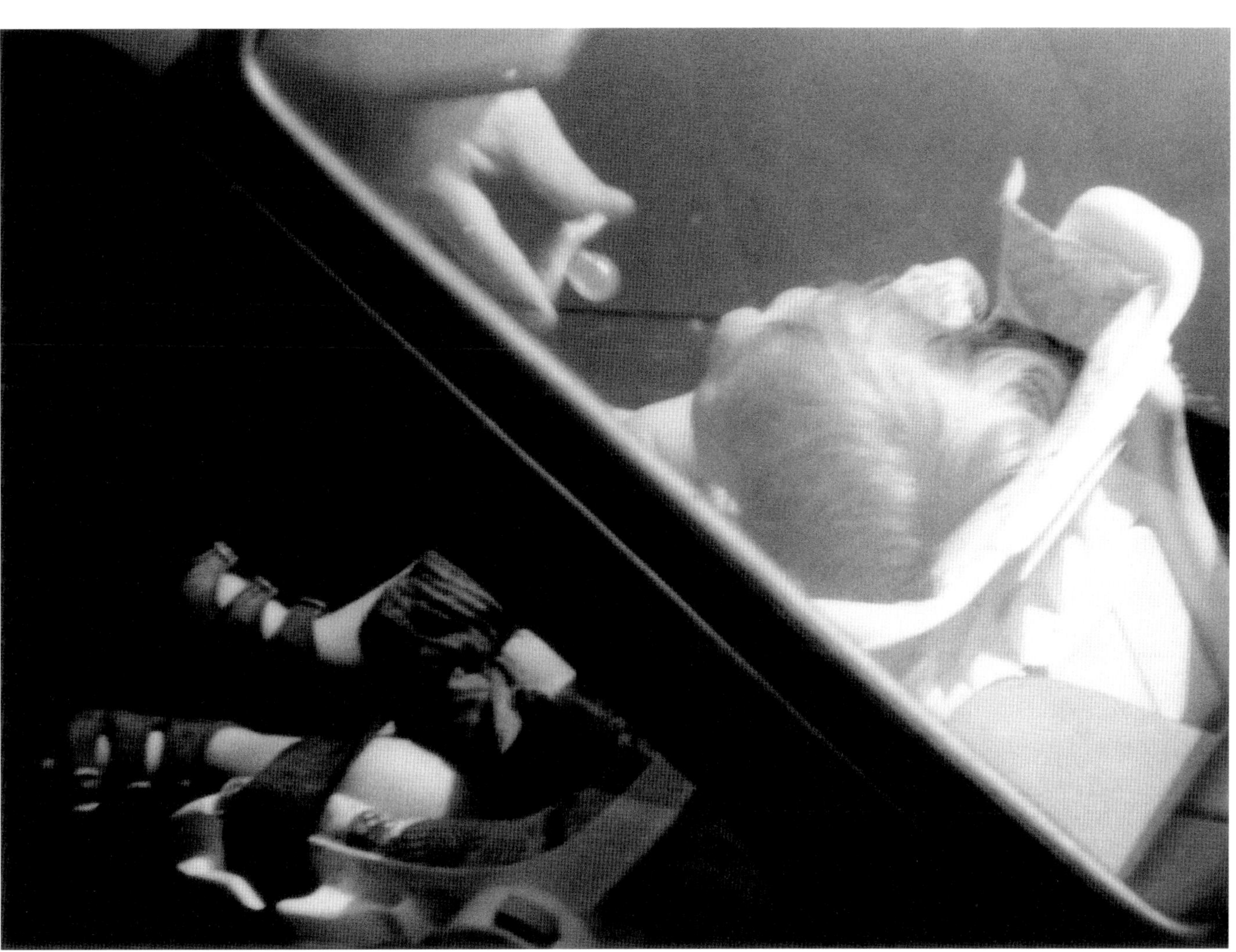

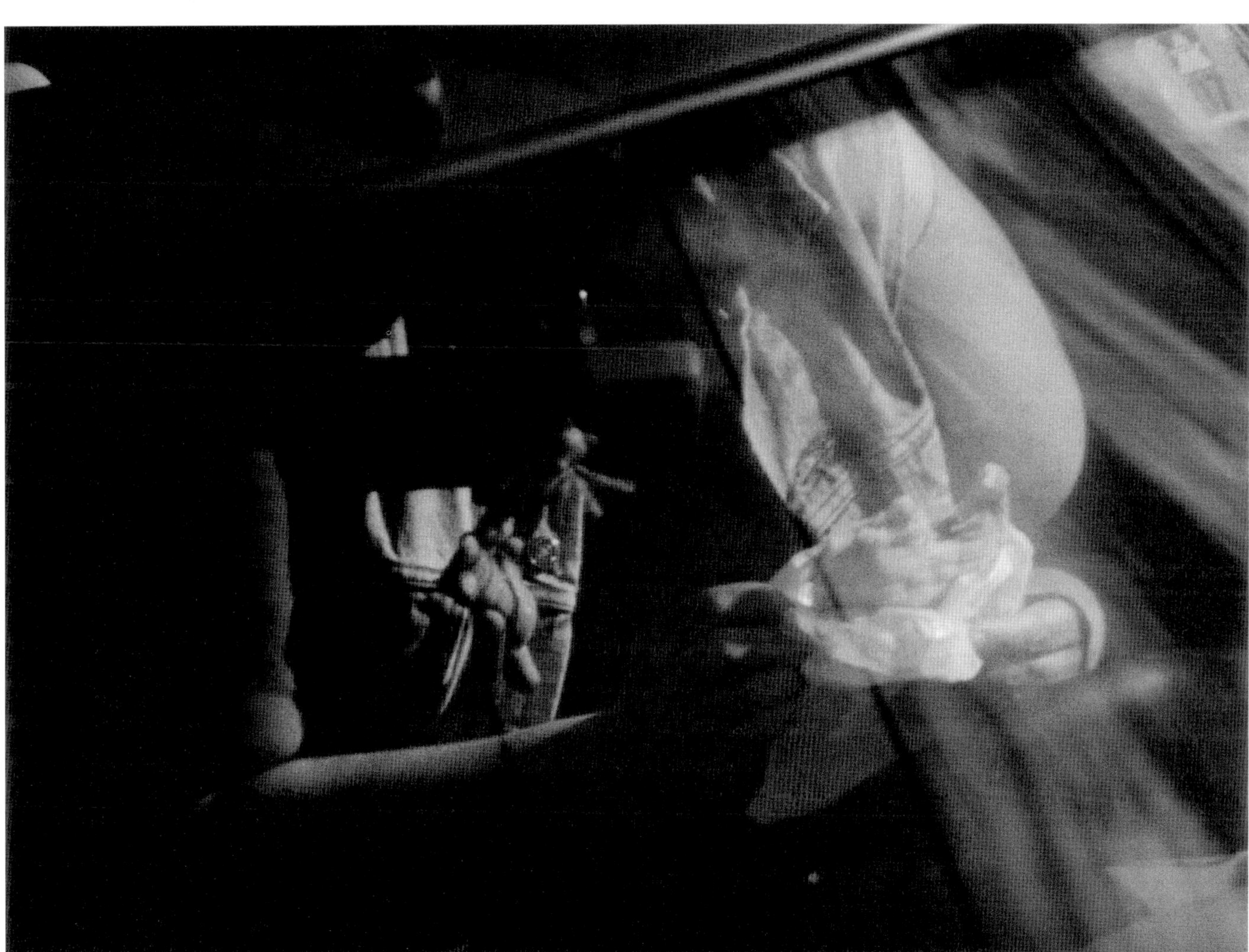

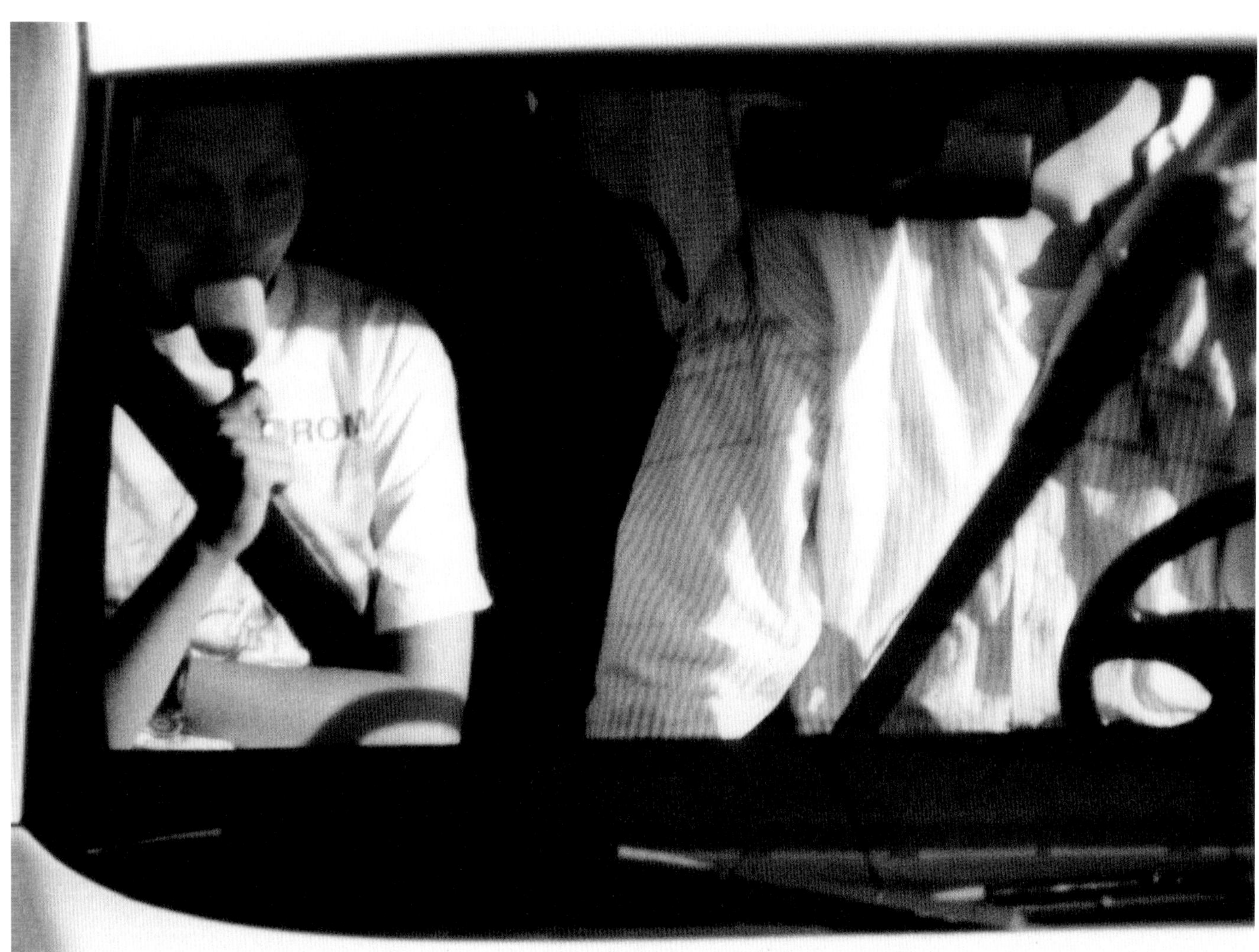
ROM

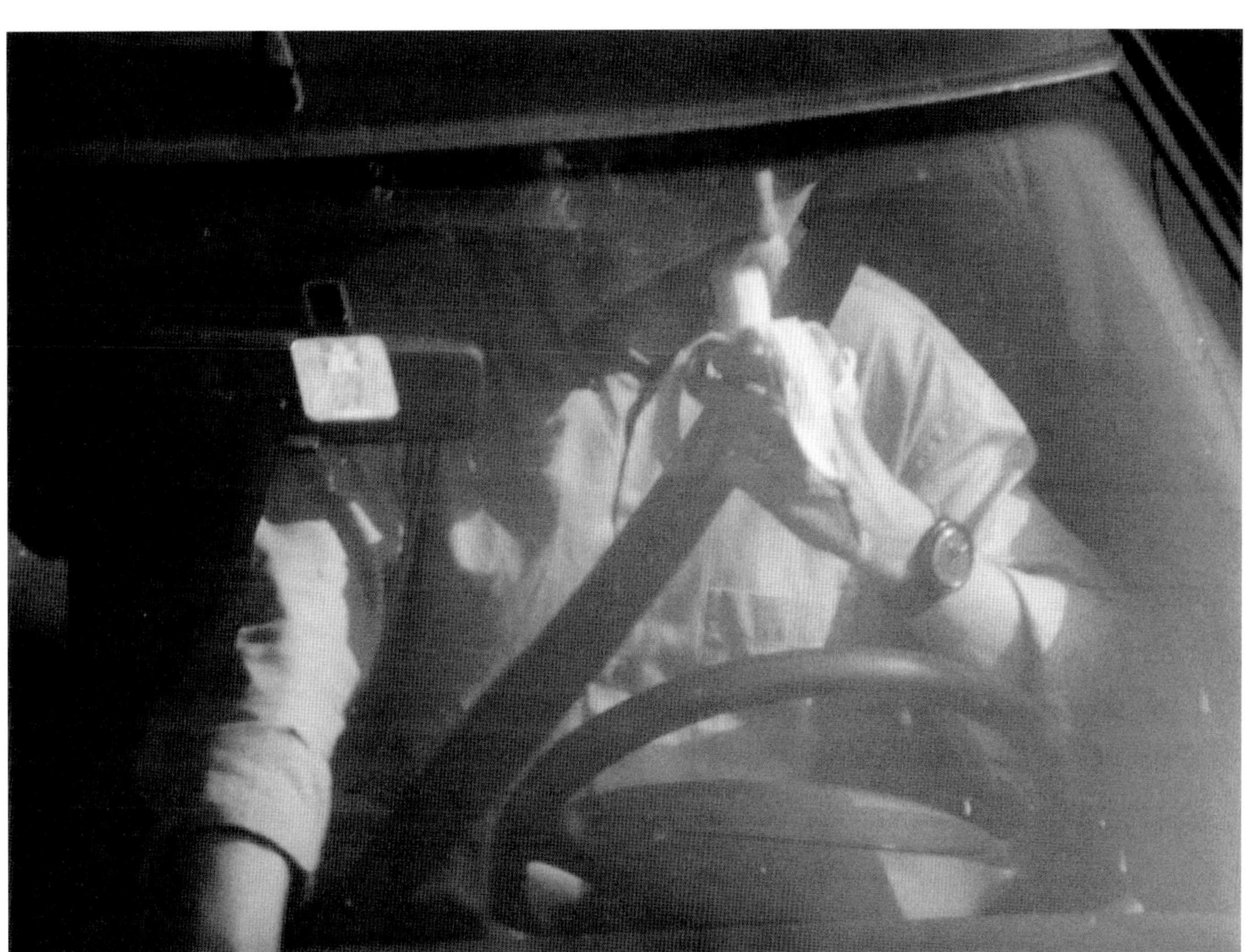

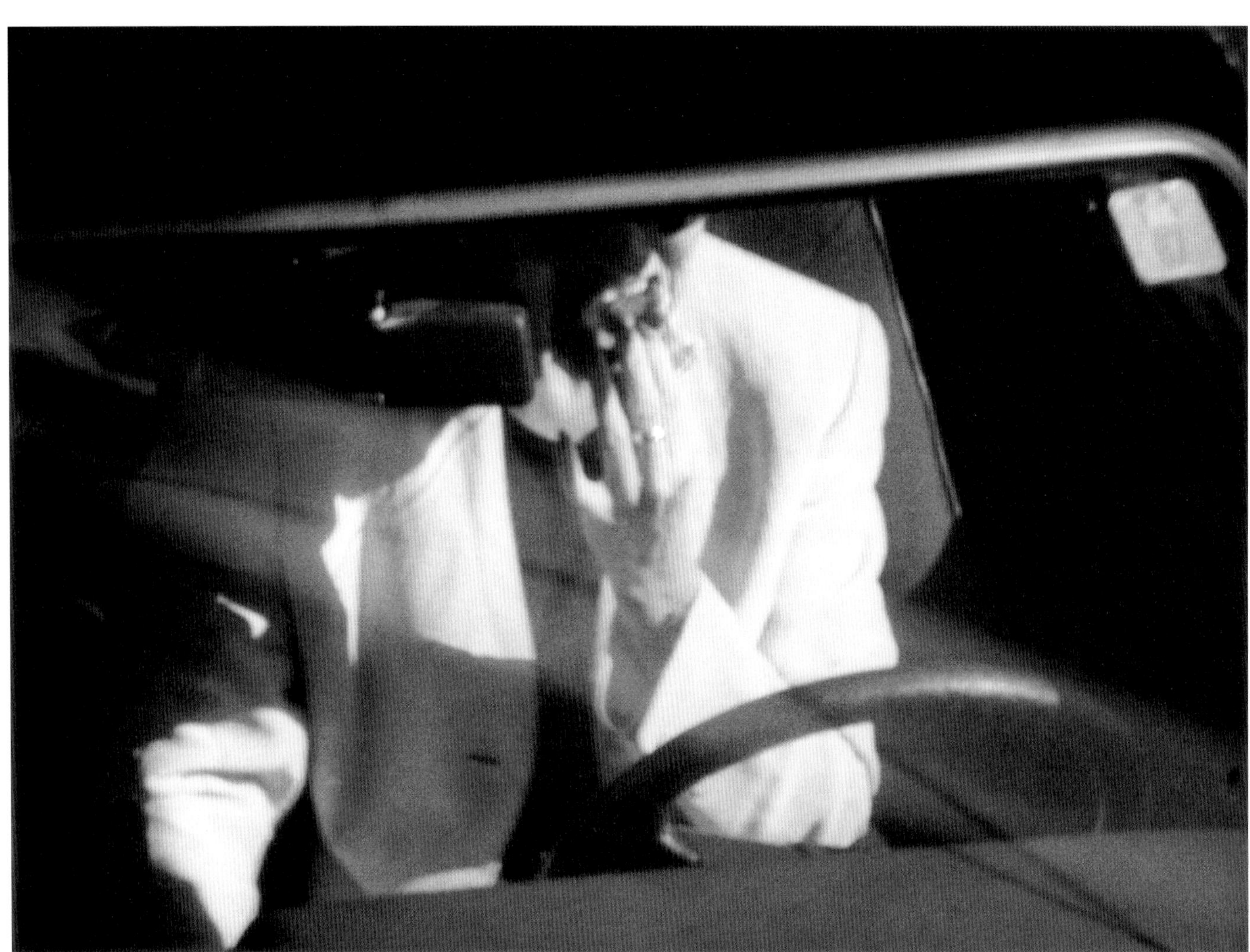

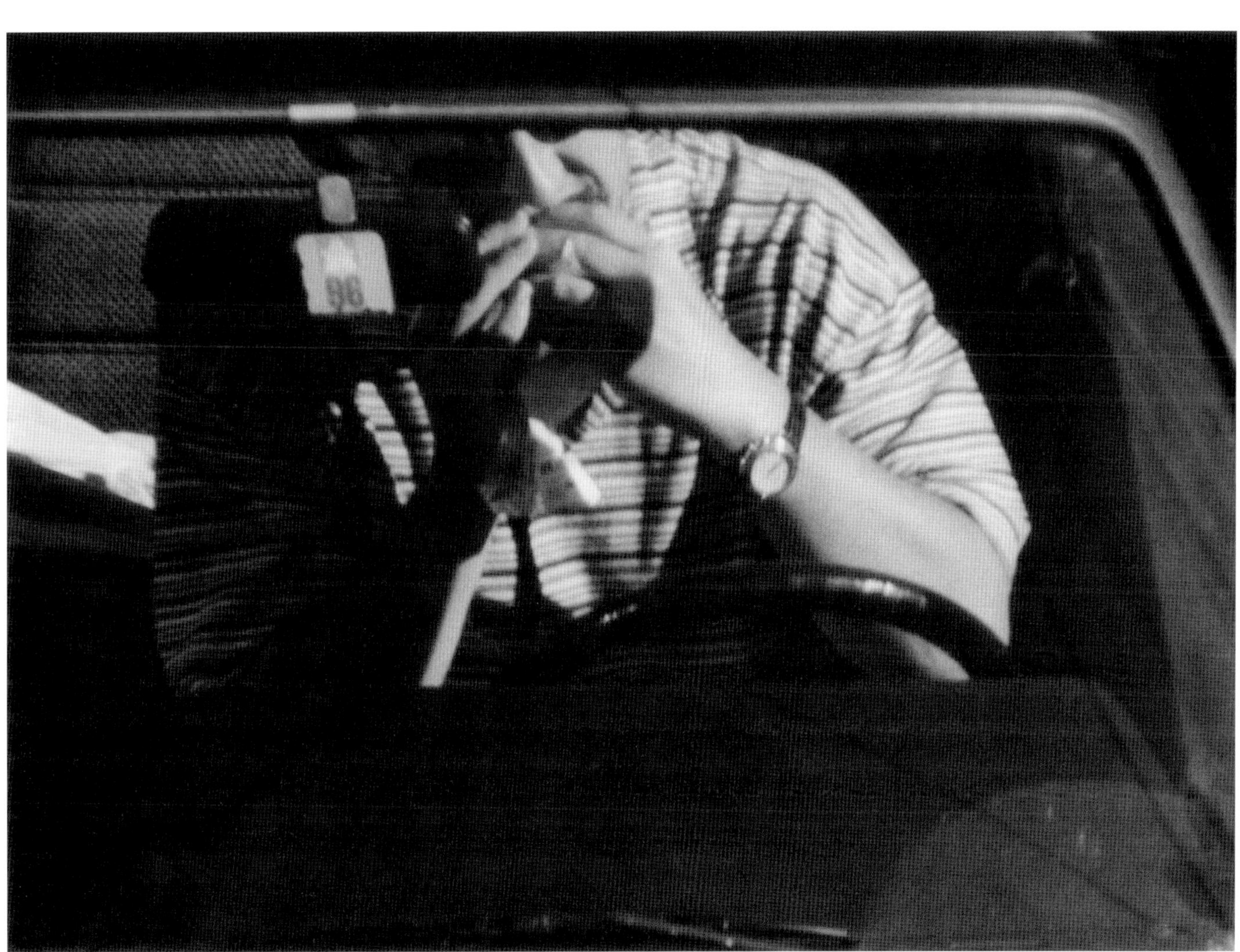

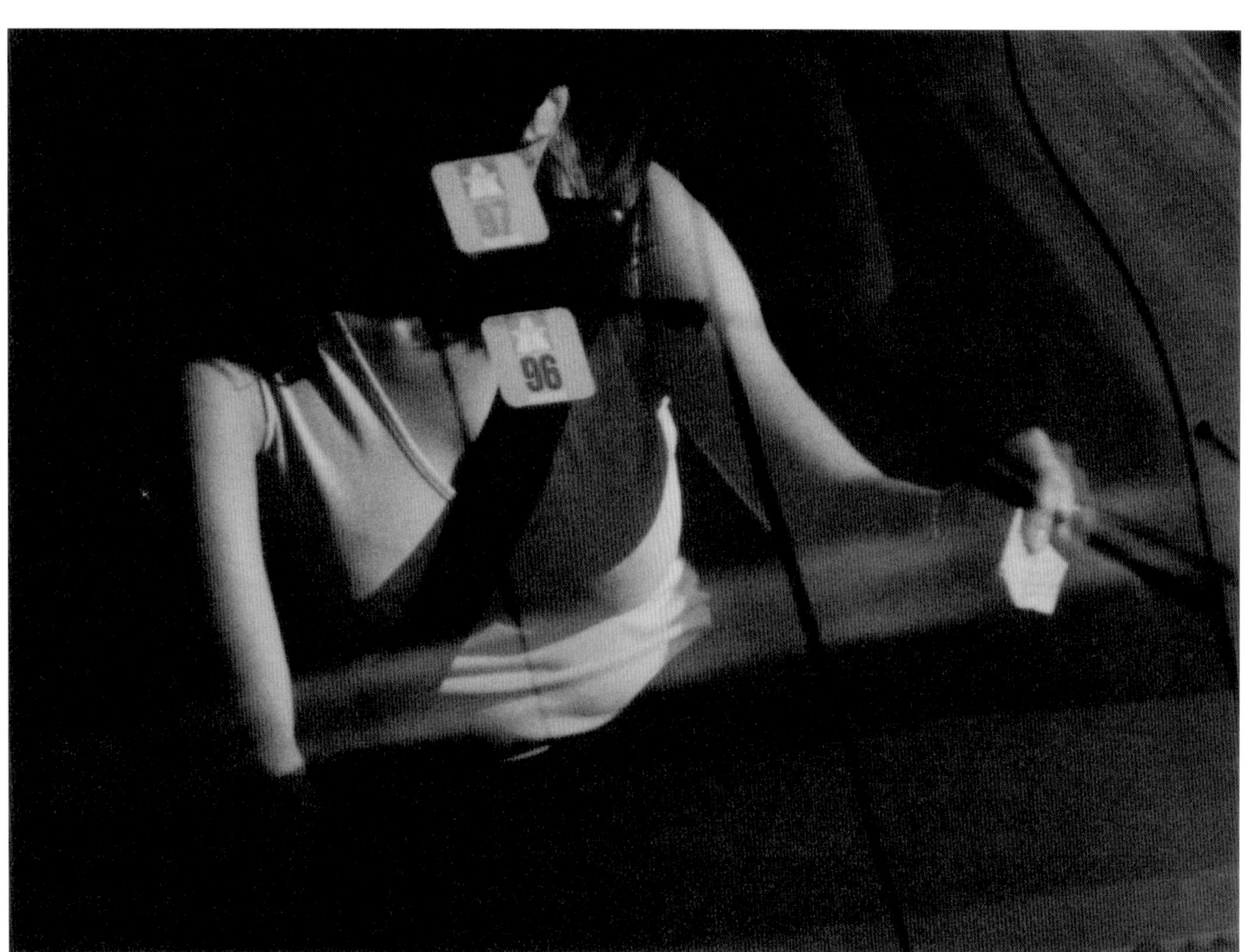

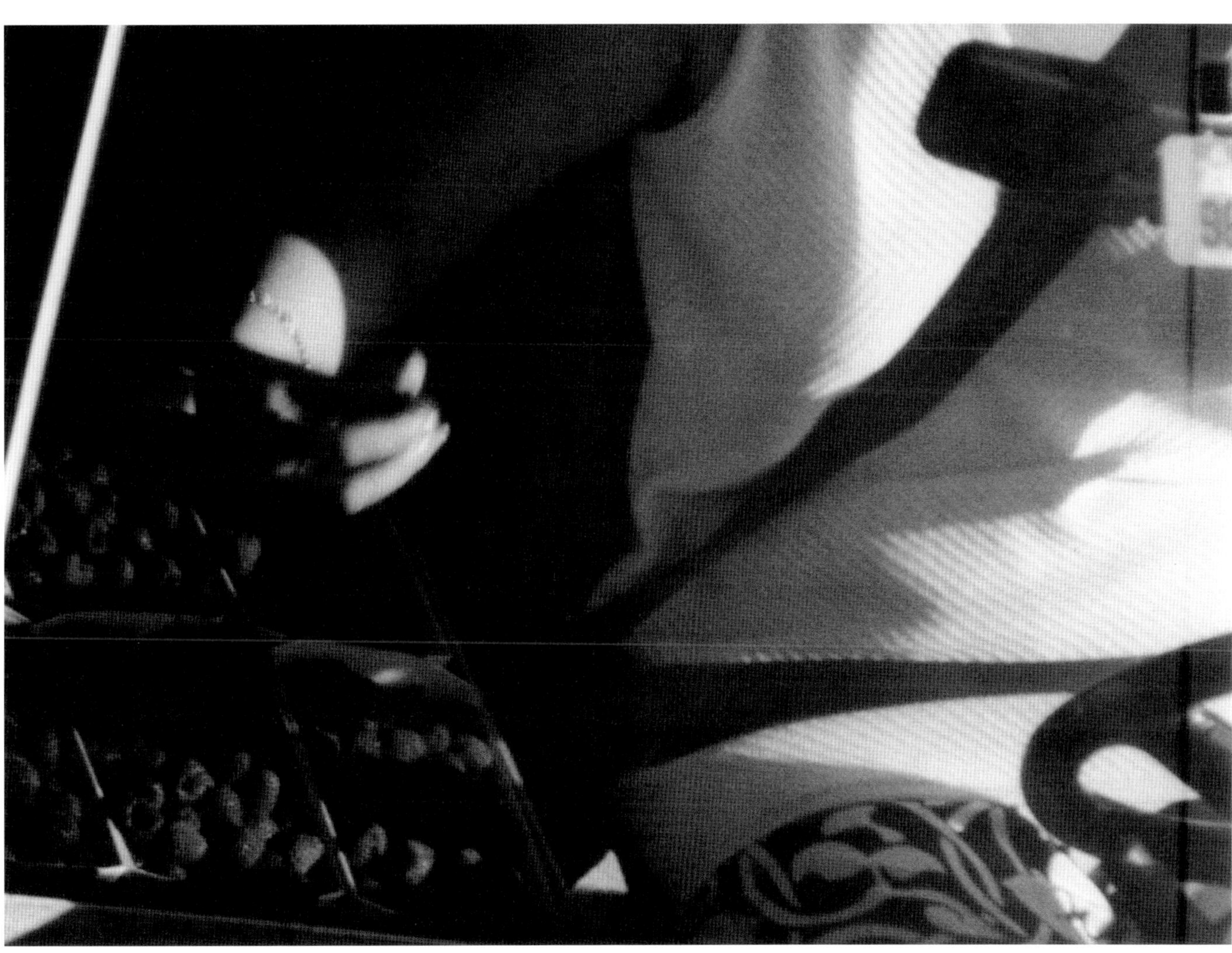

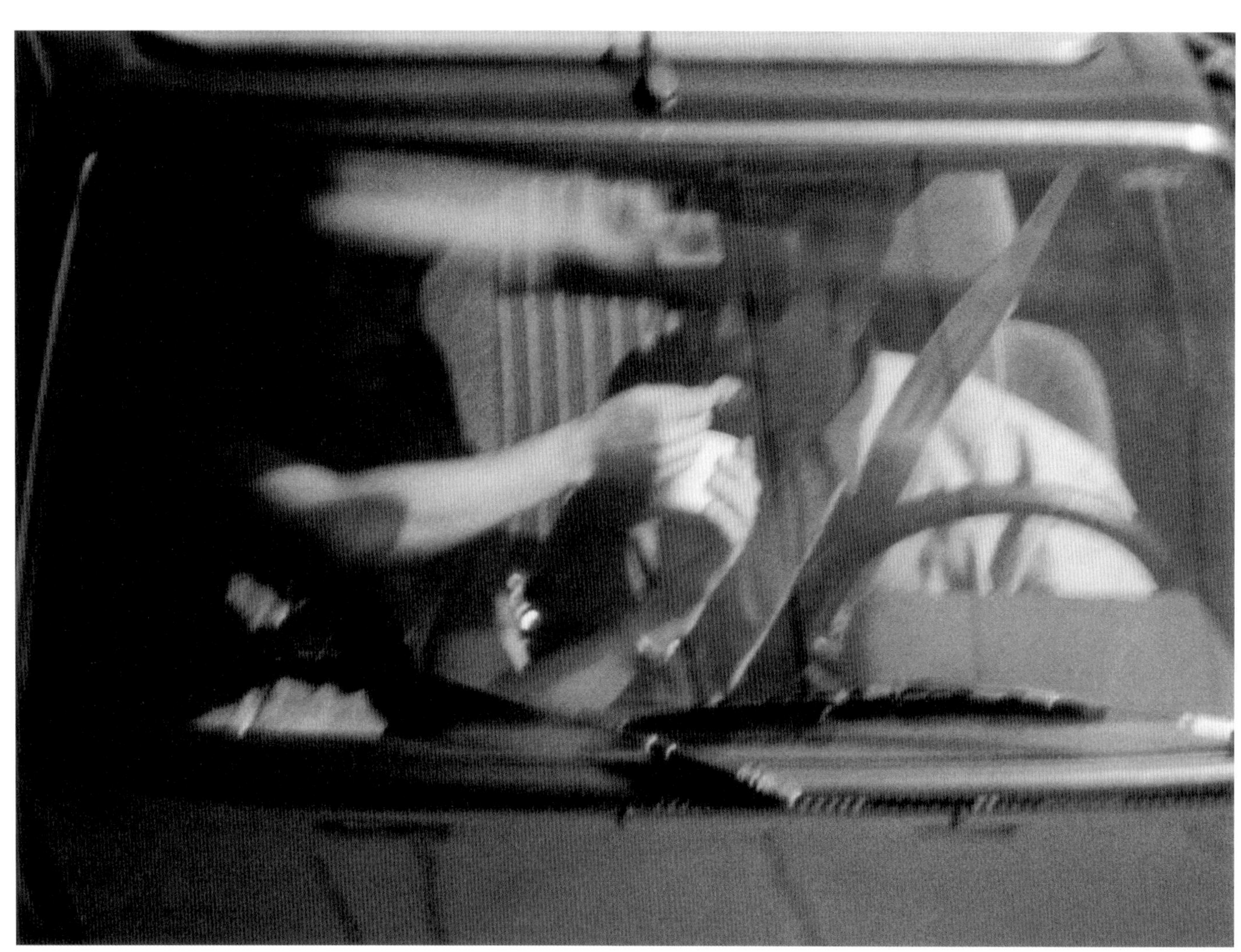

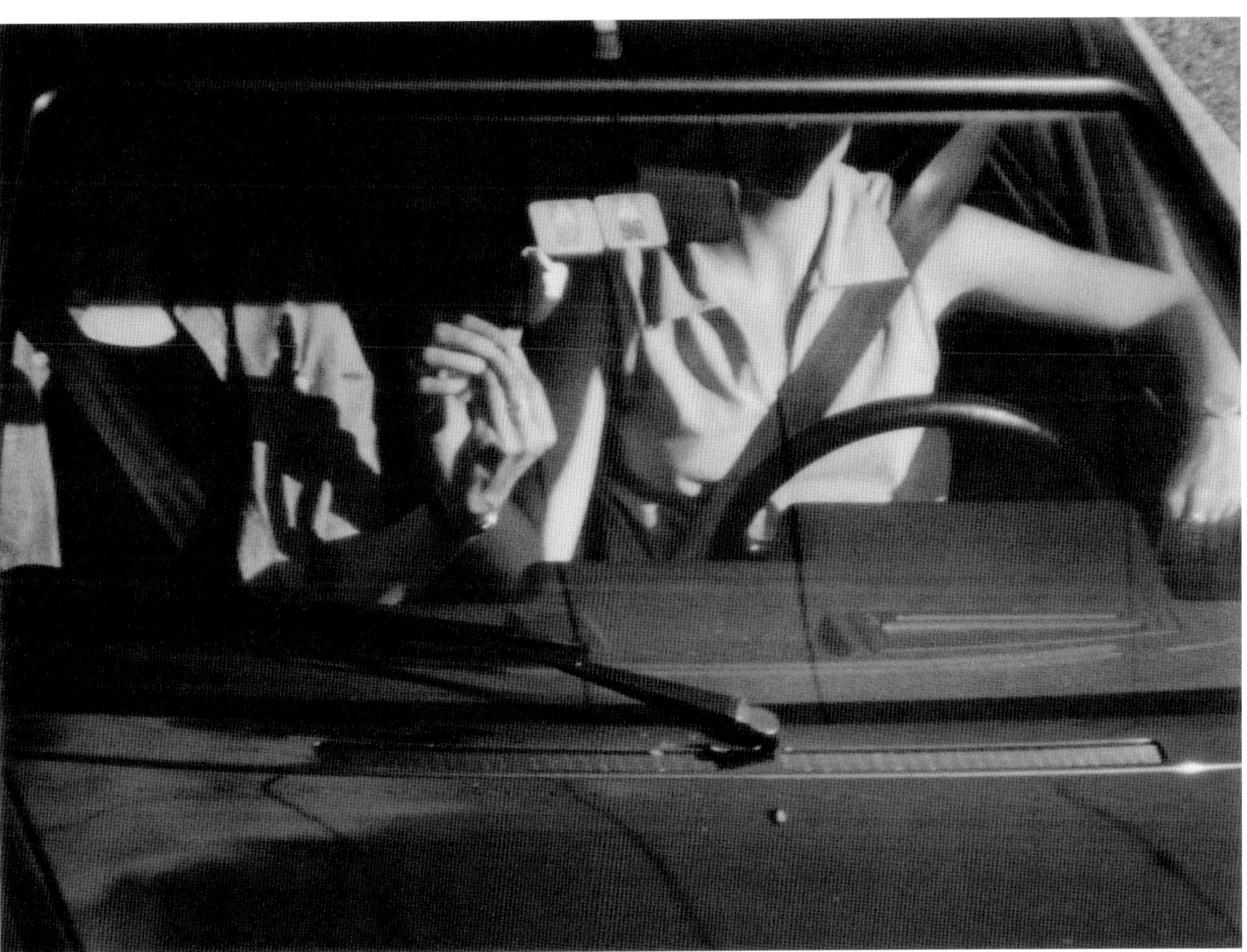

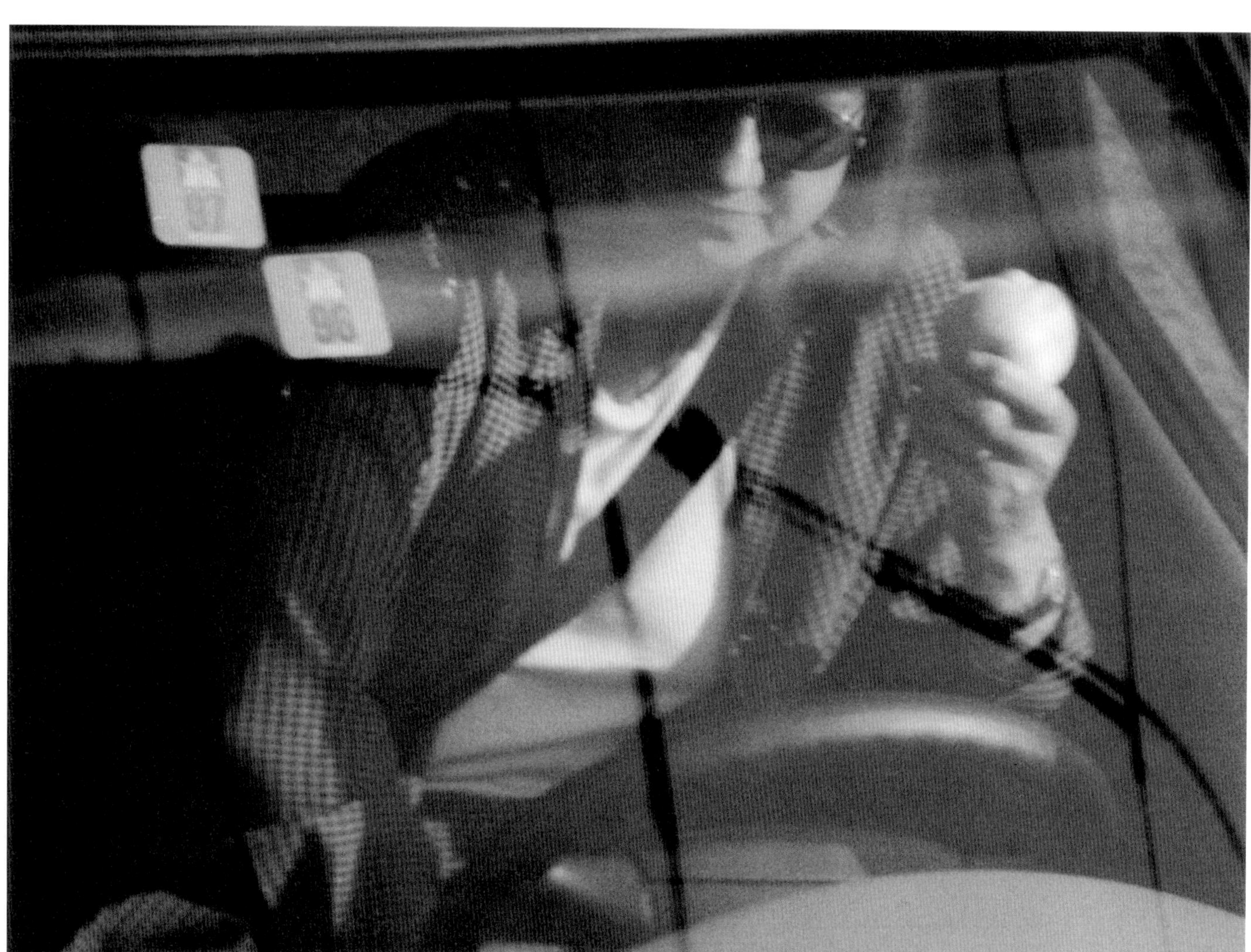

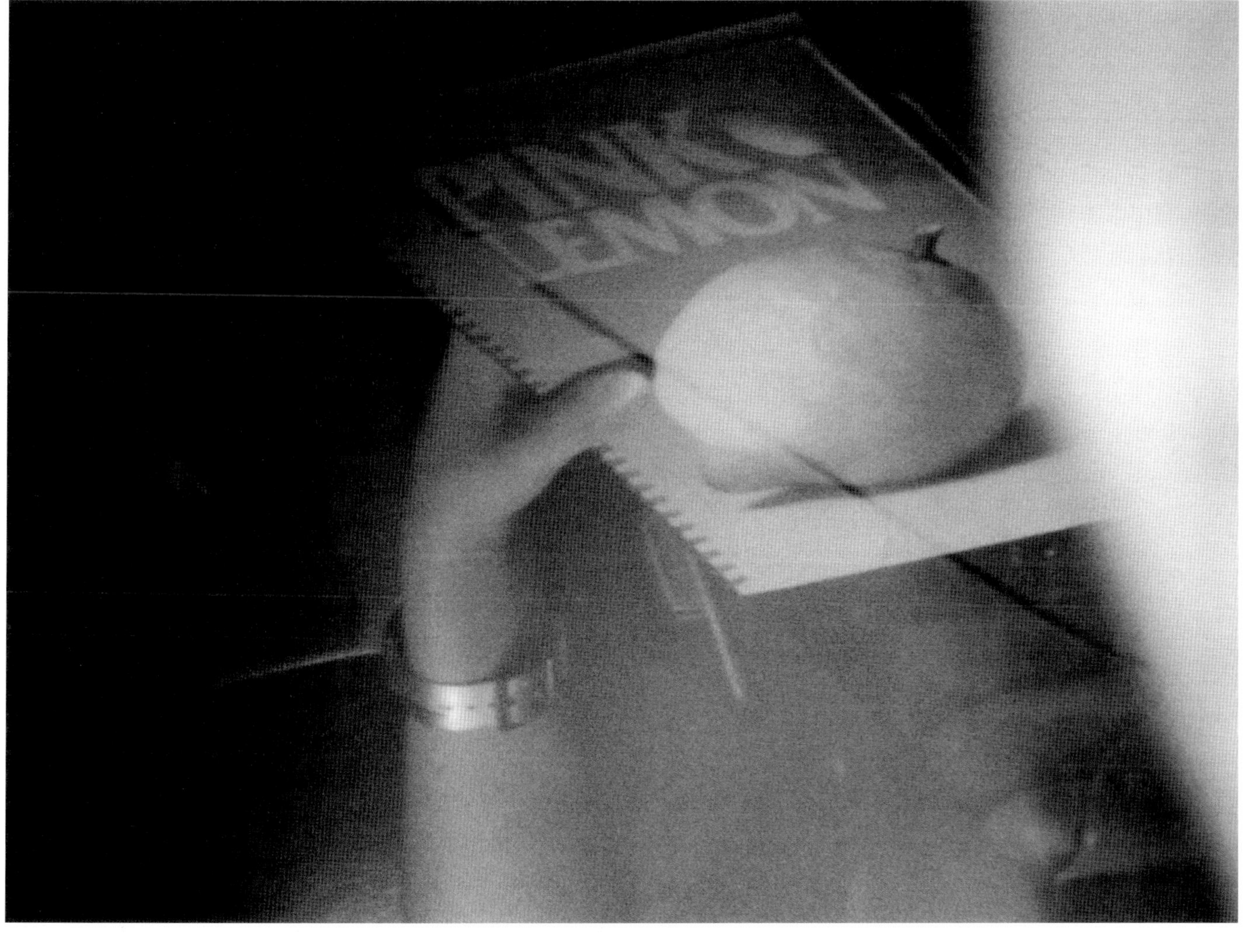
PINK
LEMON

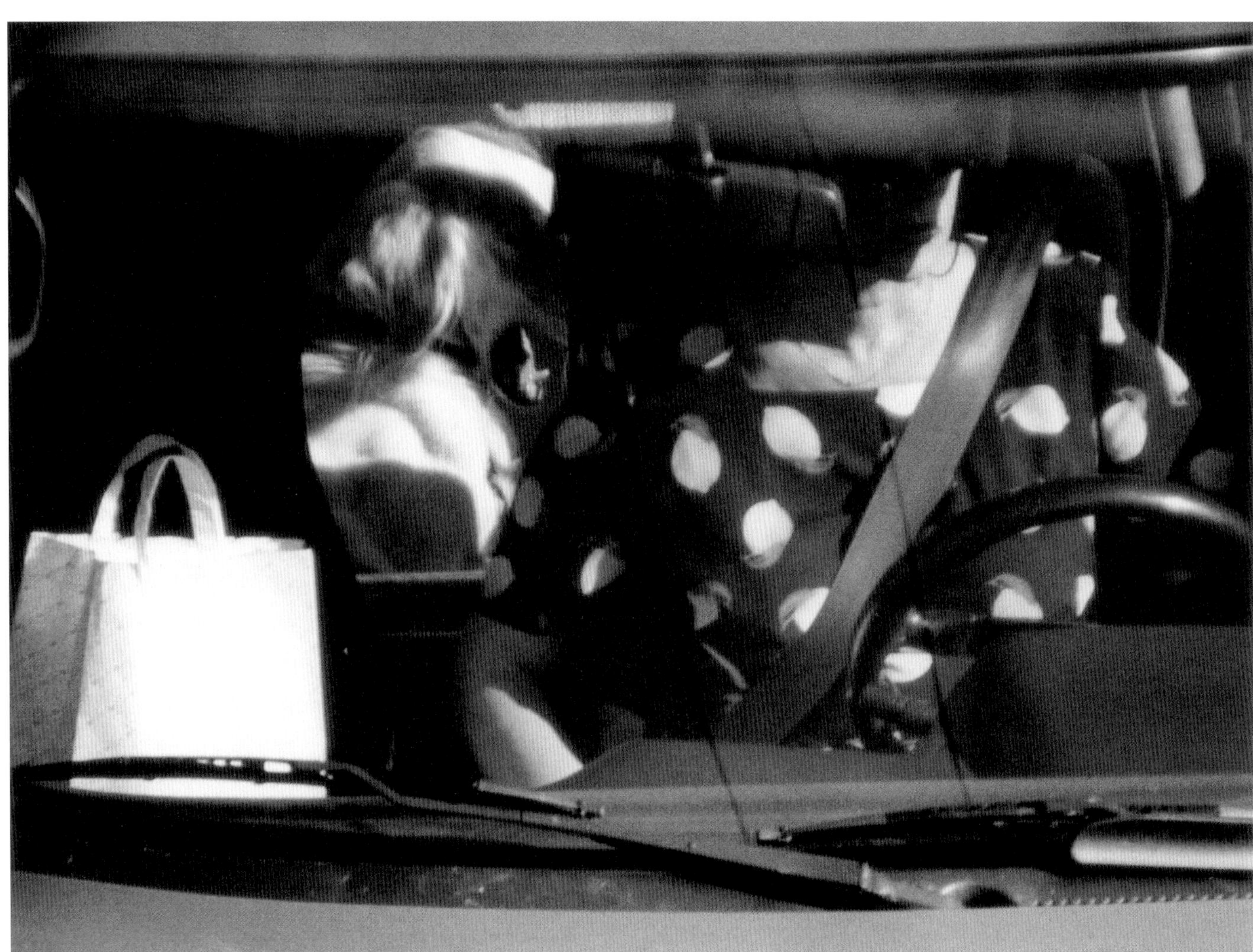

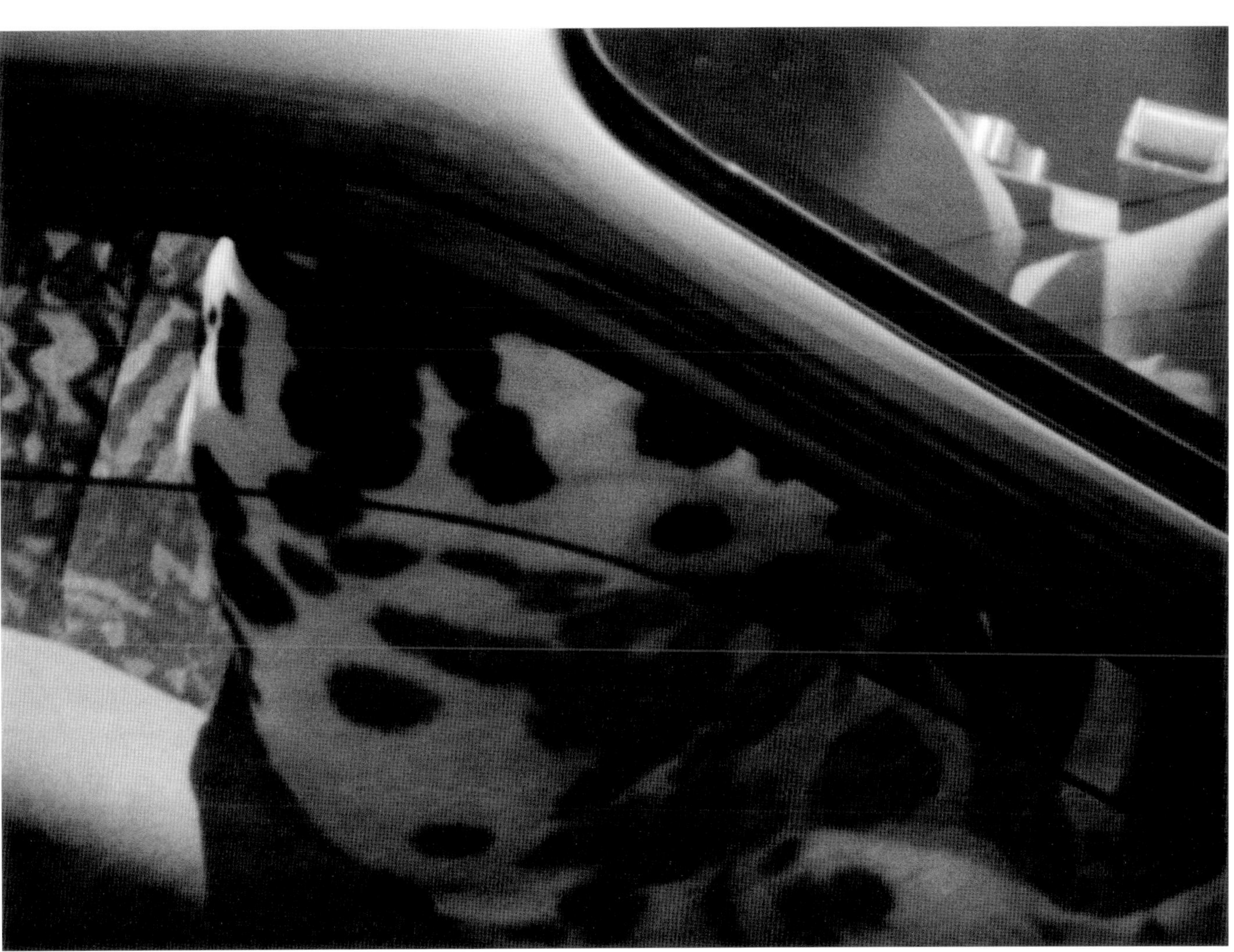

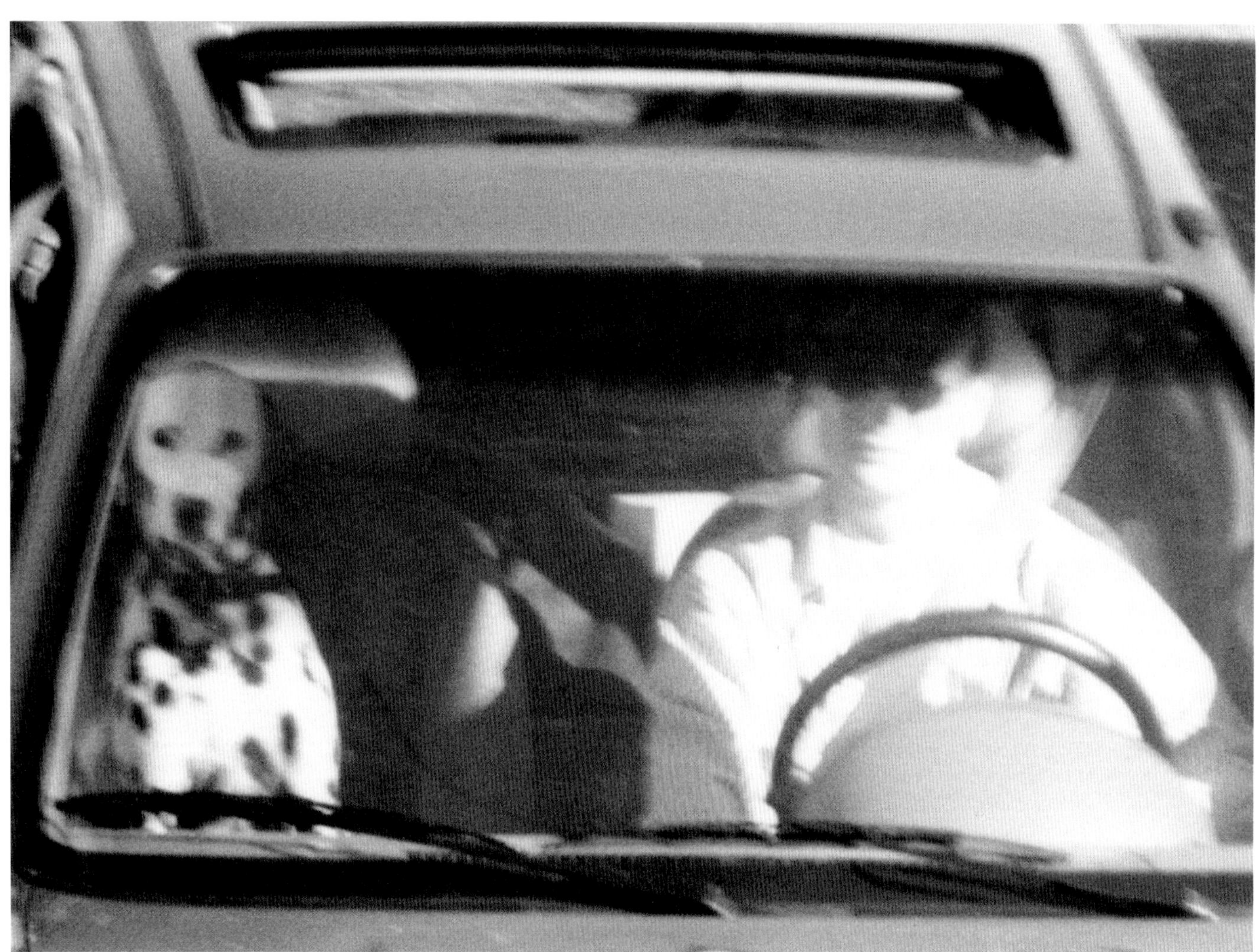

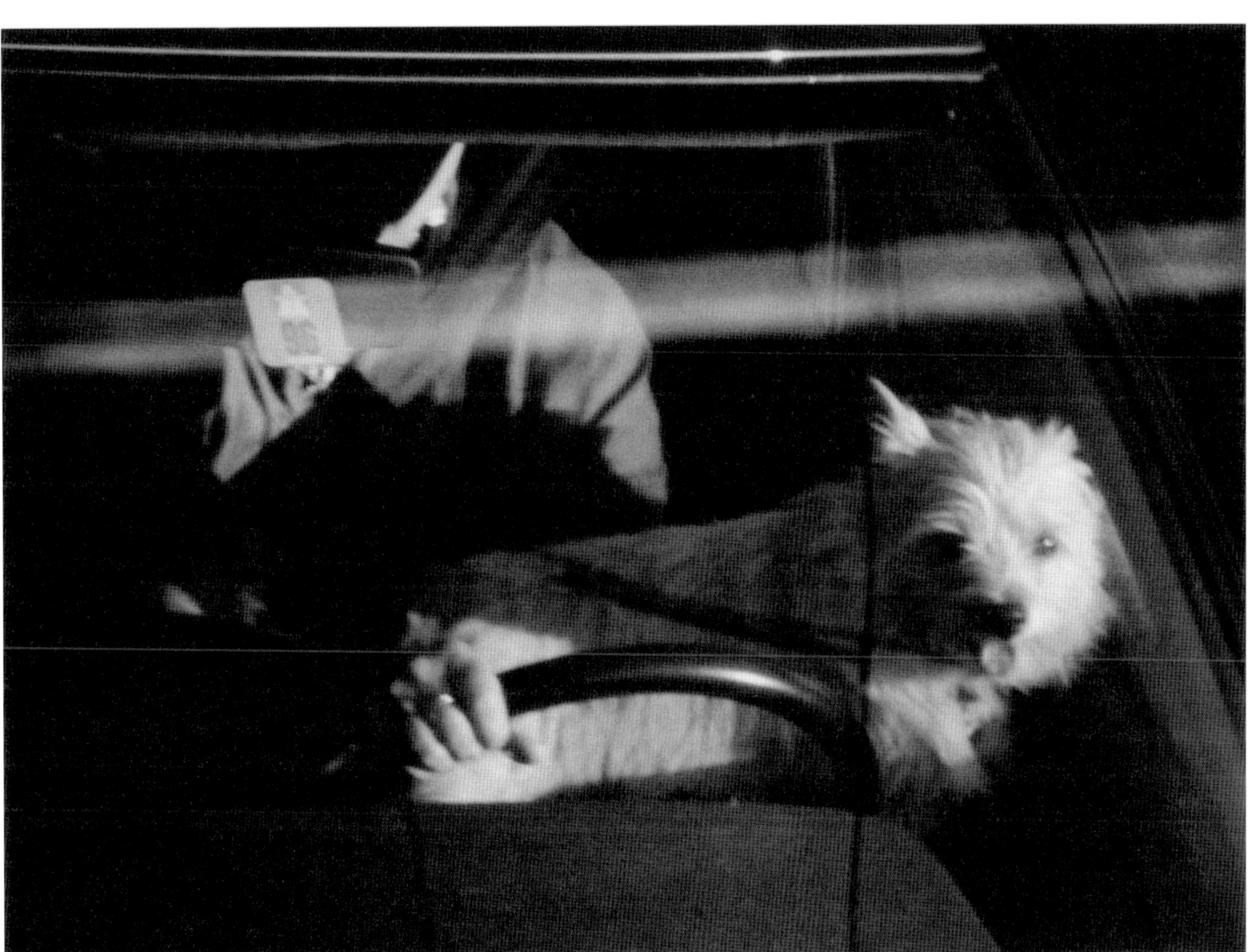

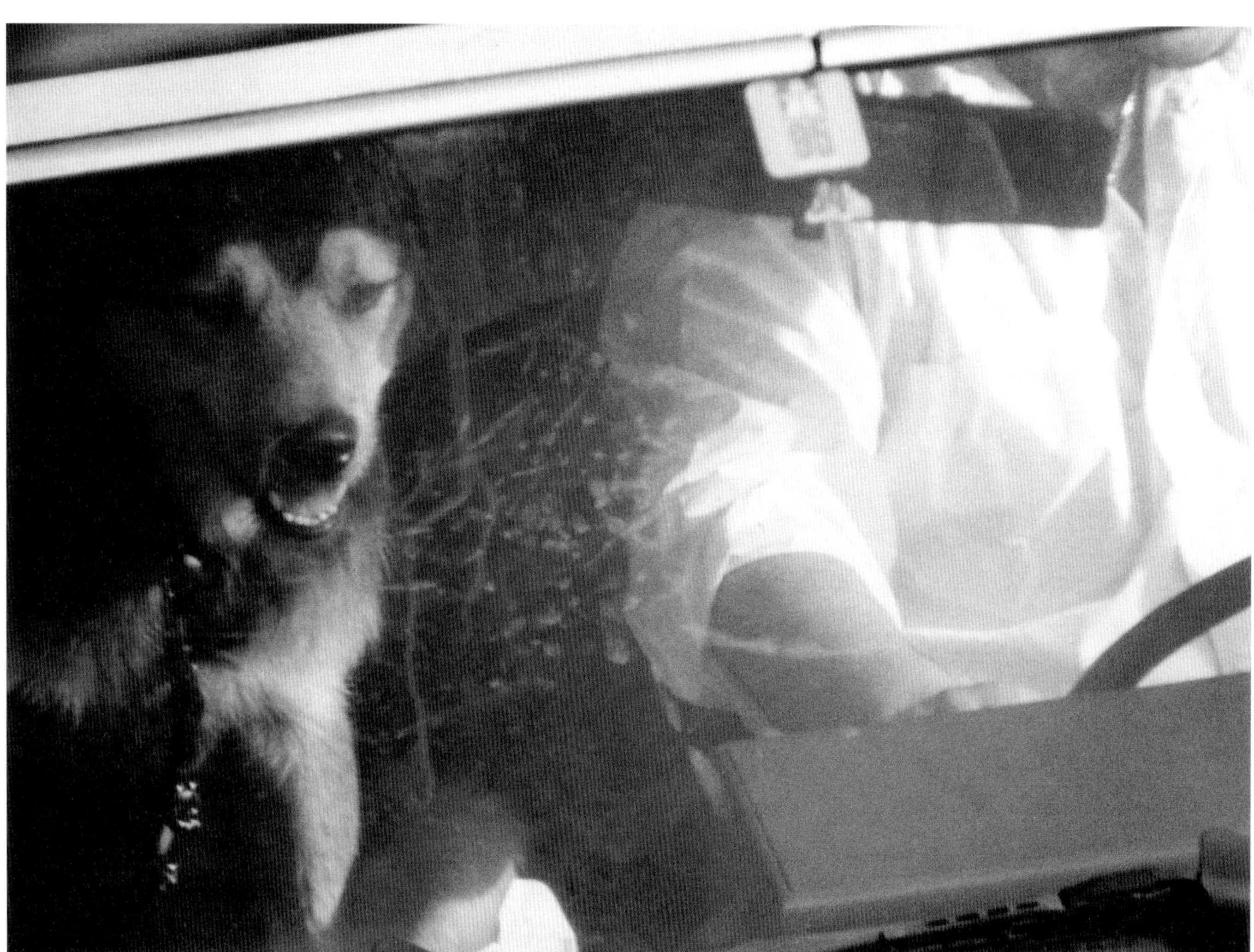

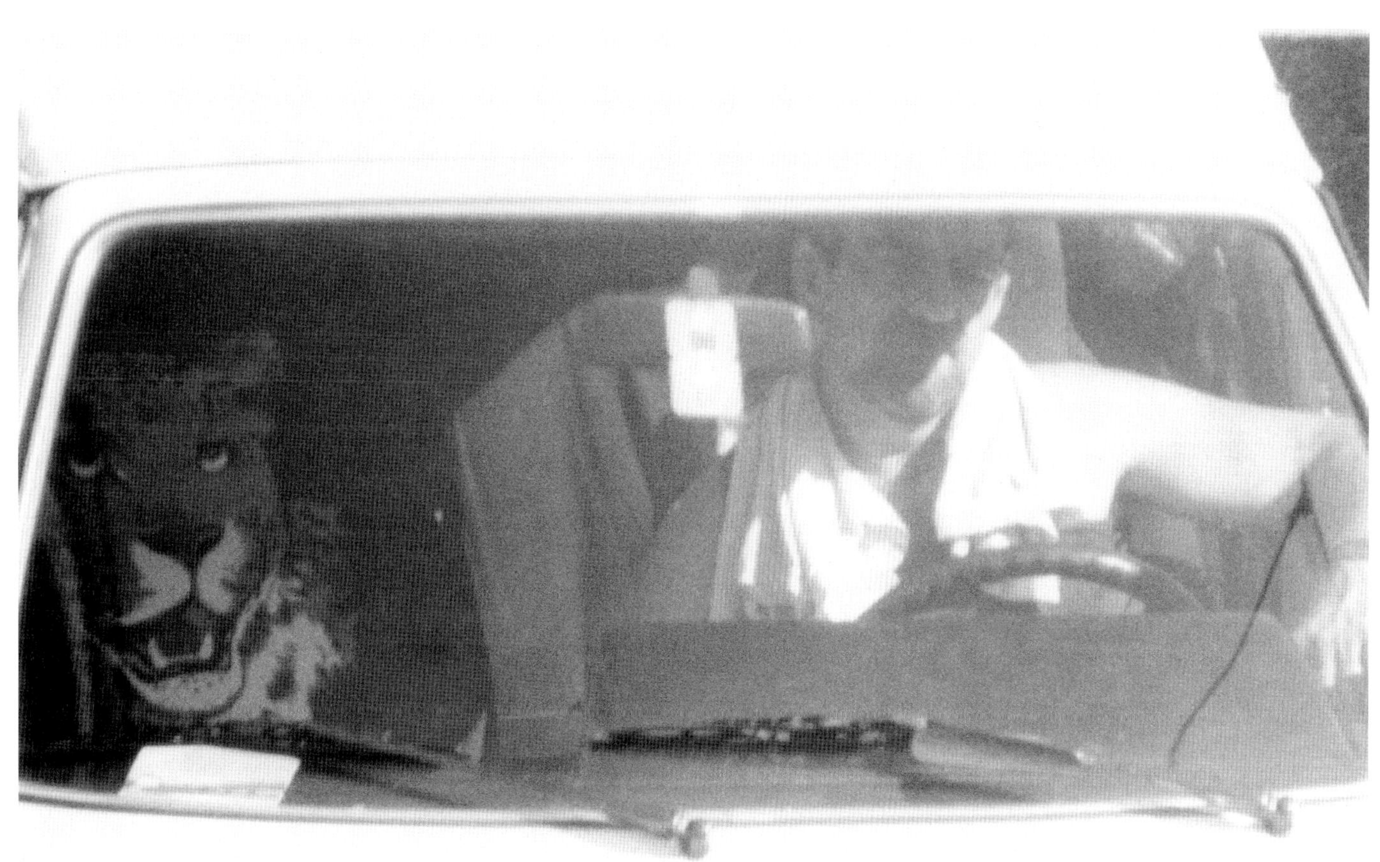

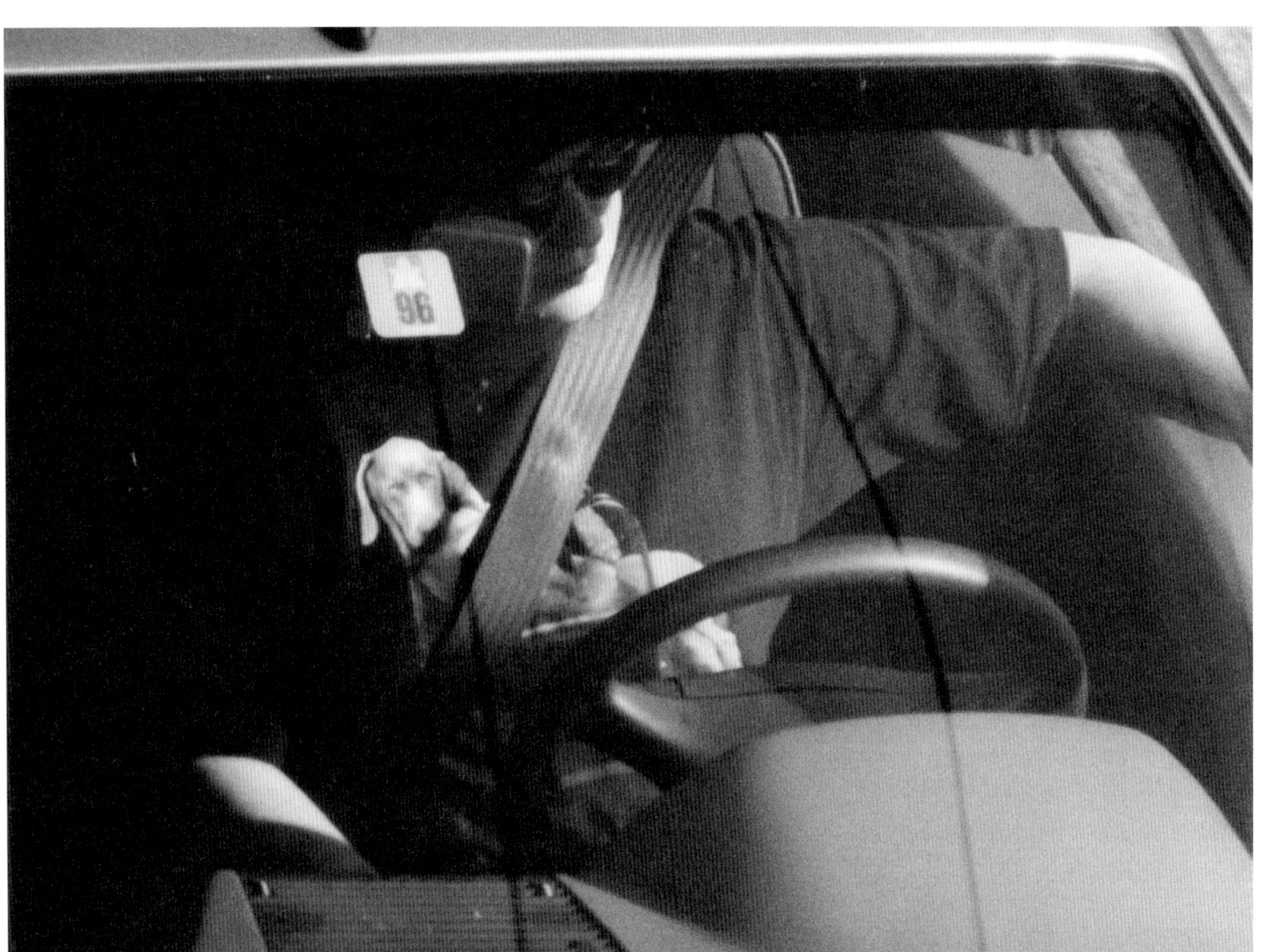
96

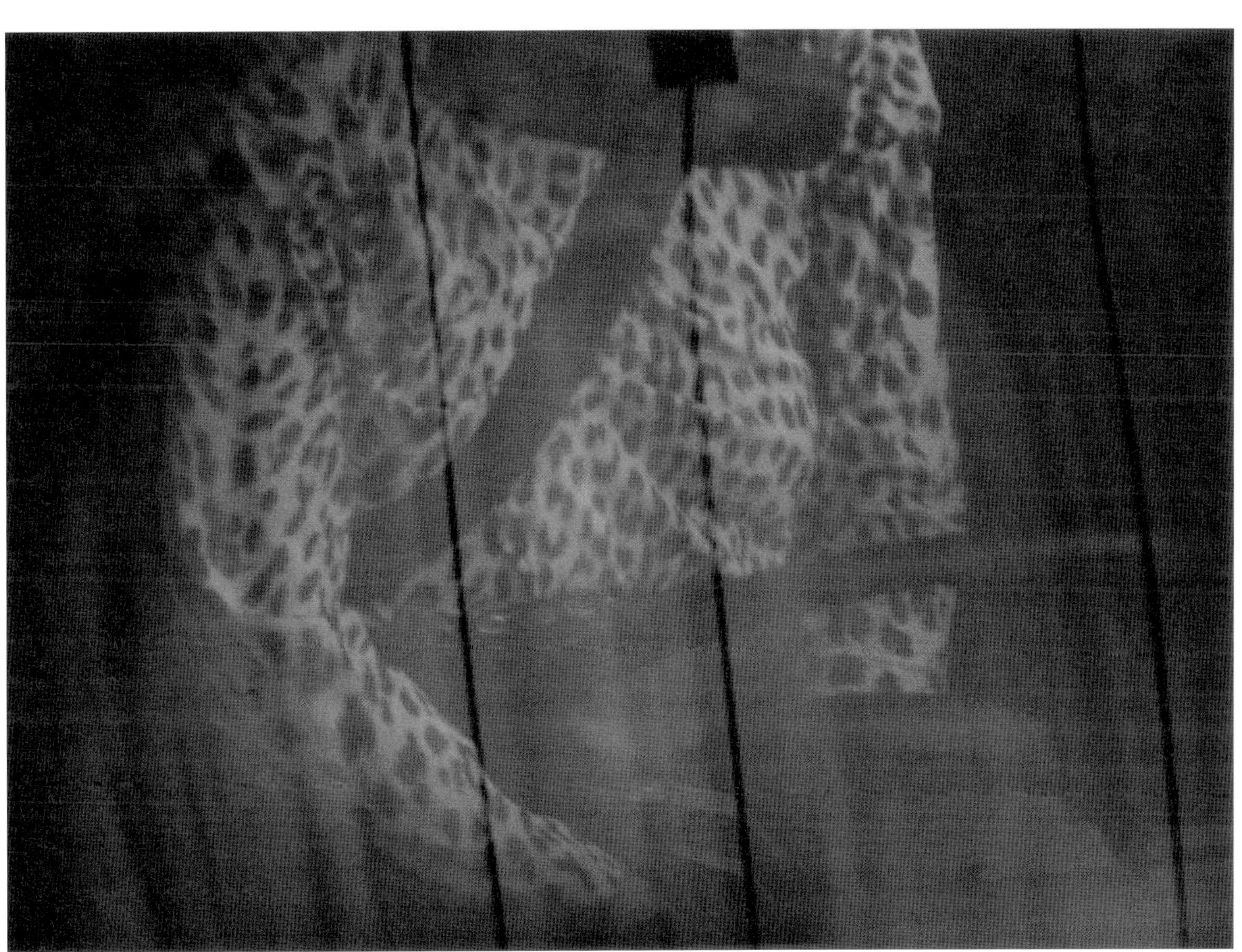

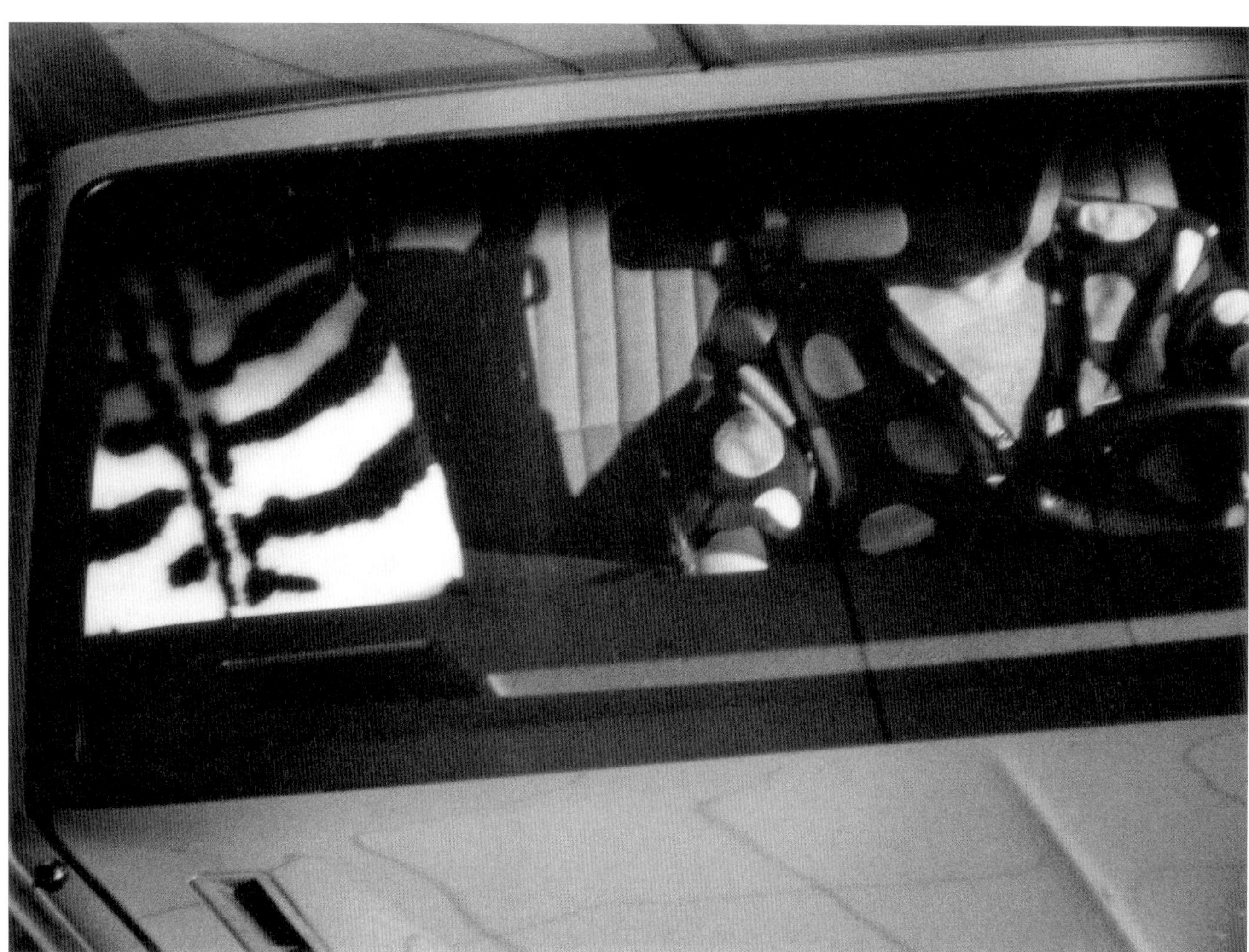

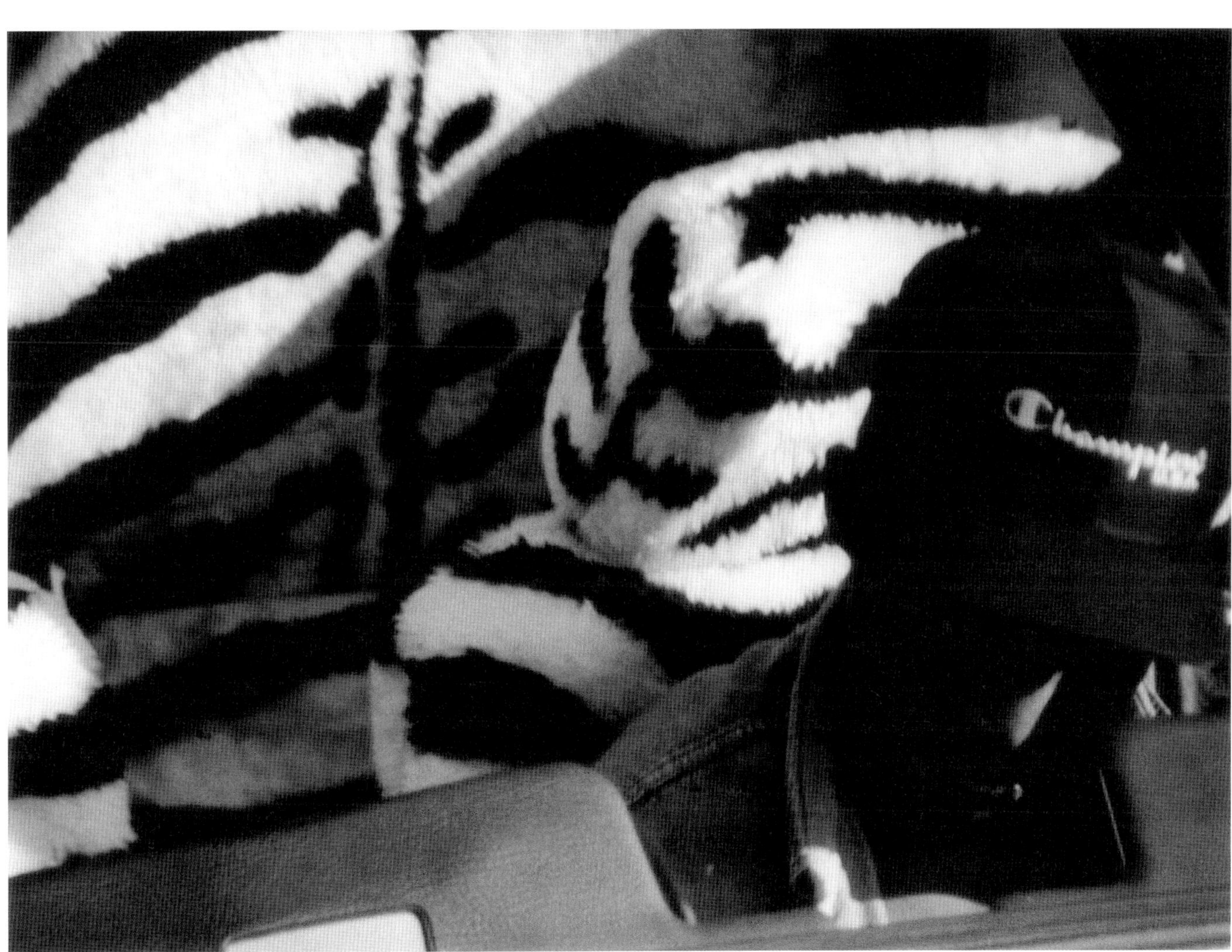
Champion

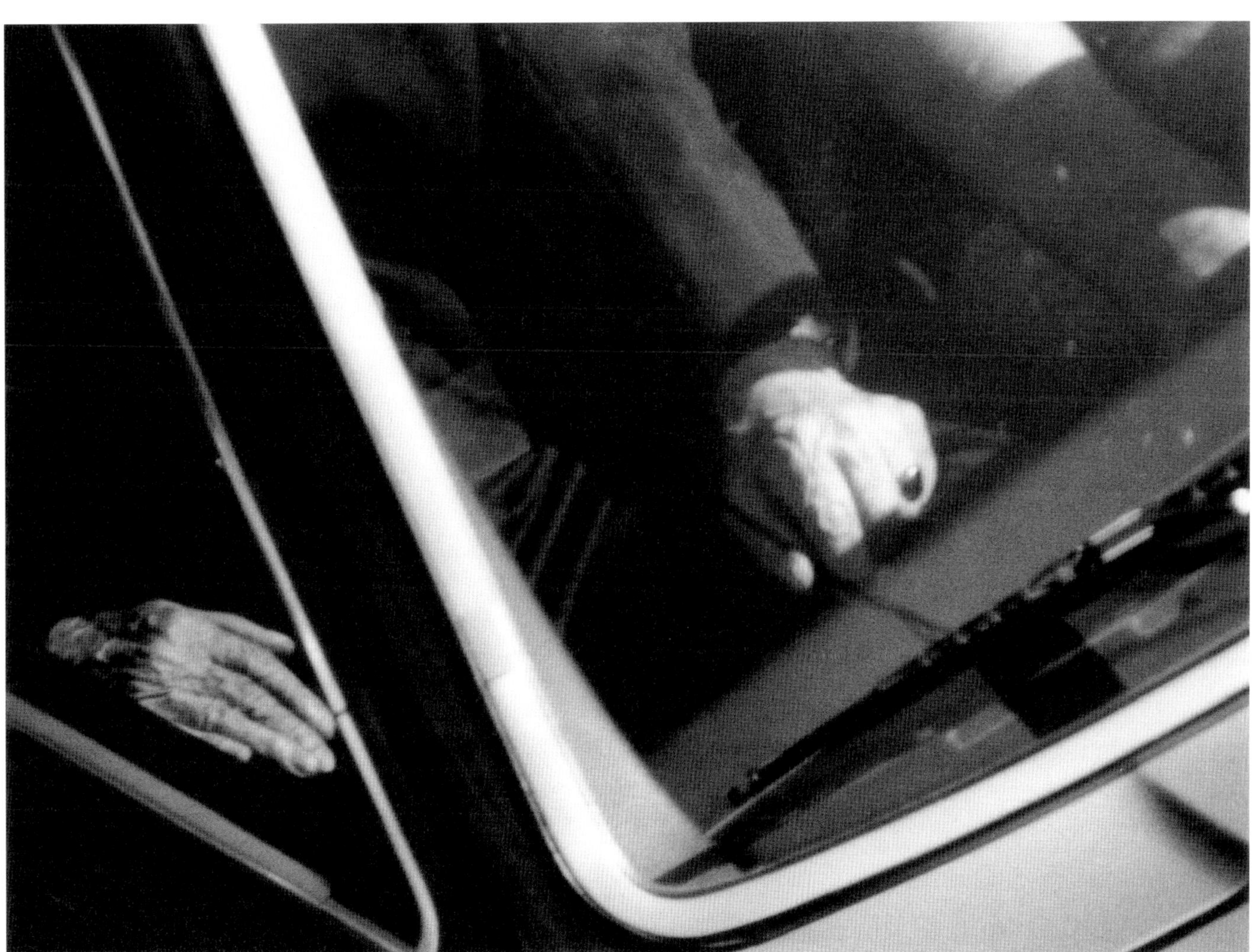

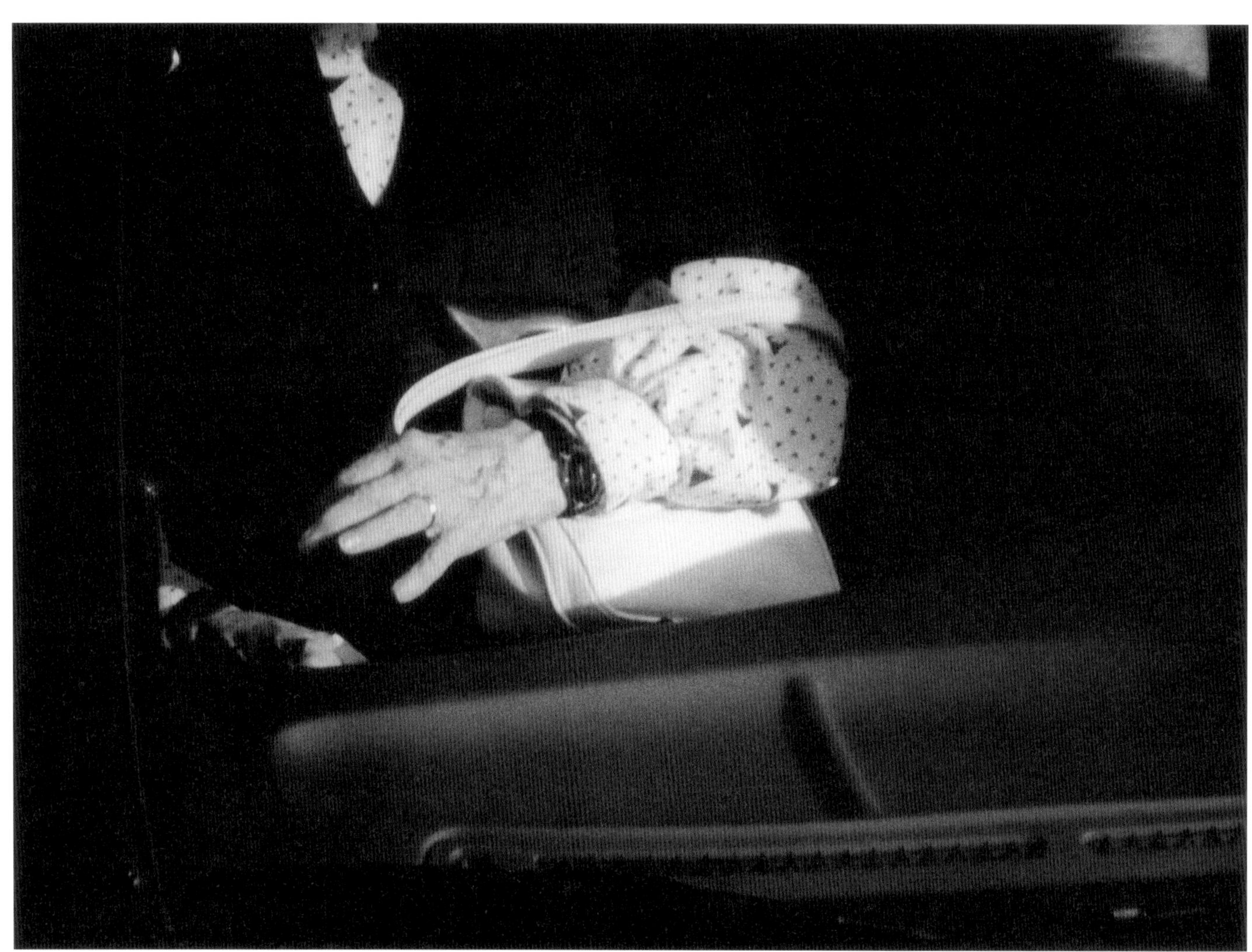

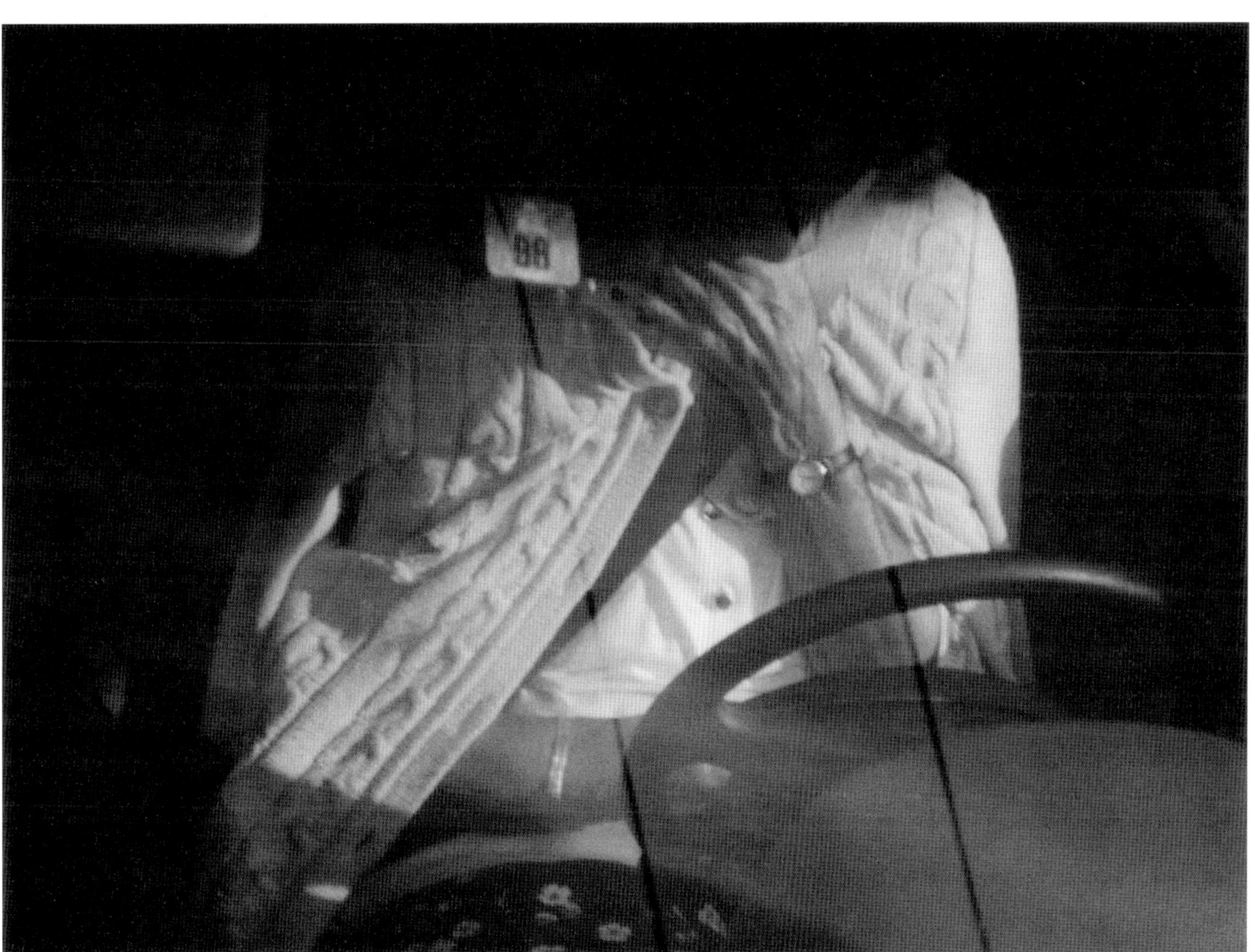

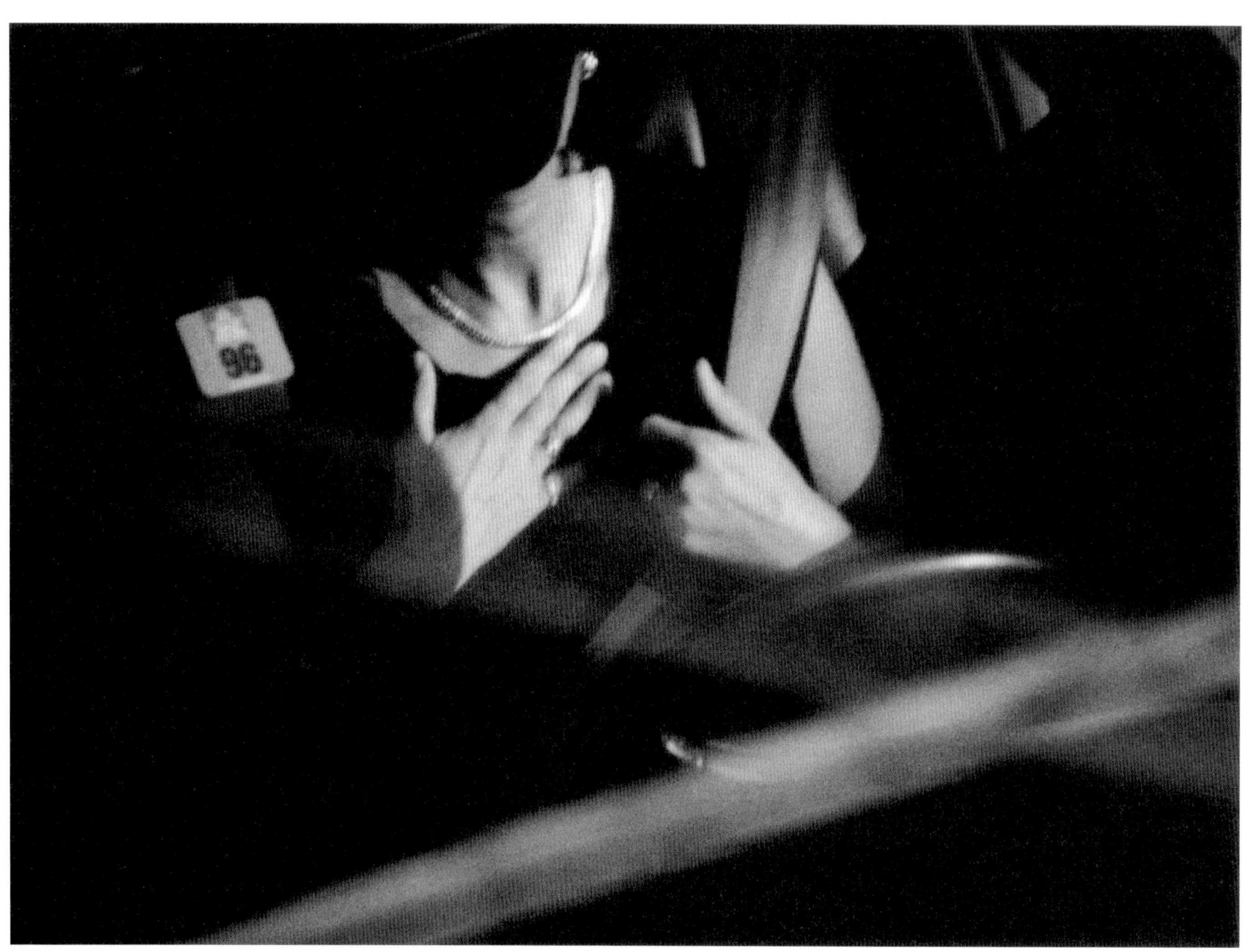

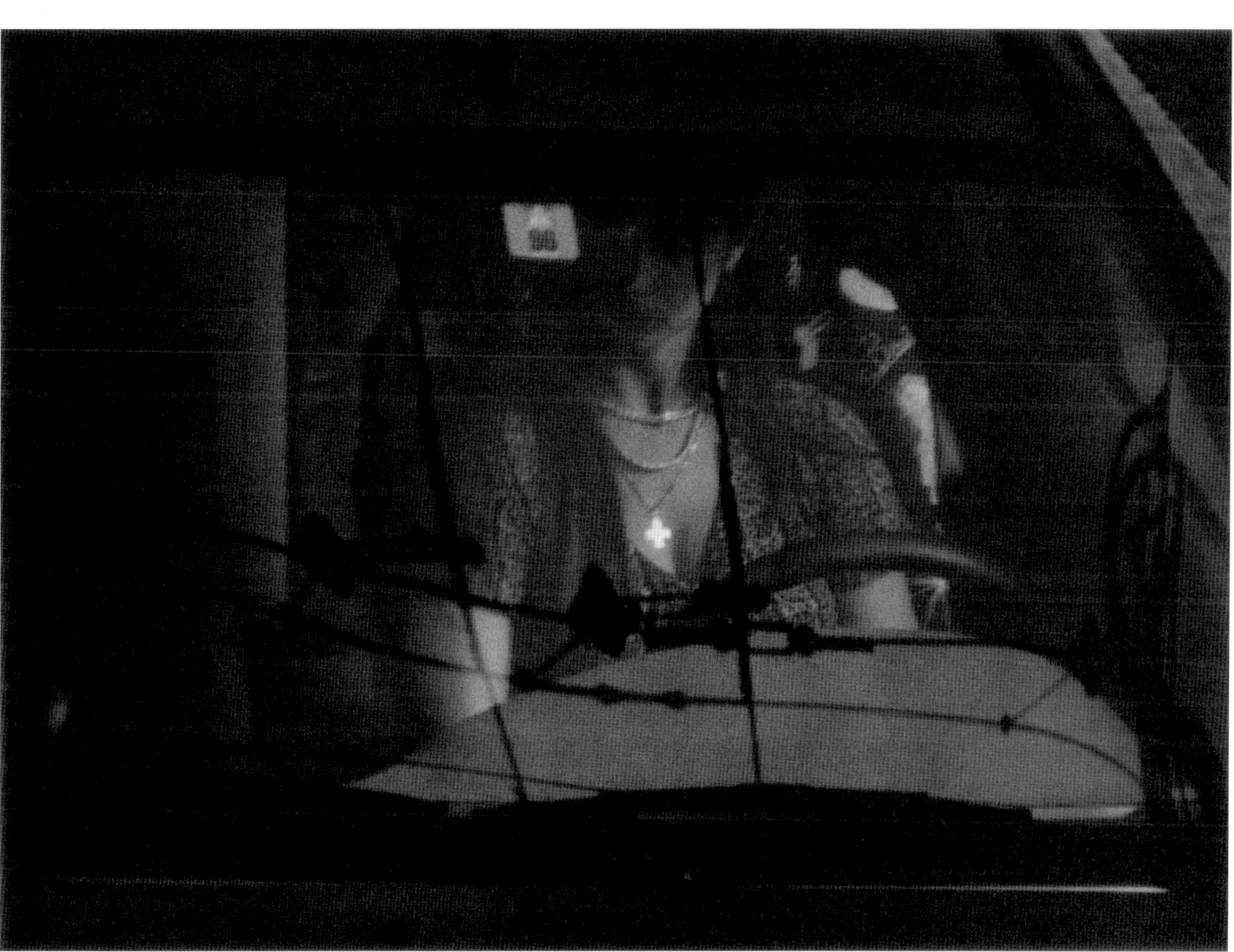

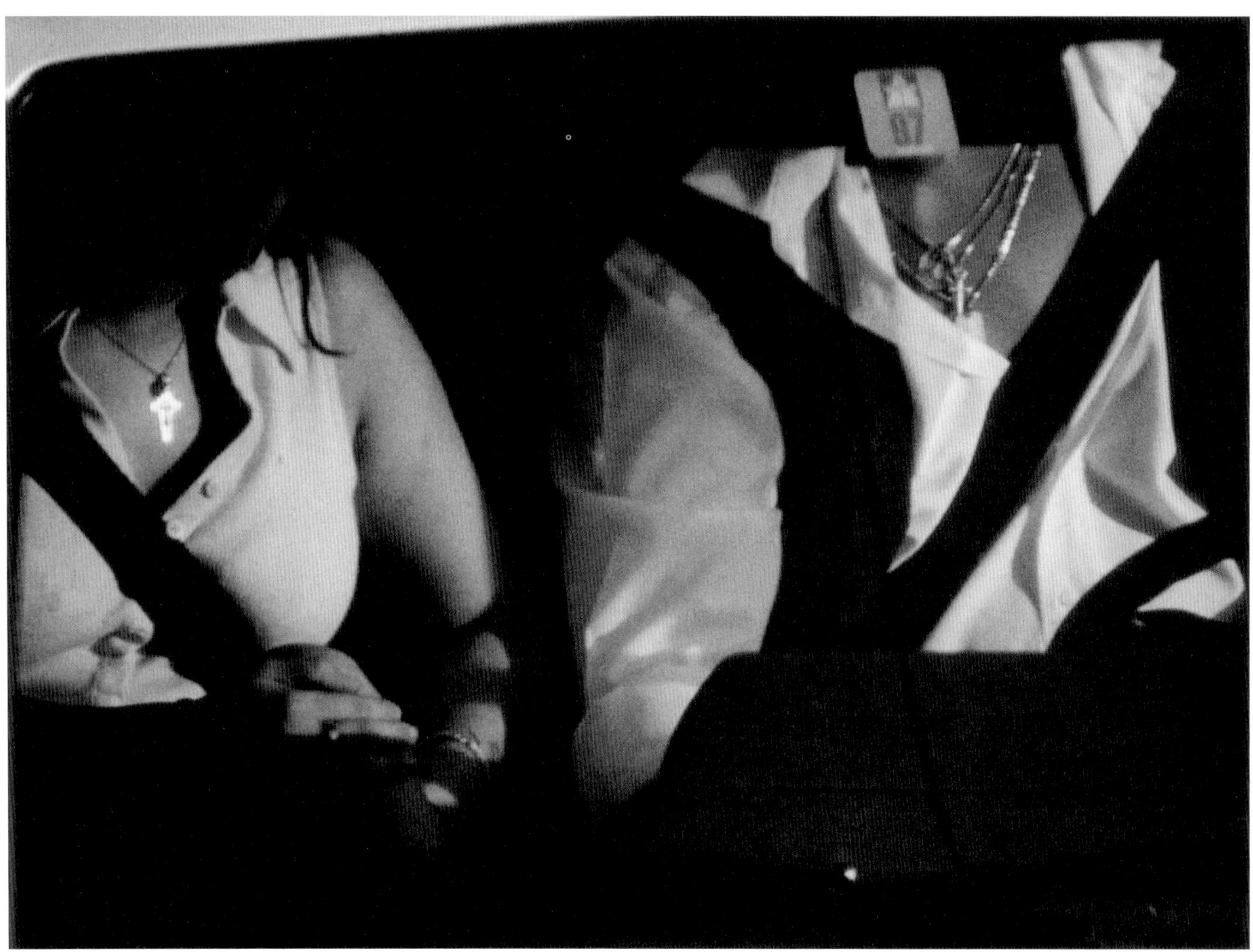

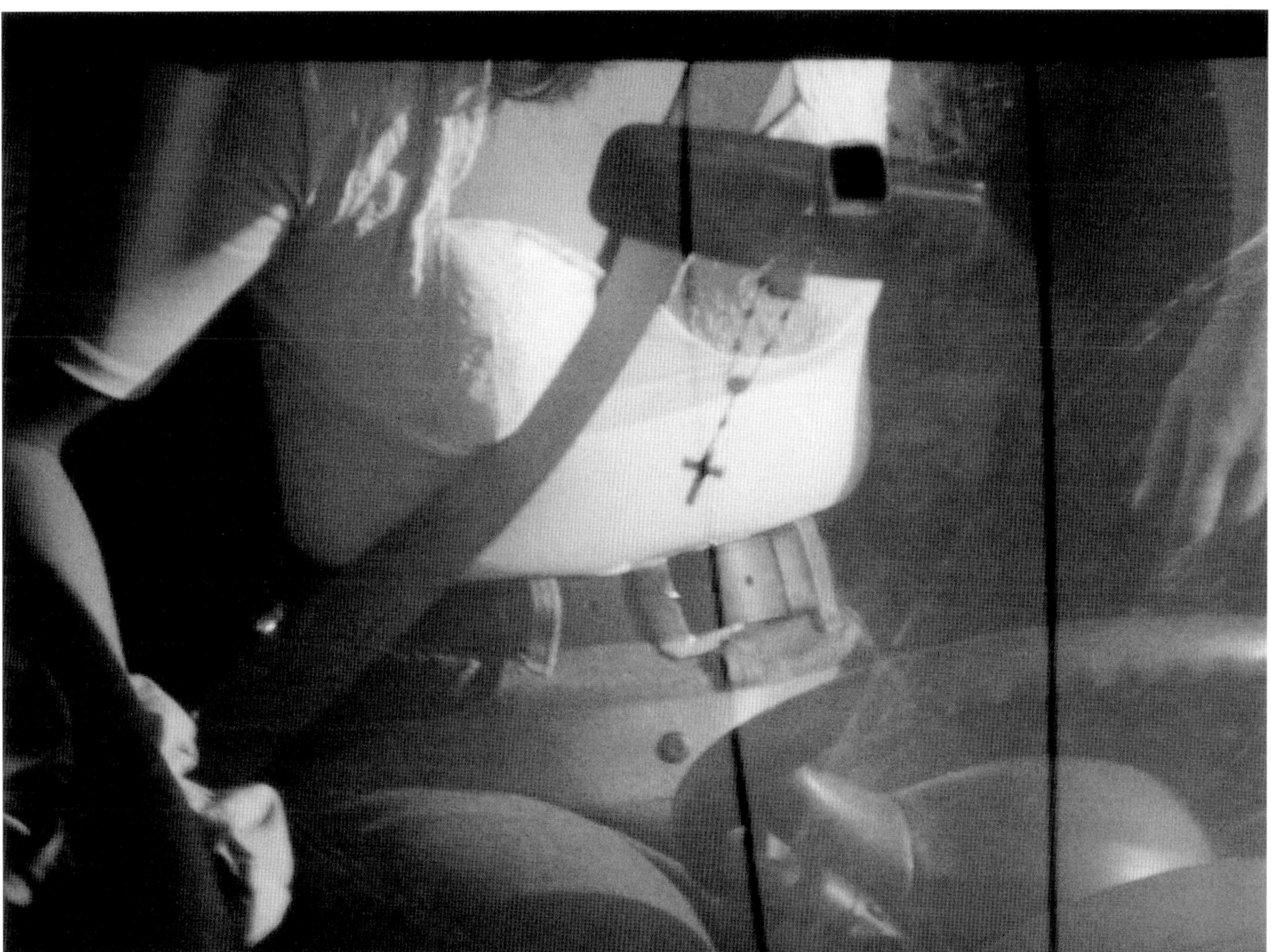

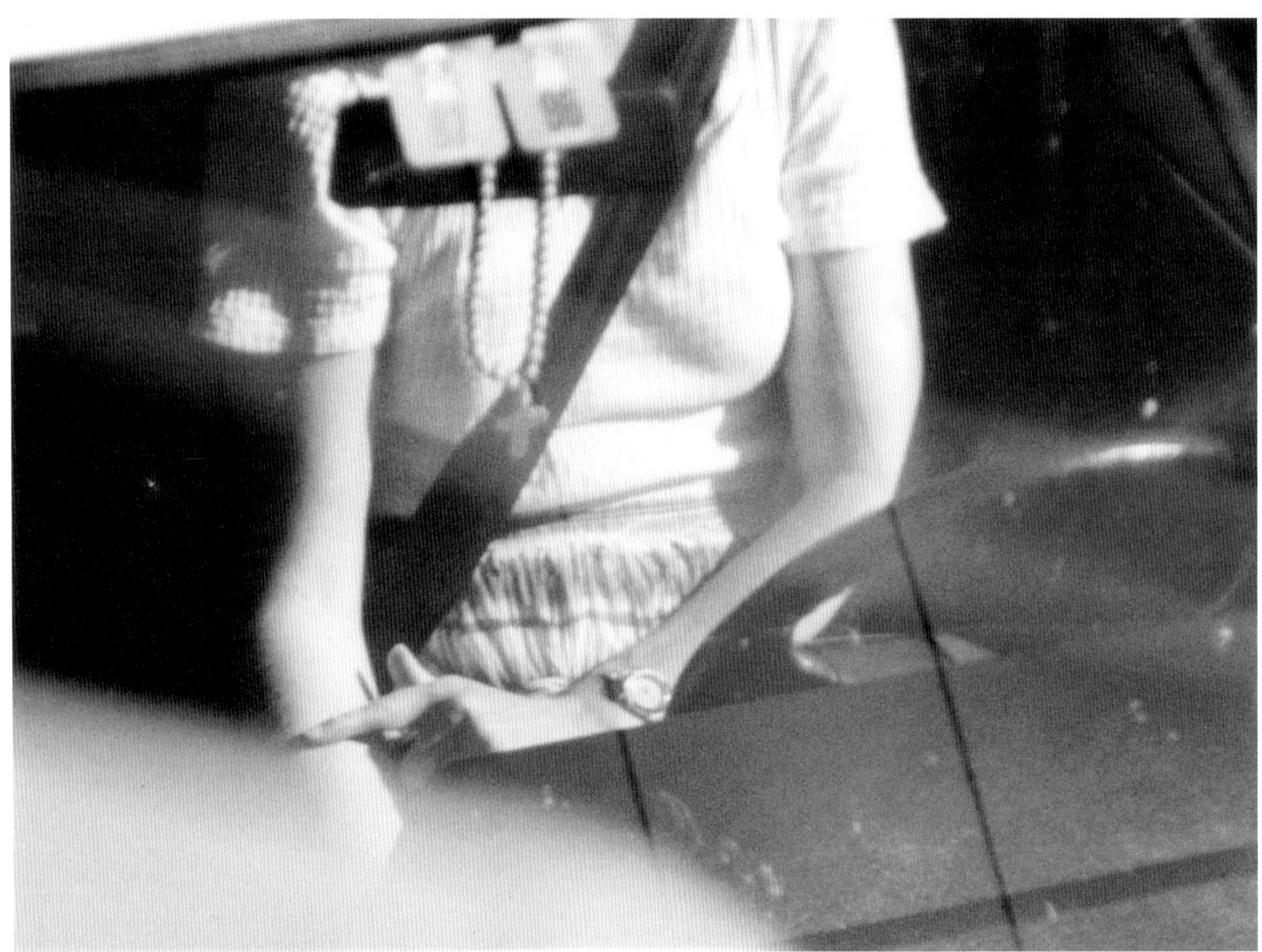

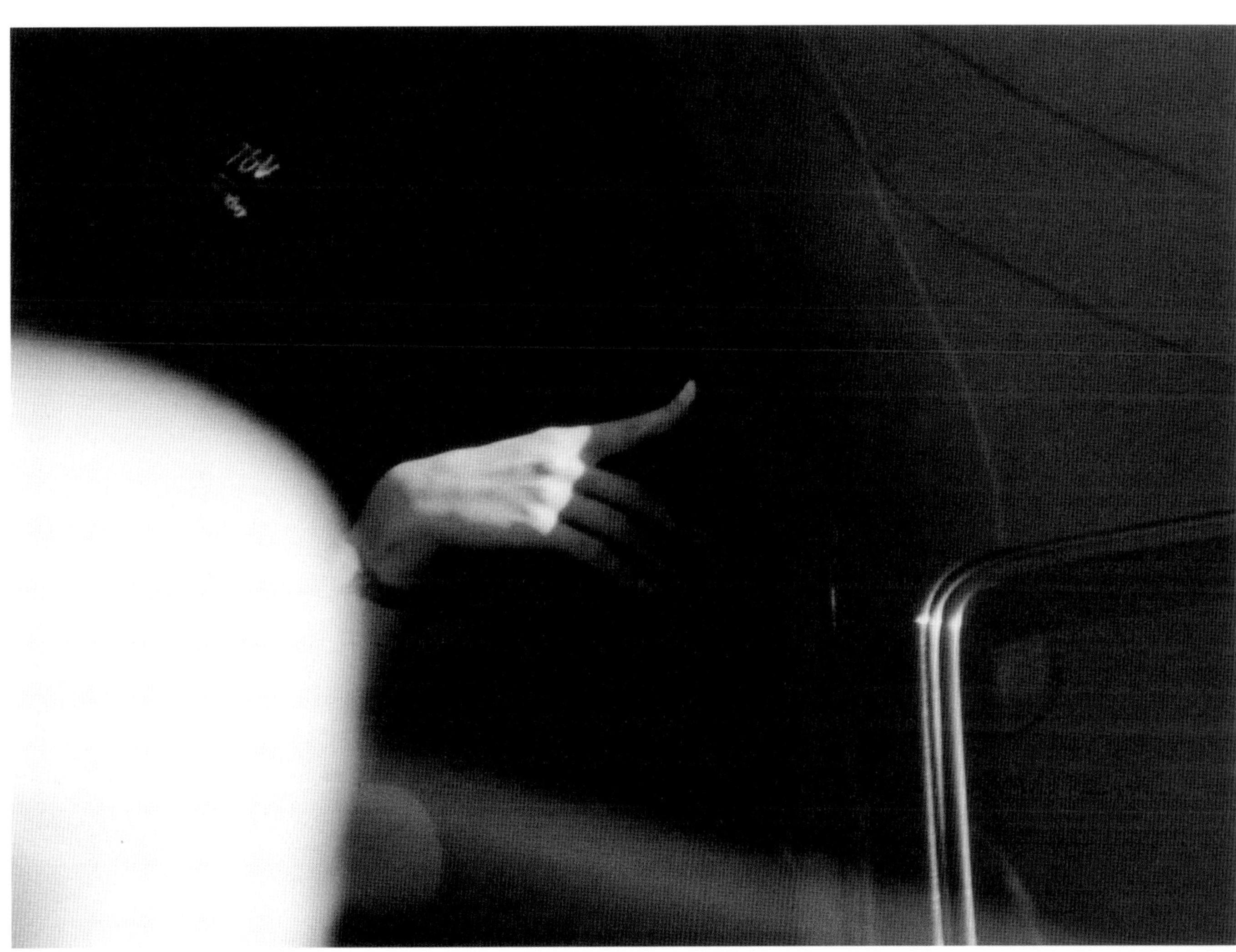

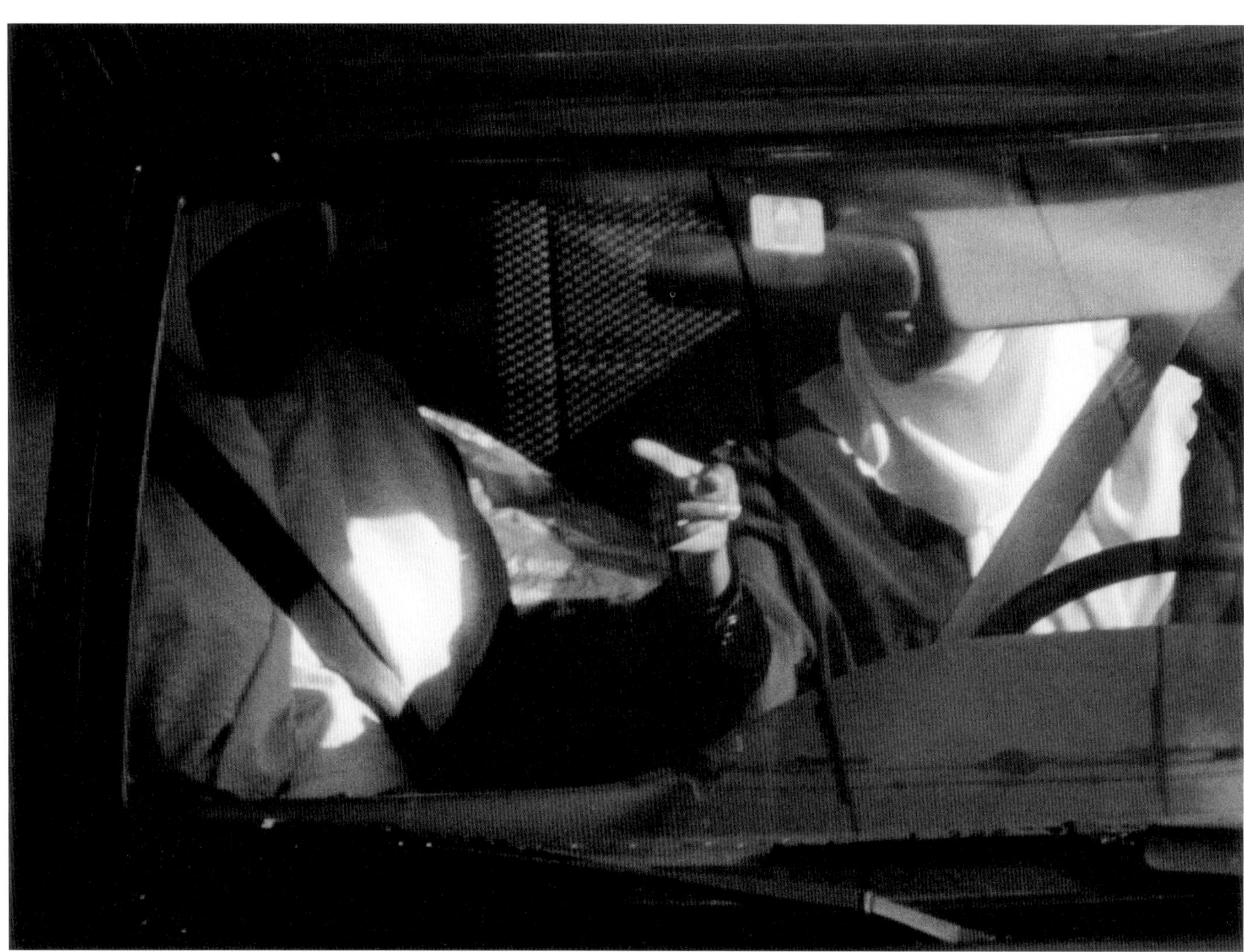

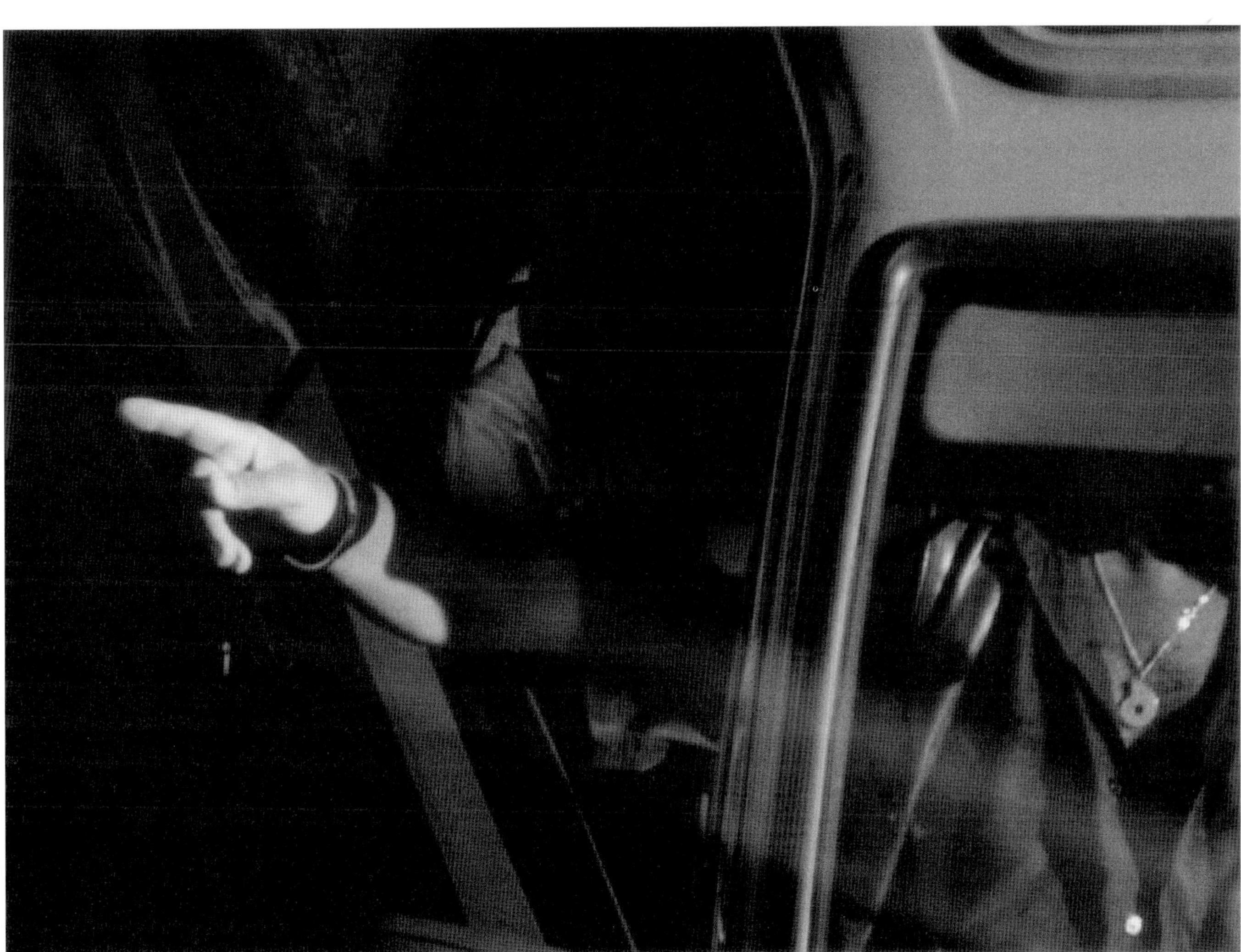

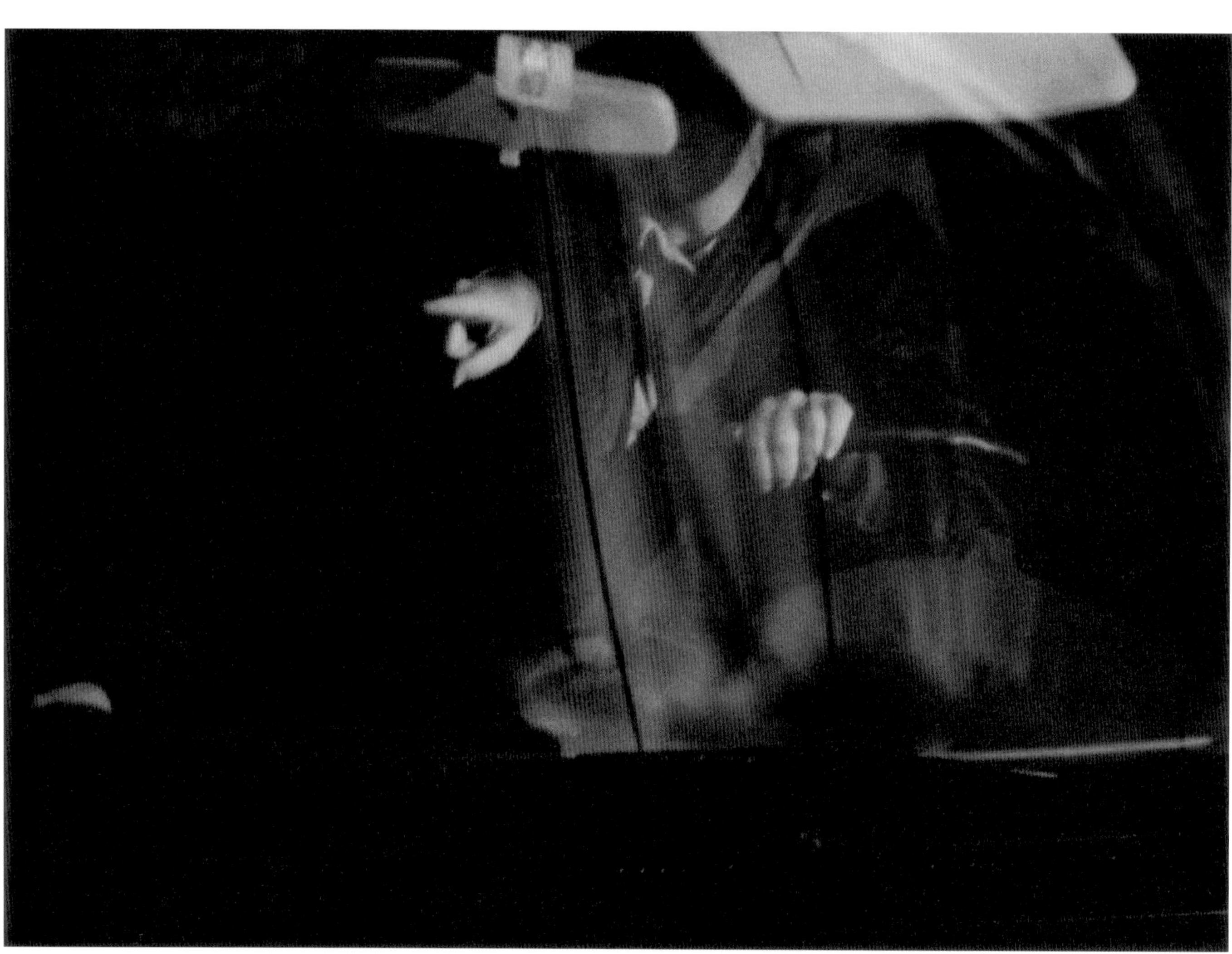

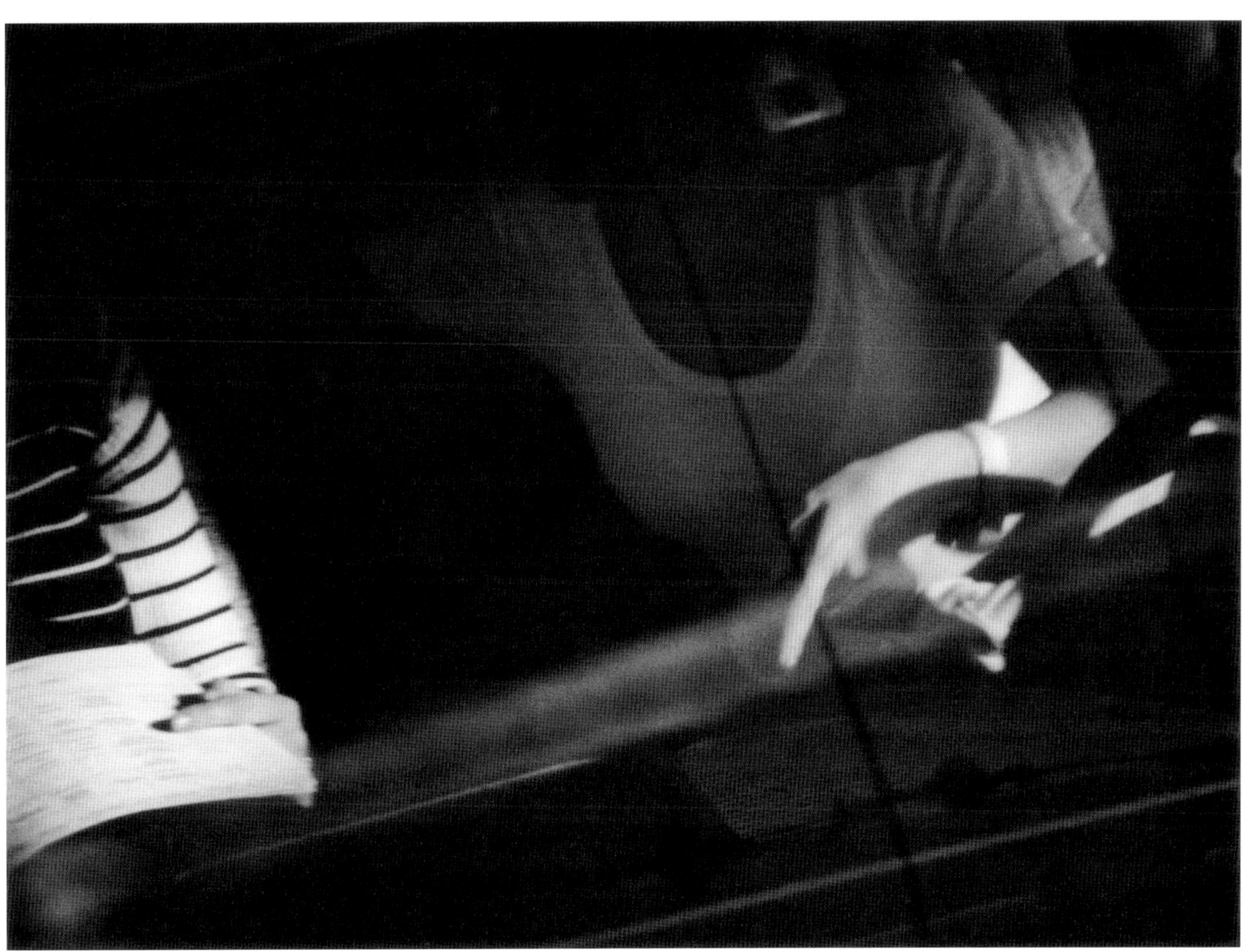

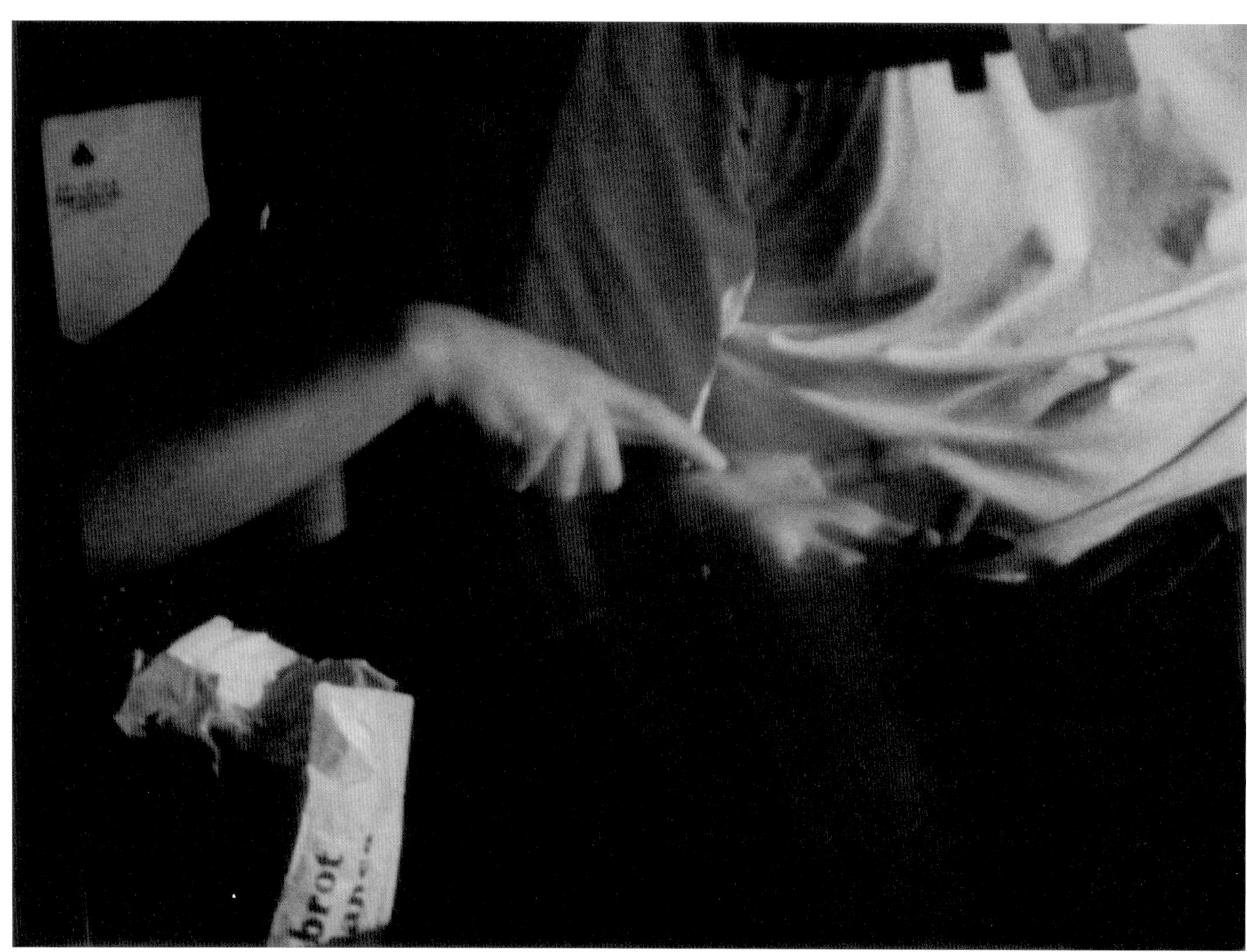

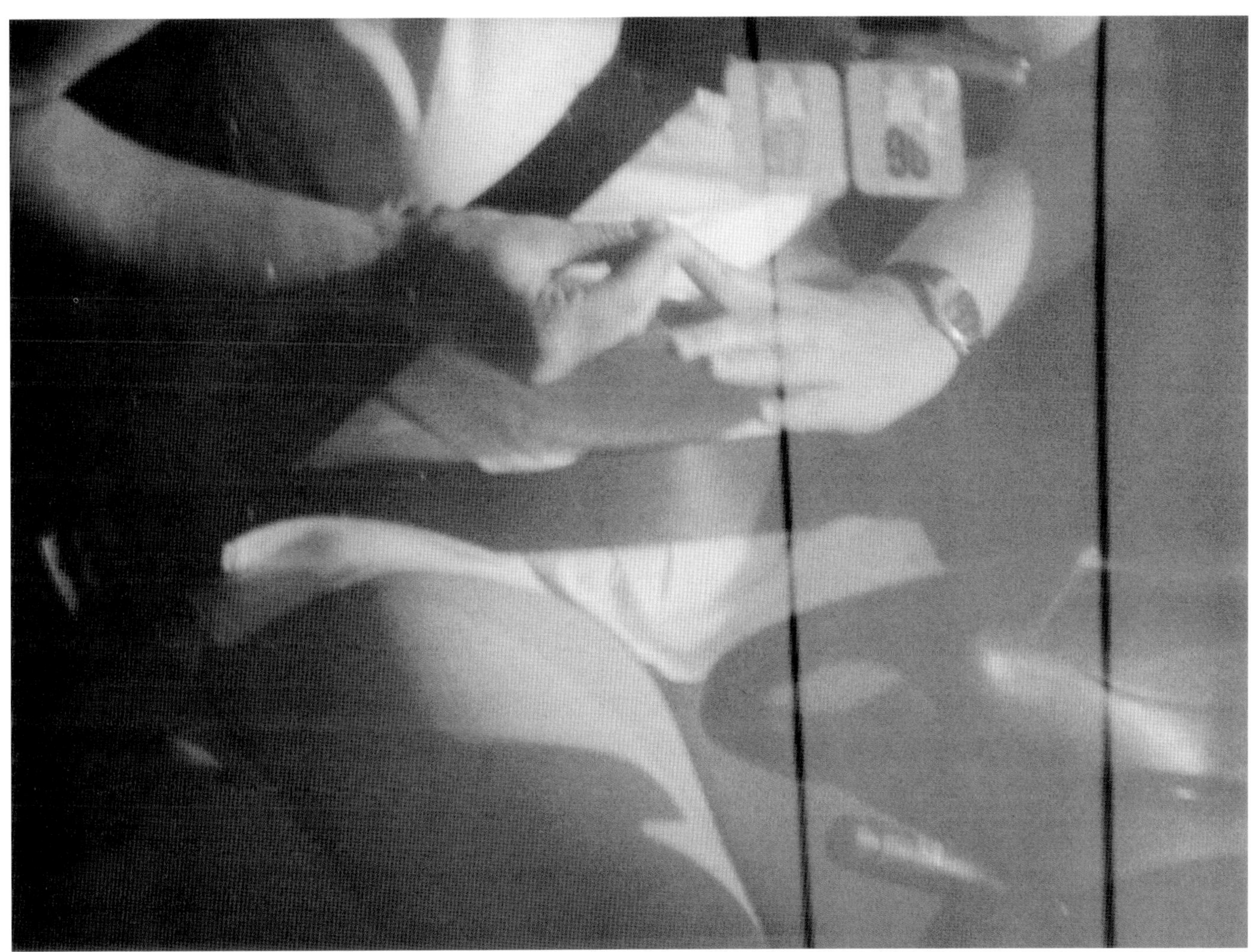

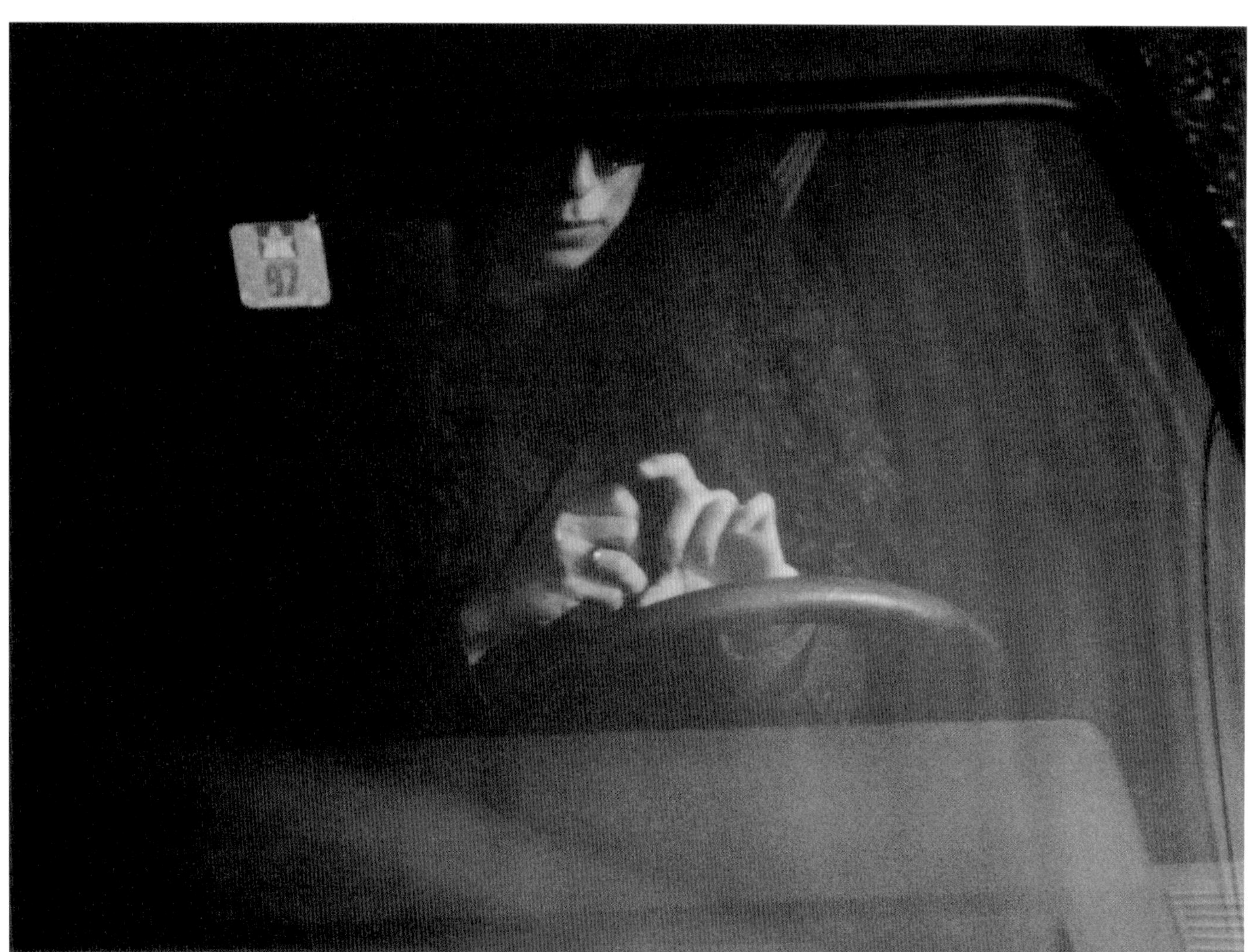

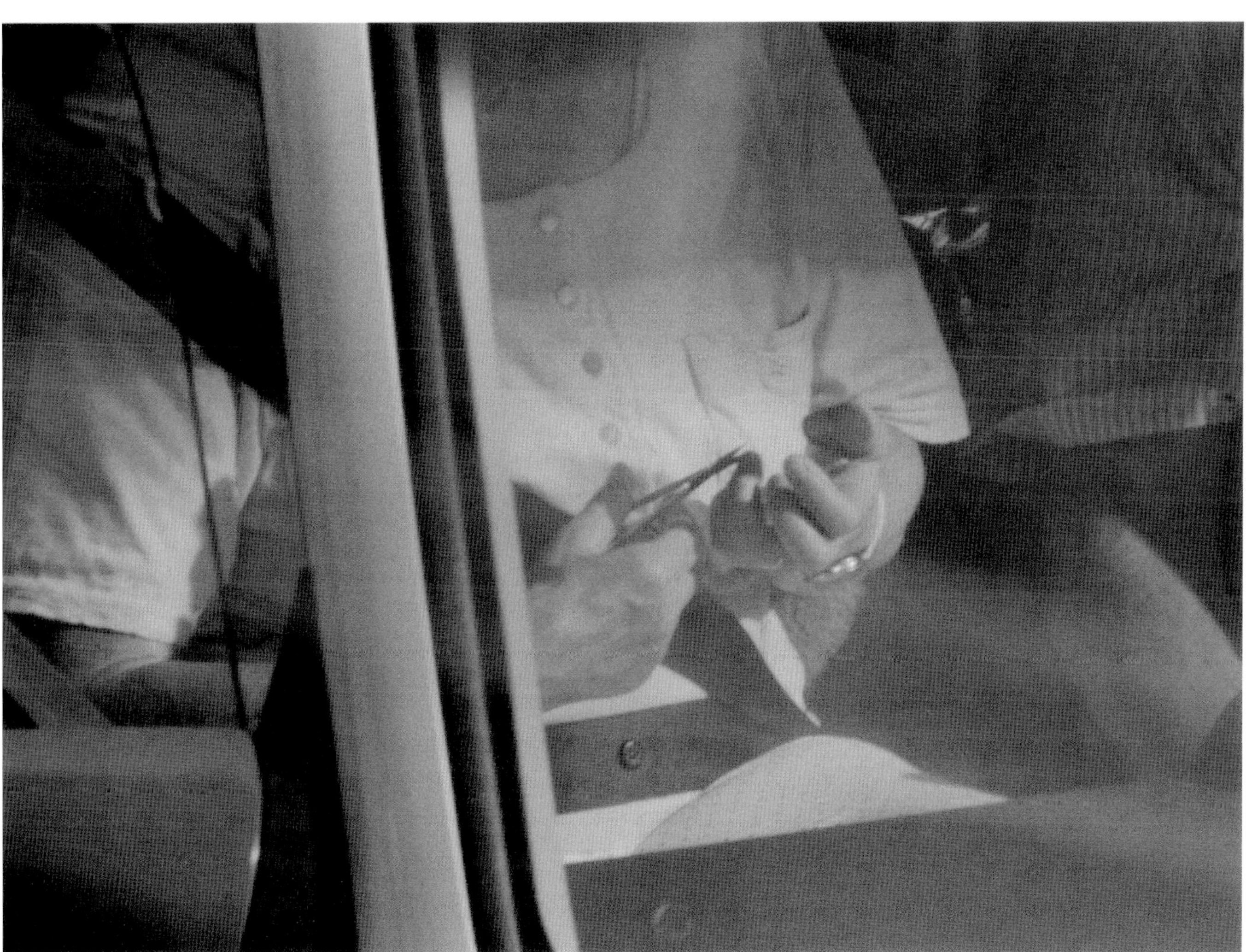

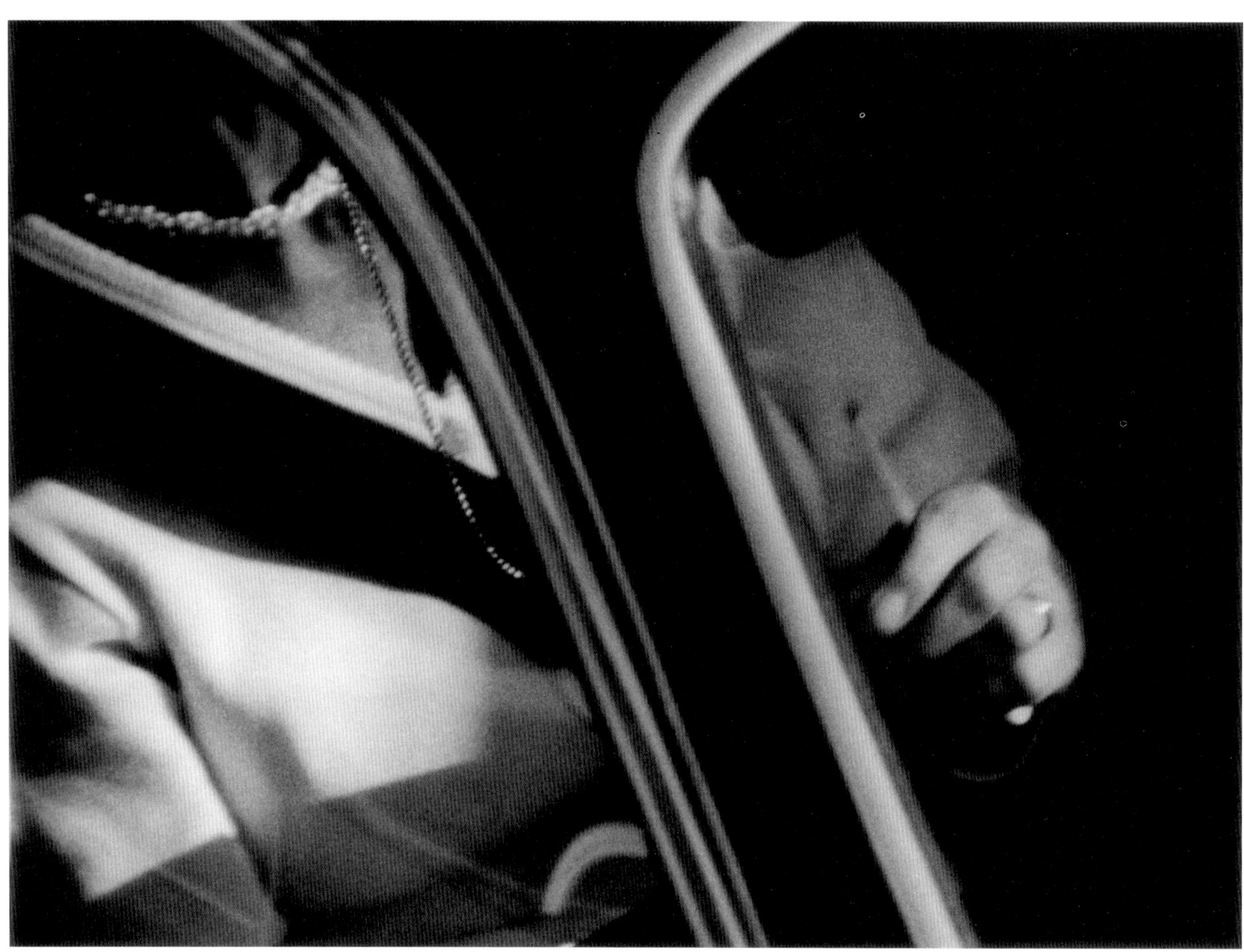

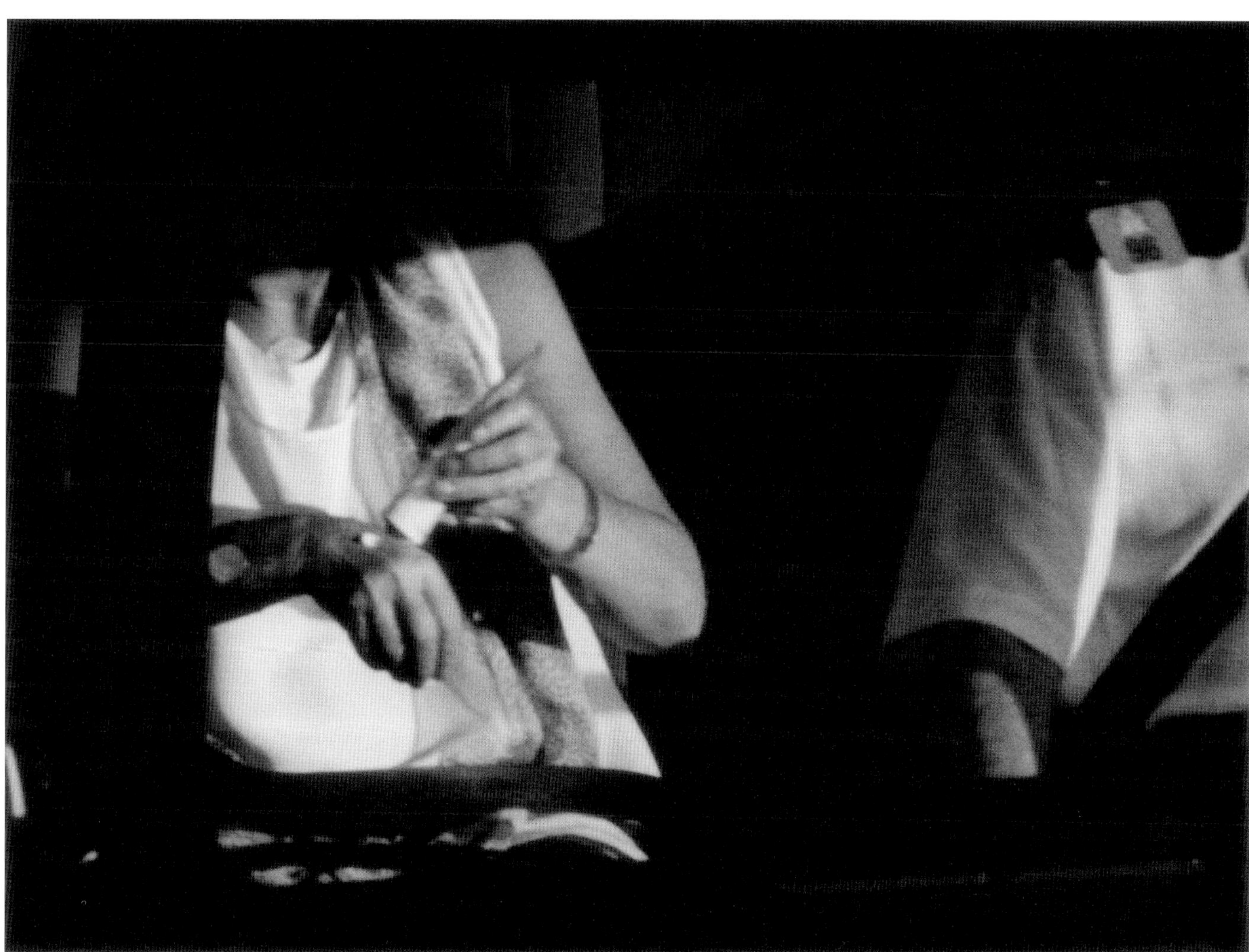

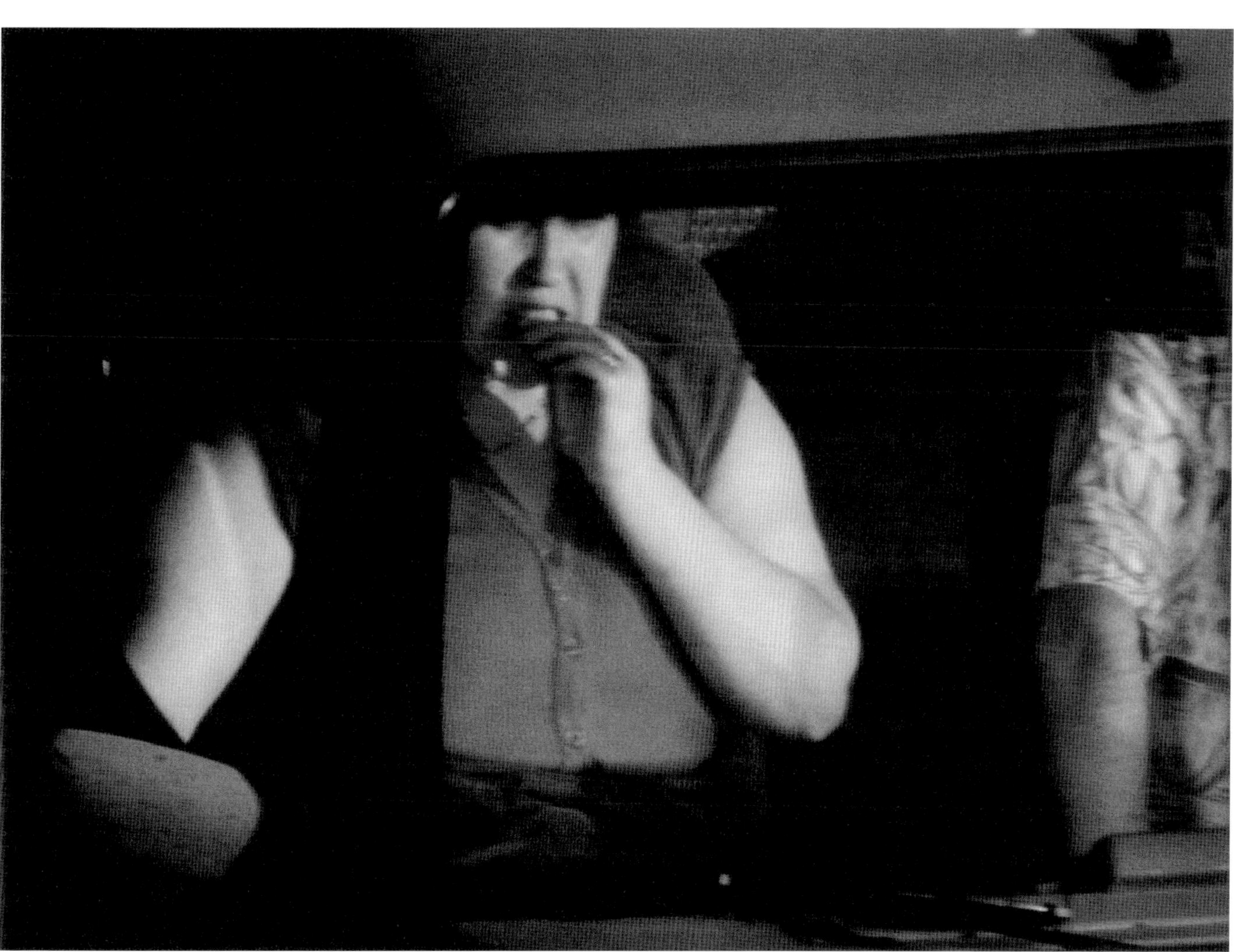

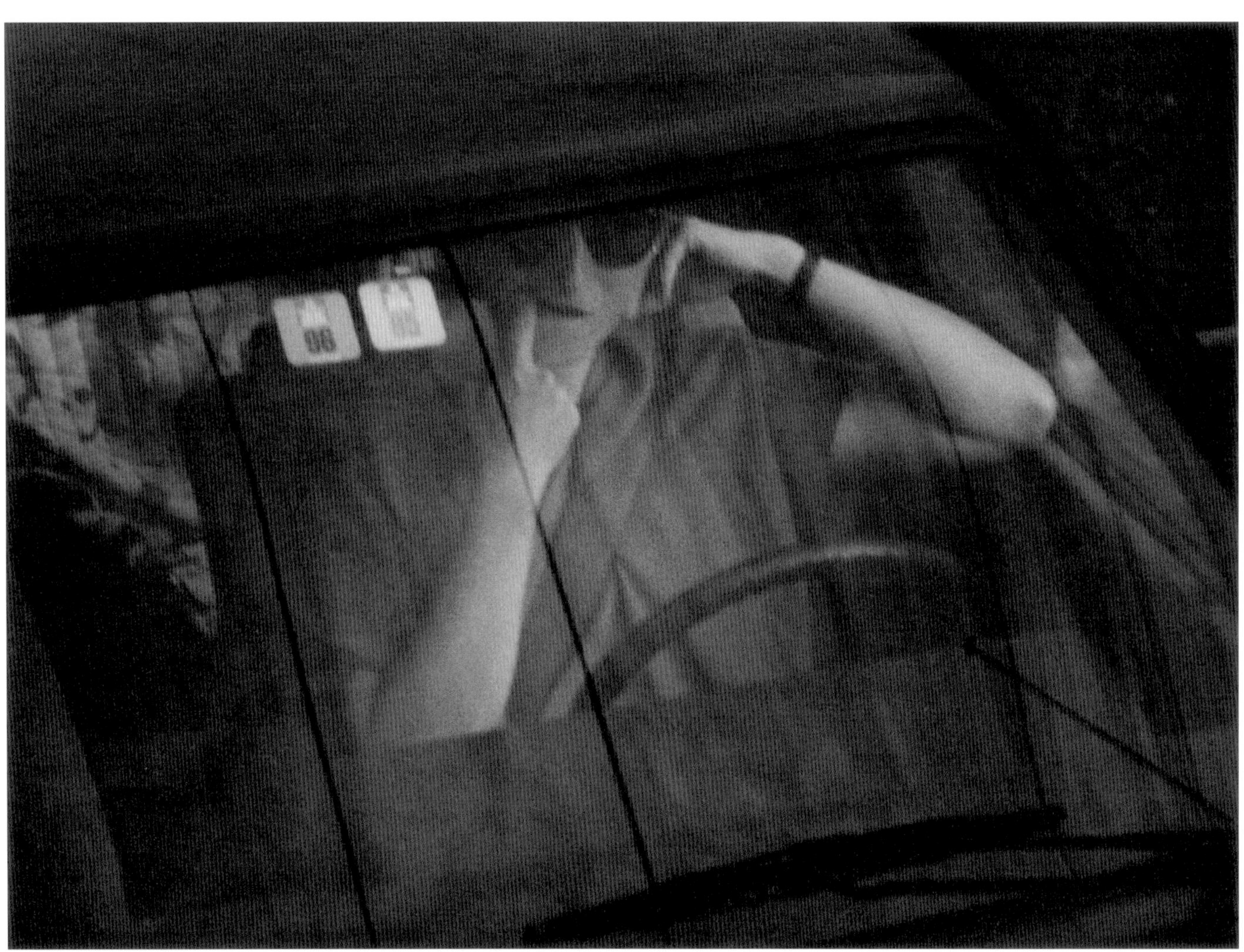

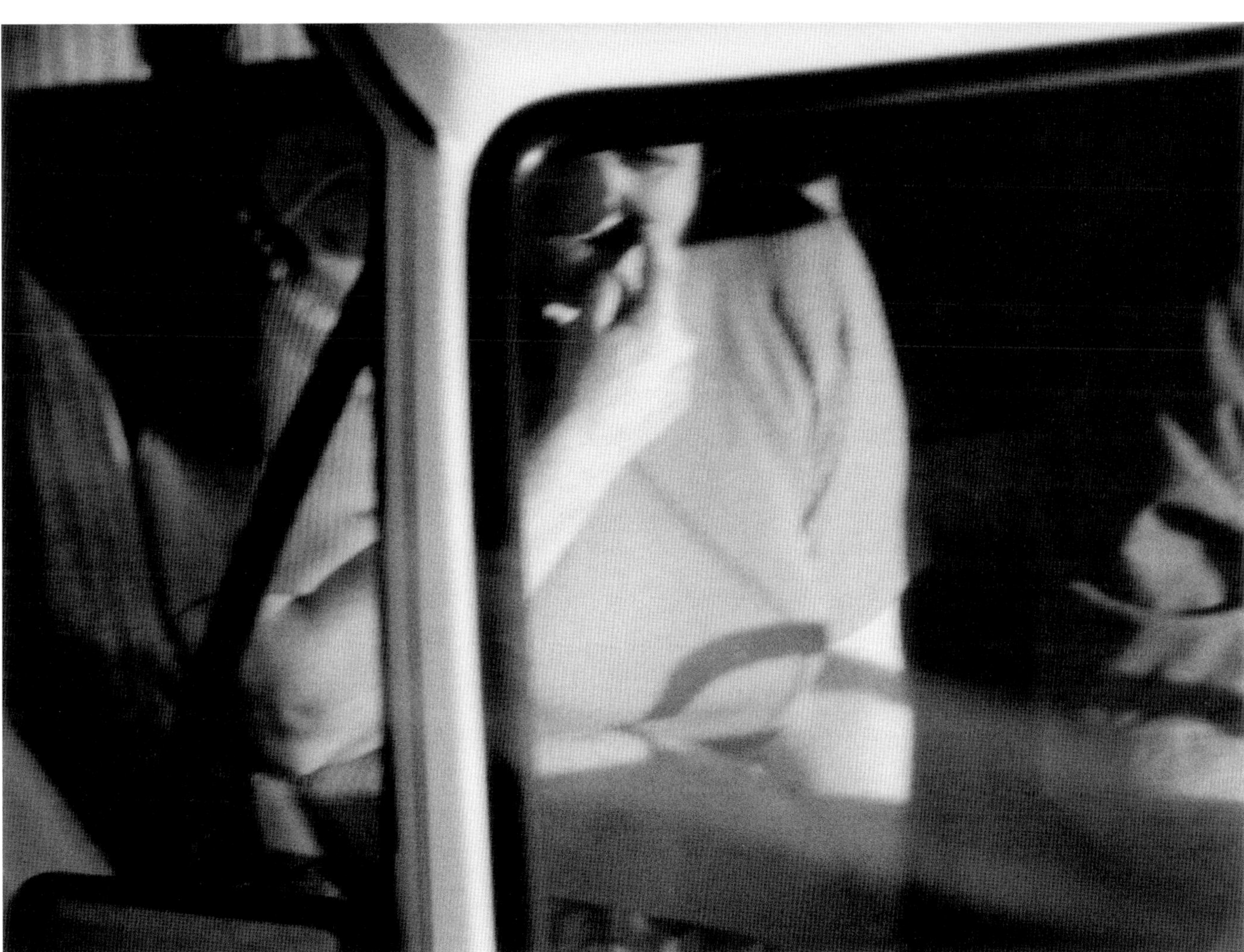

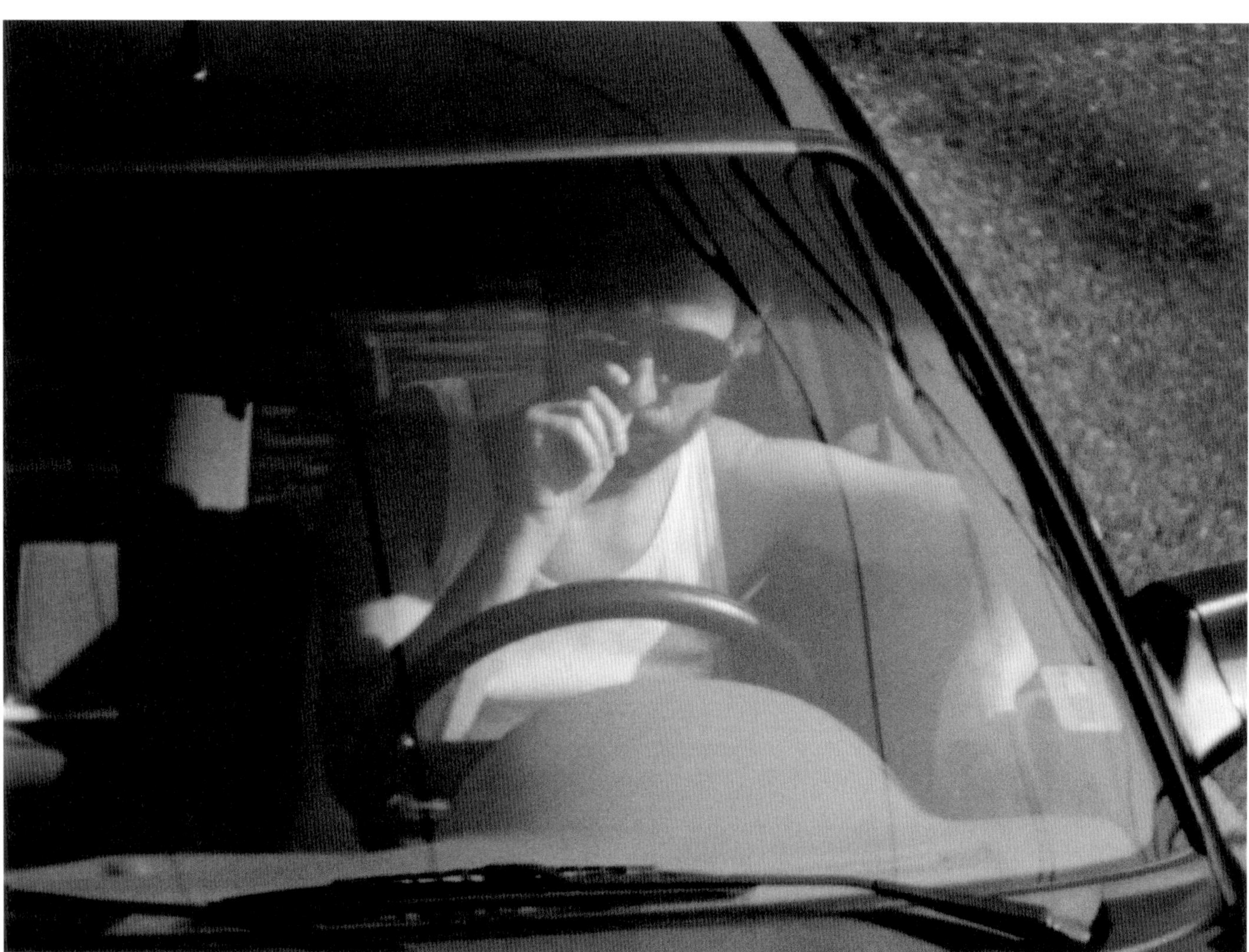

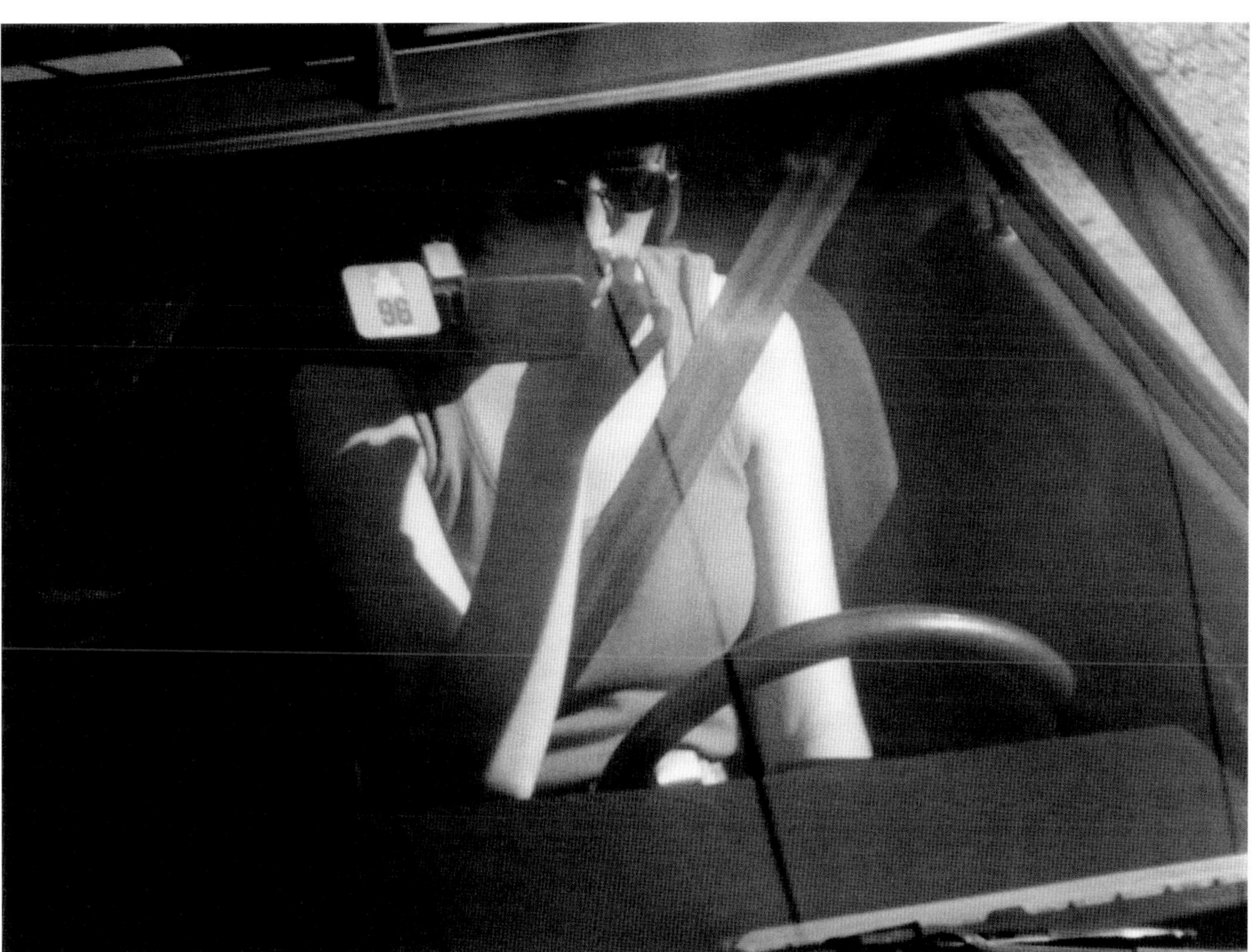

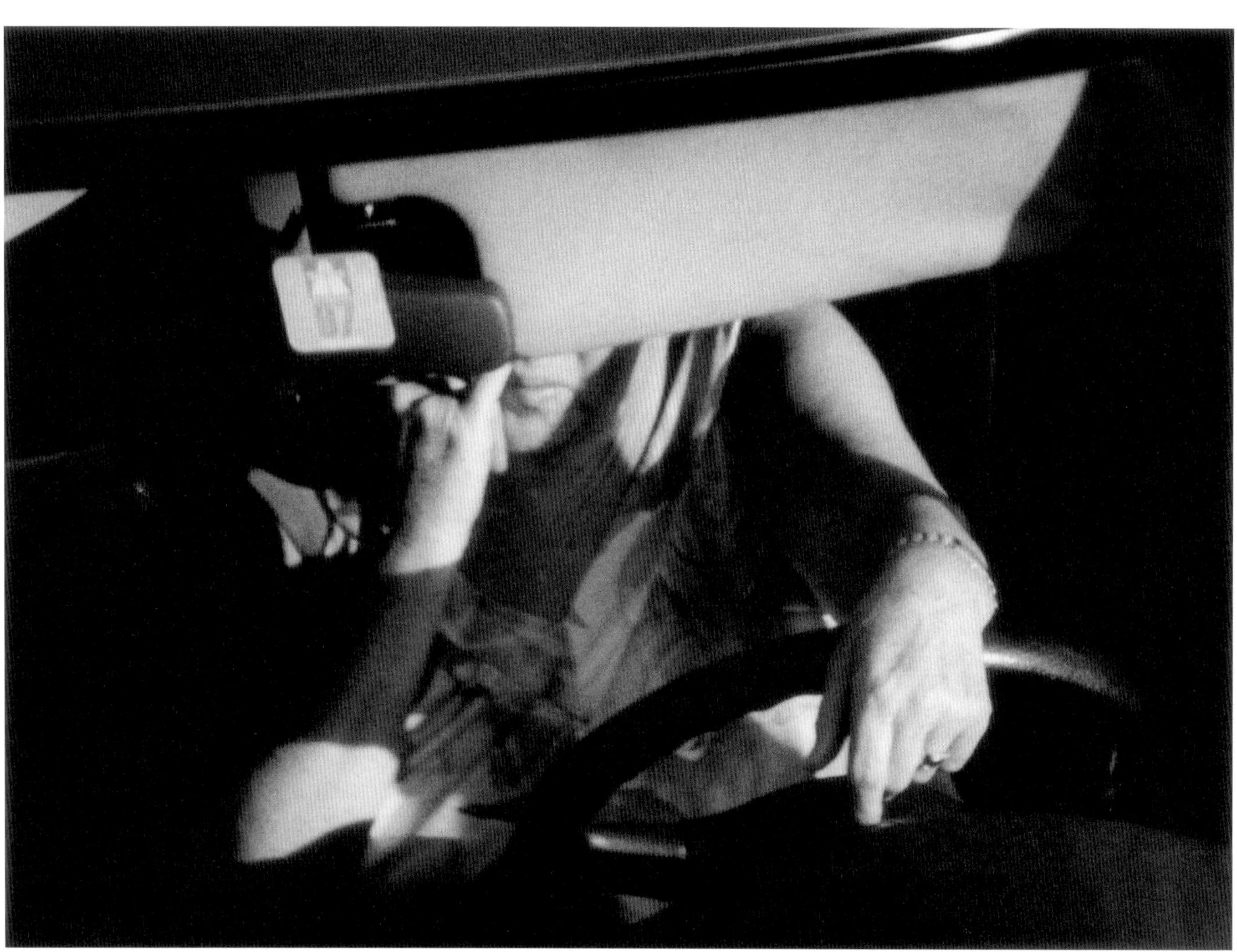

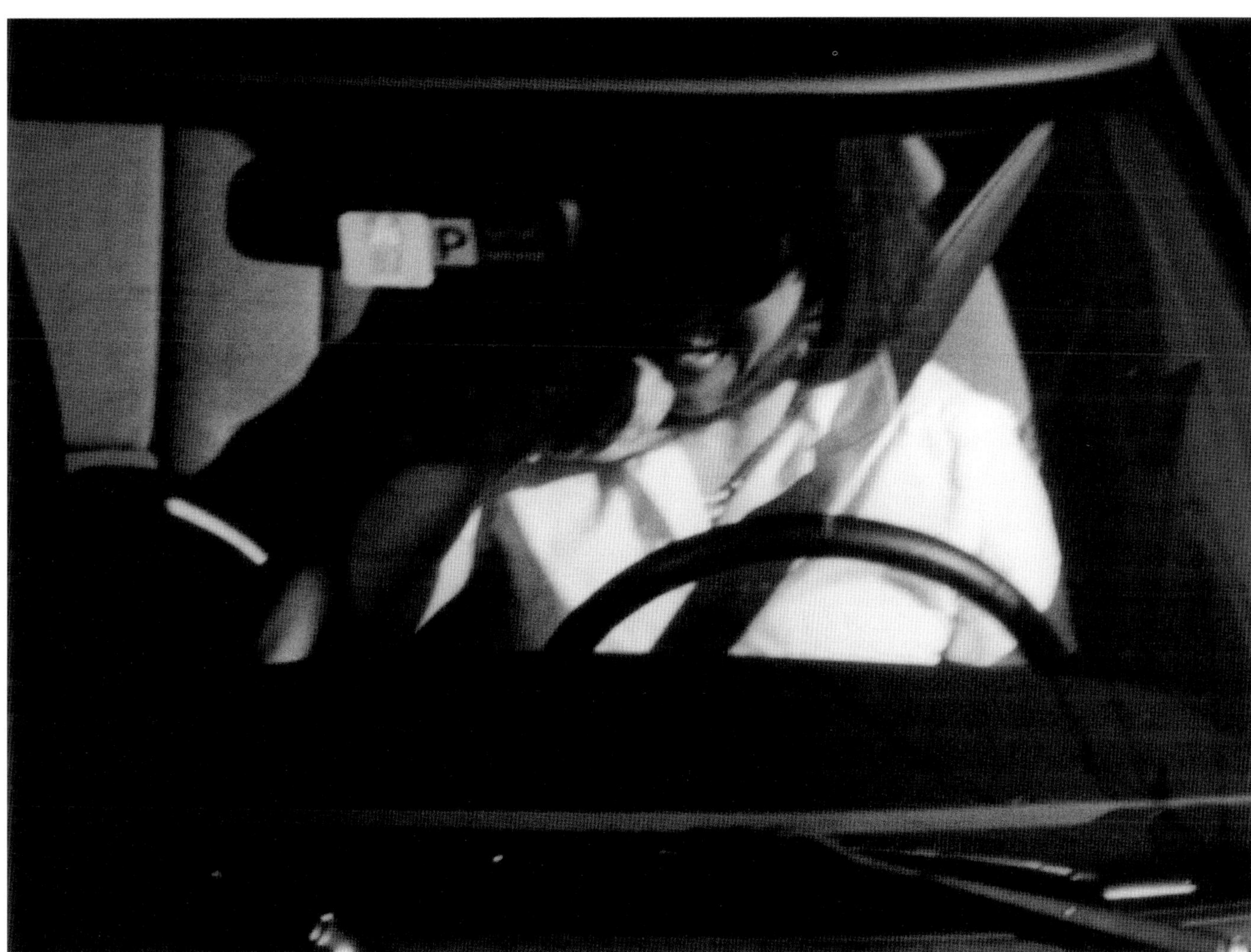

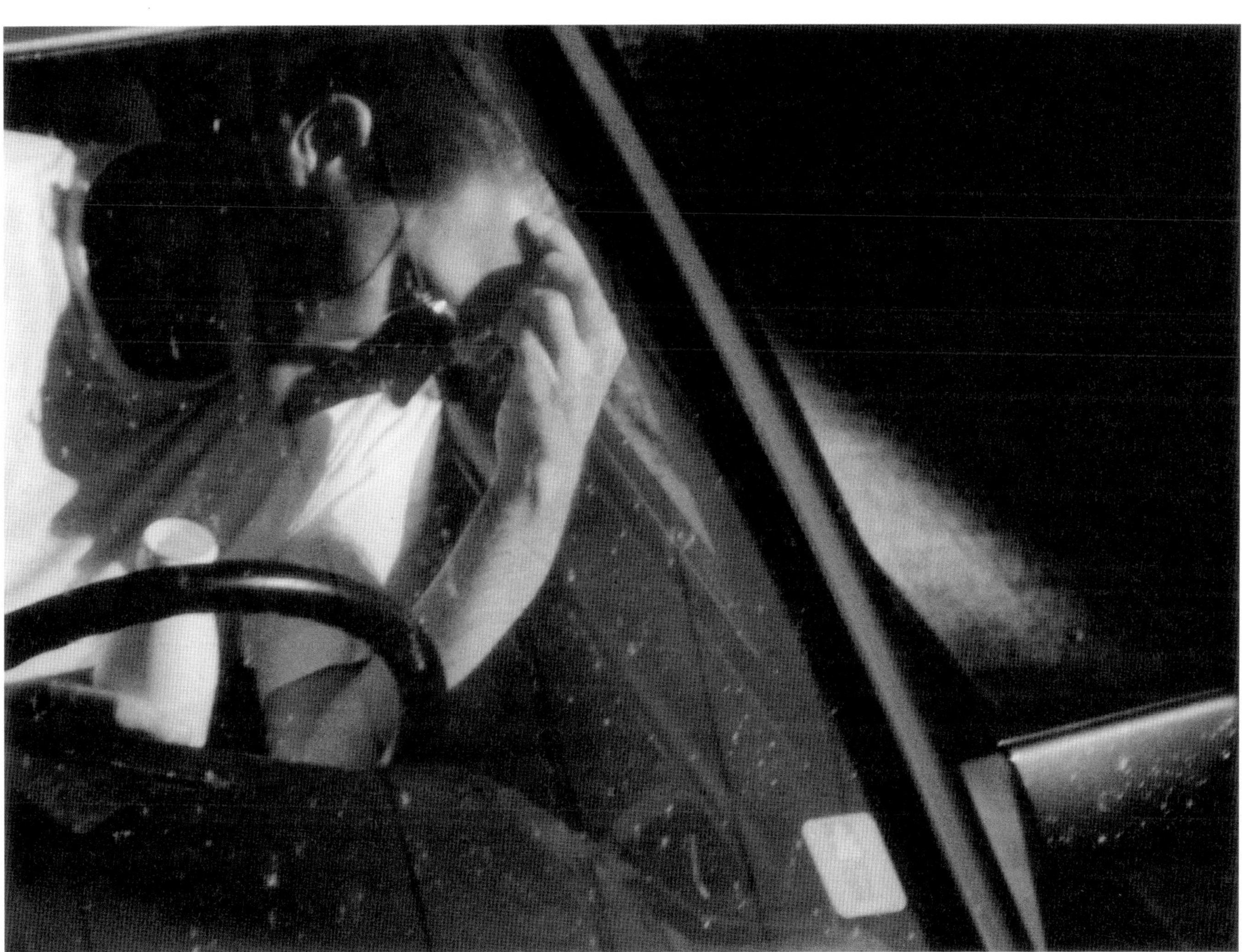

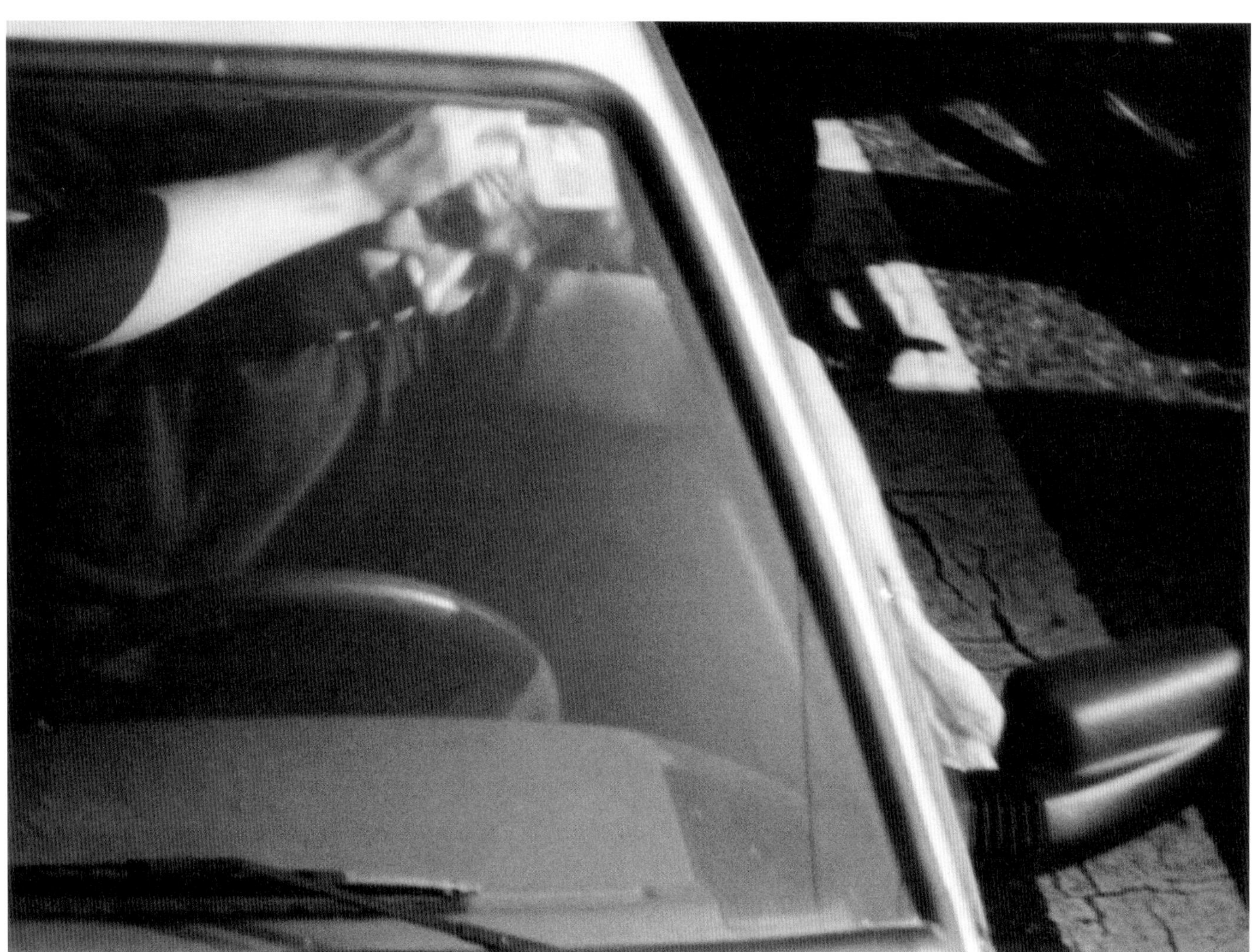

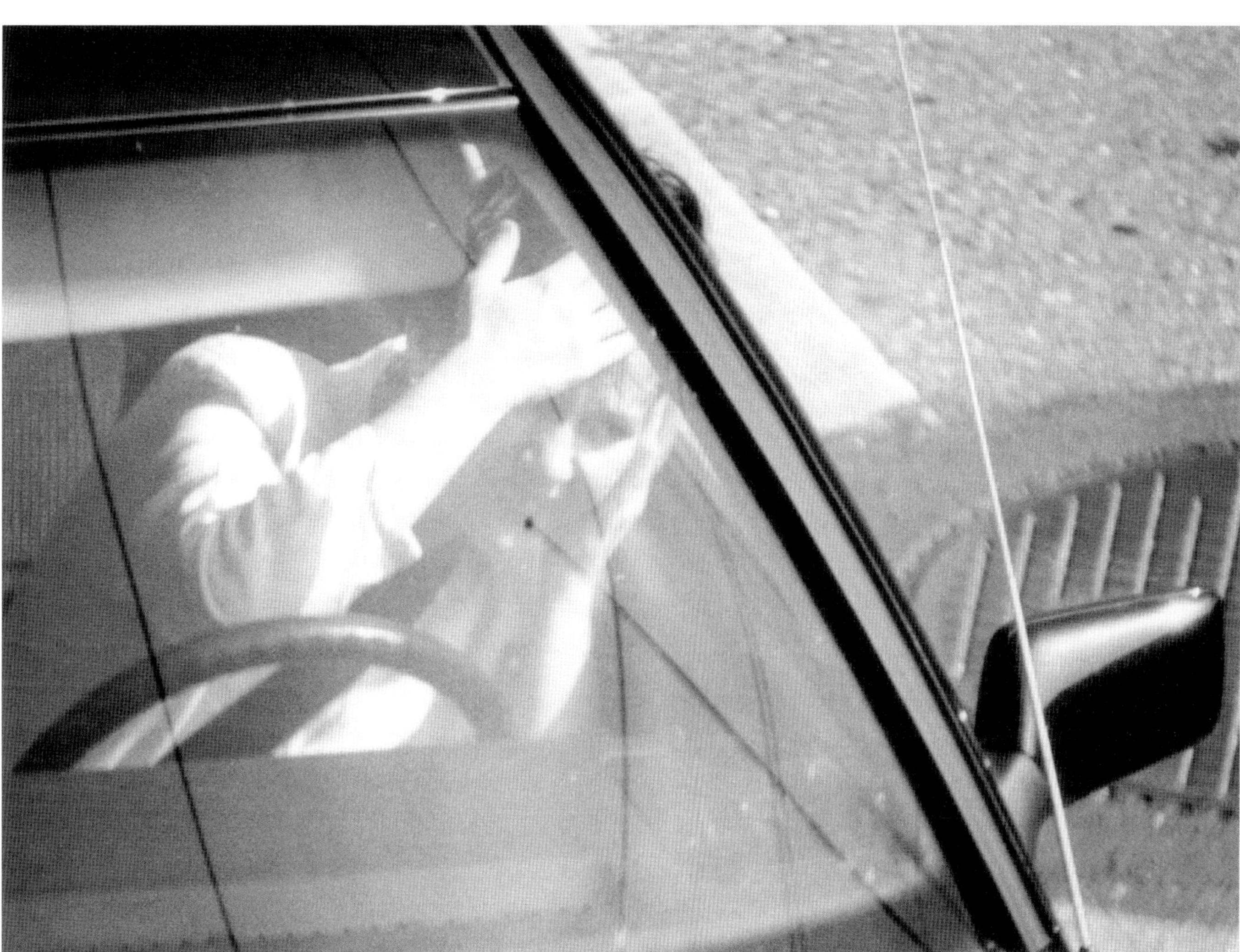

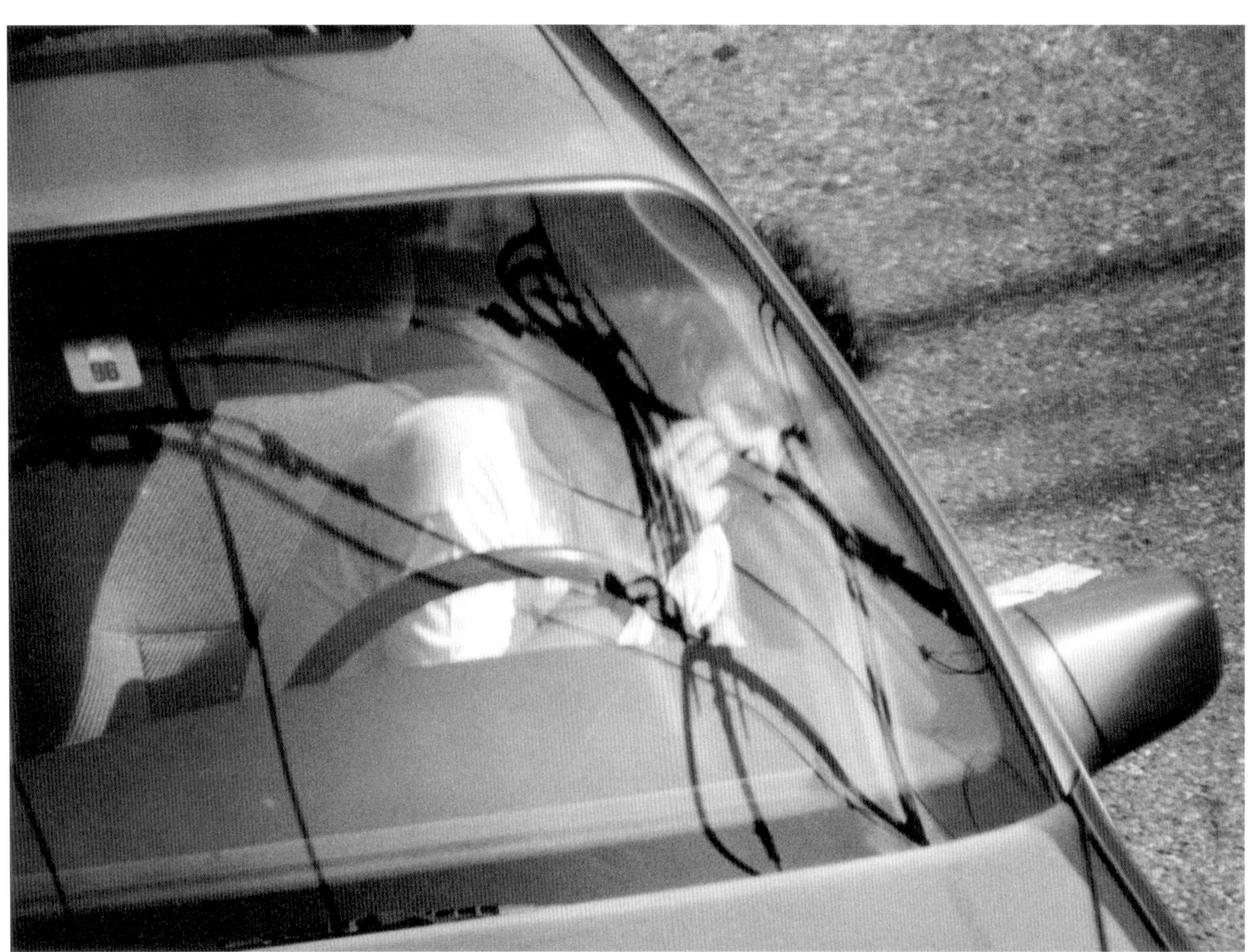

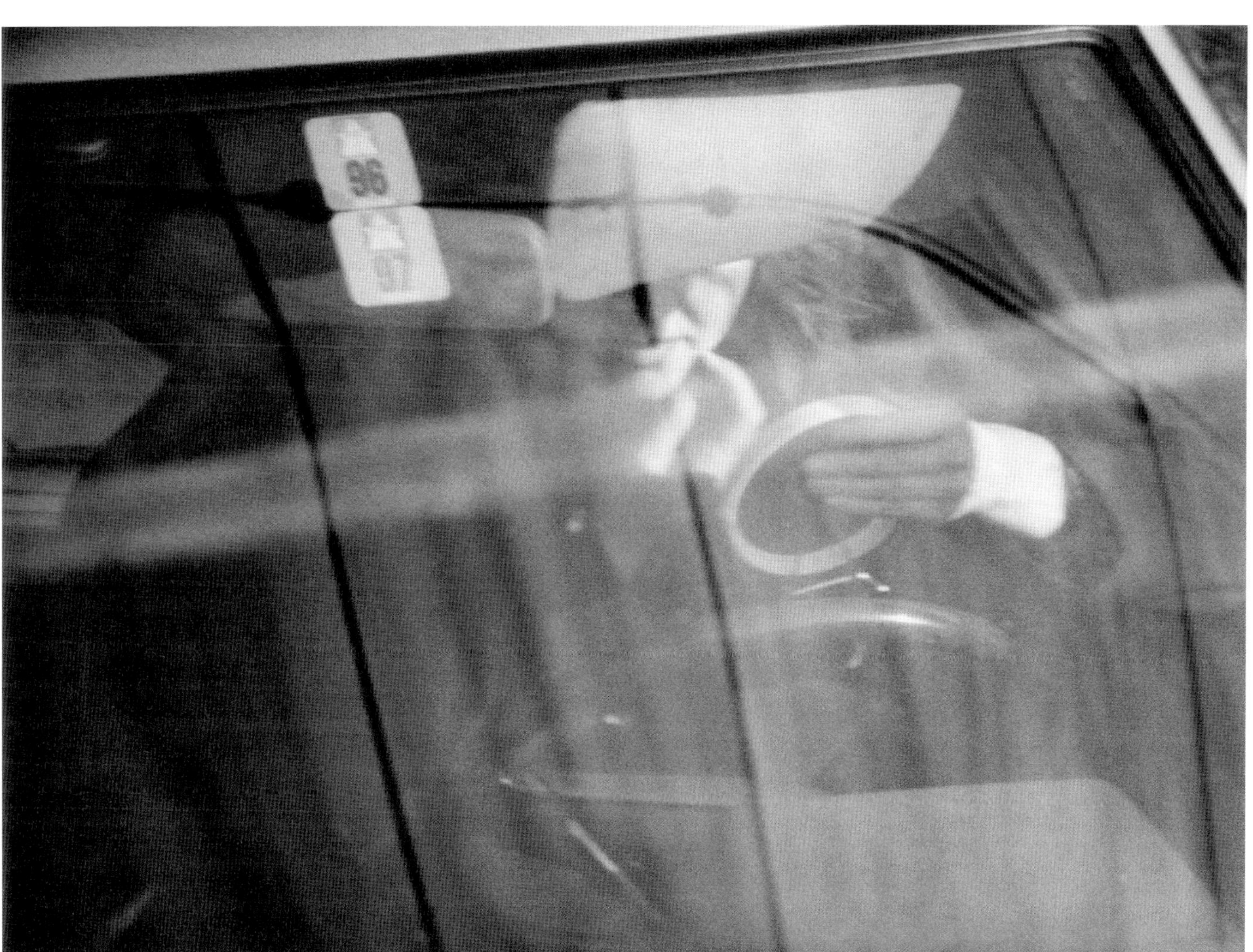

96
97

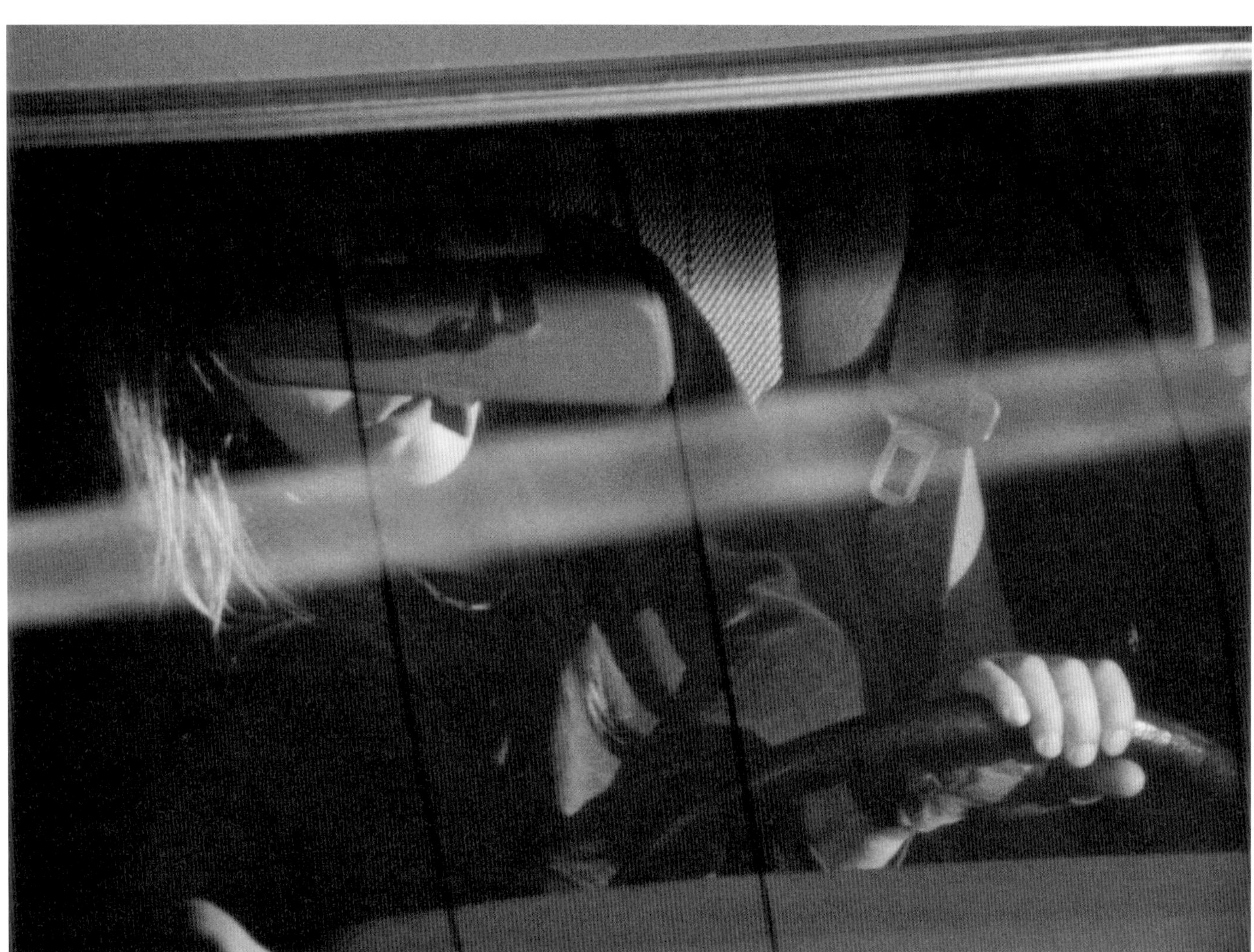

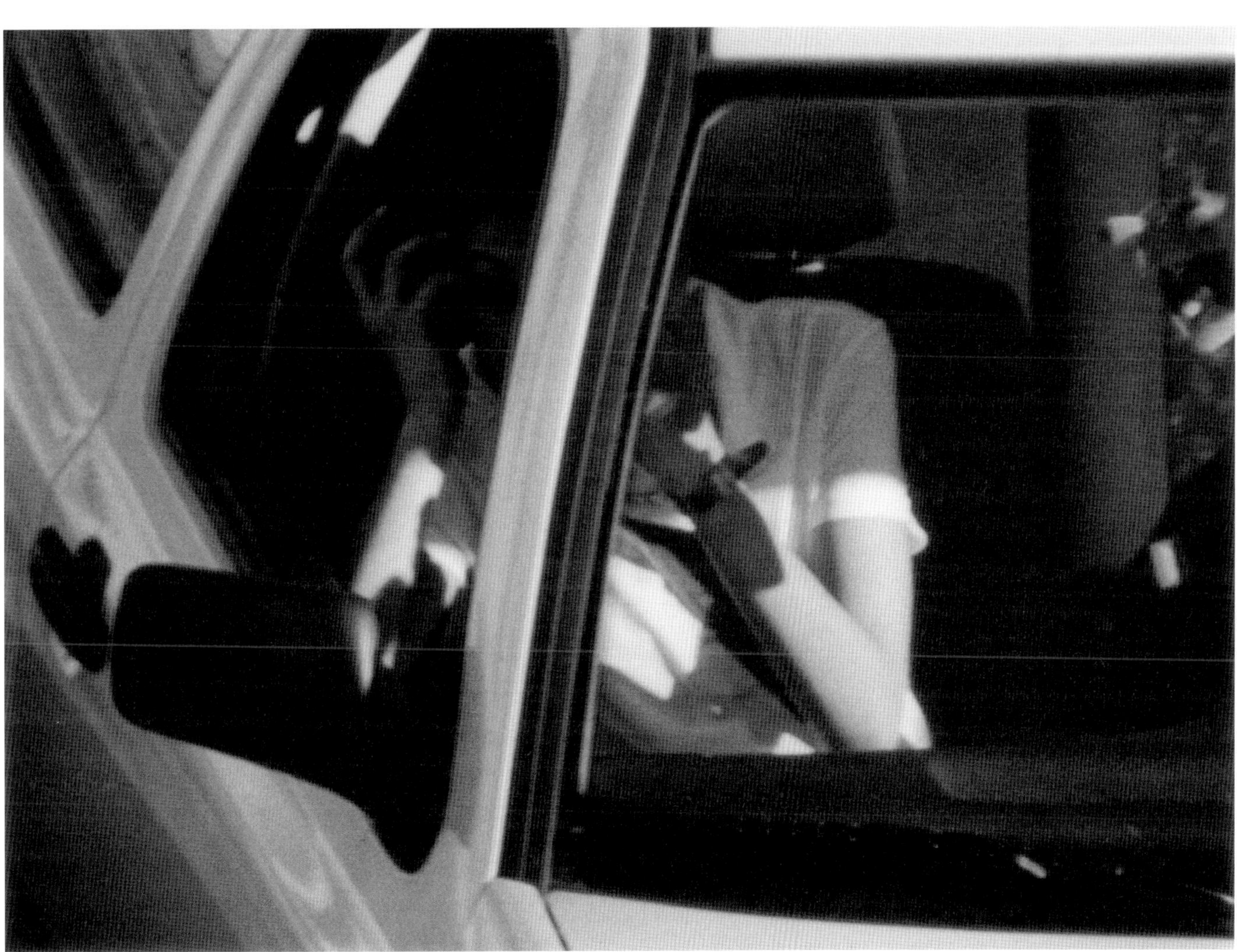

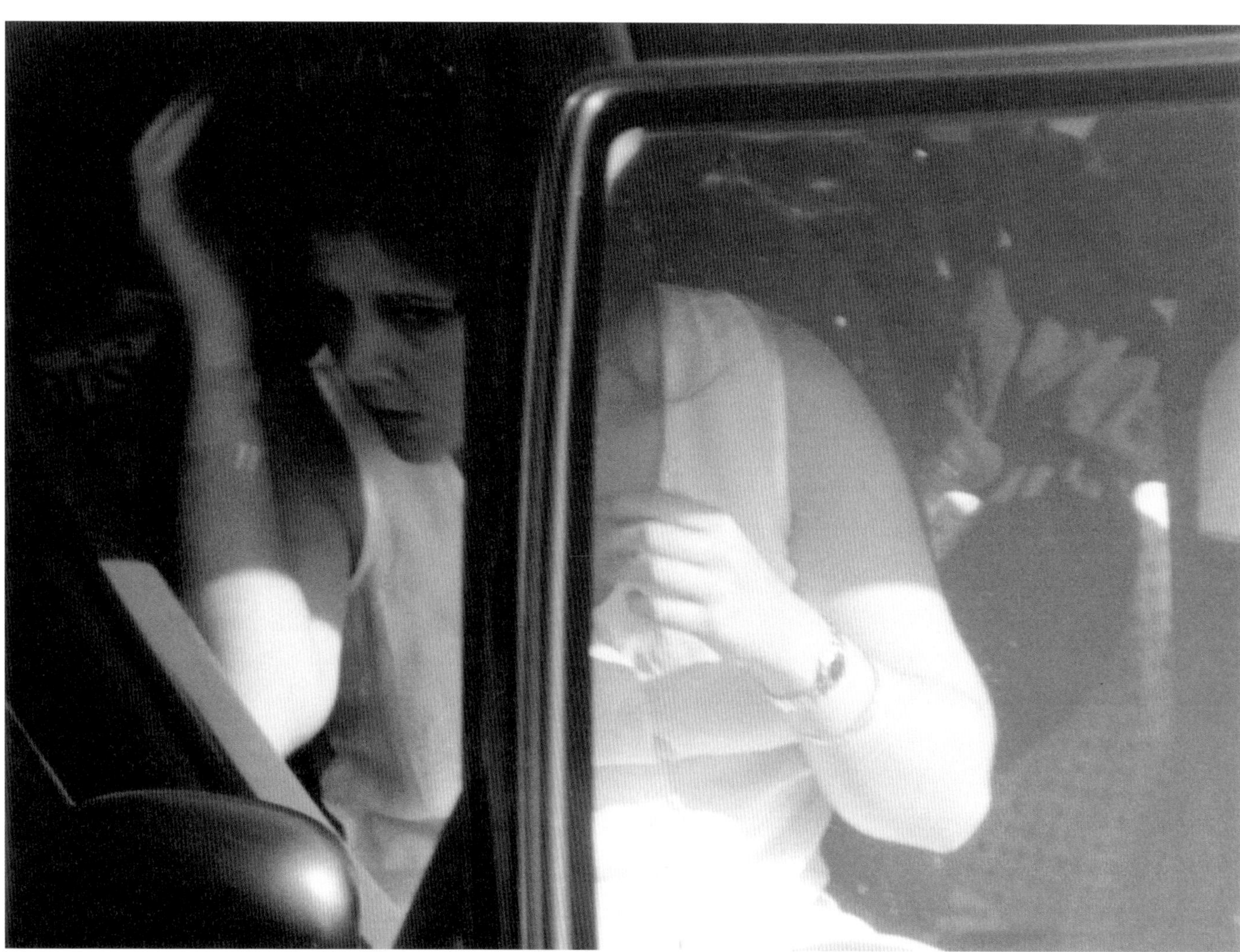

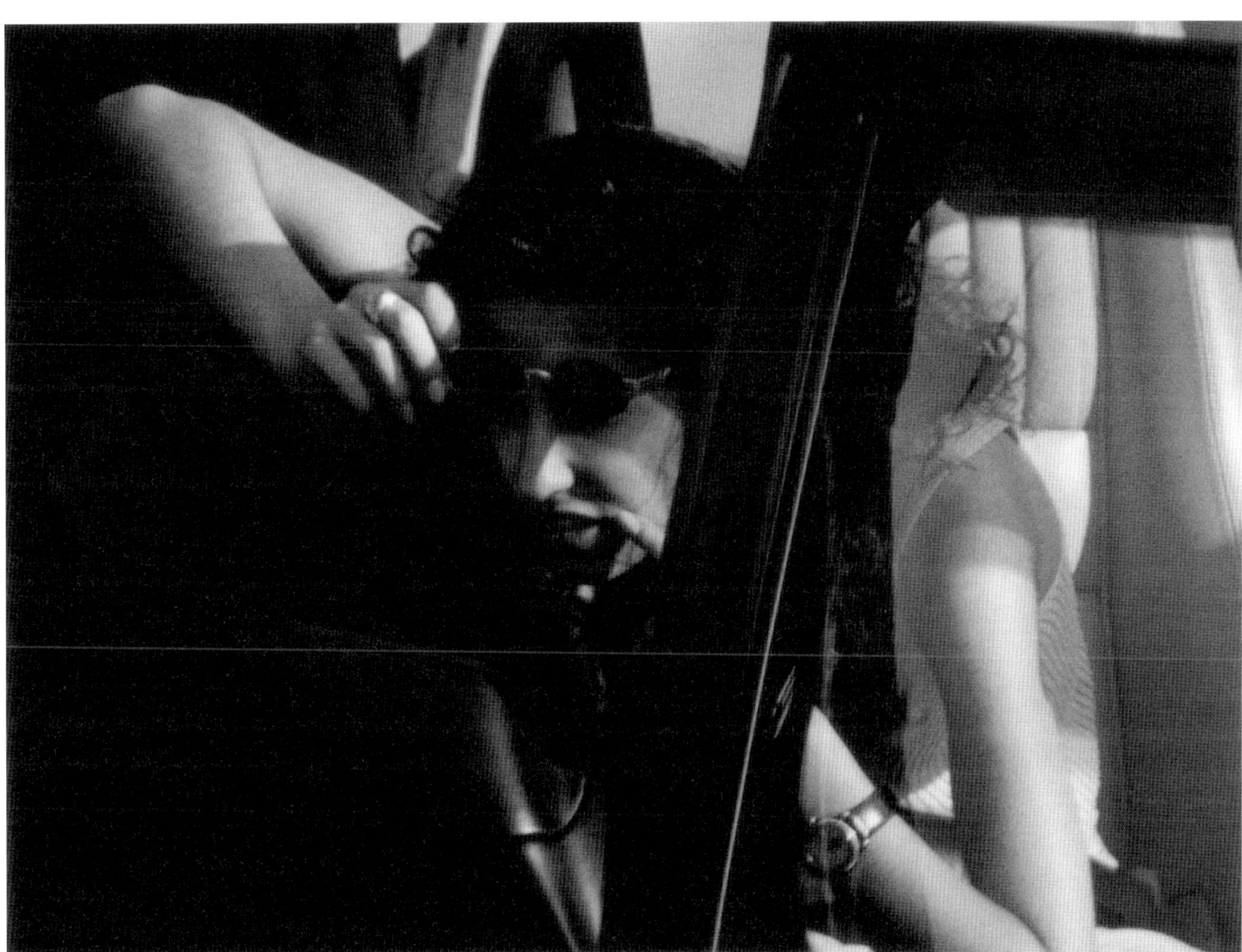

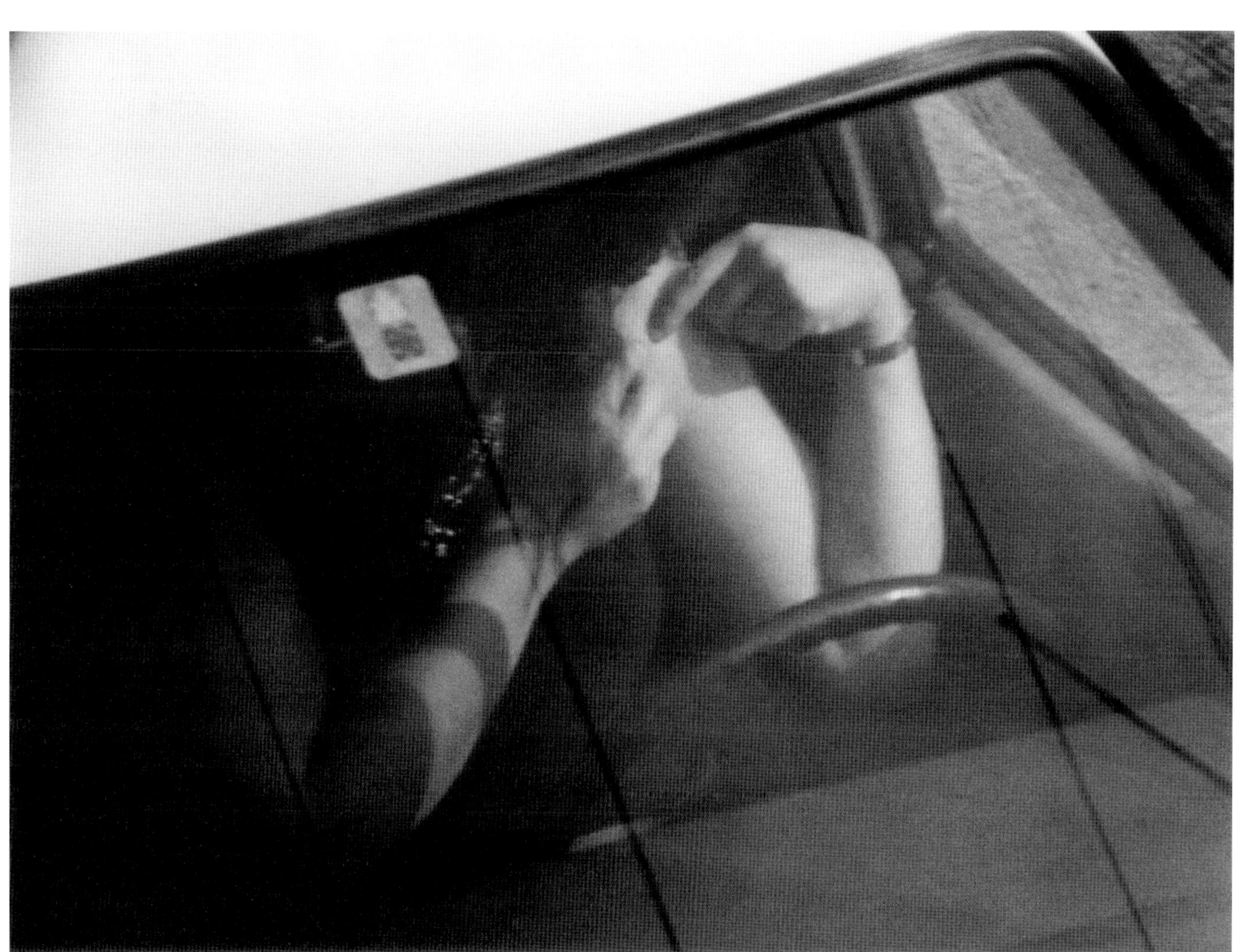

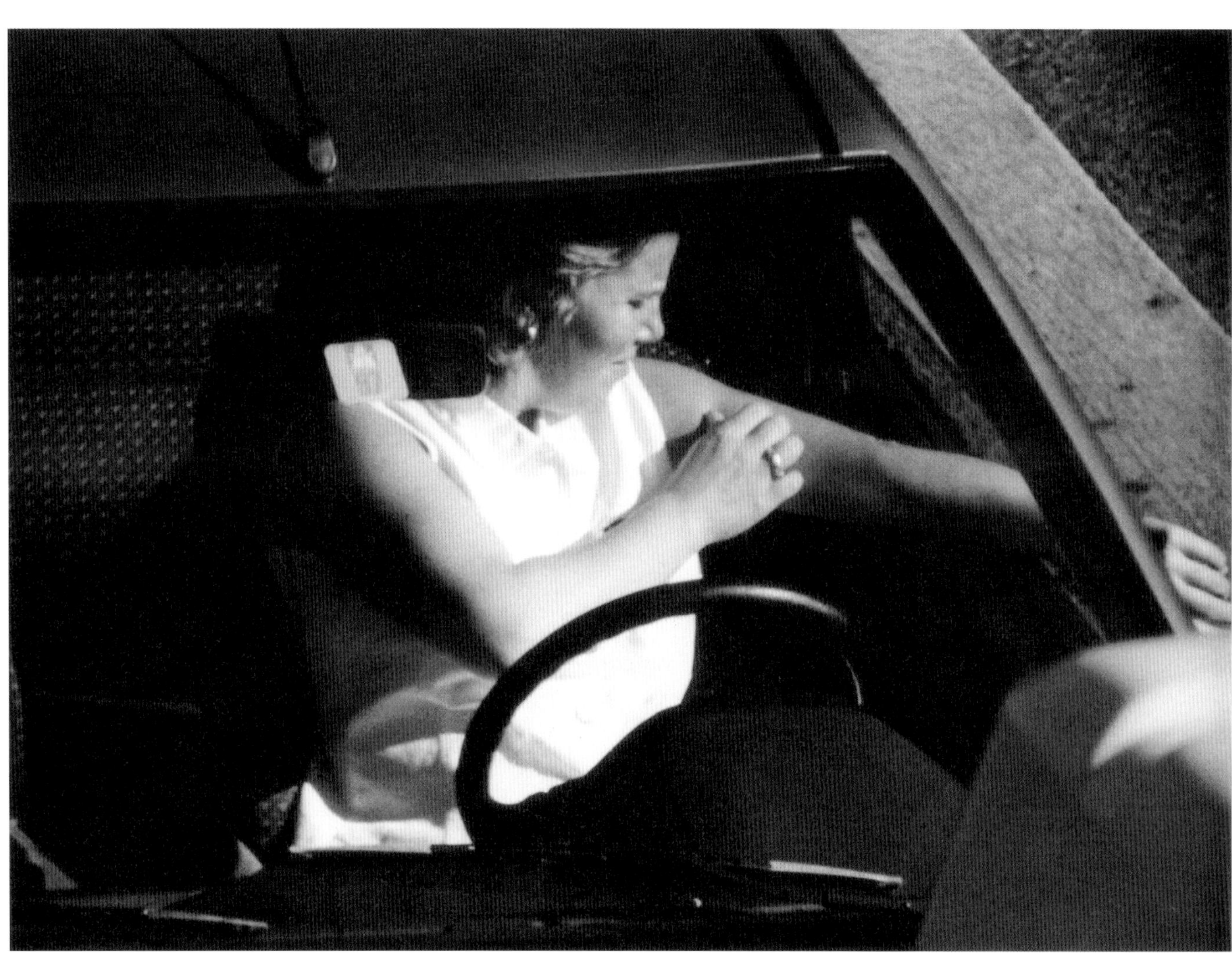

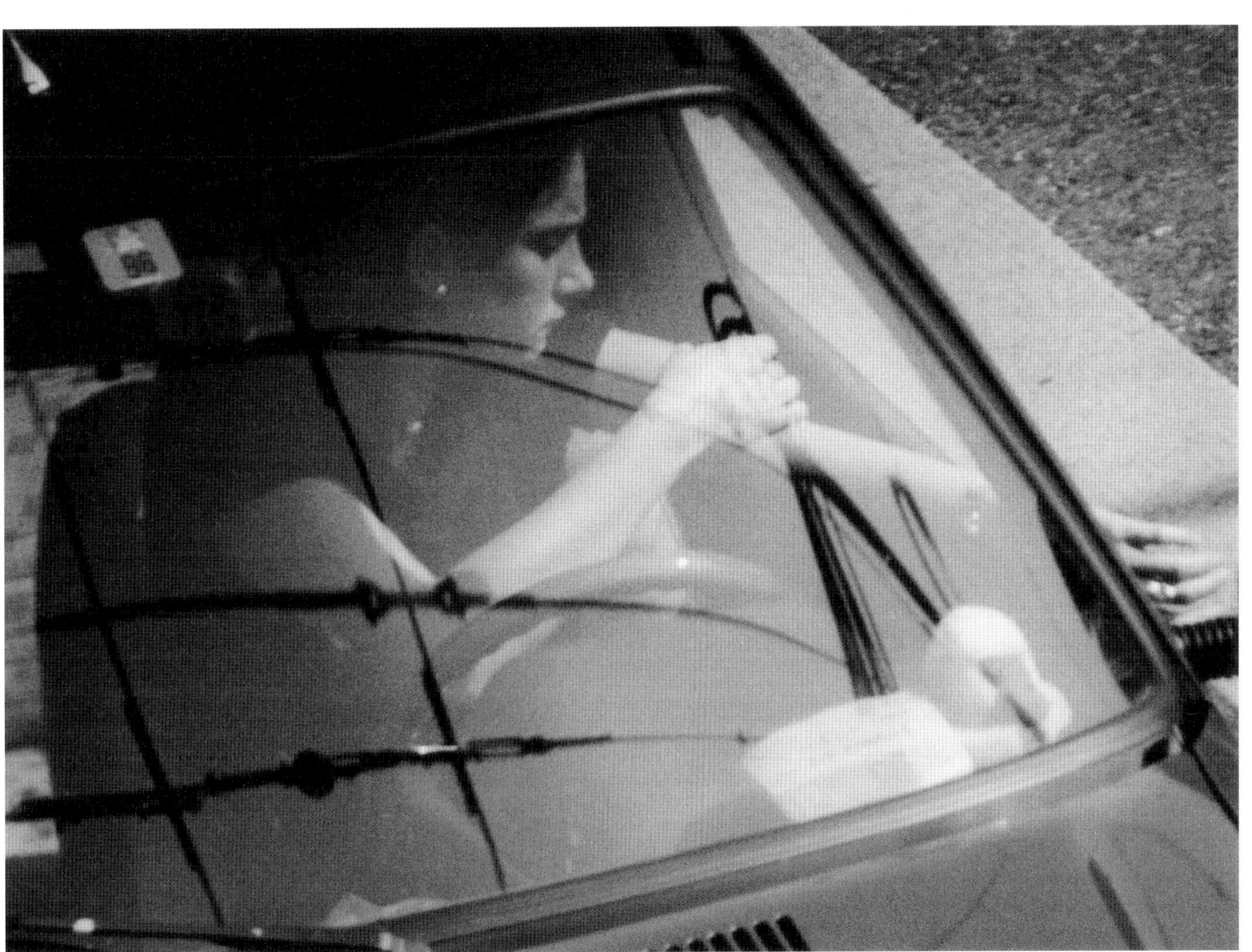

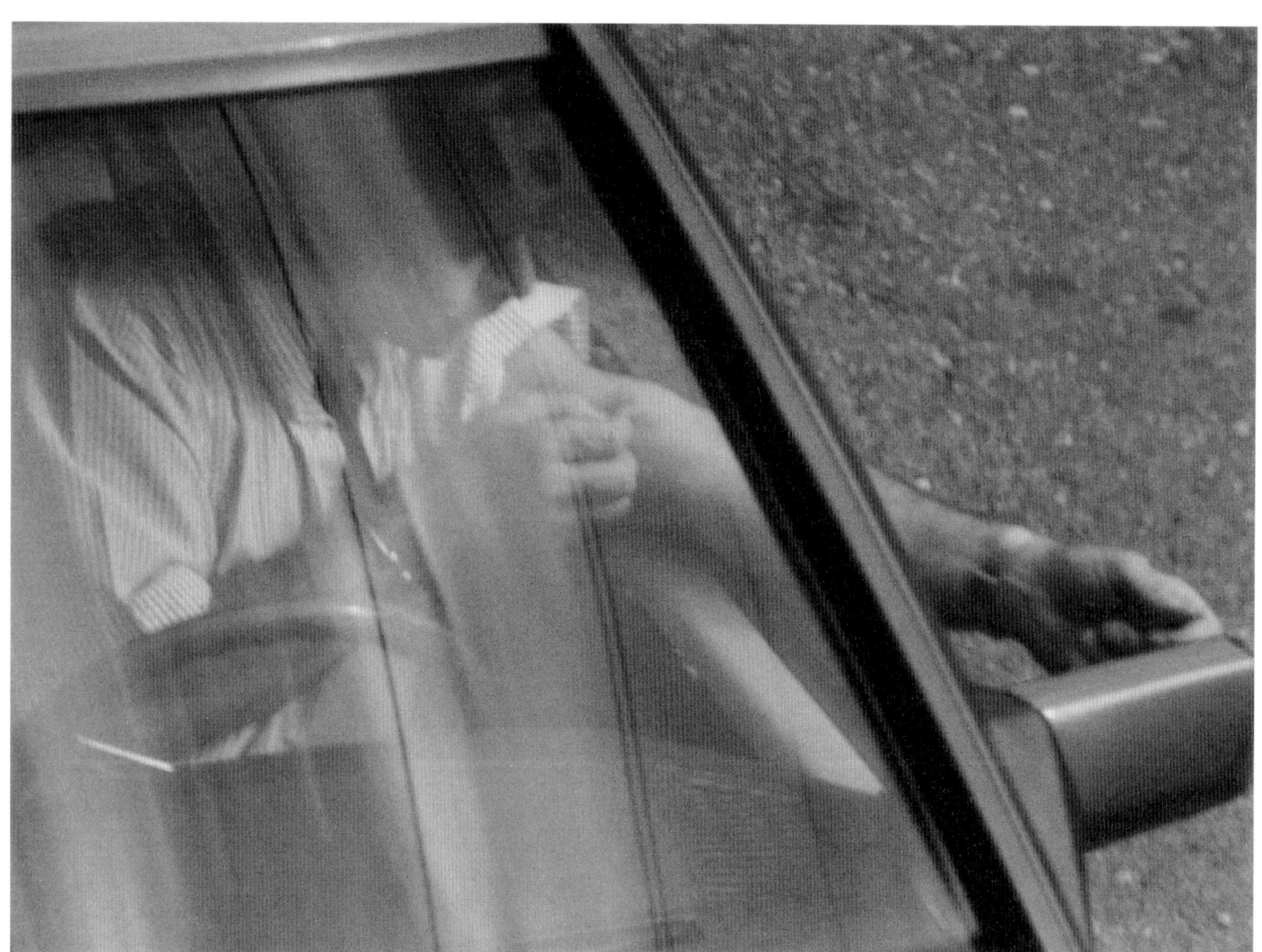

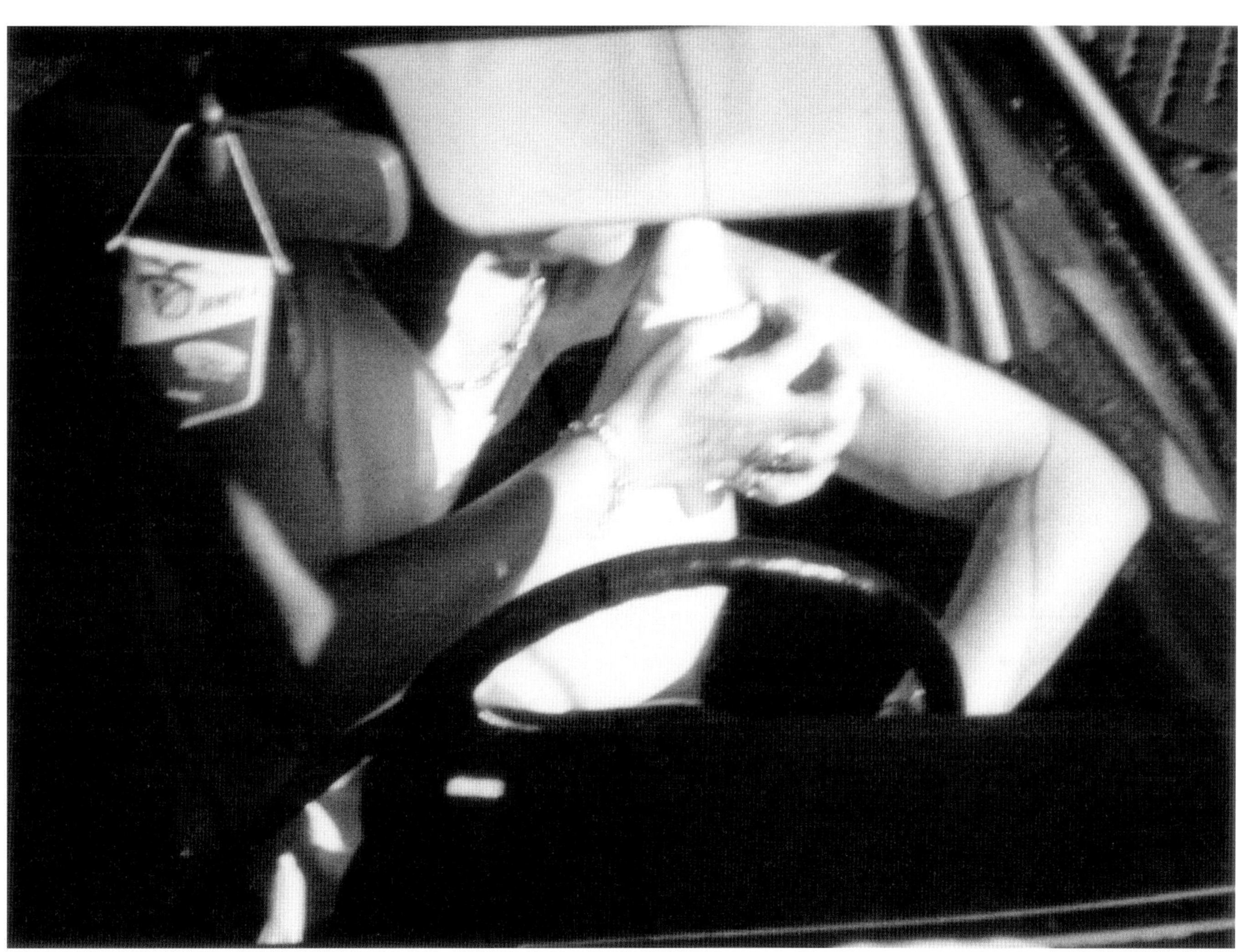

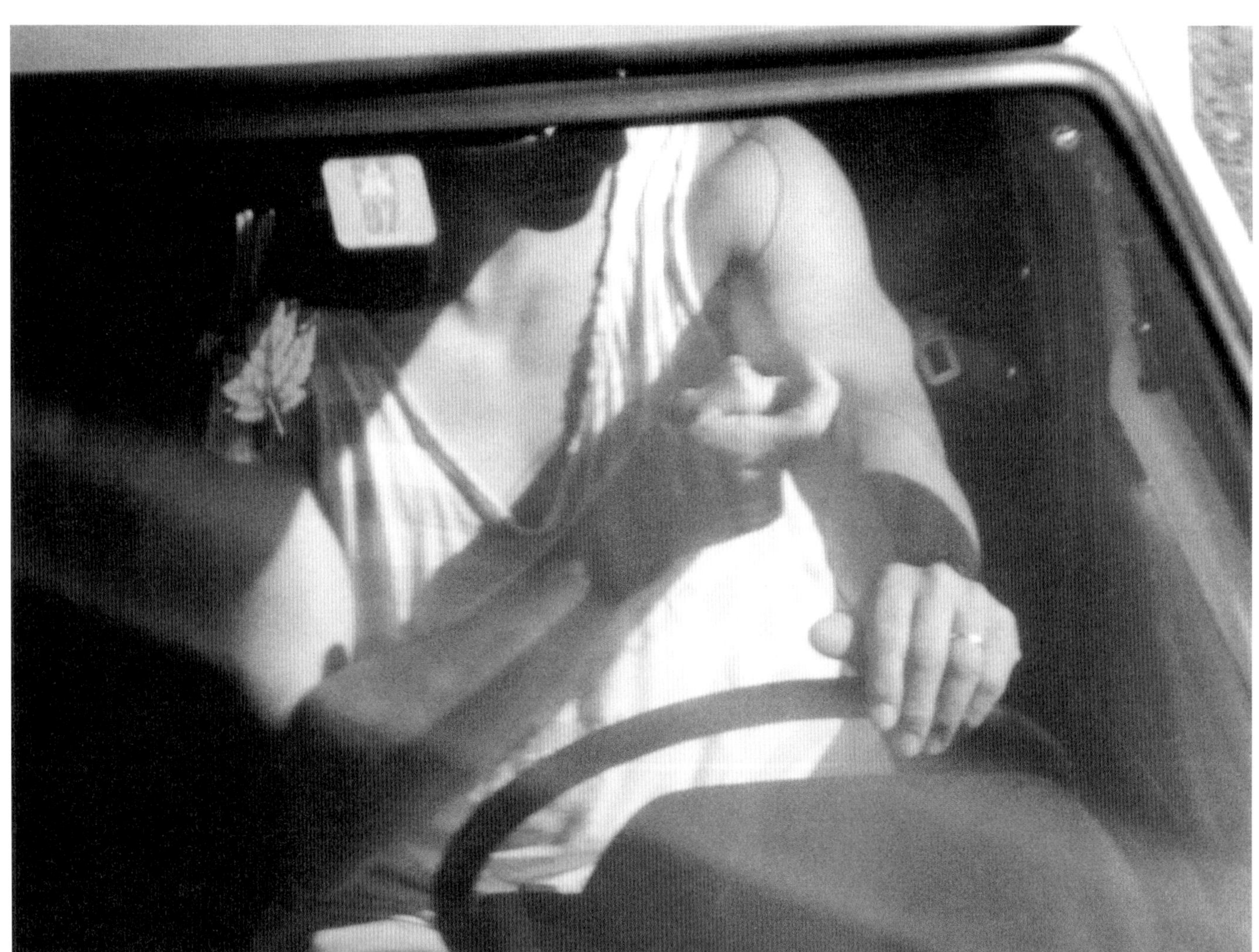

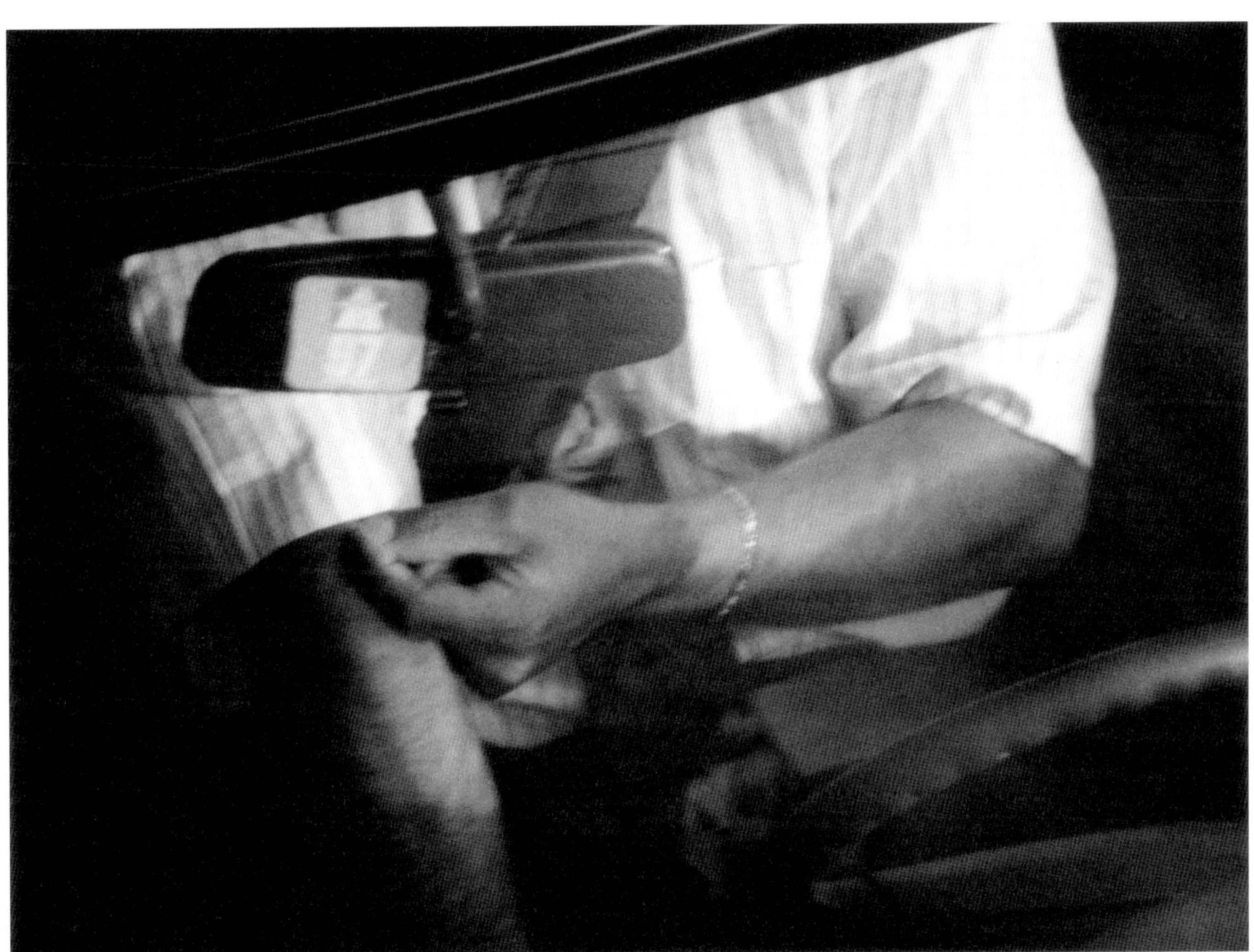

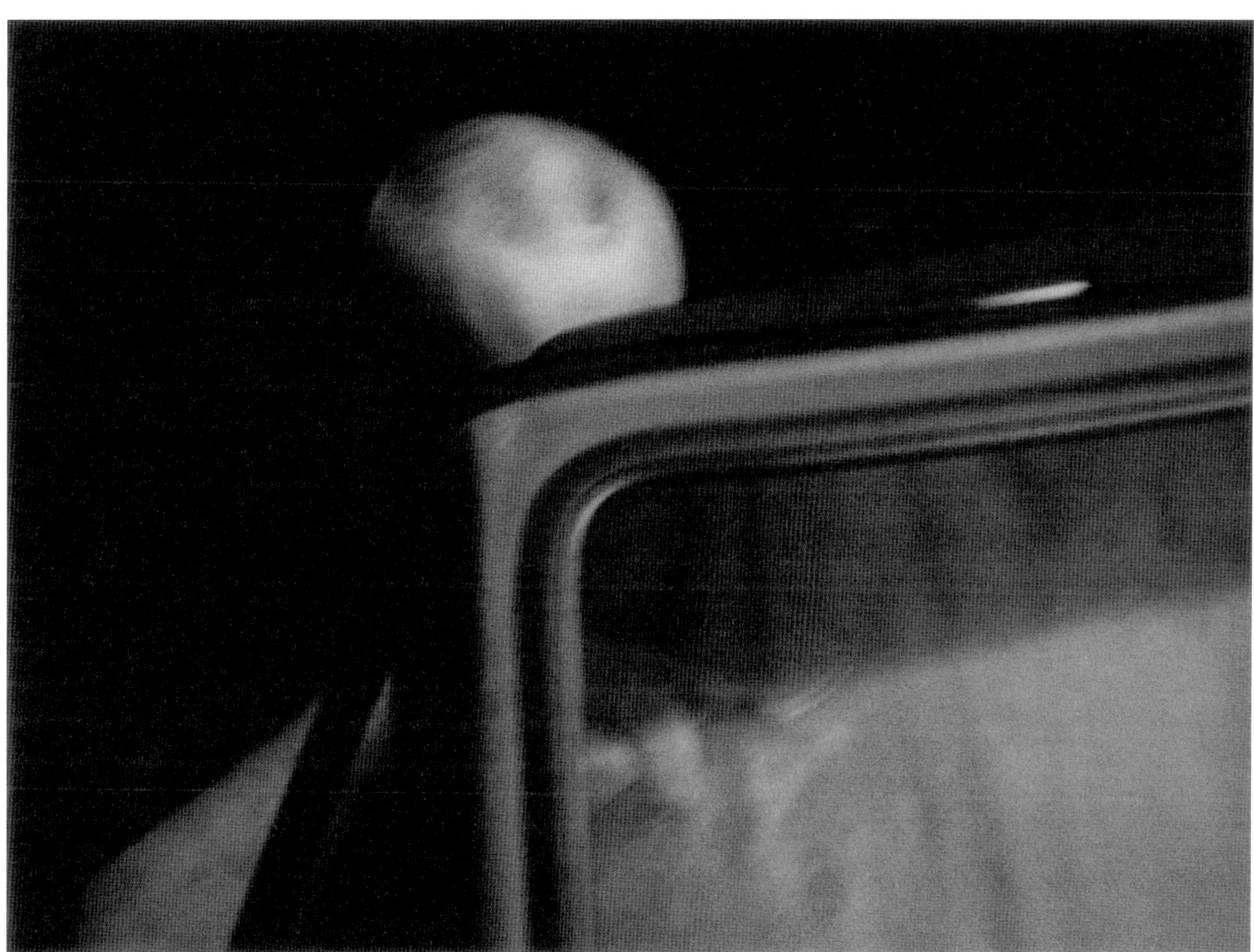

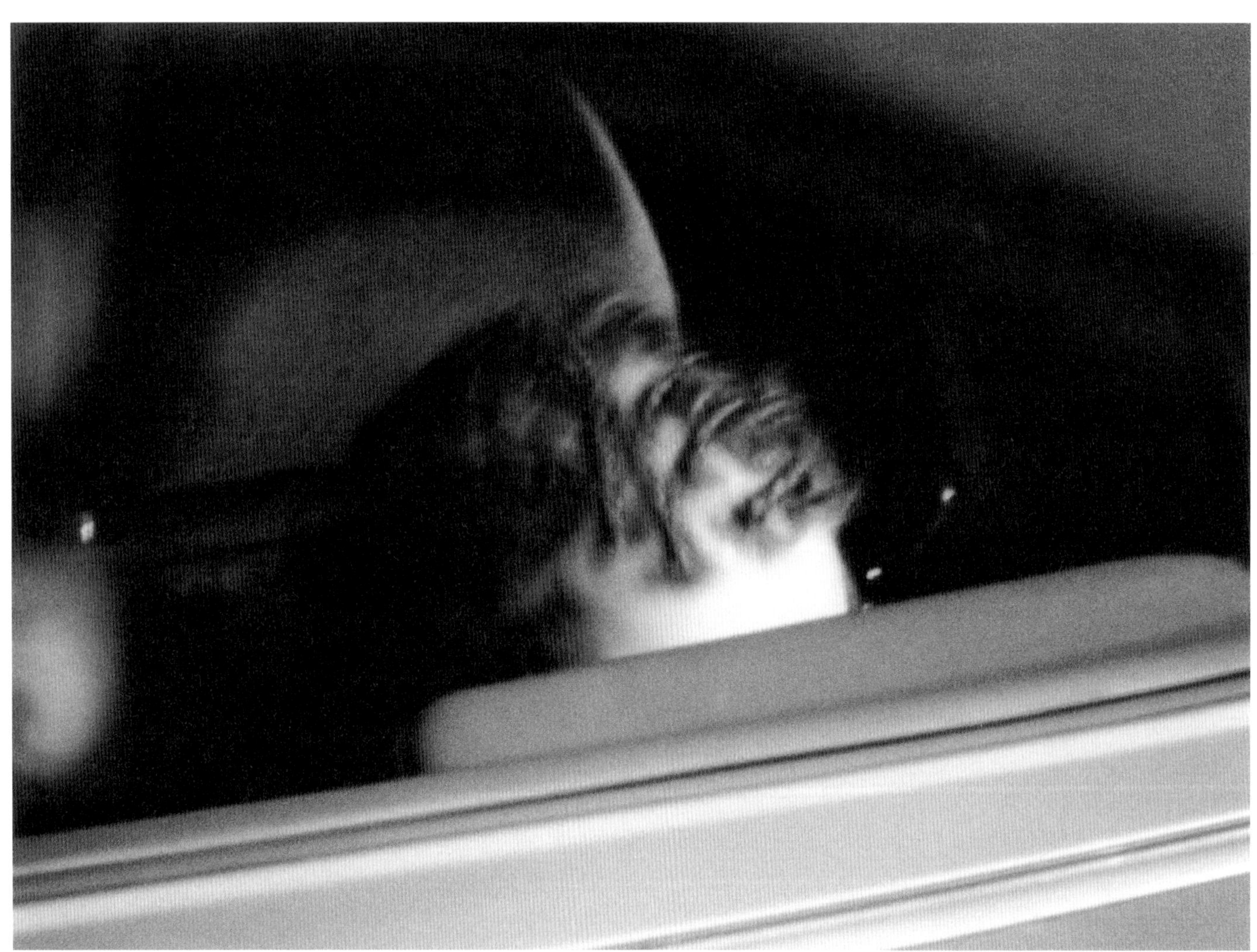

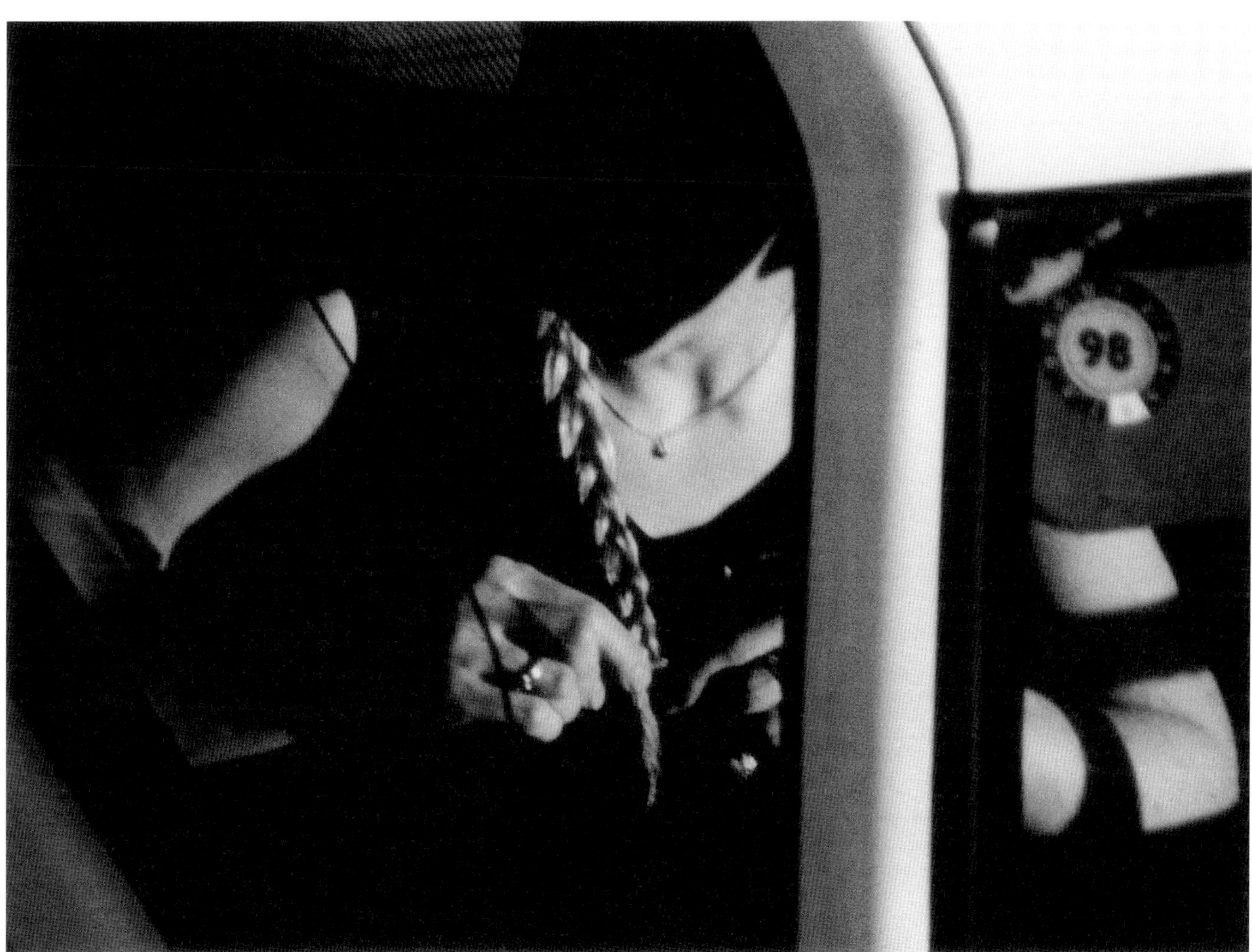

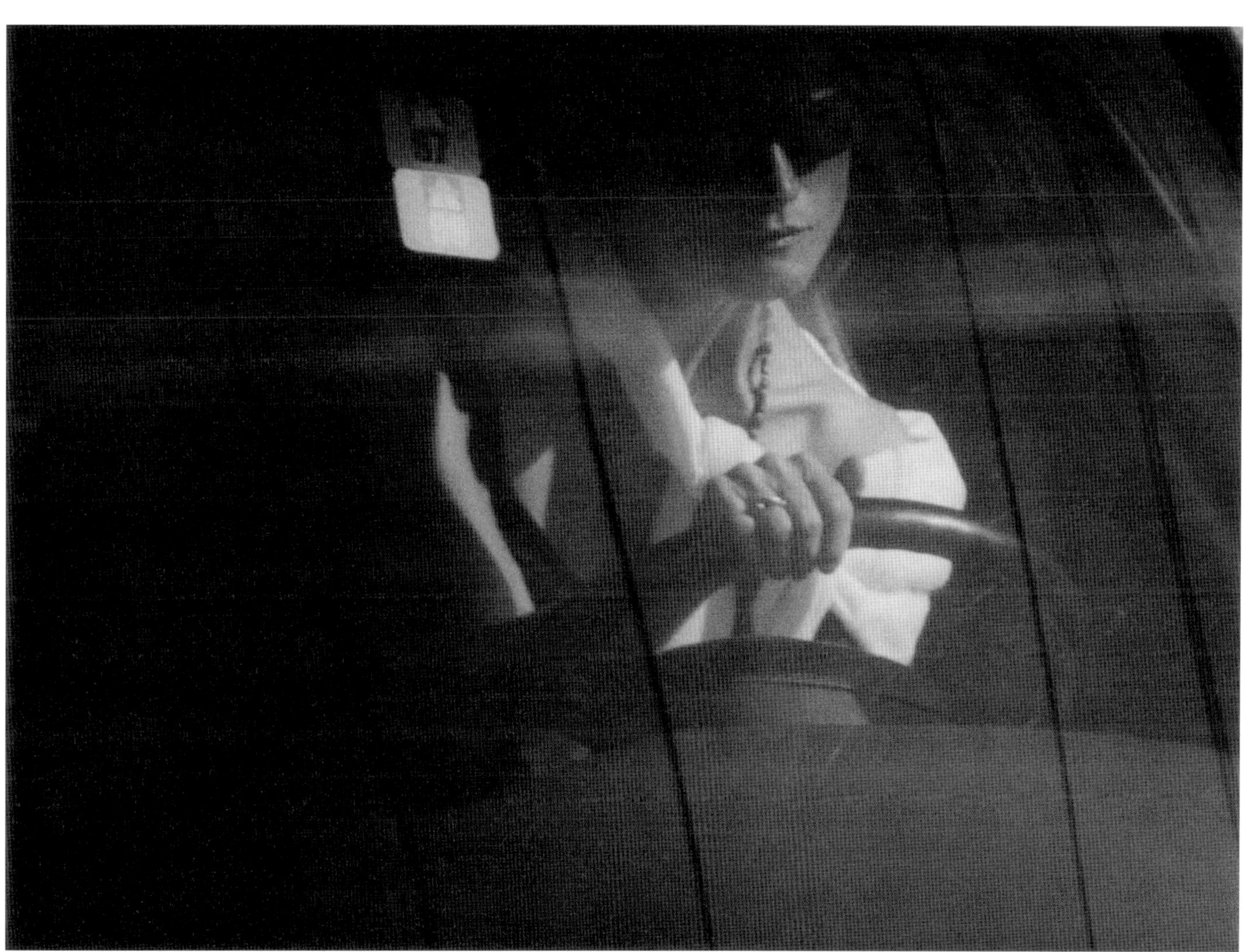

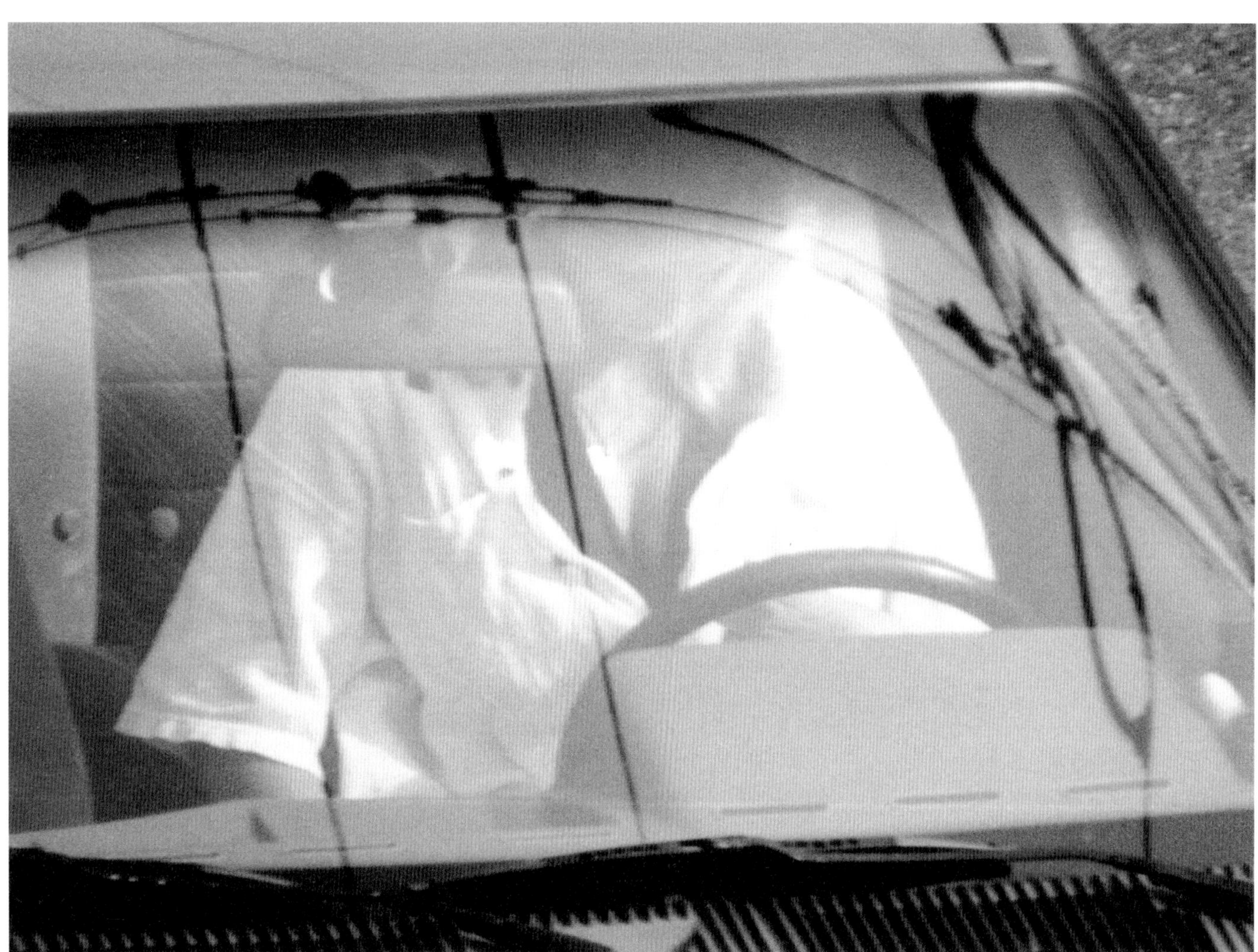

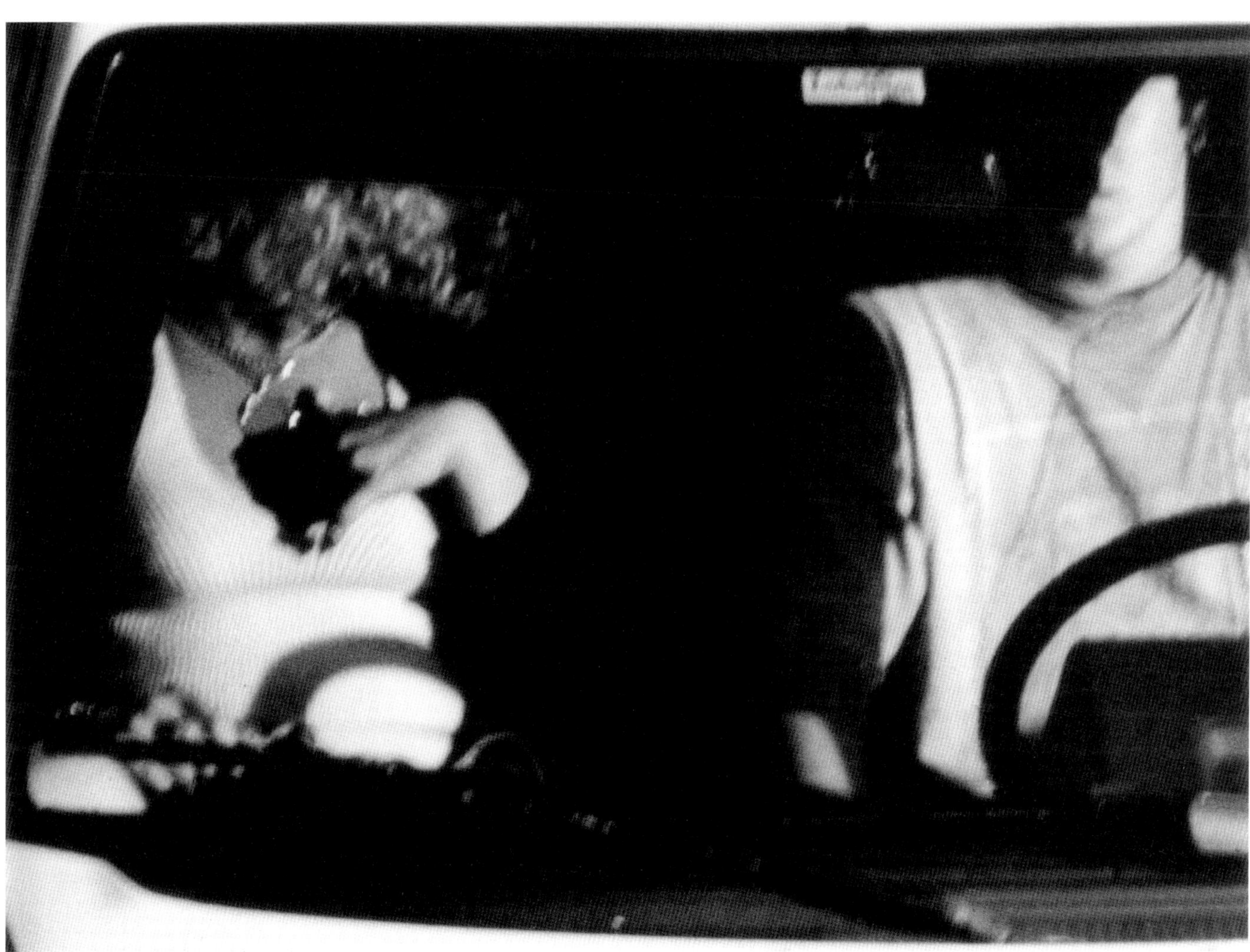

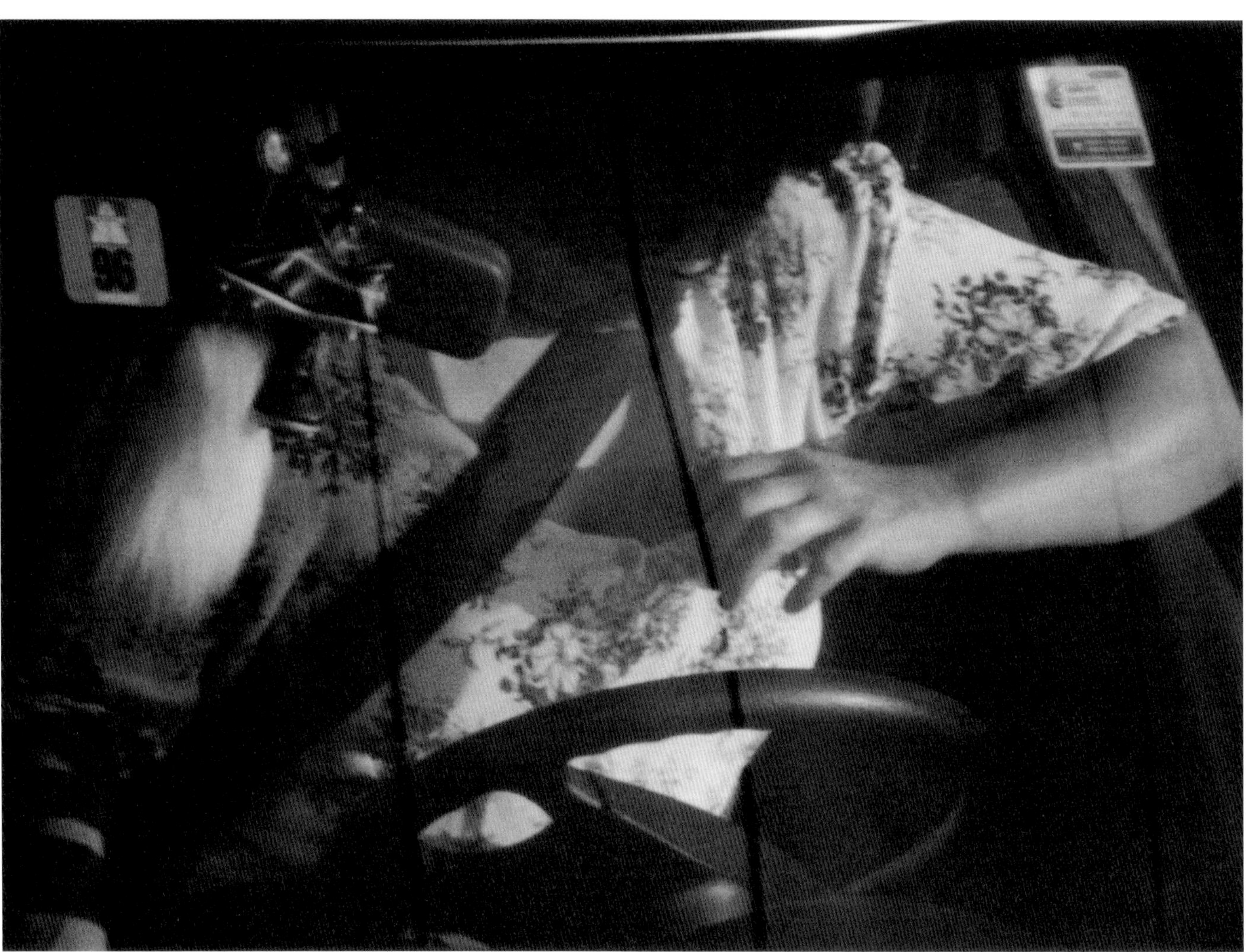

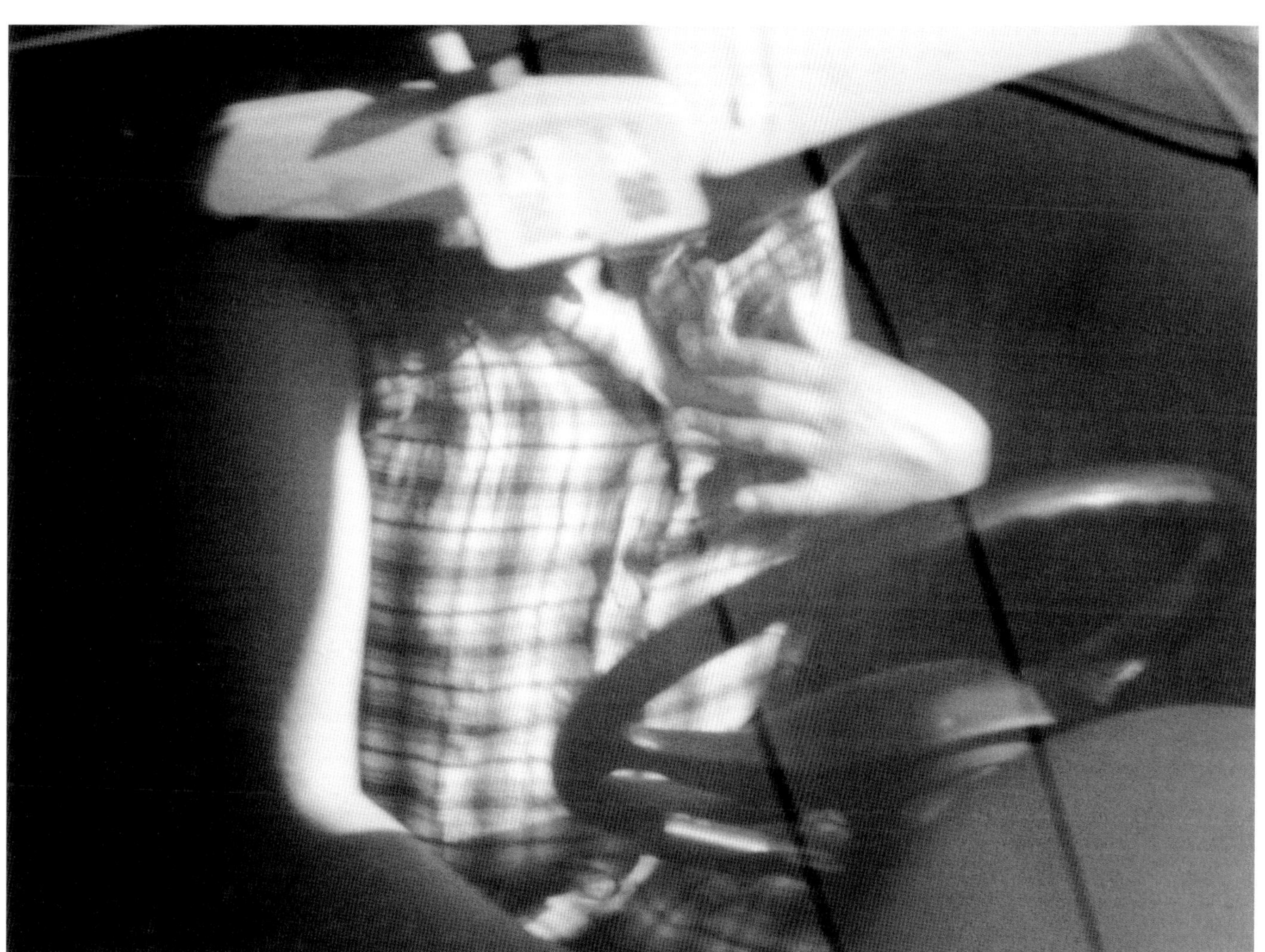

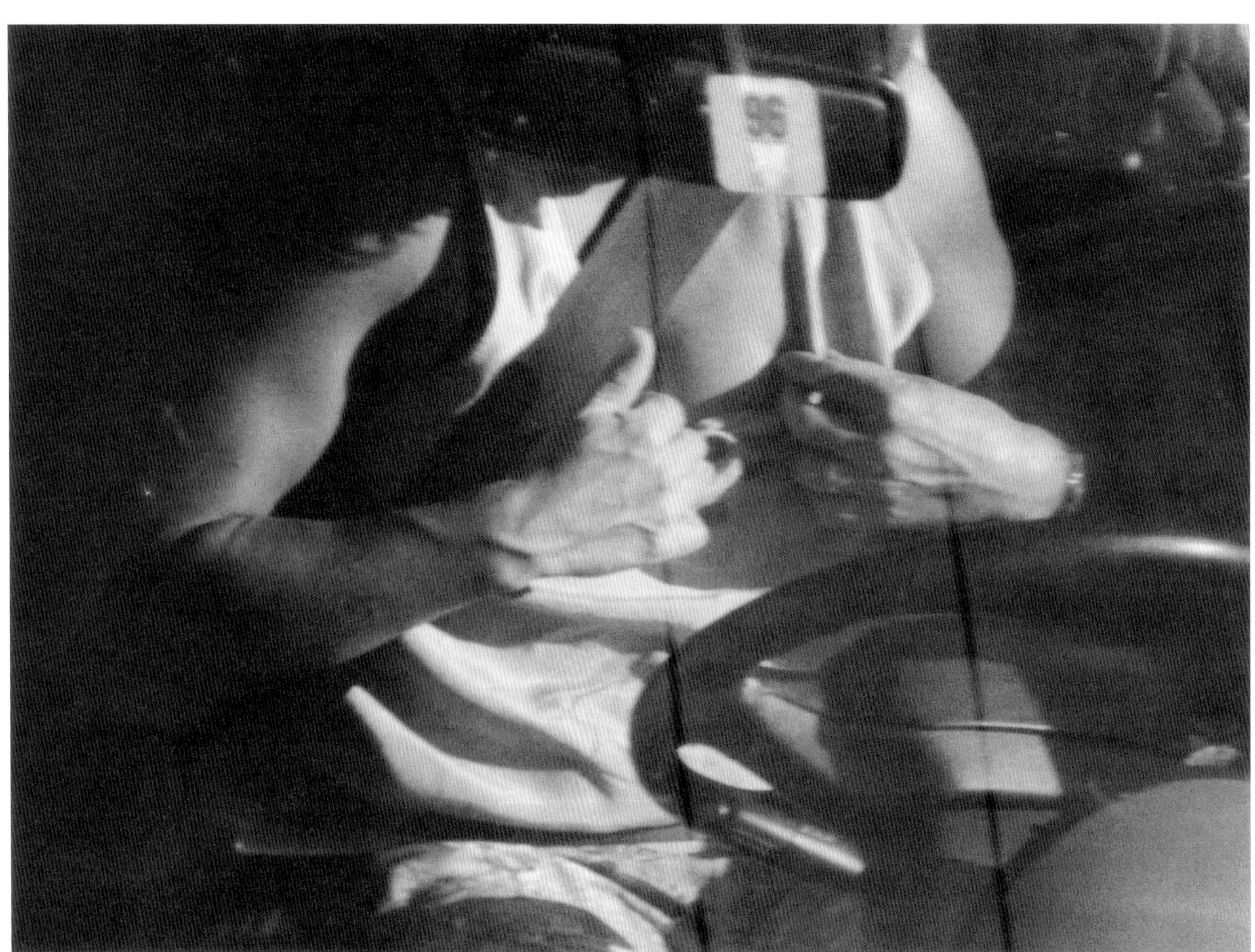

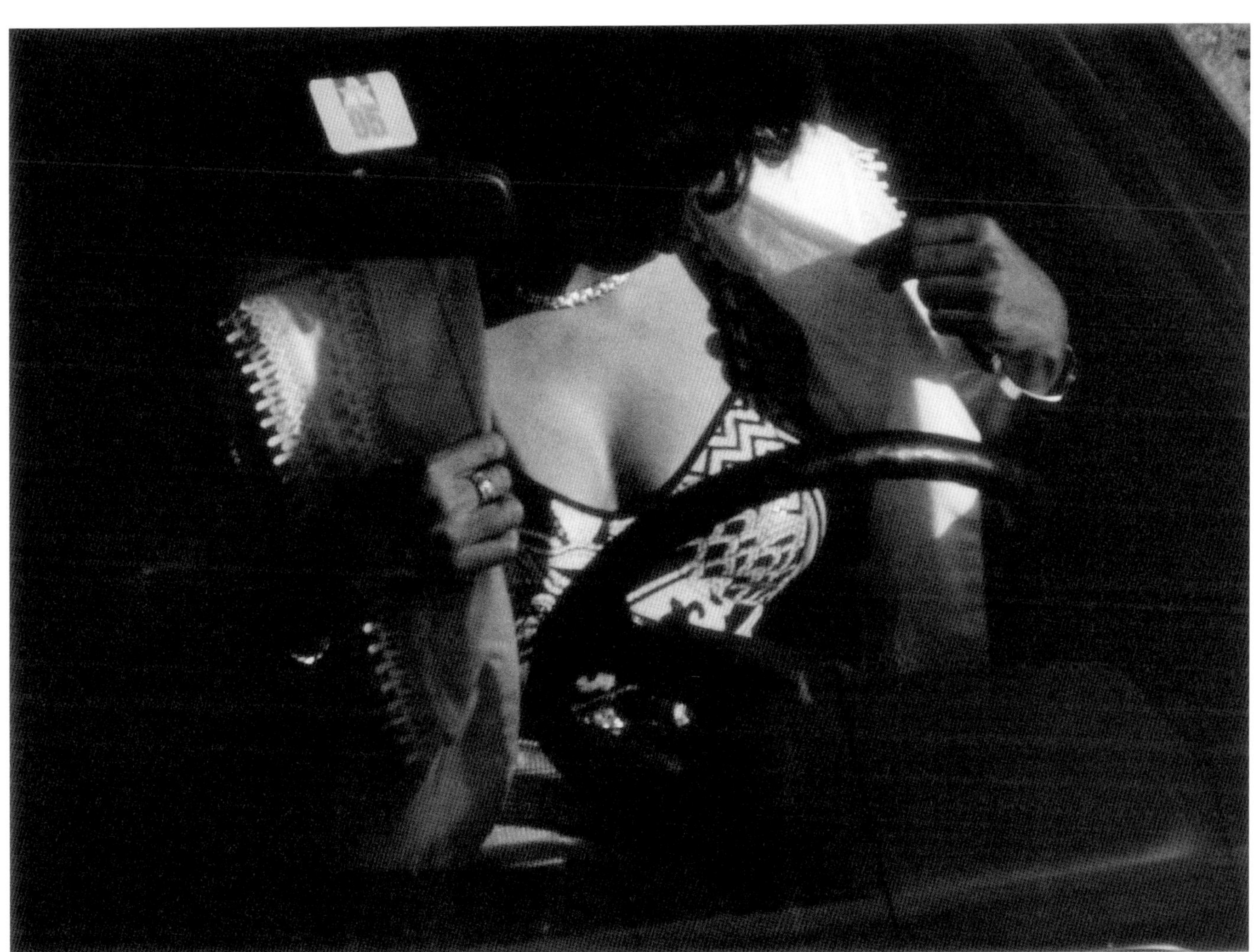

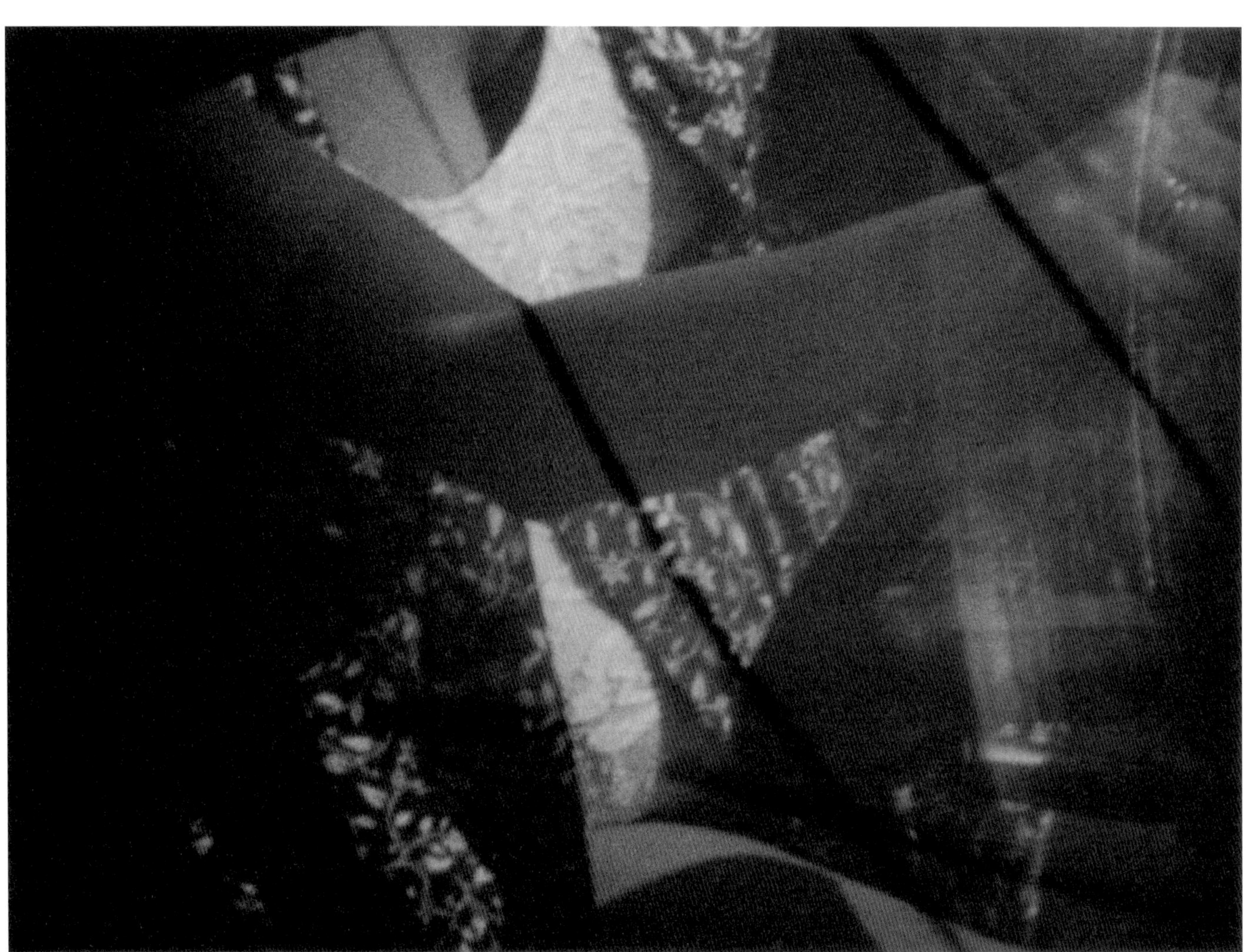

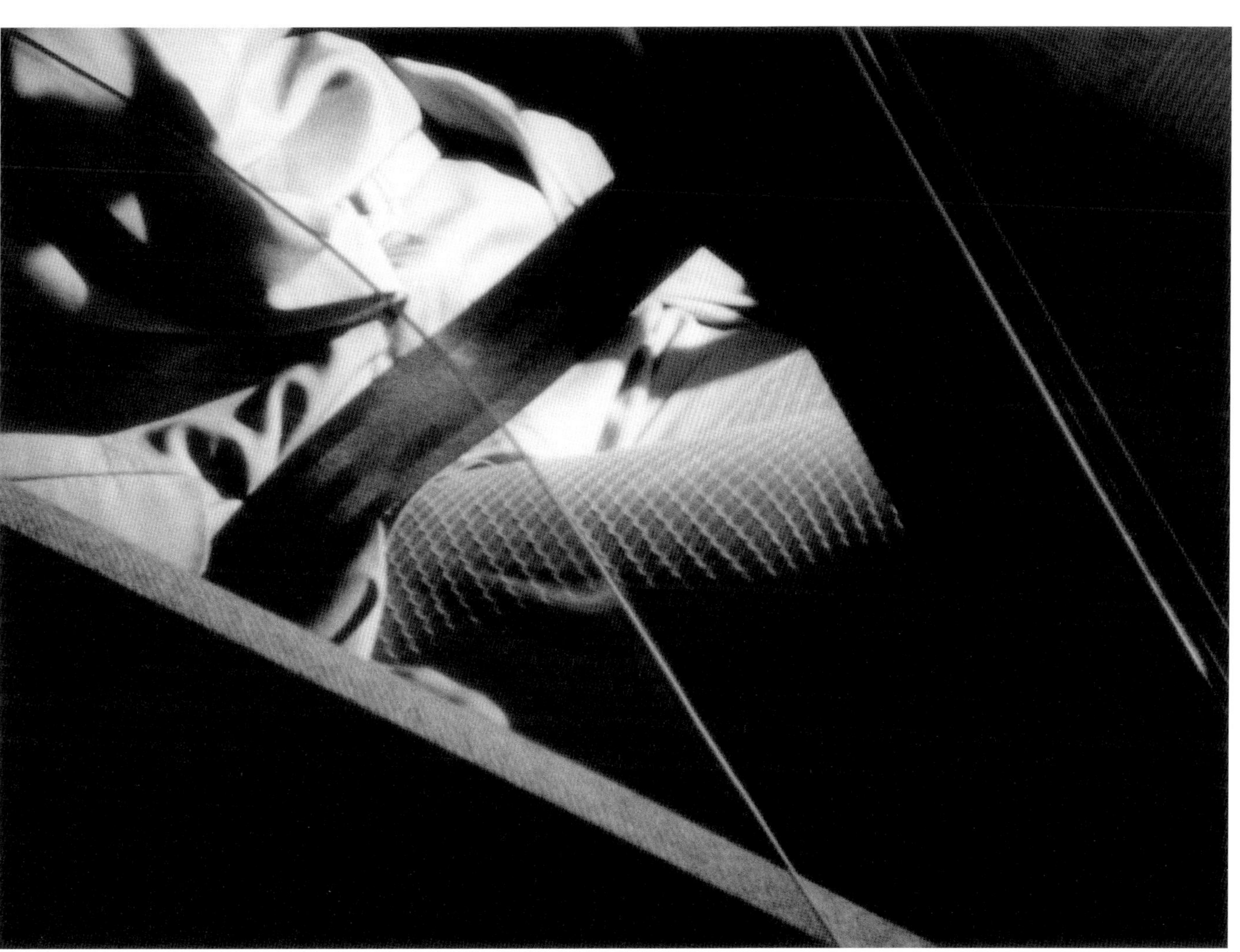

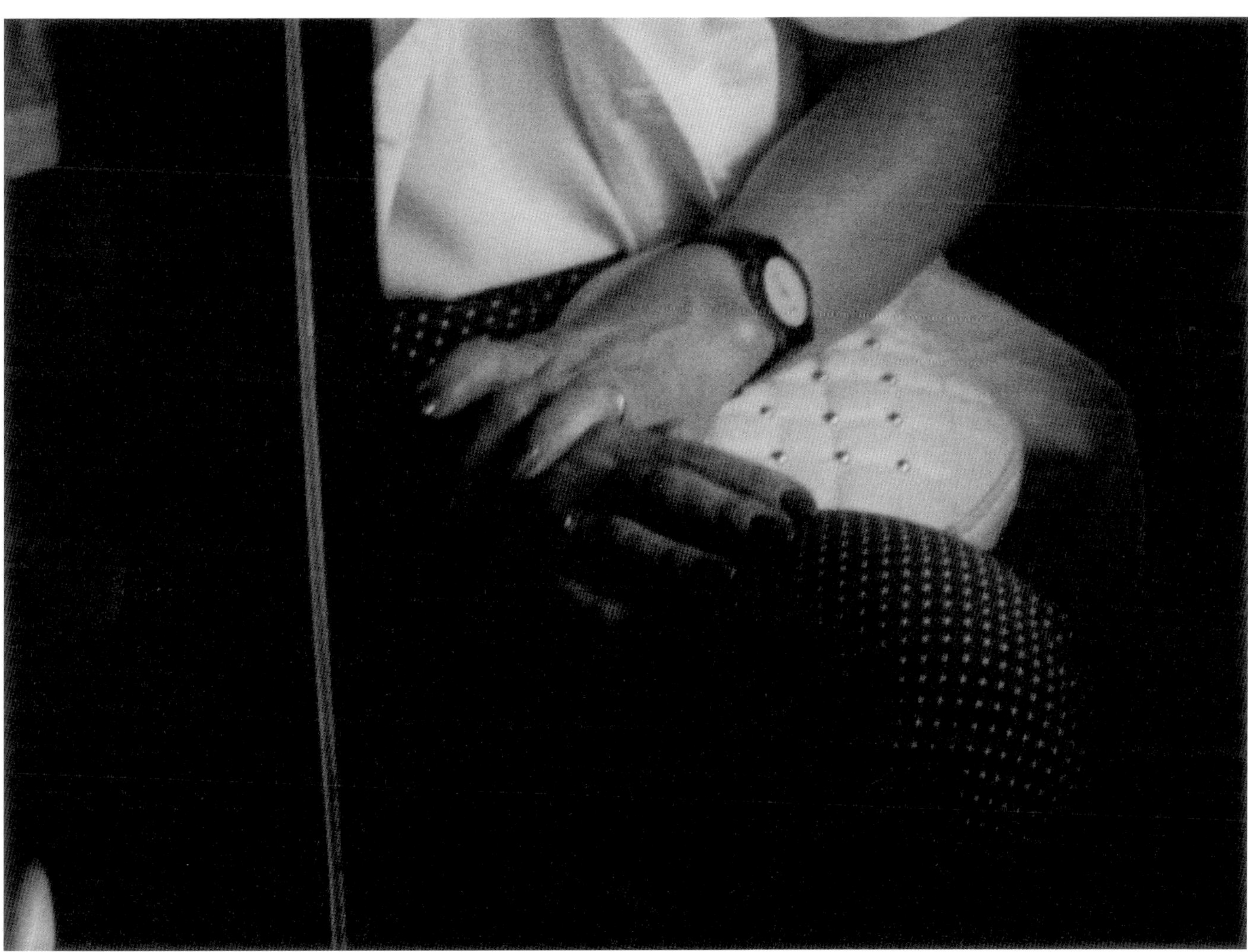

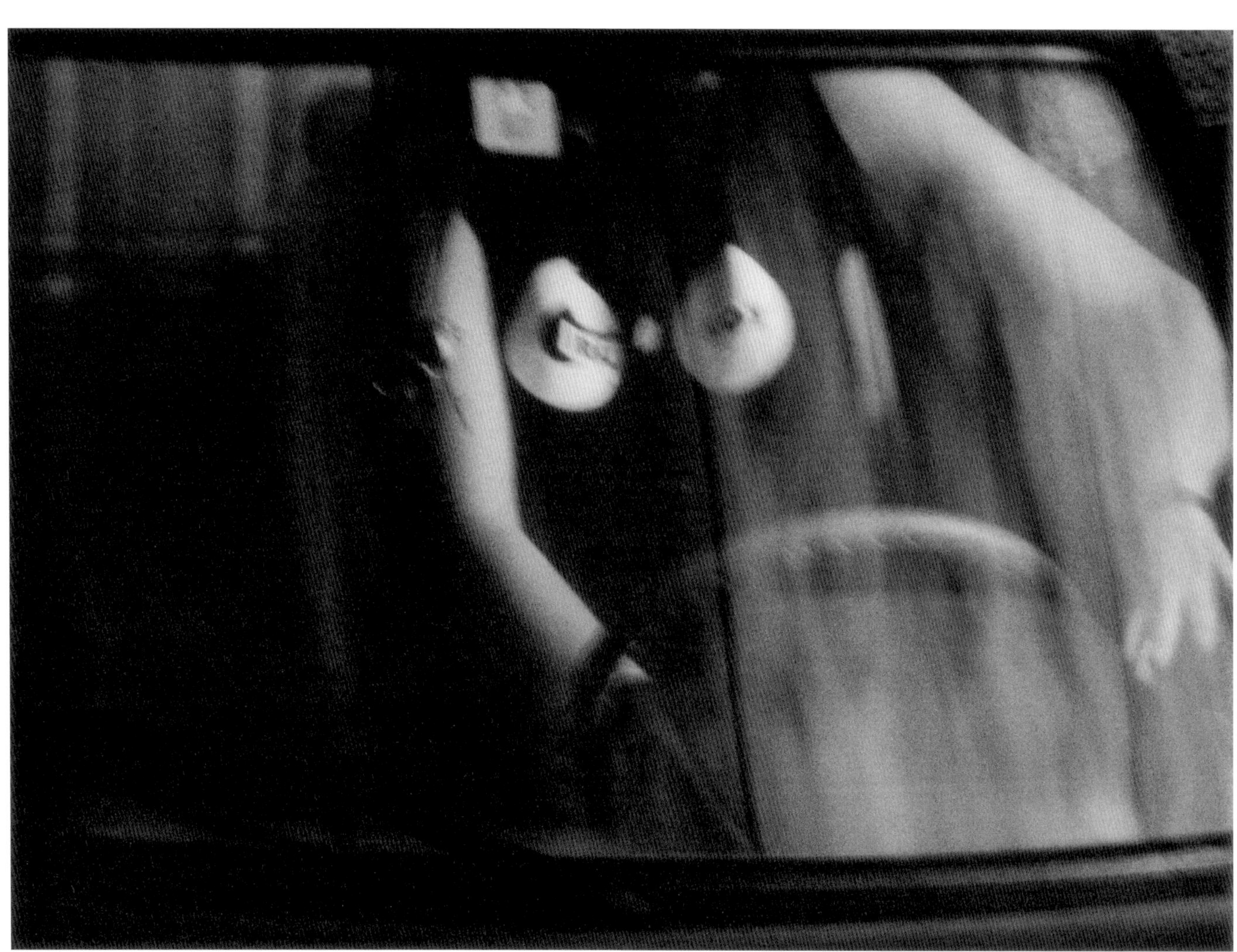

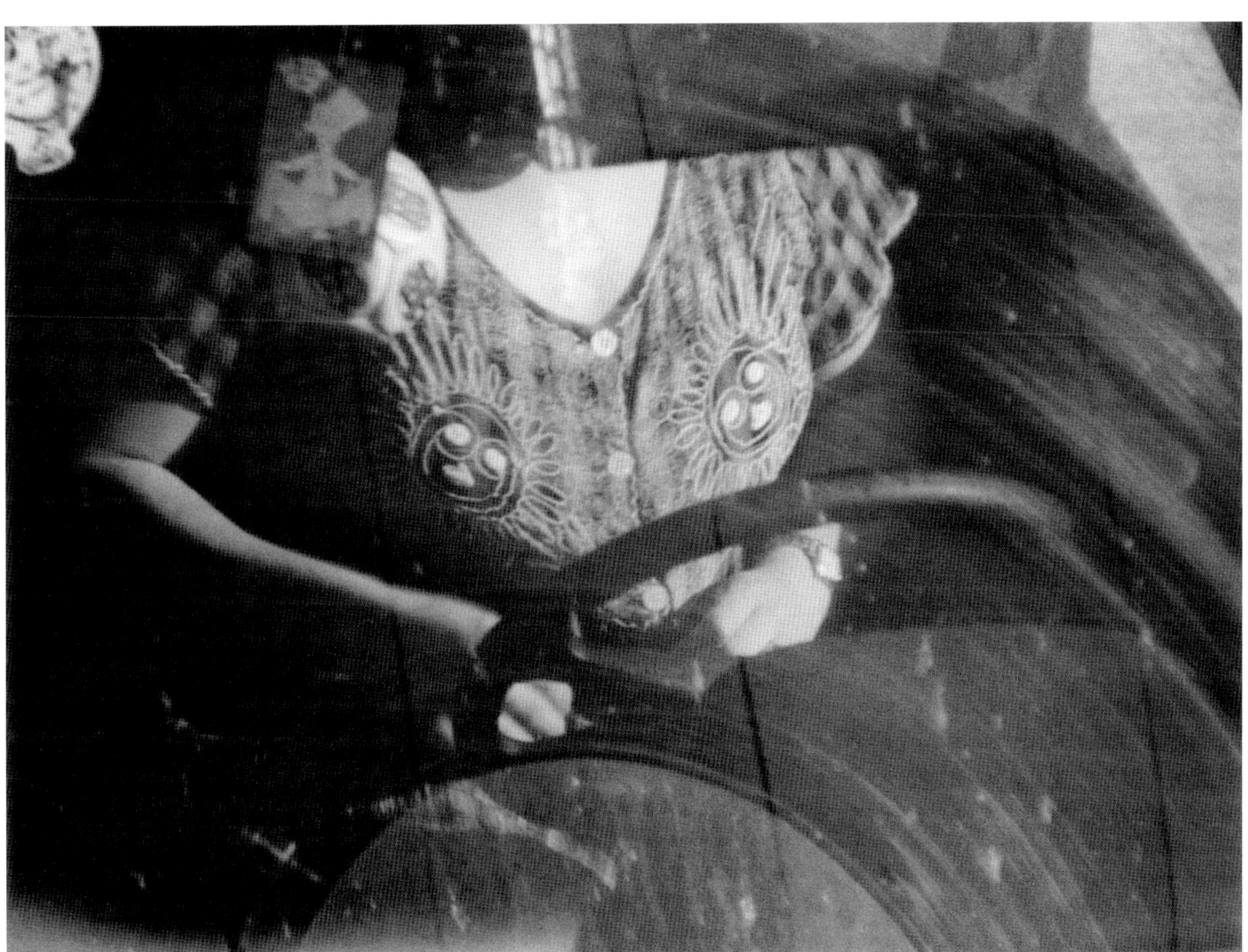

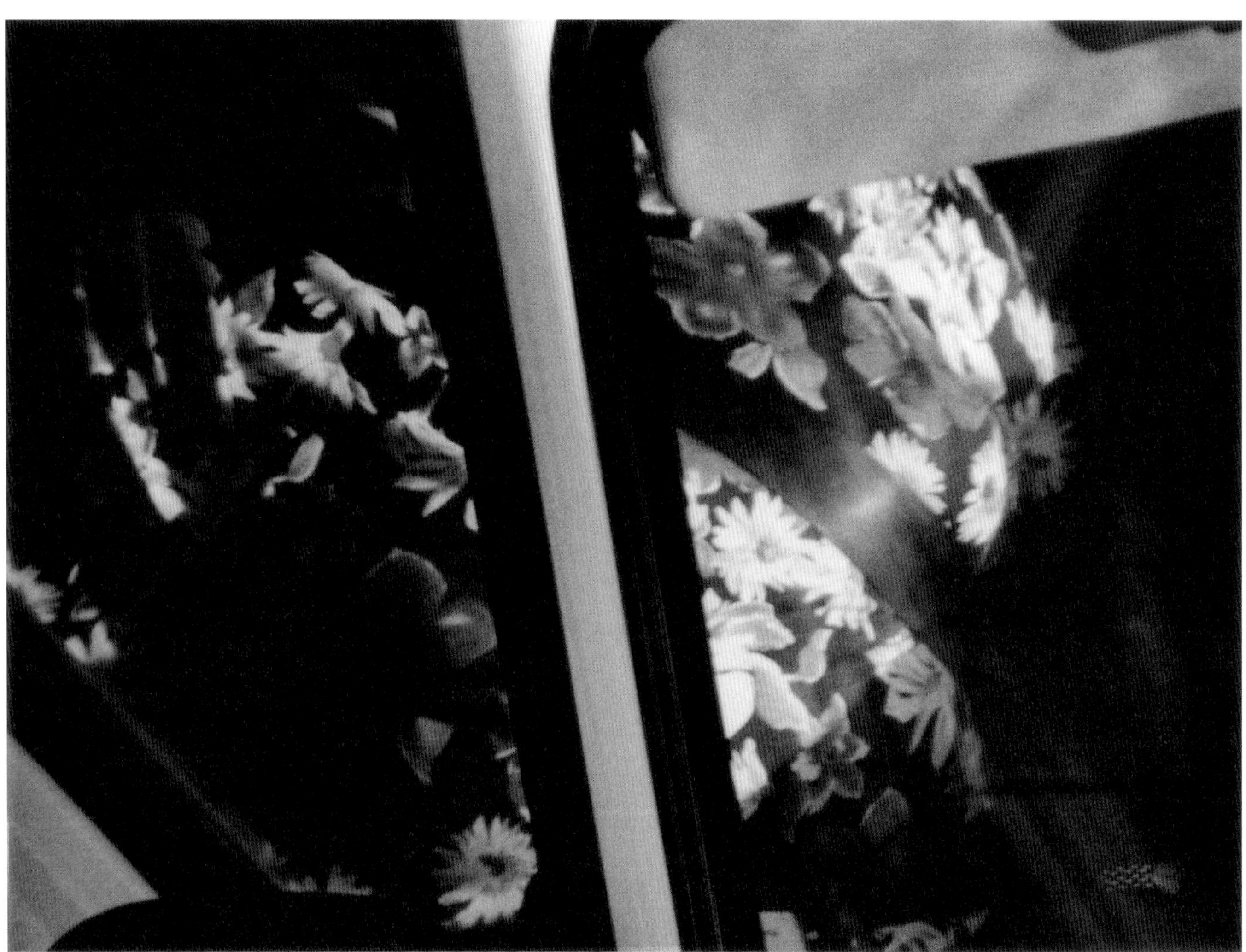

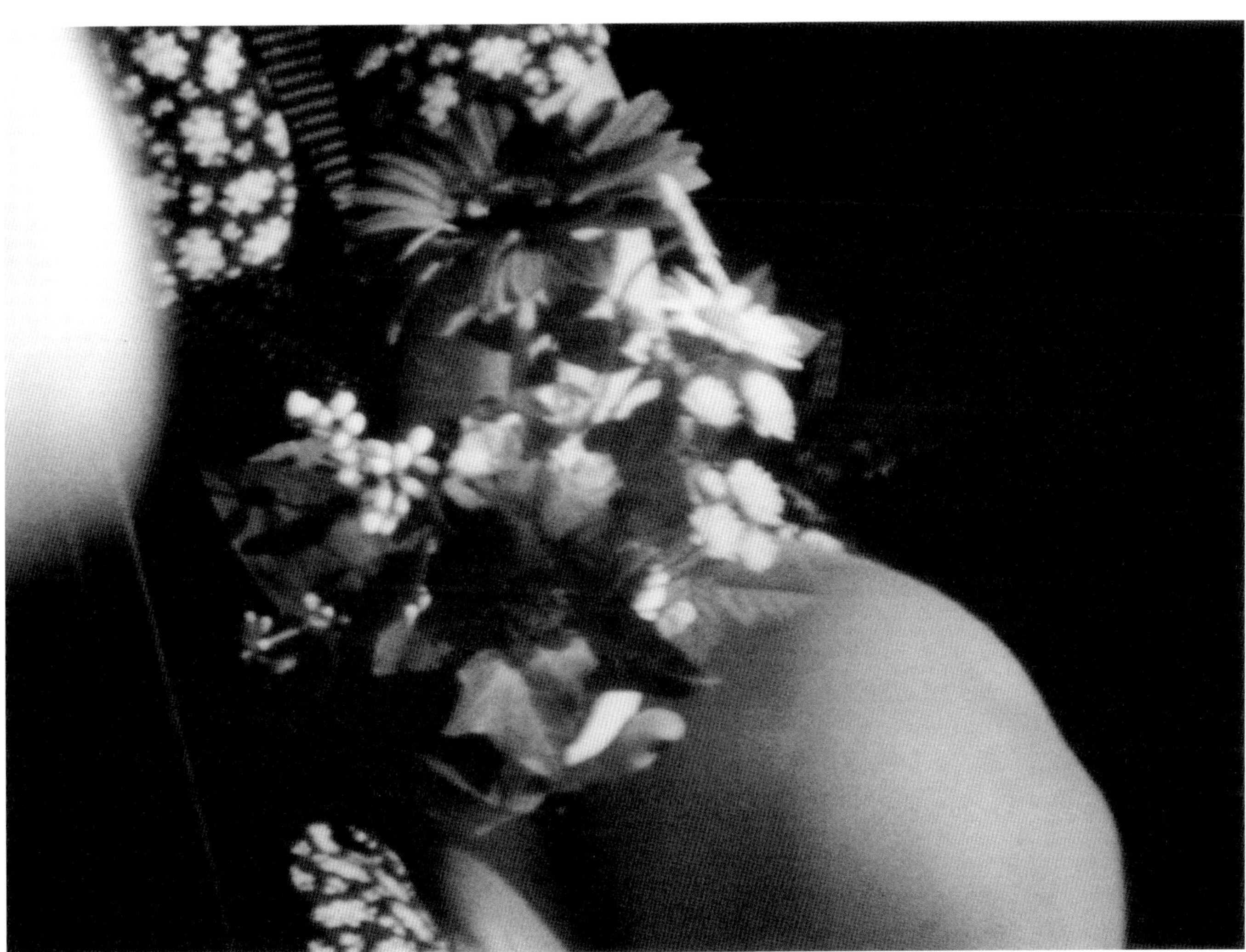

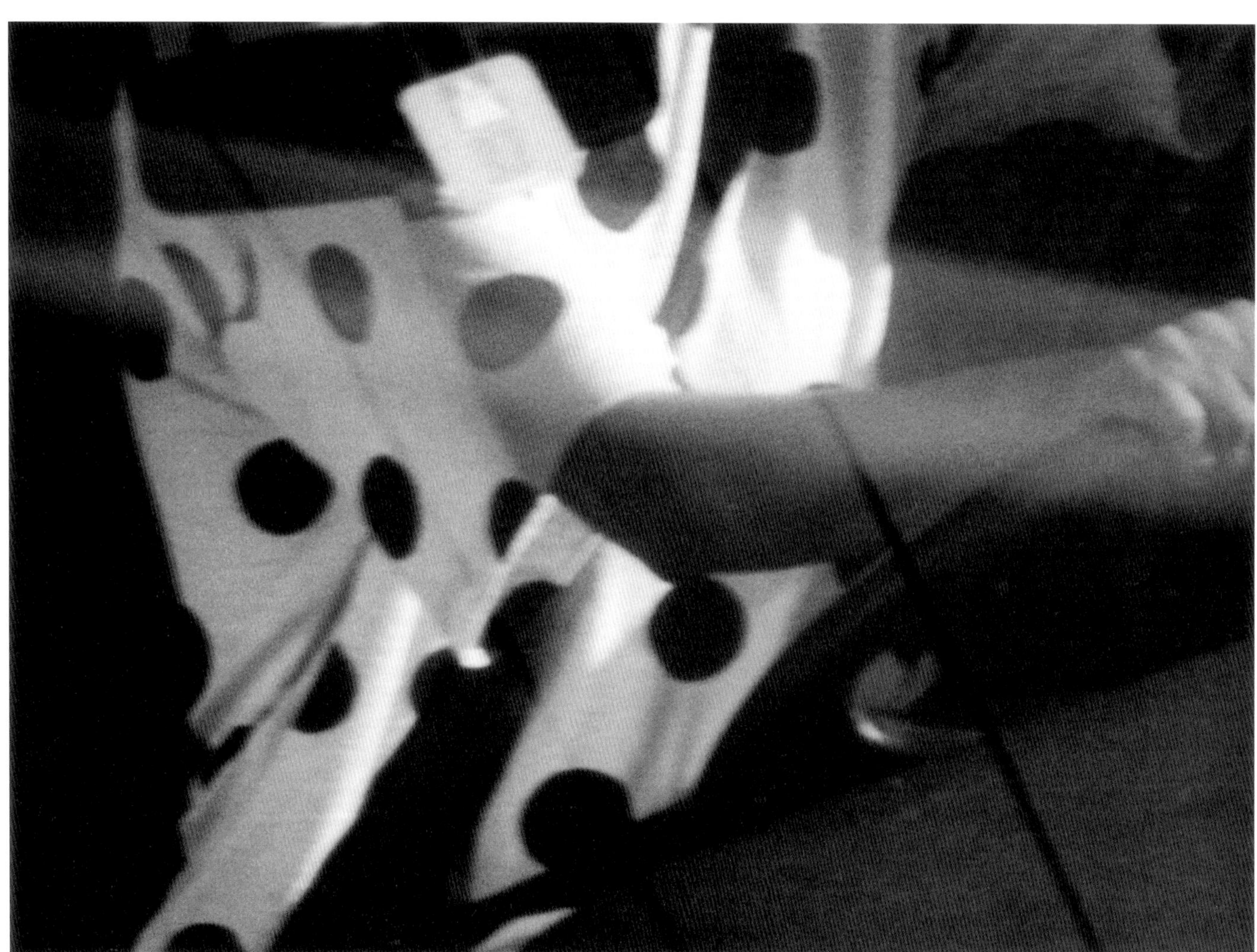

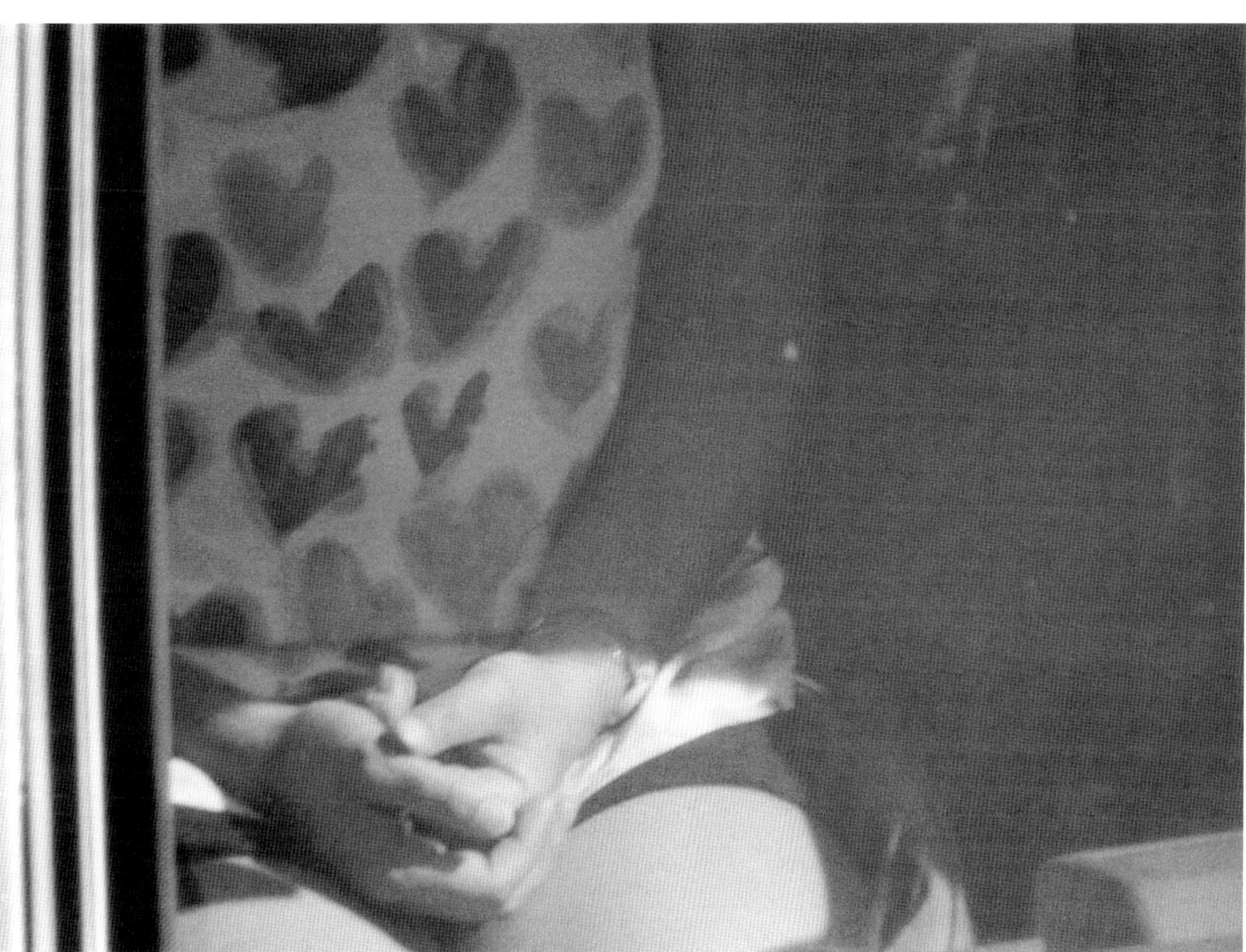

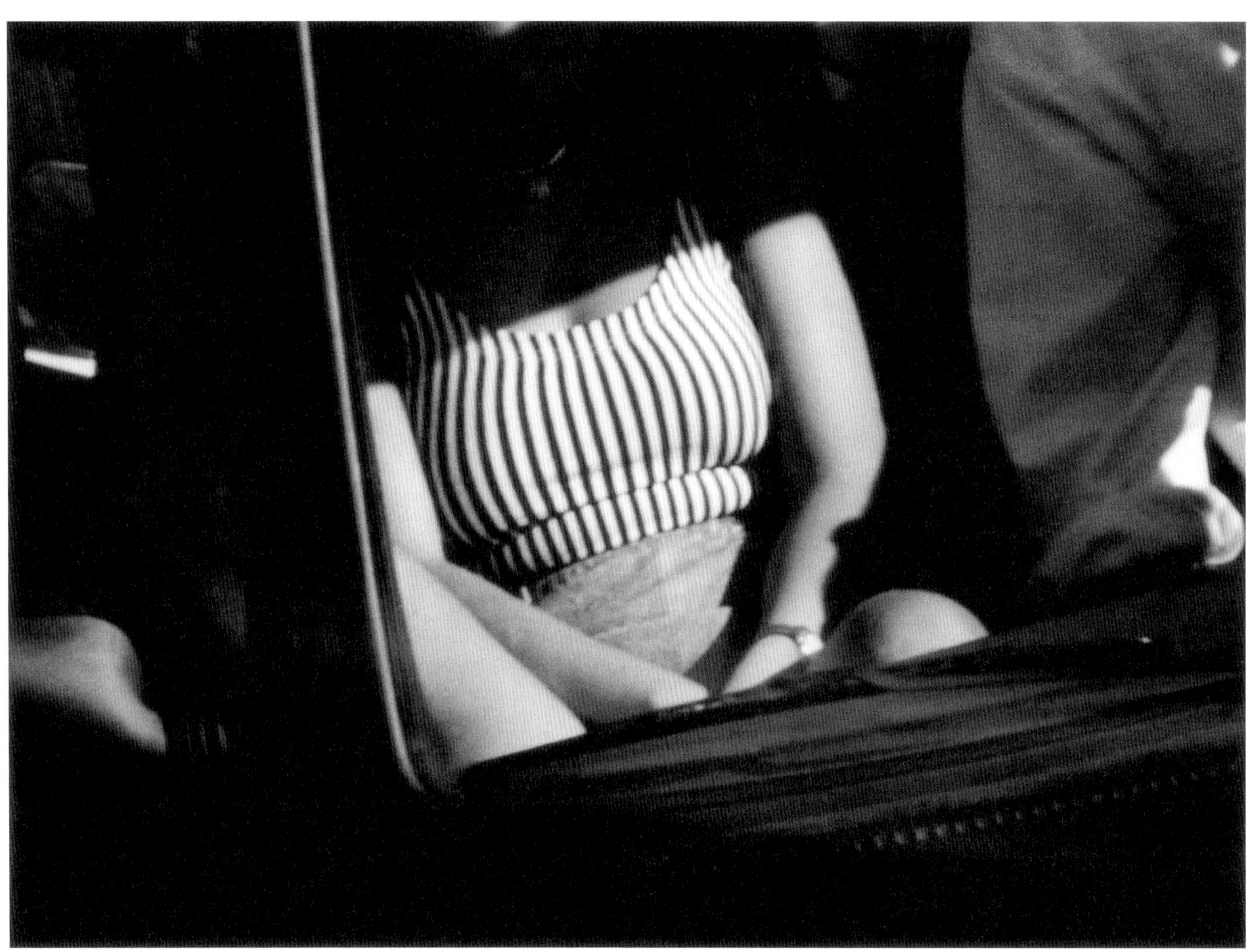

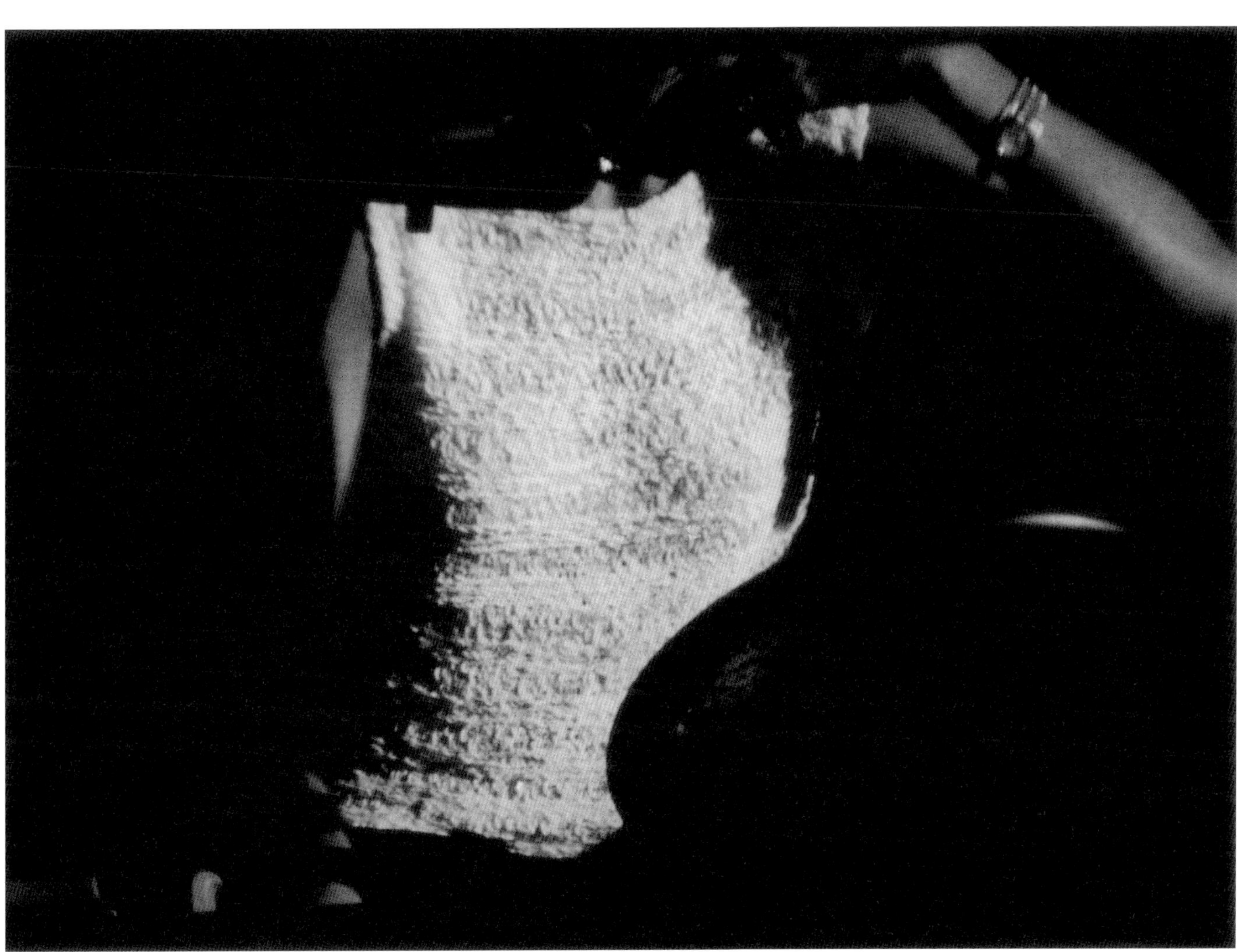

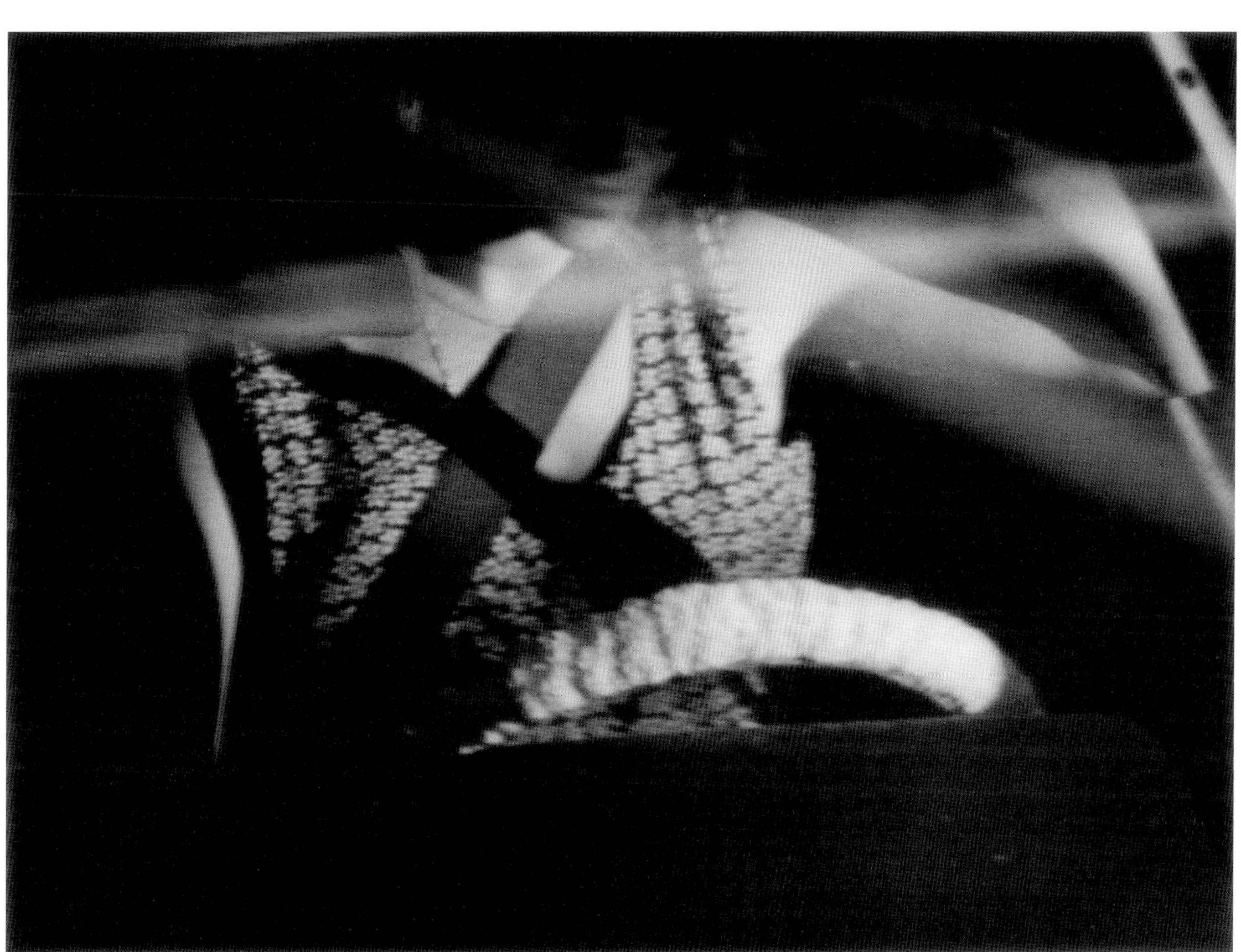

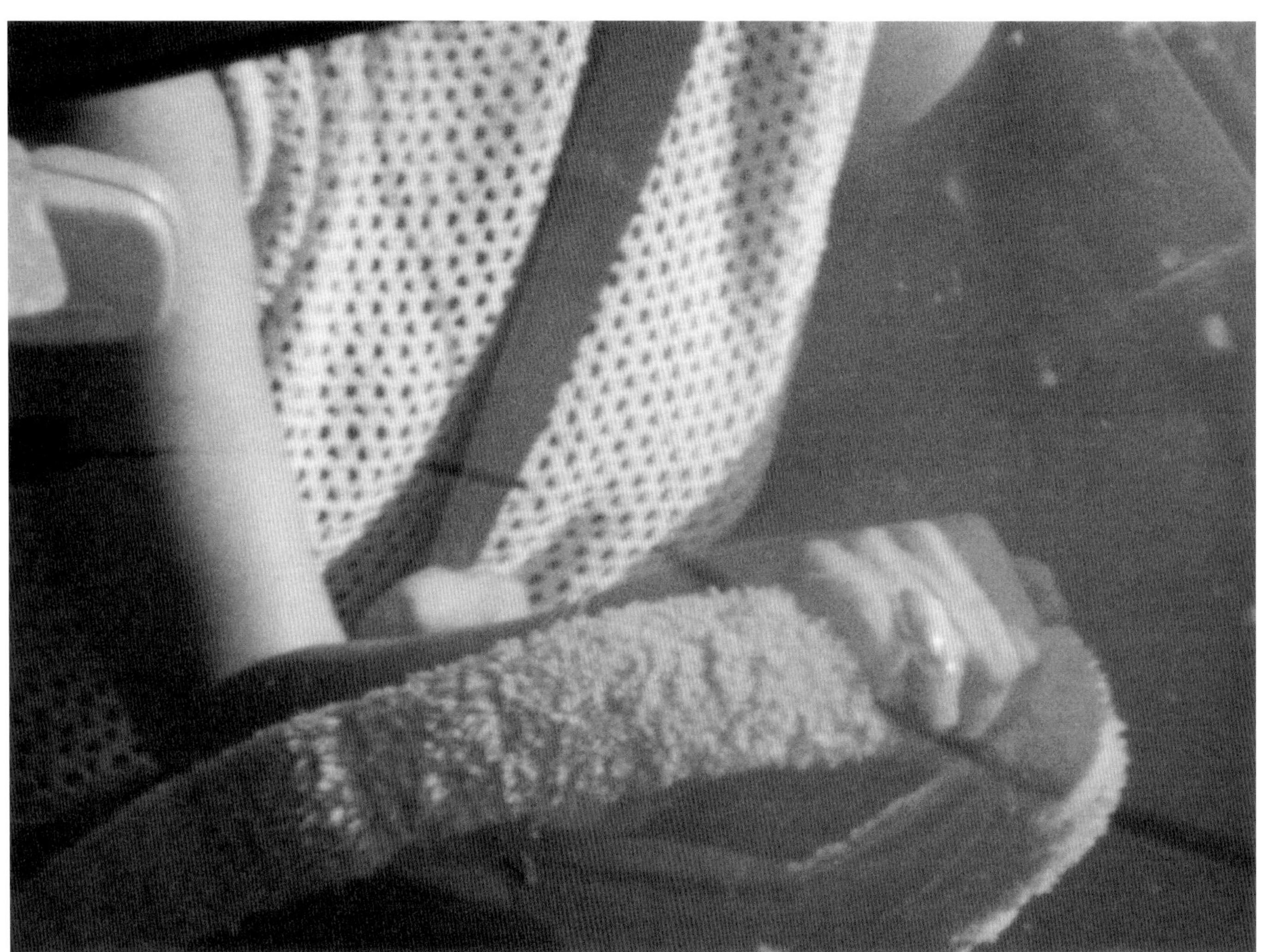

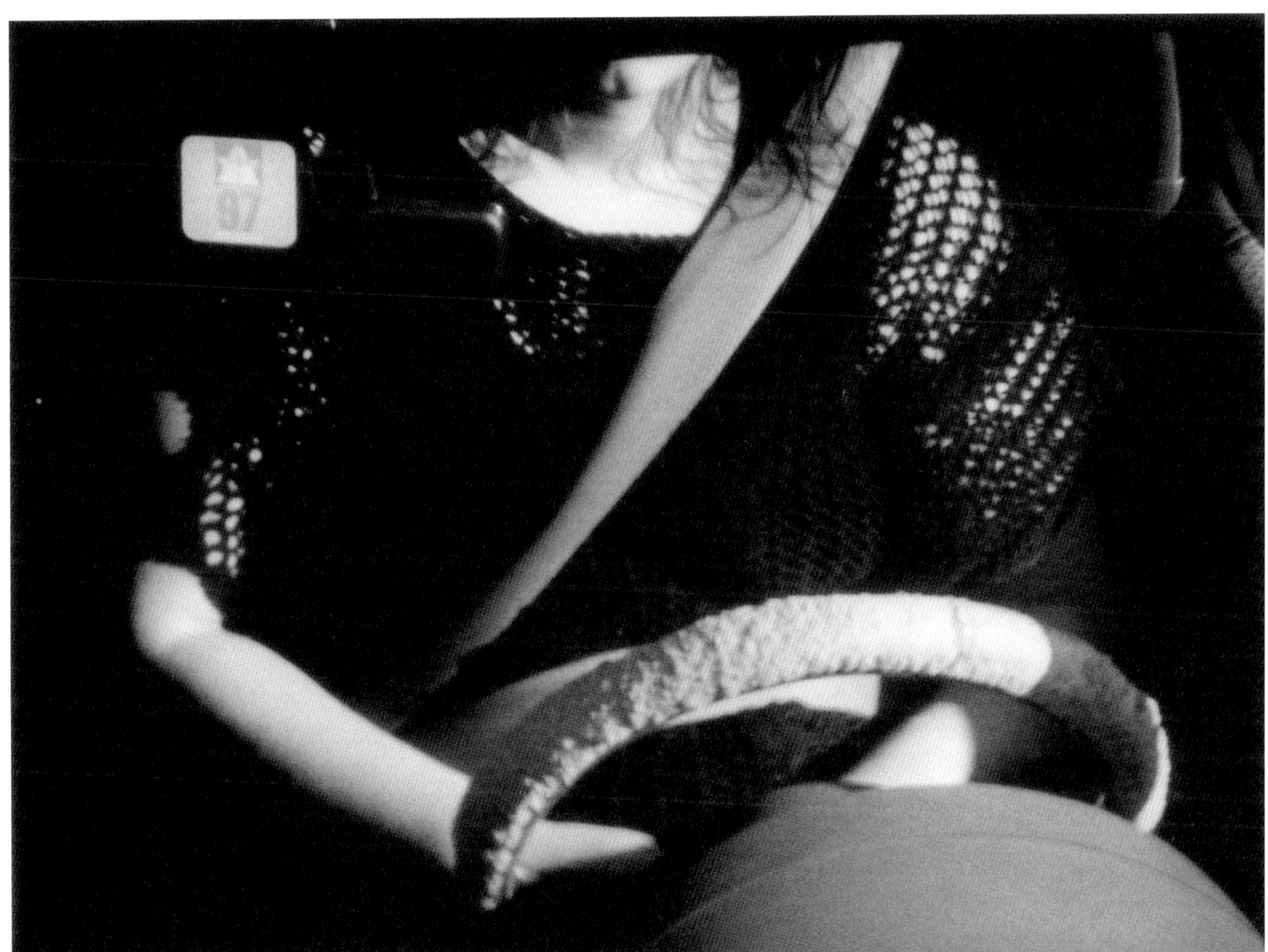

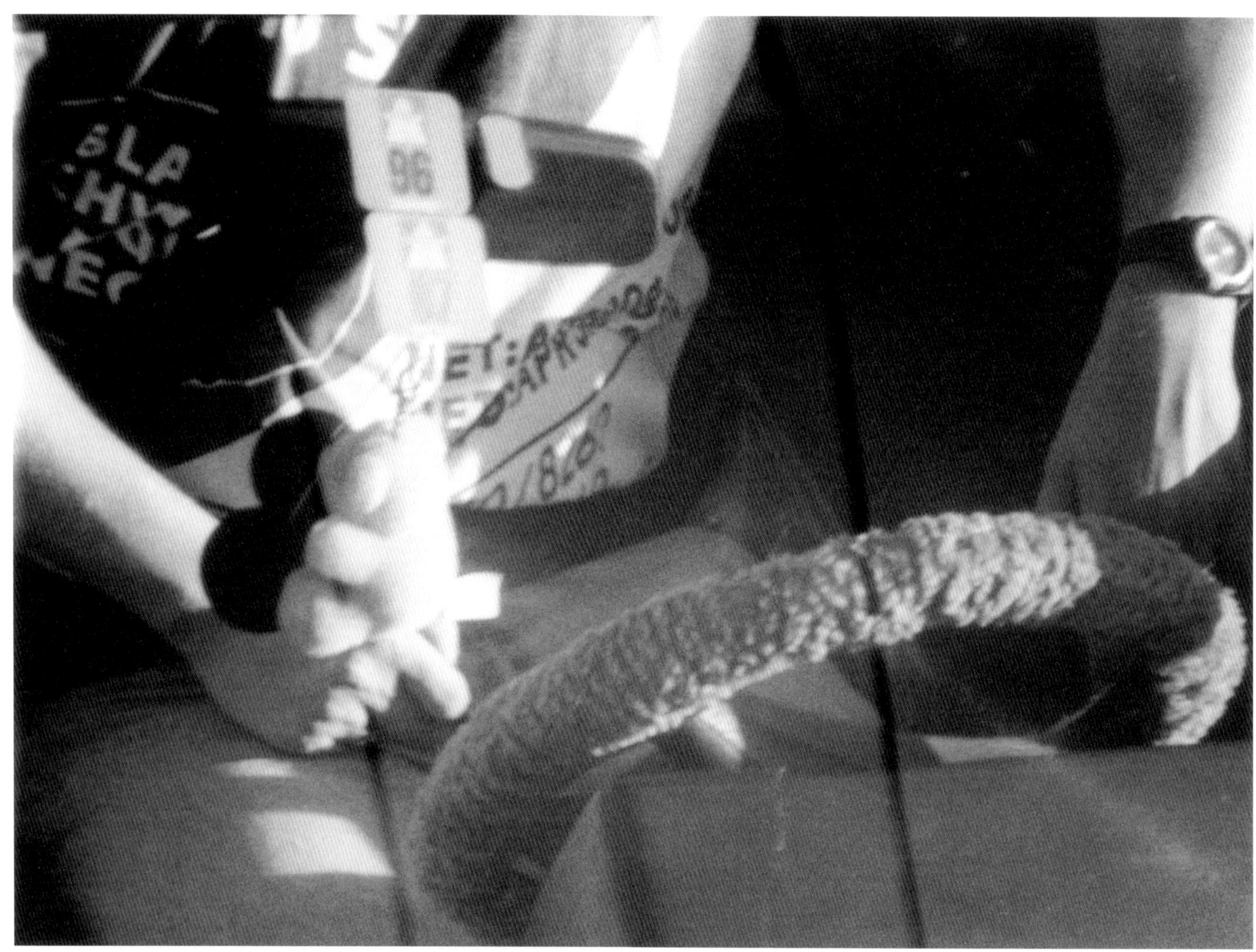

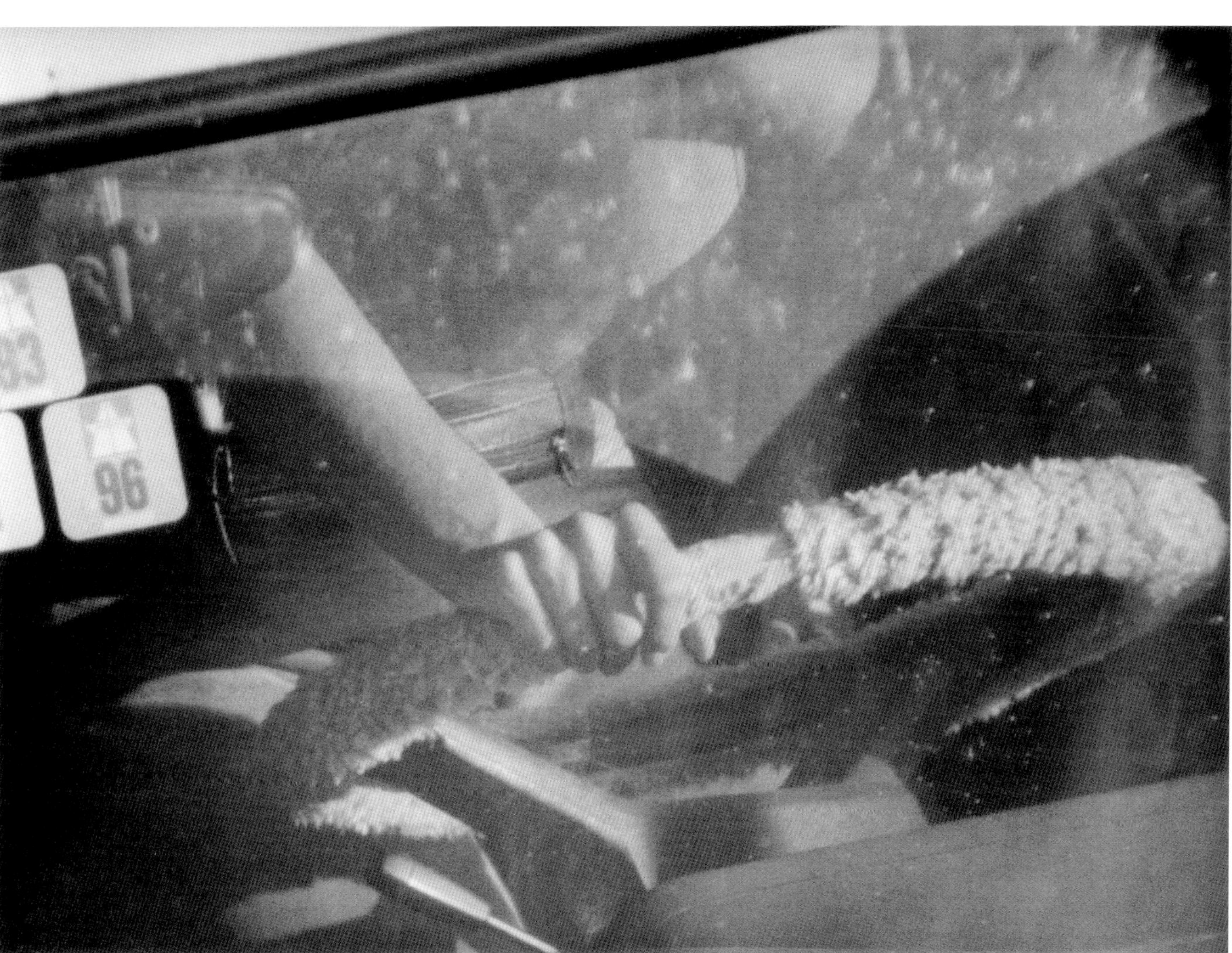

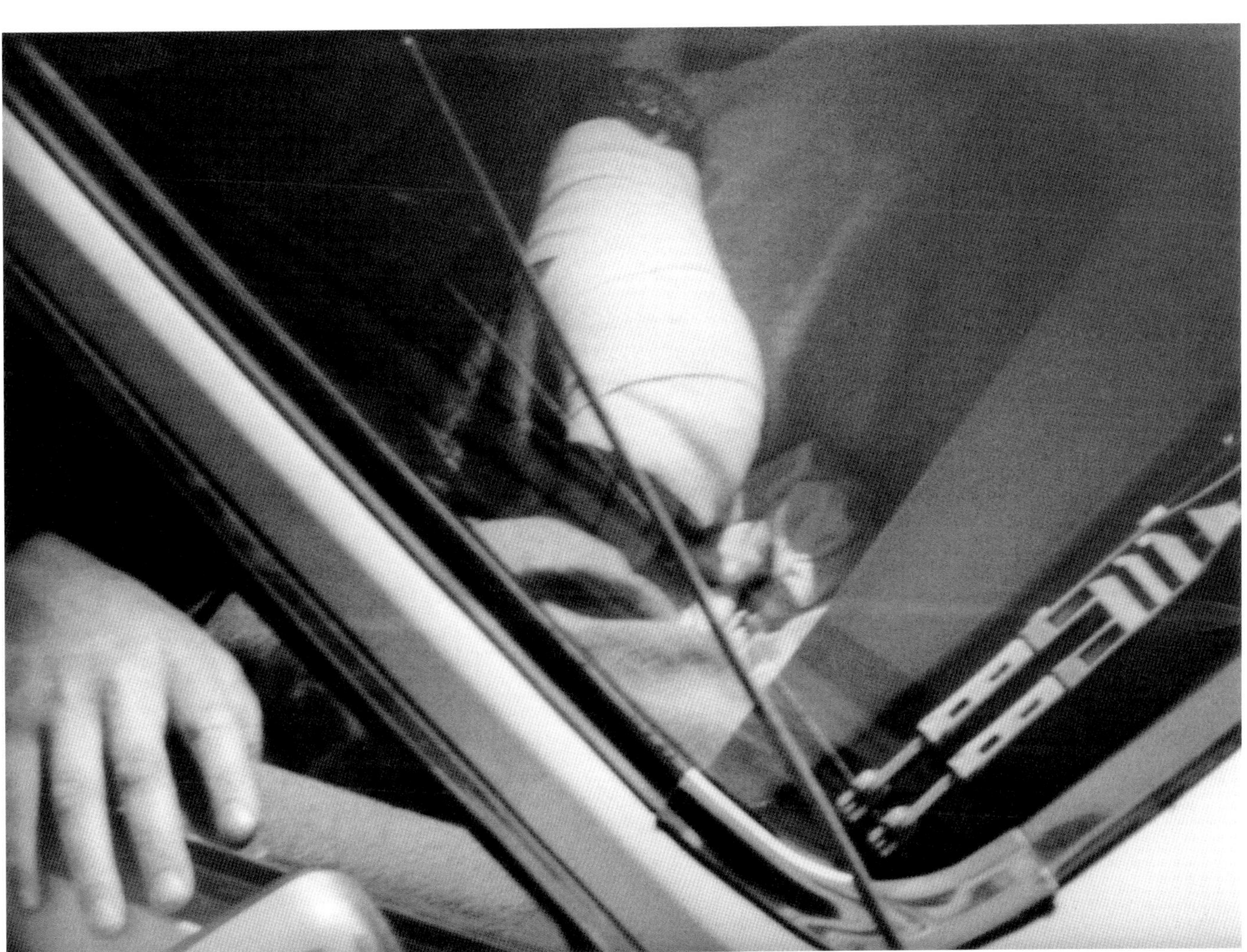

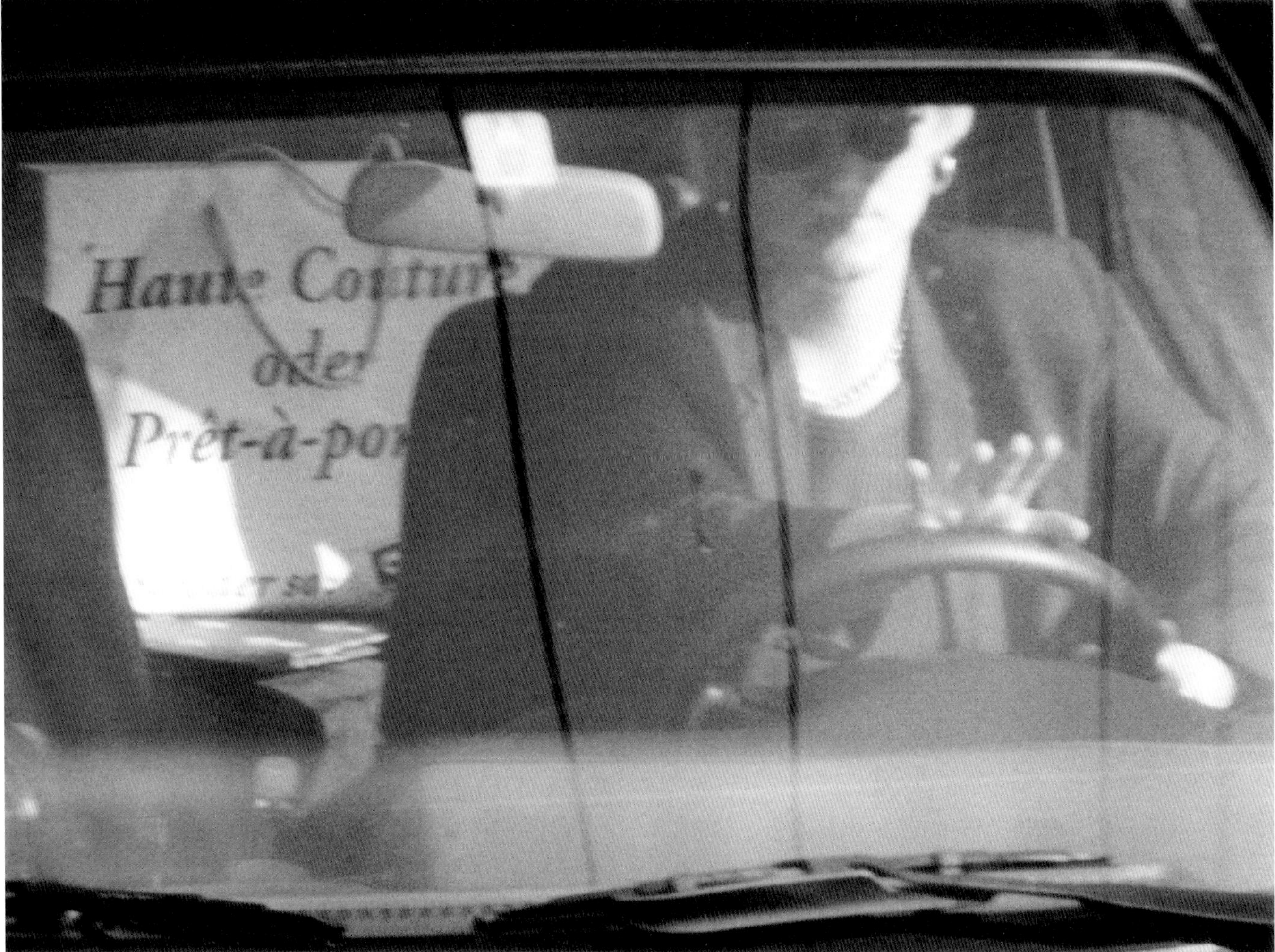

Haute Couture
oder
Prêt-à-por

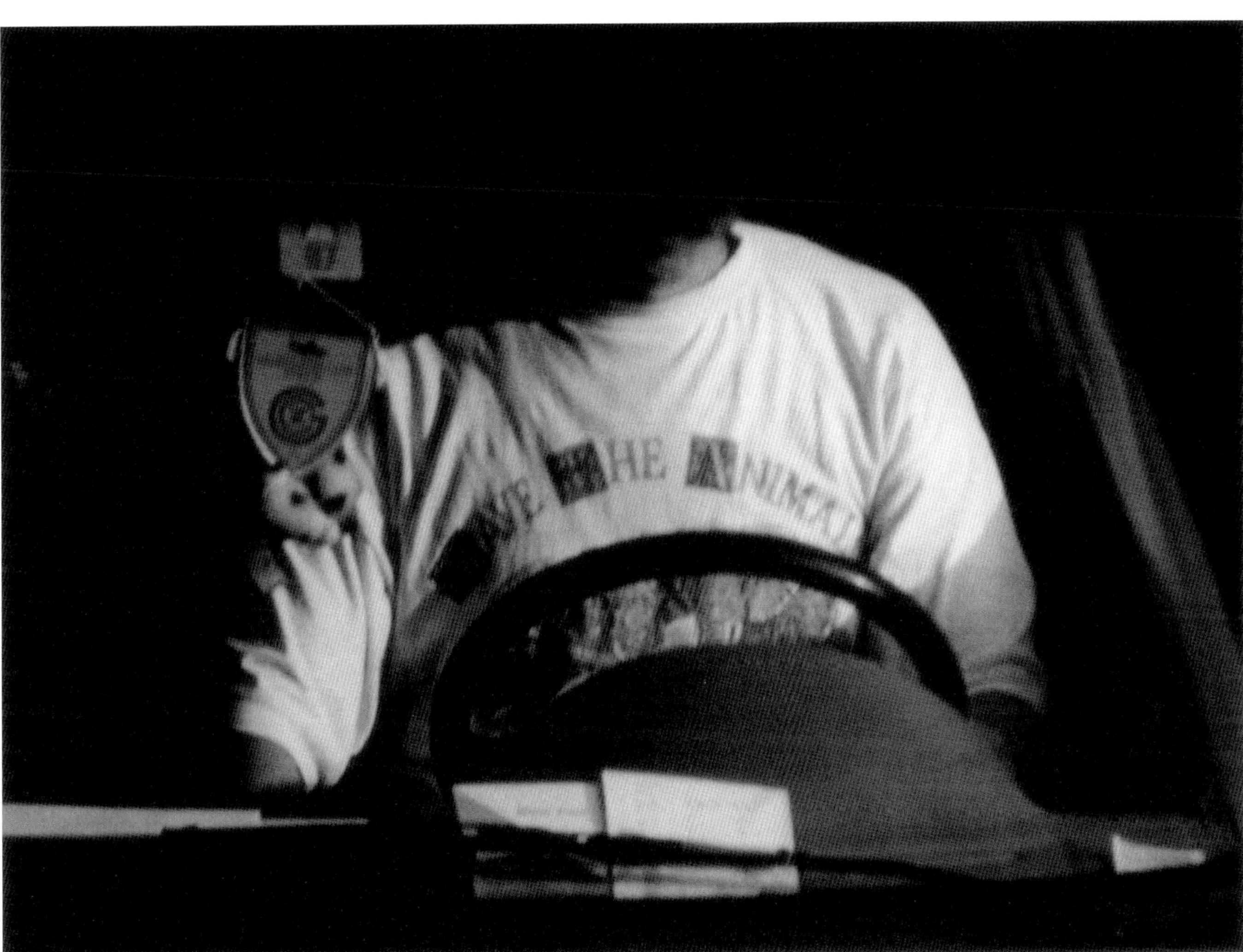

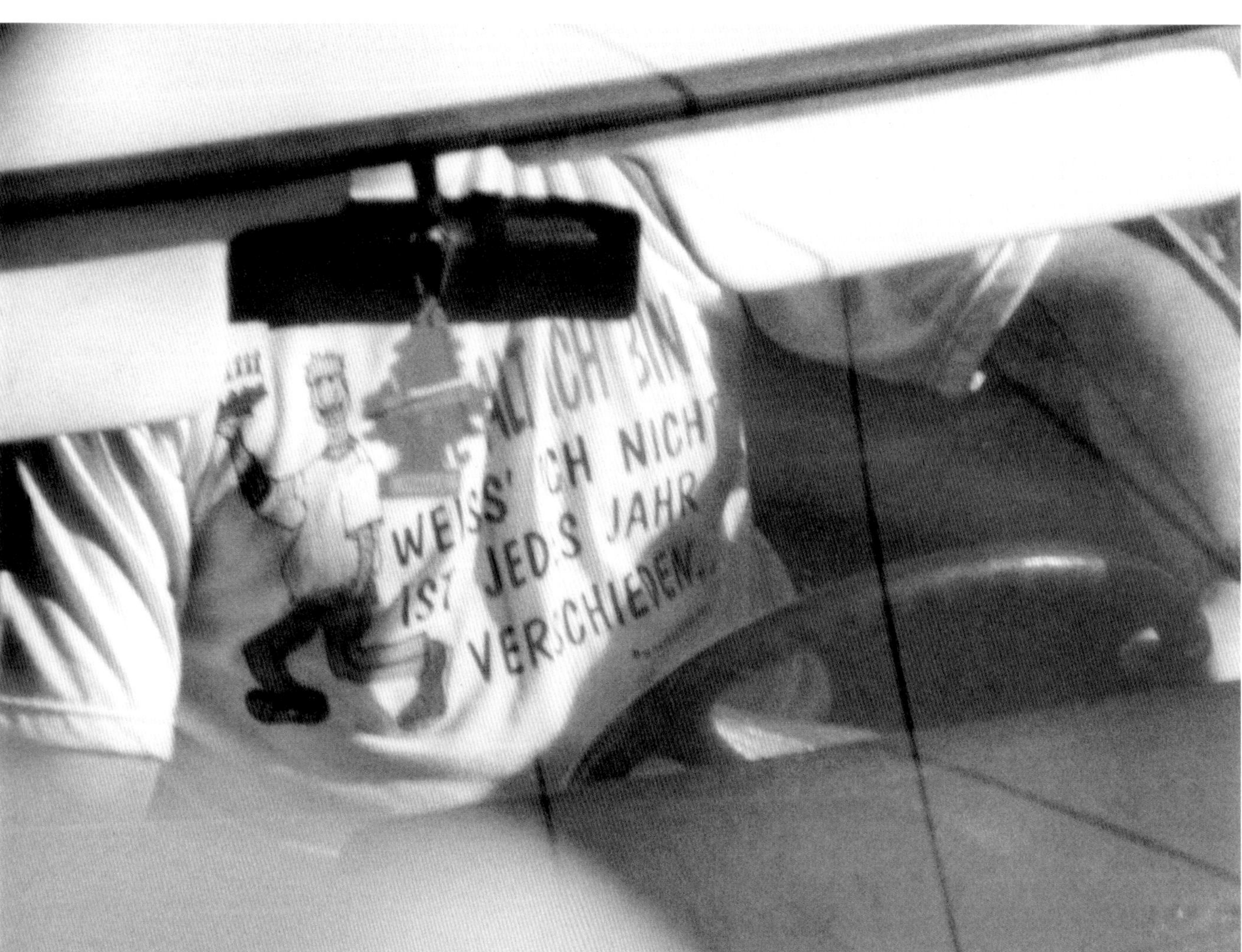
WIE ALT ICH BIN
WEISS' ICH NICHT
IST JED.S JAHR
VERSCHIEDEN.

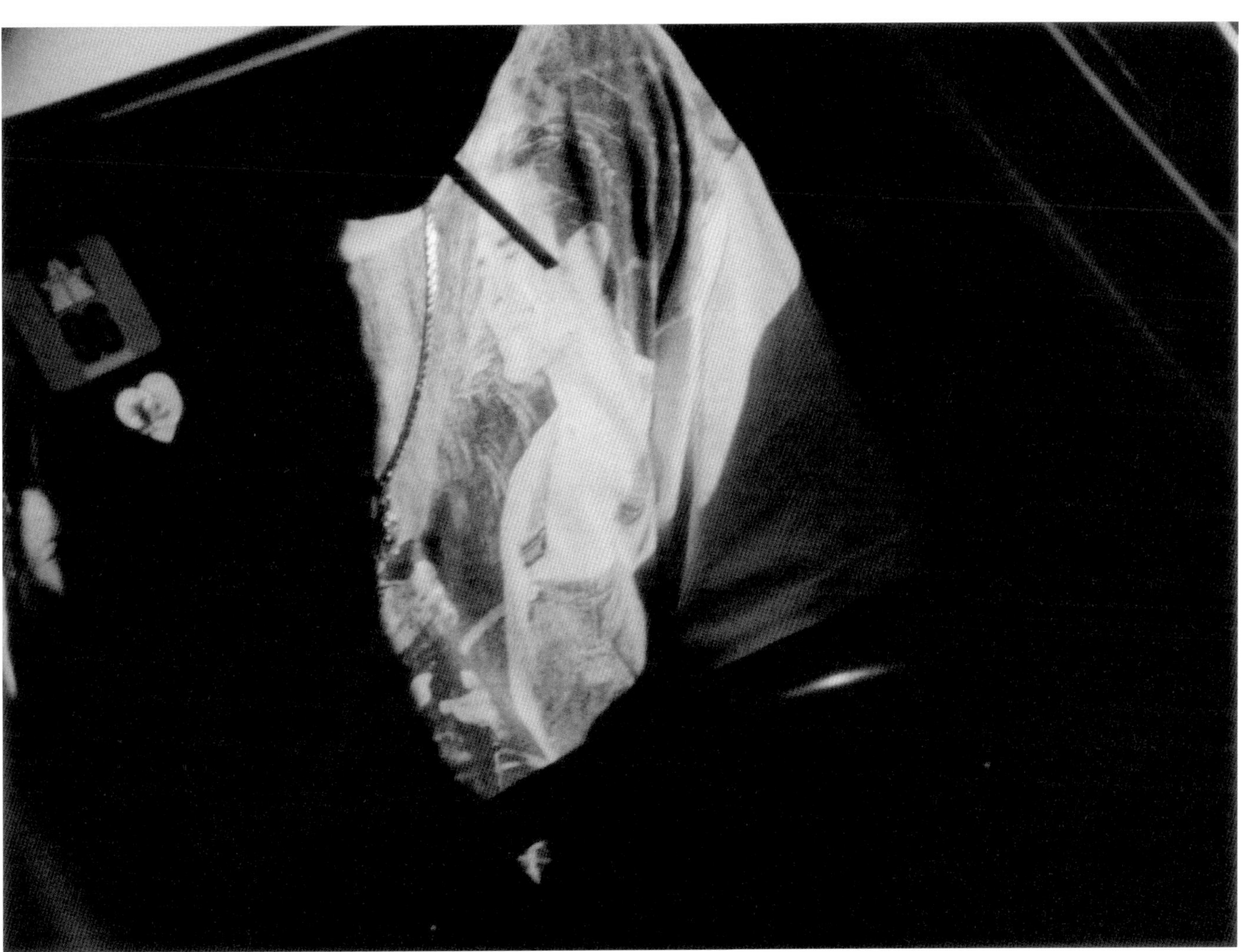

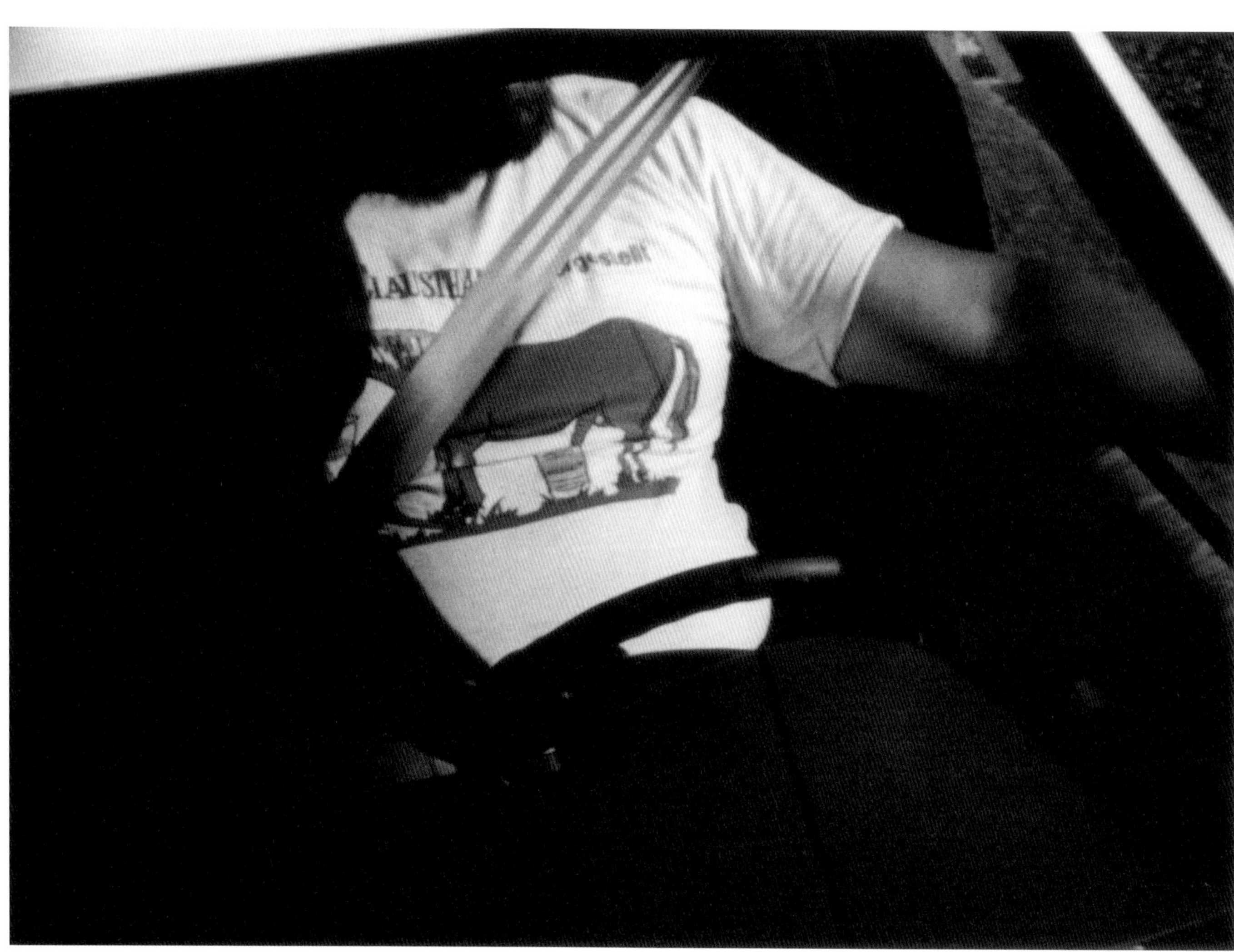

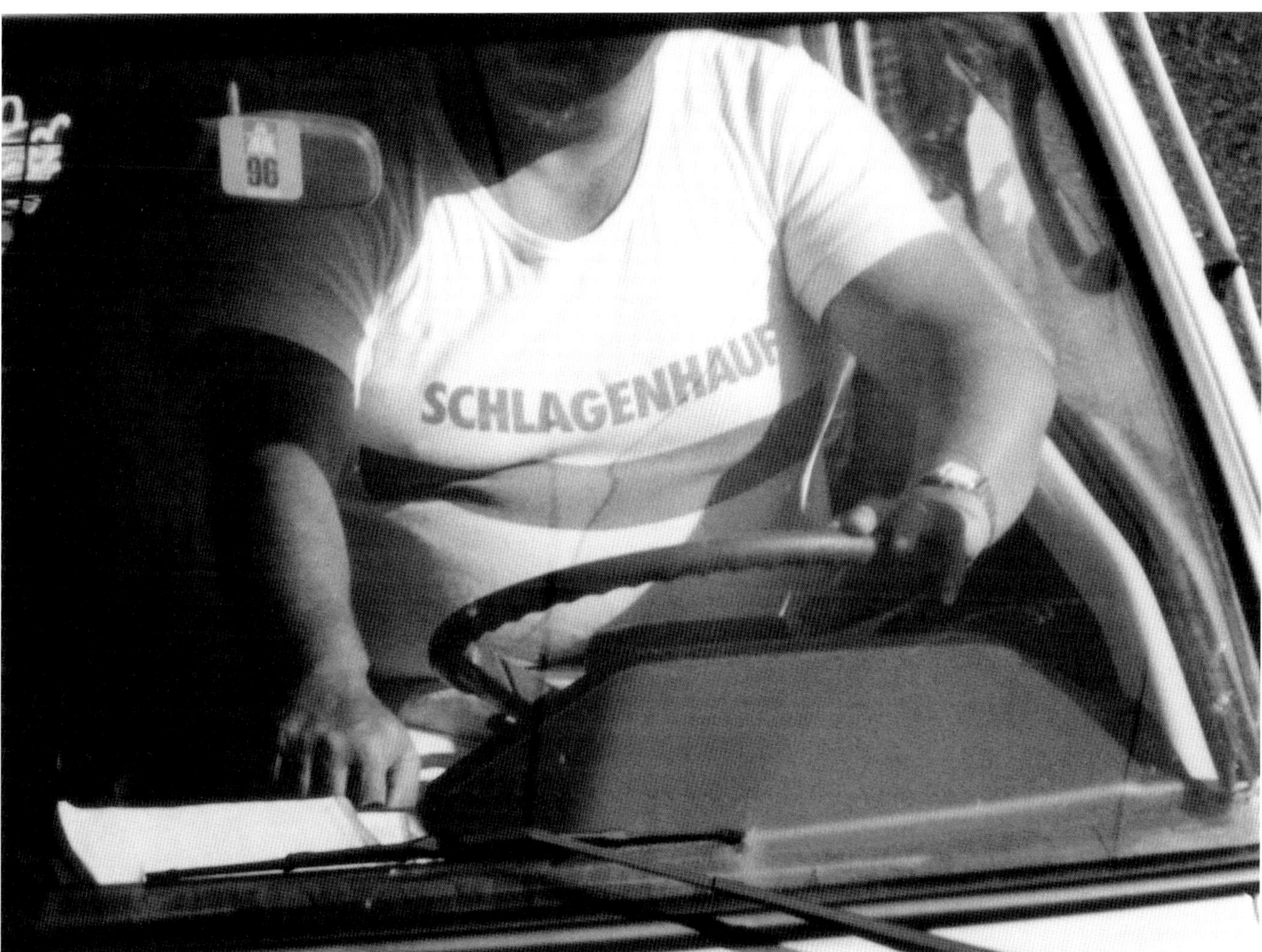
SCHLAGENHAU

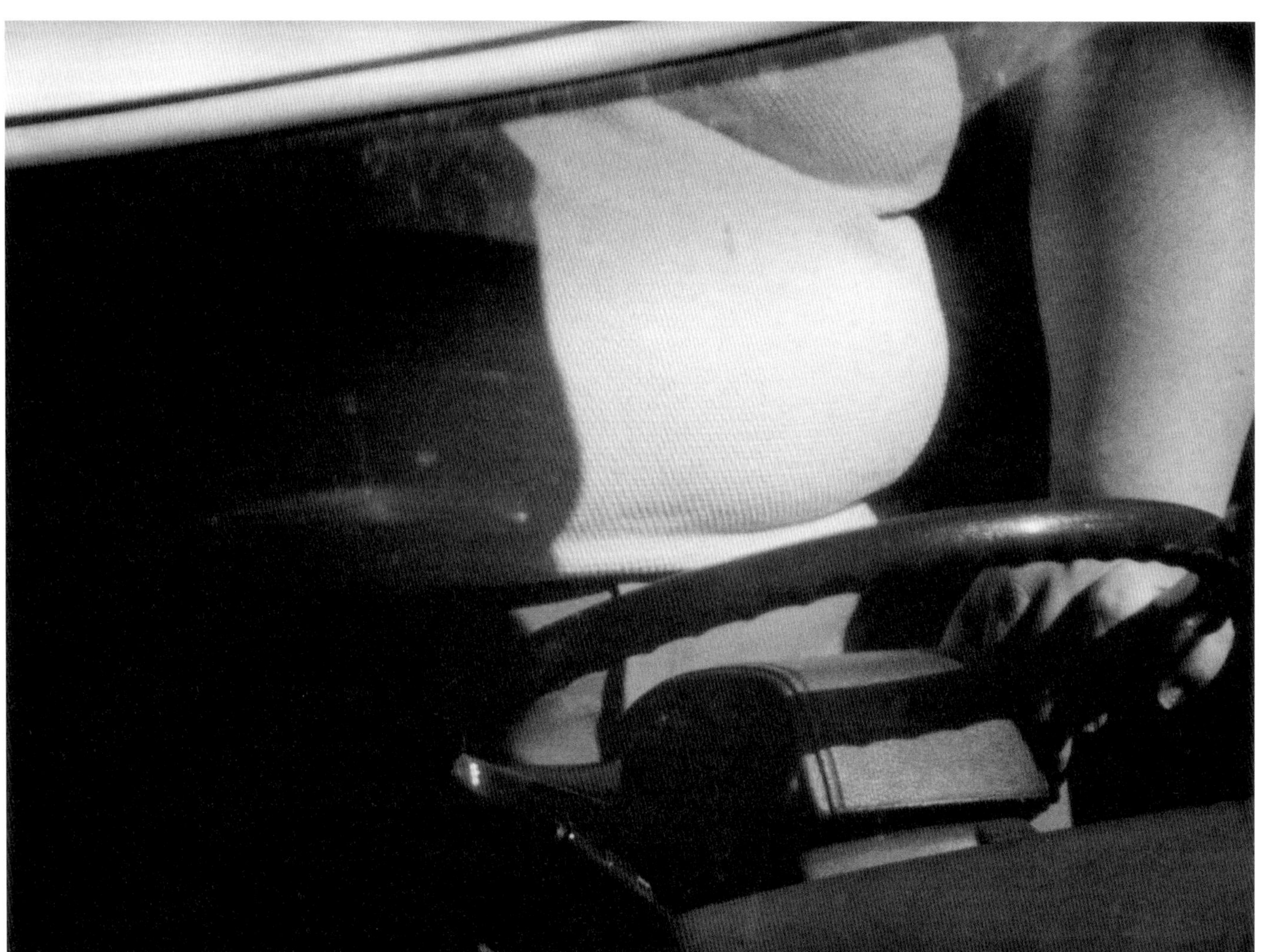

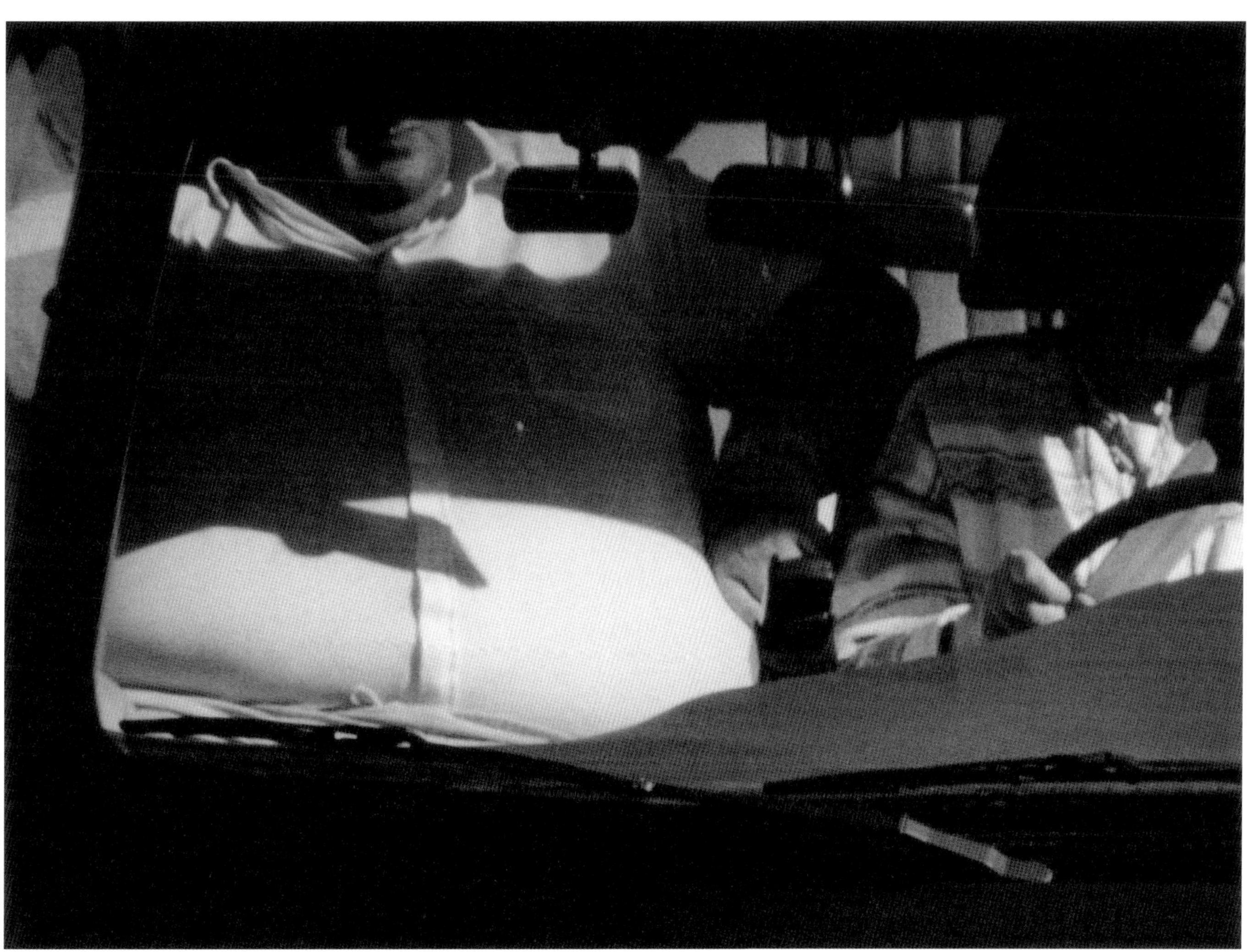

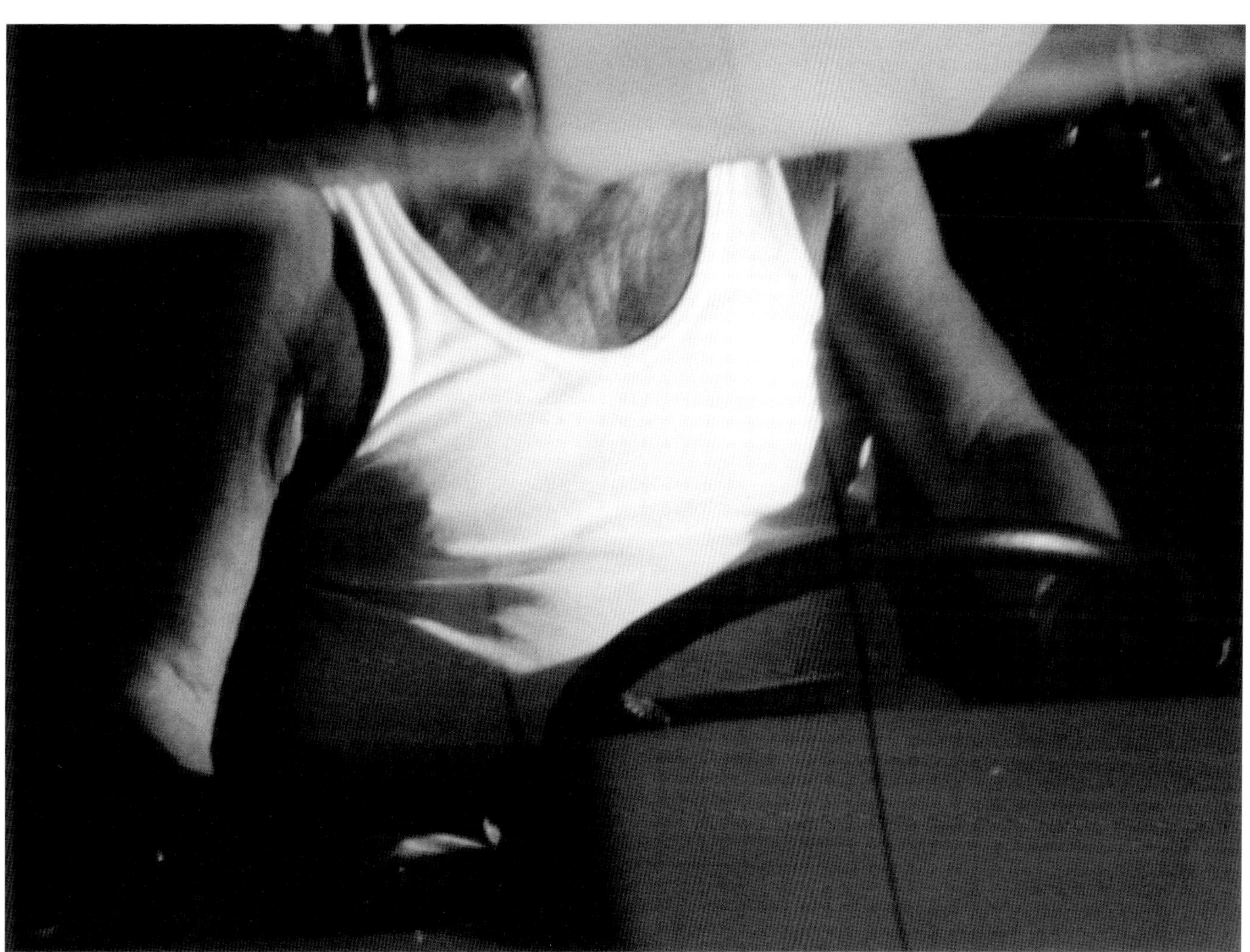

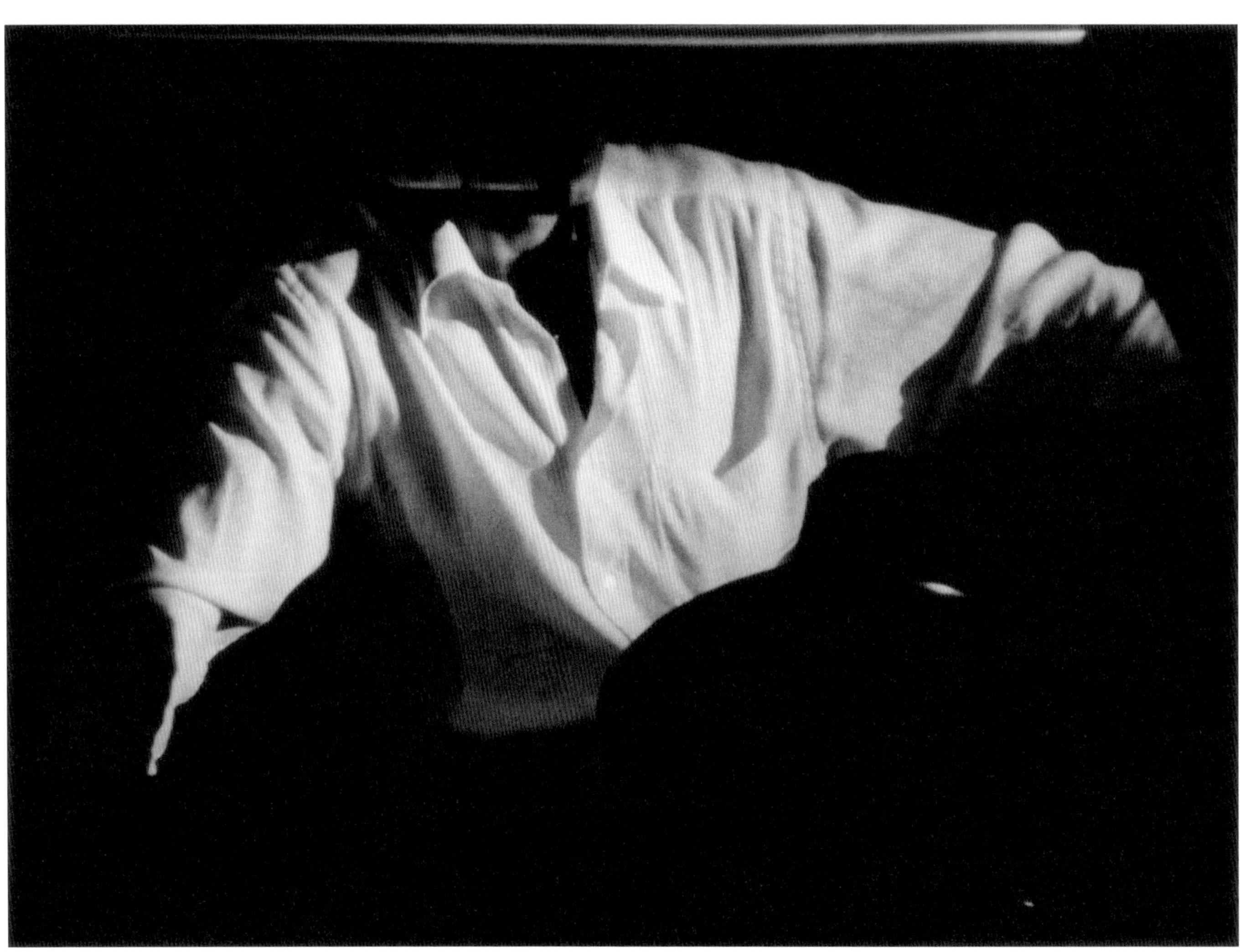

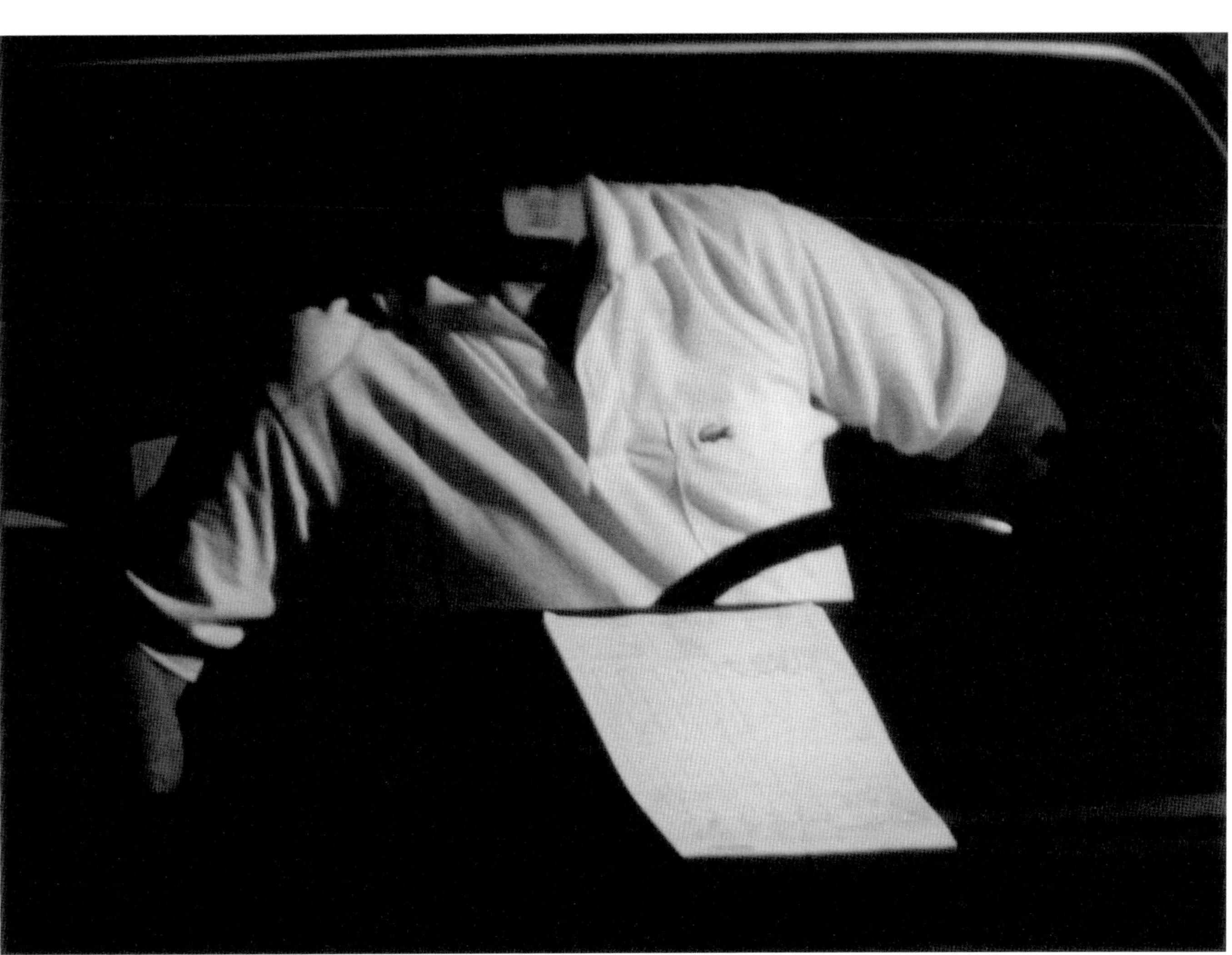

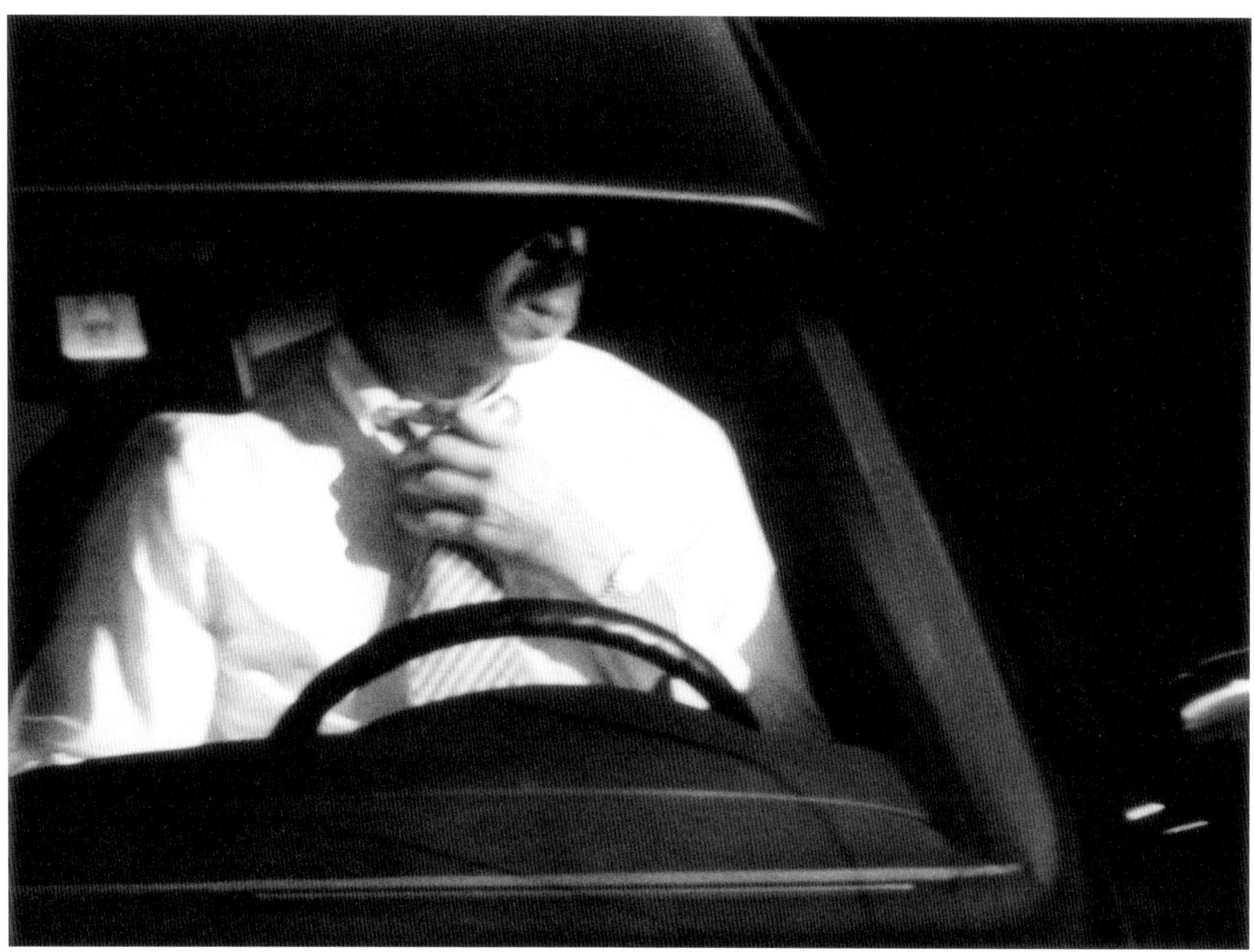

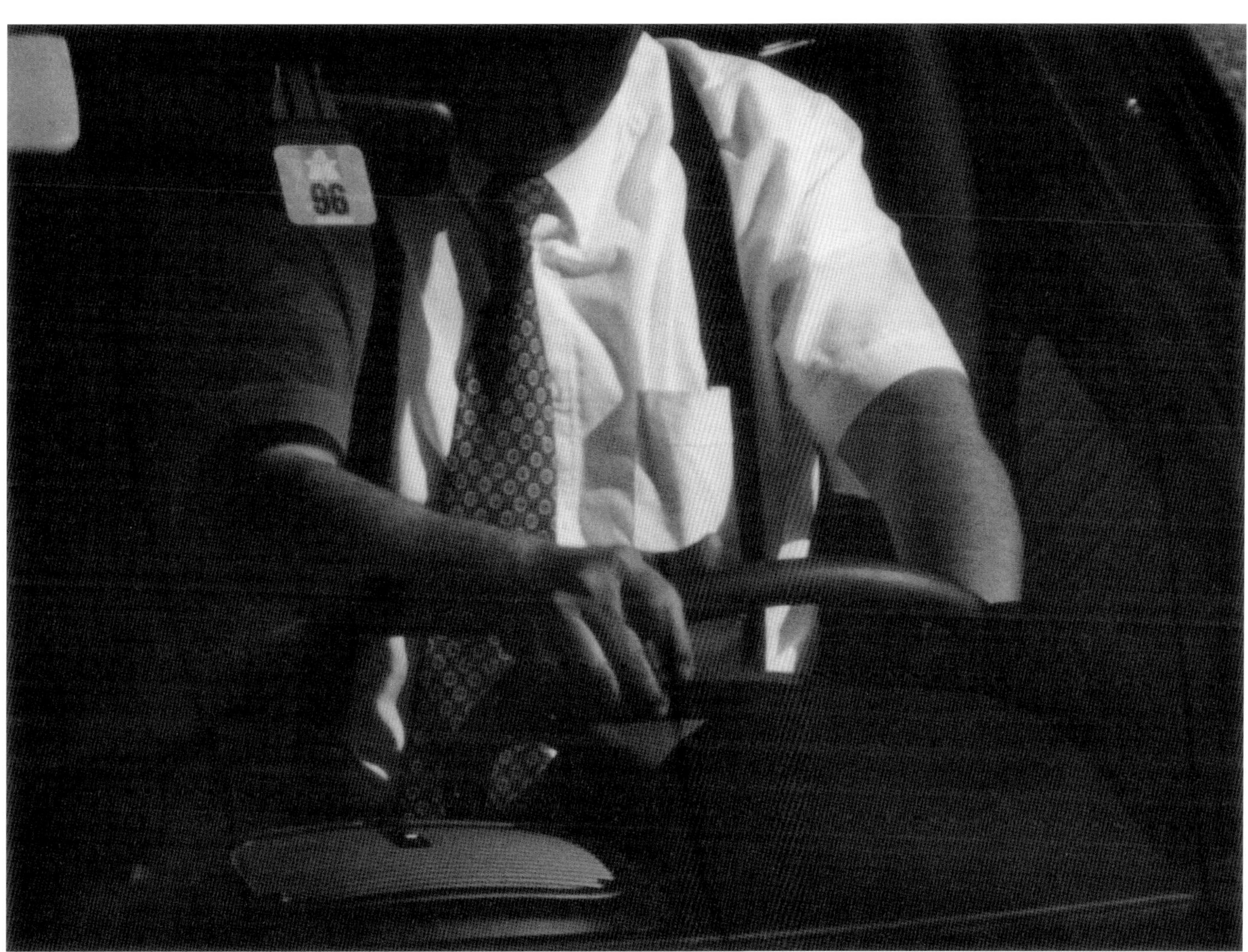

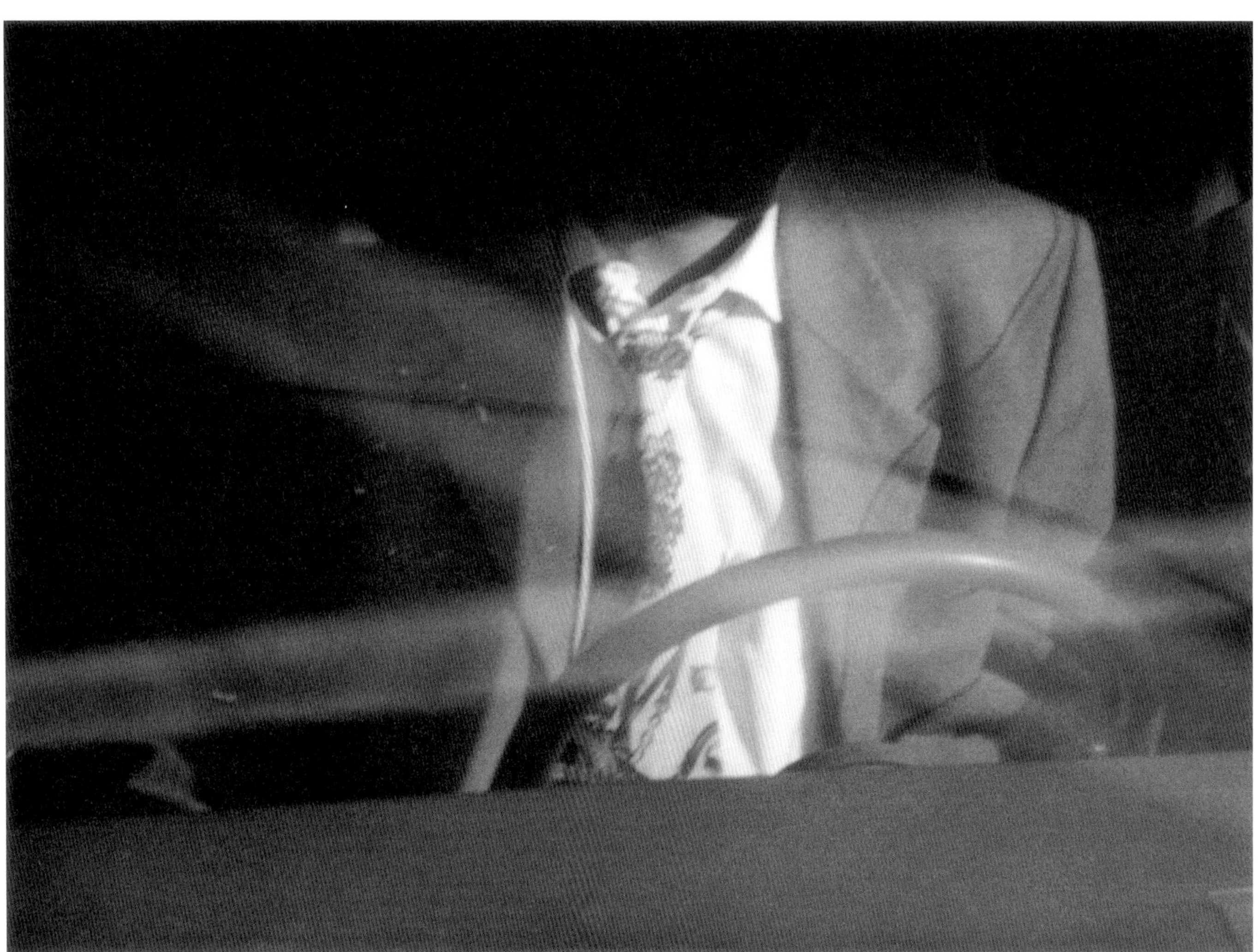

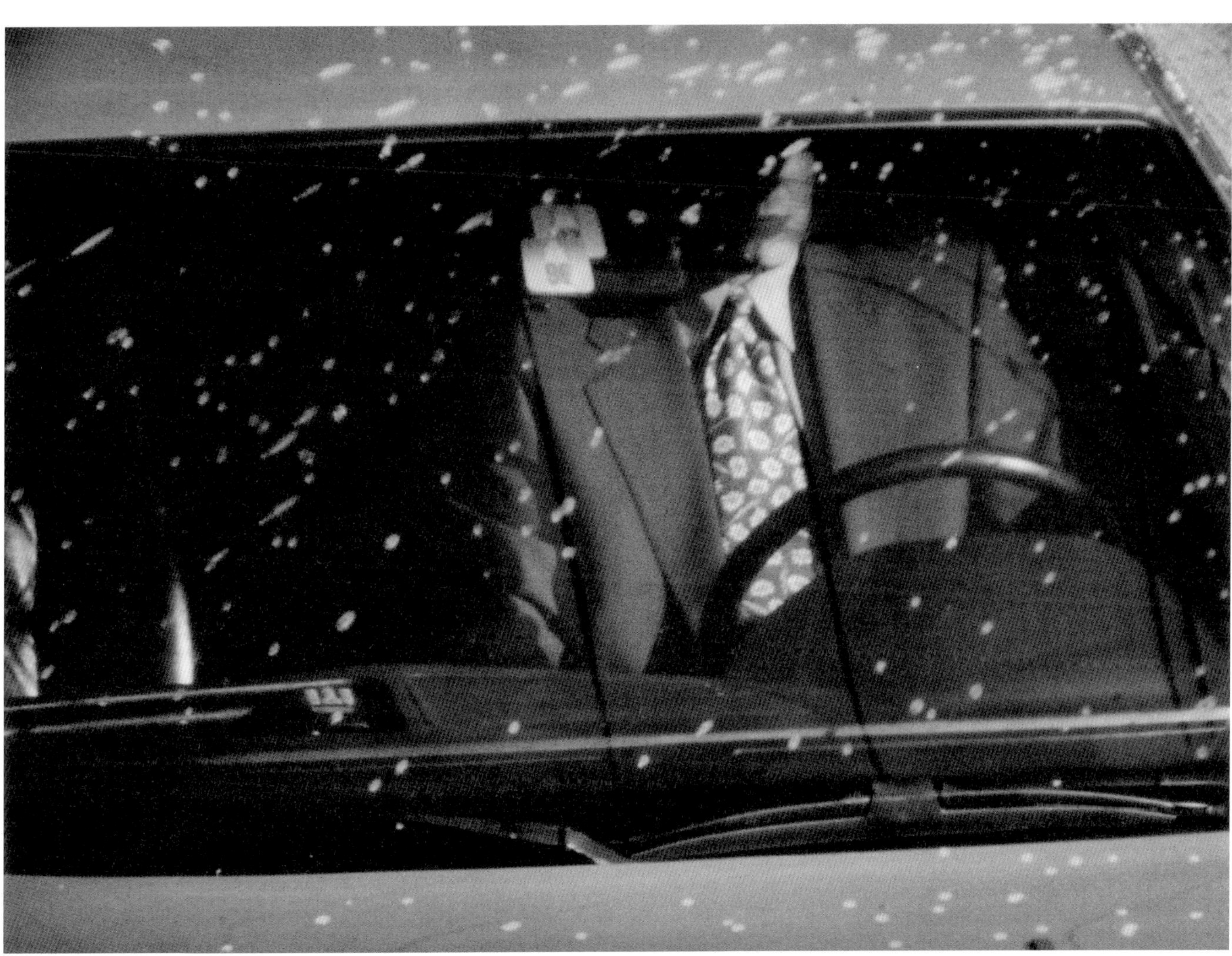

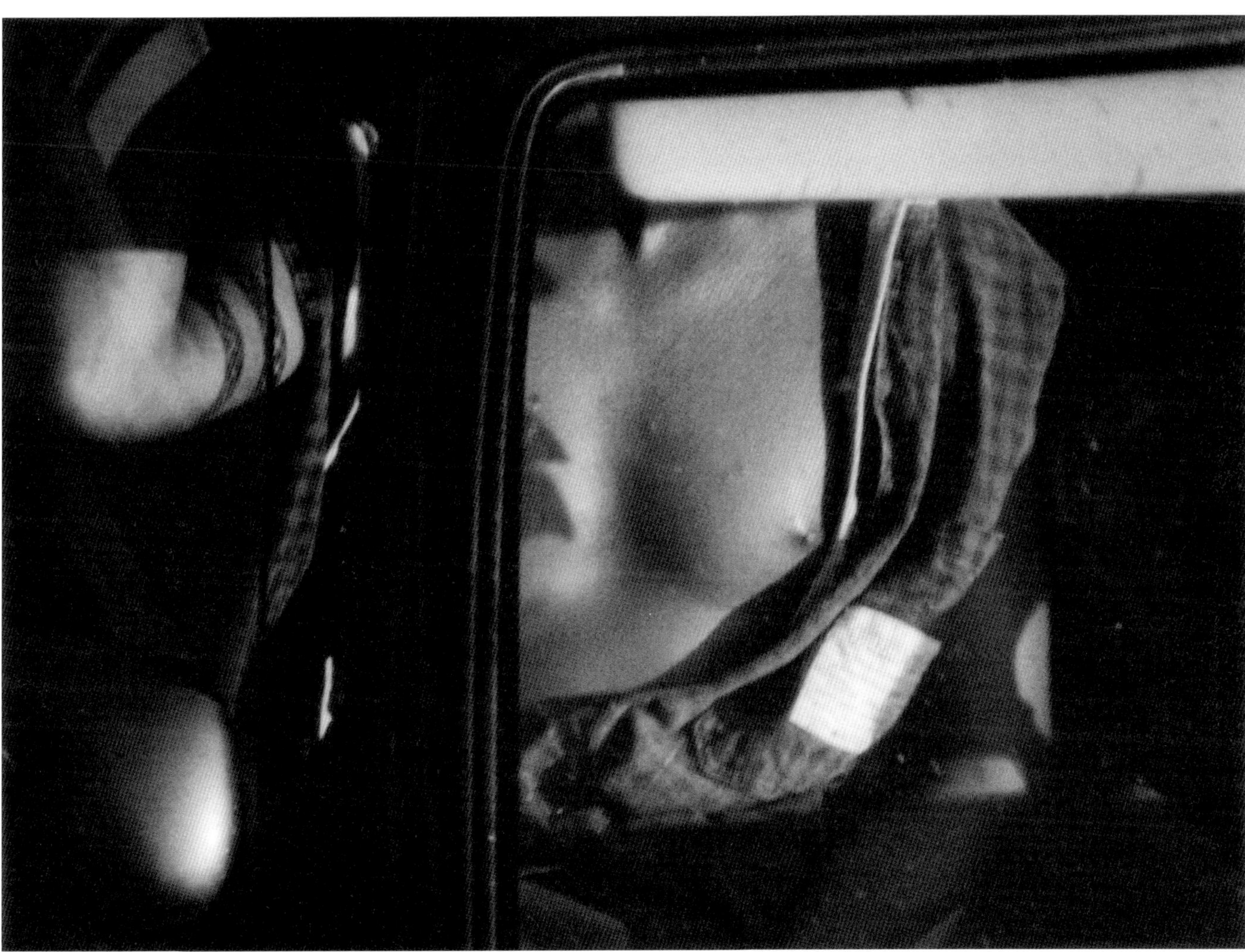

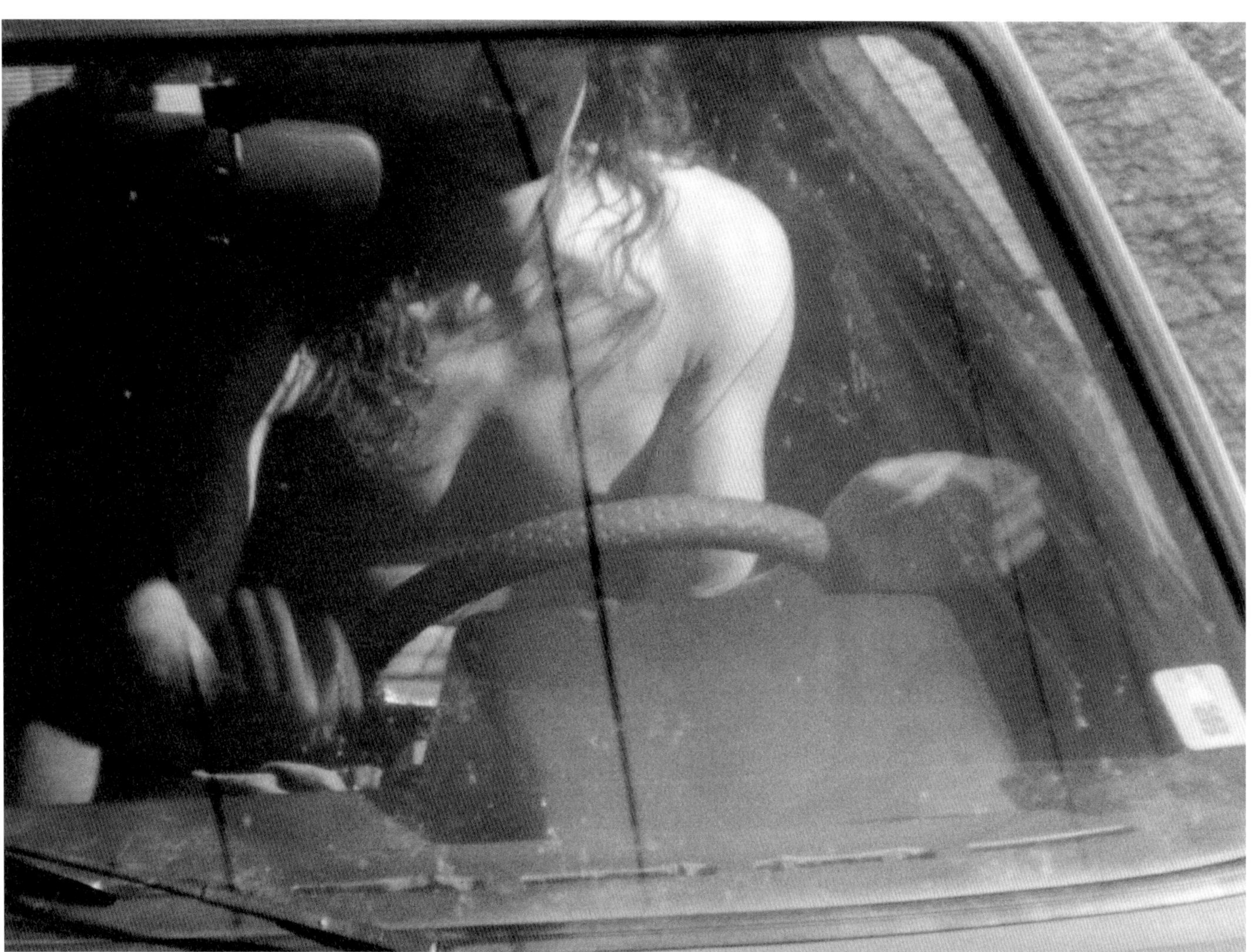

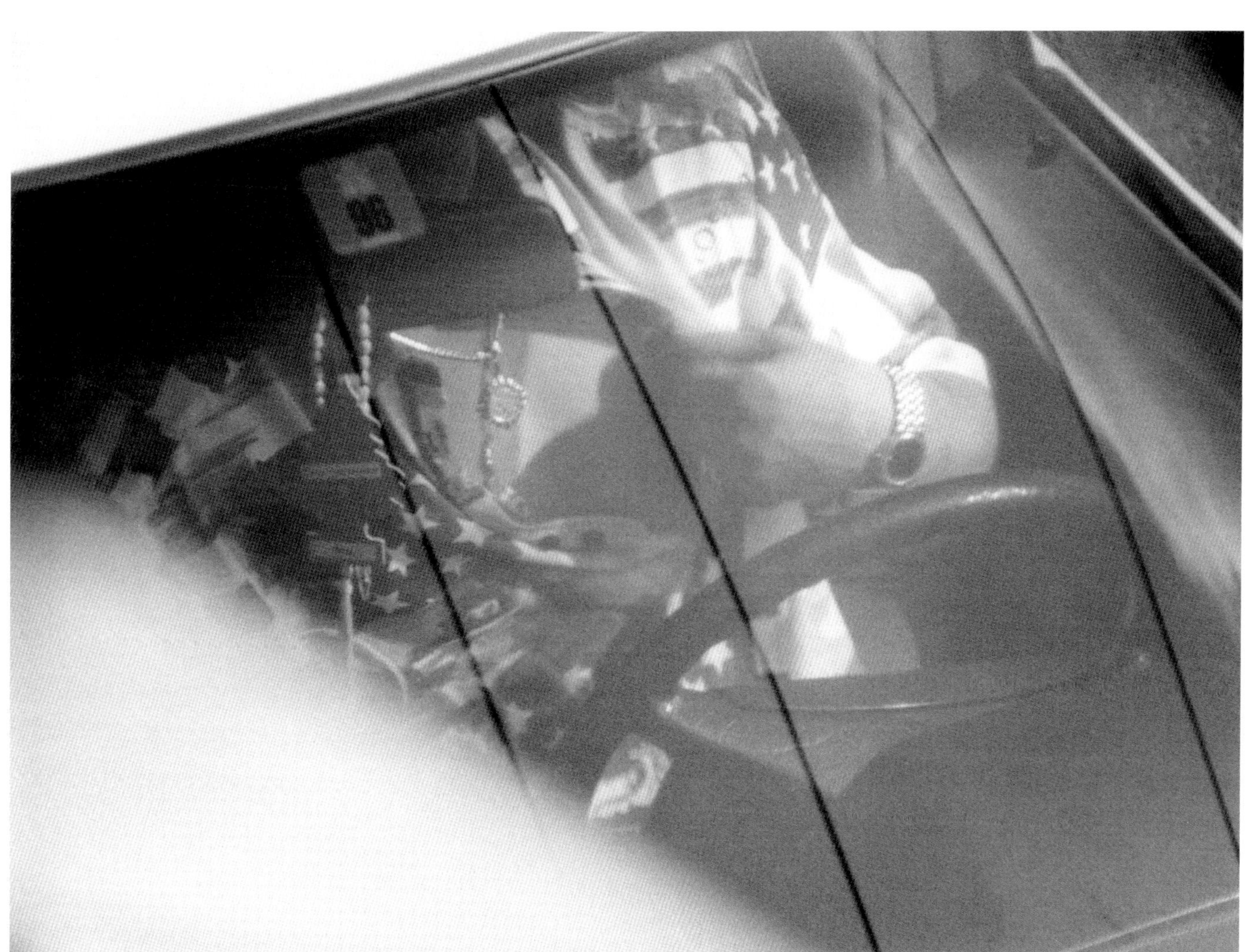

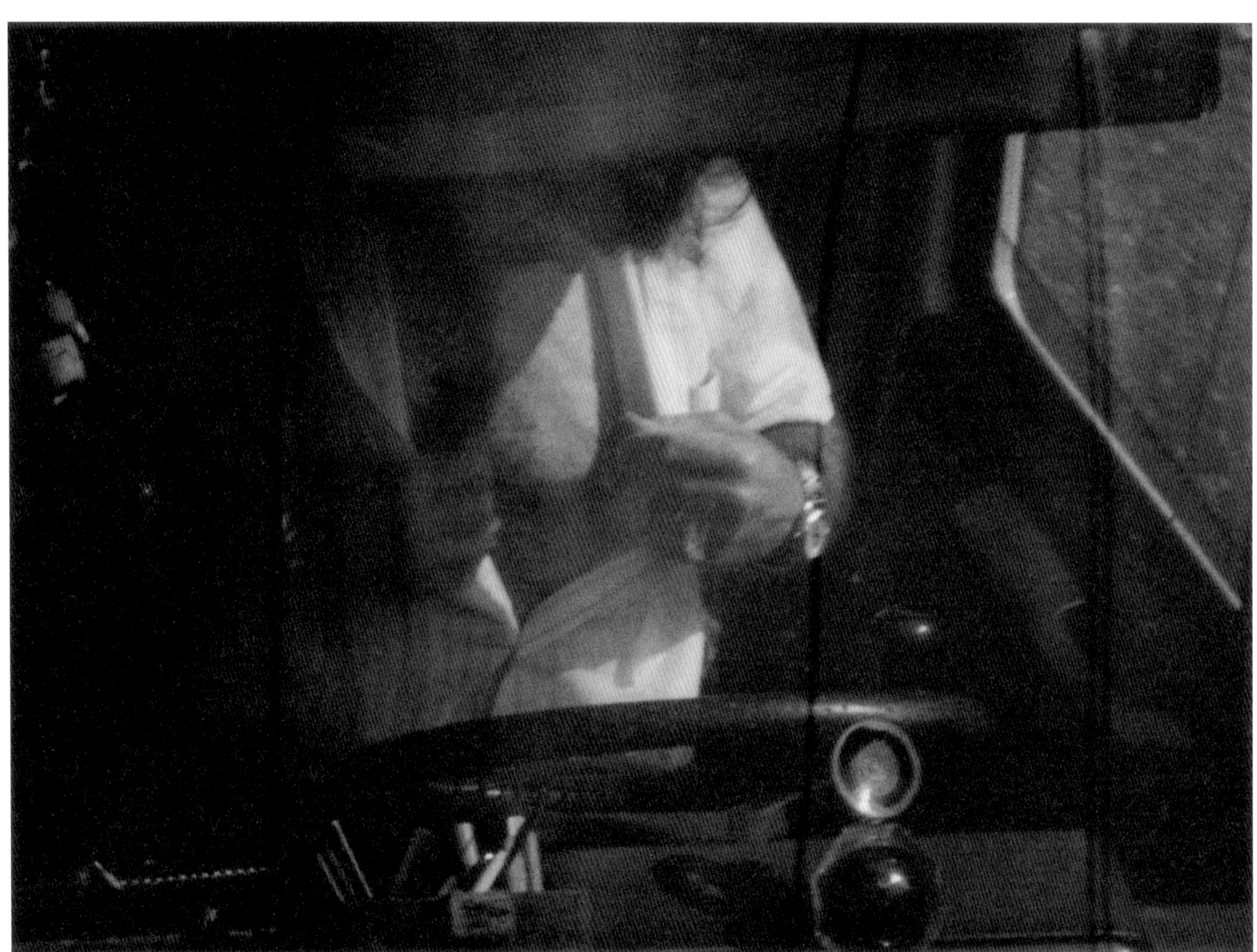

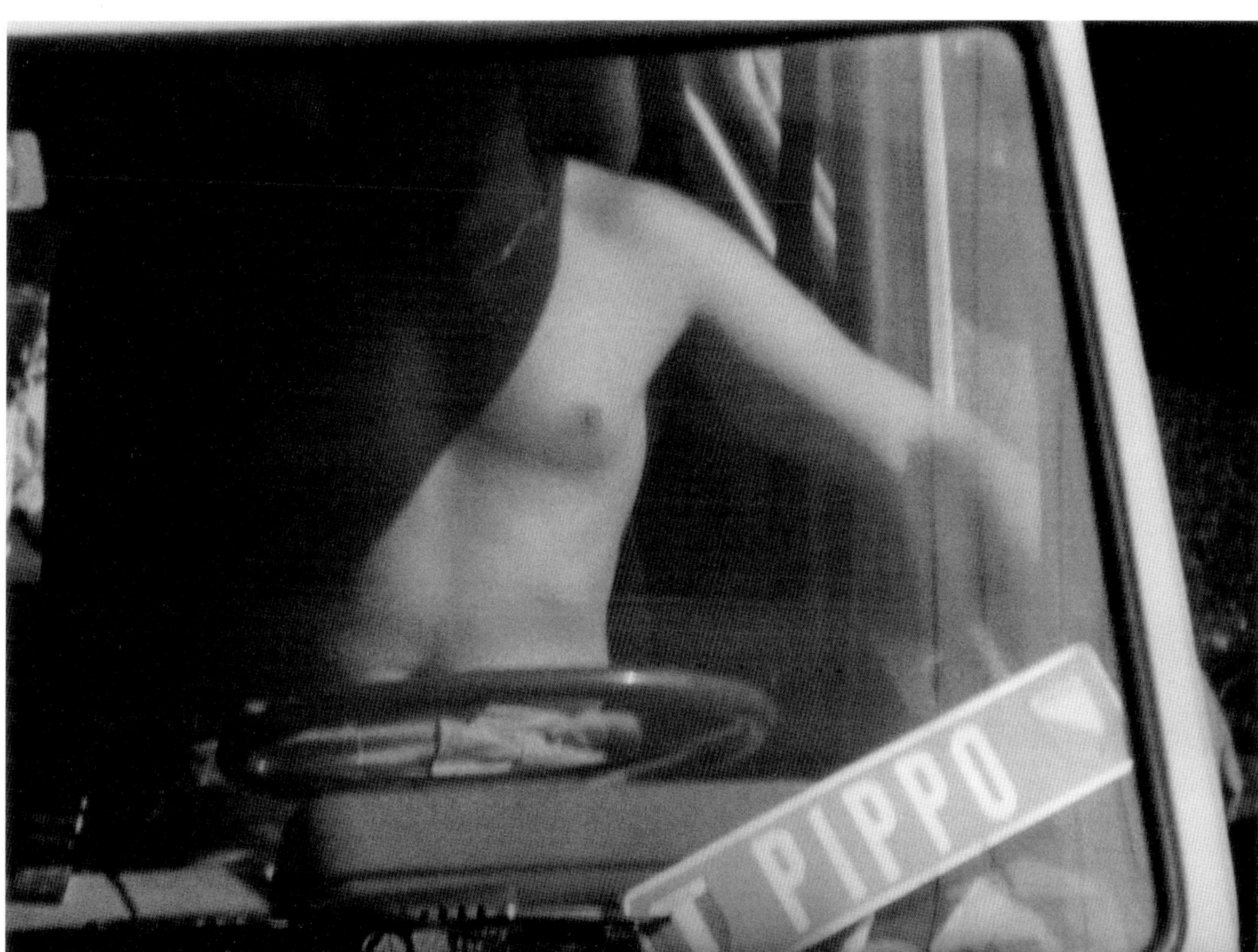
PIPPO

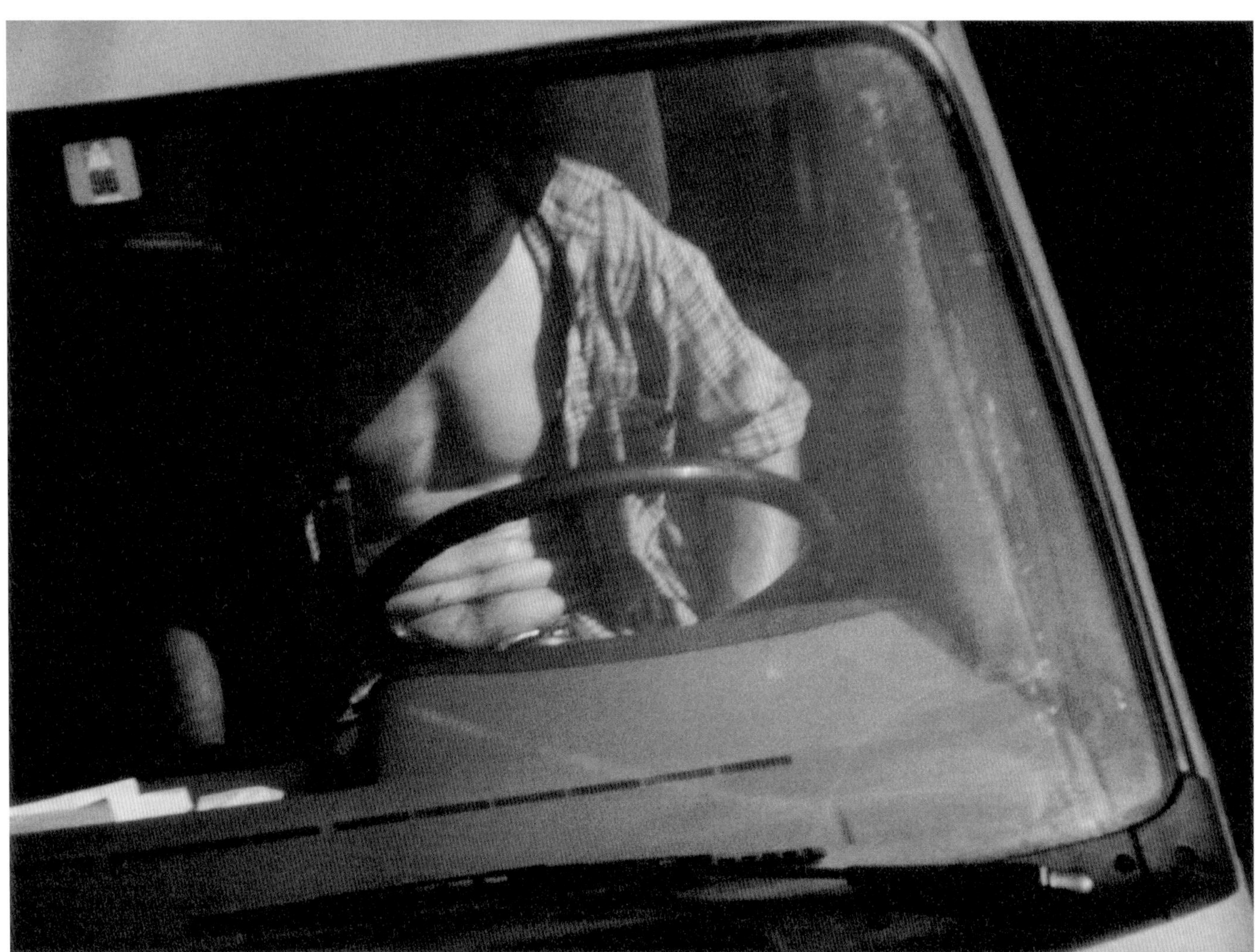

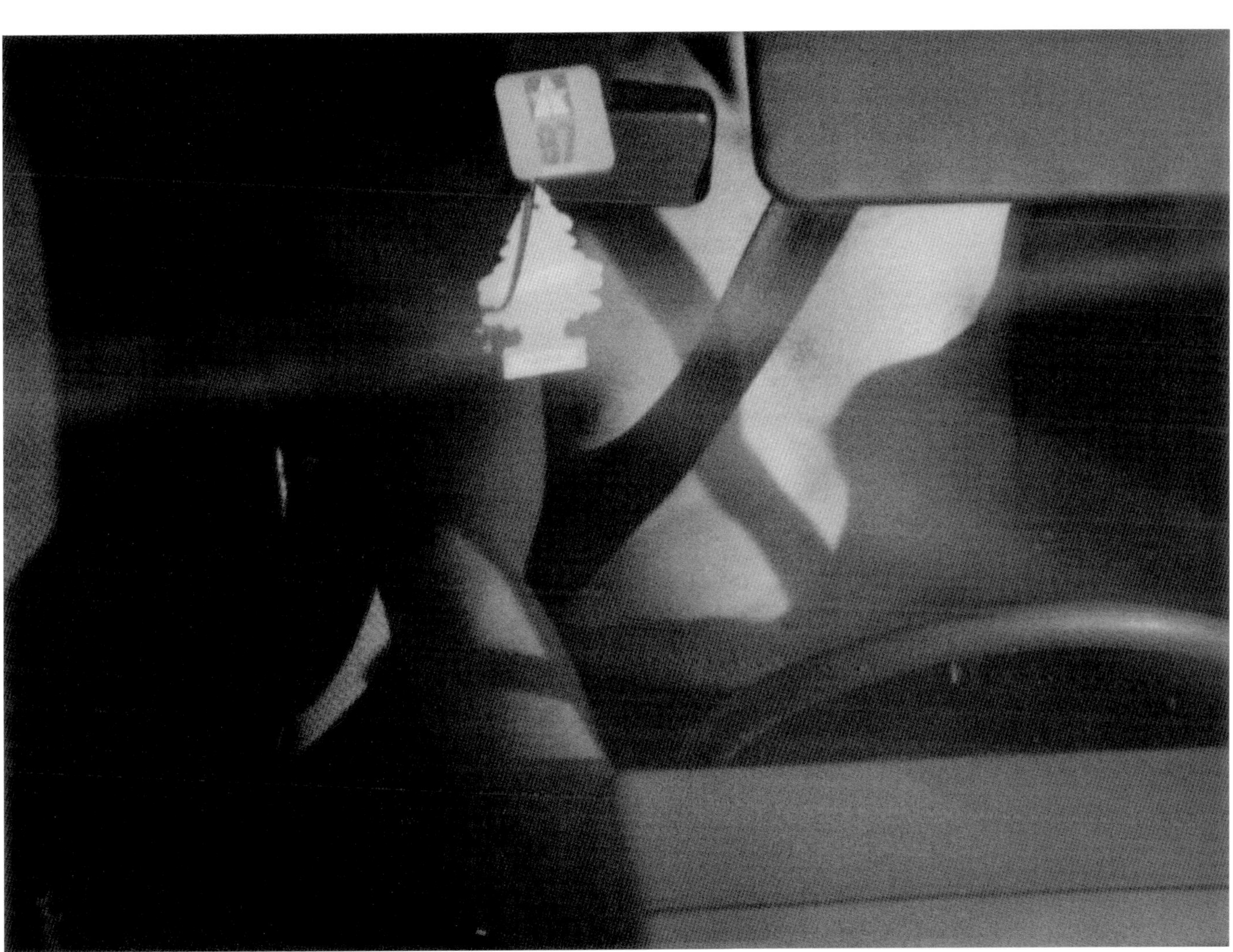

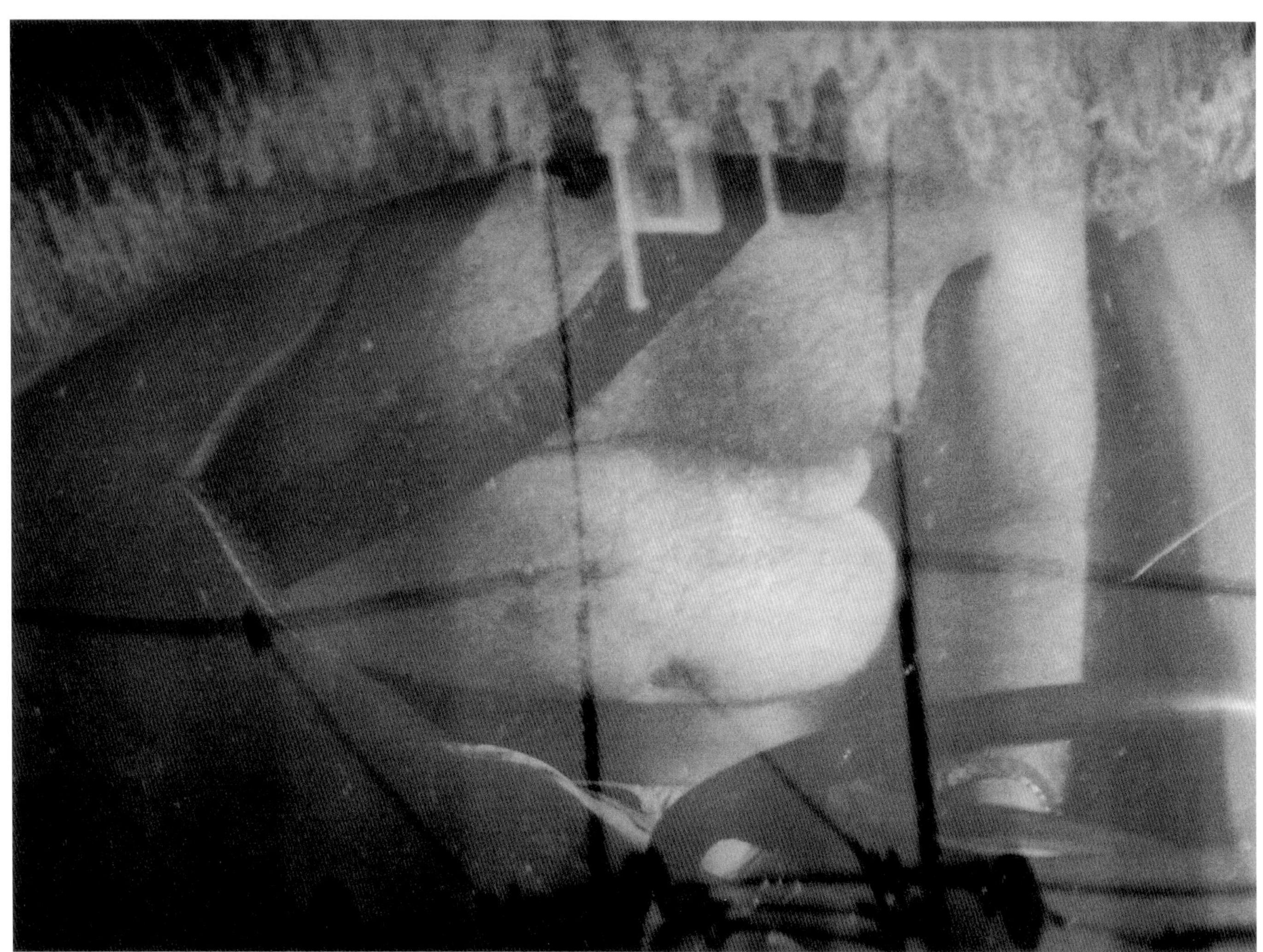

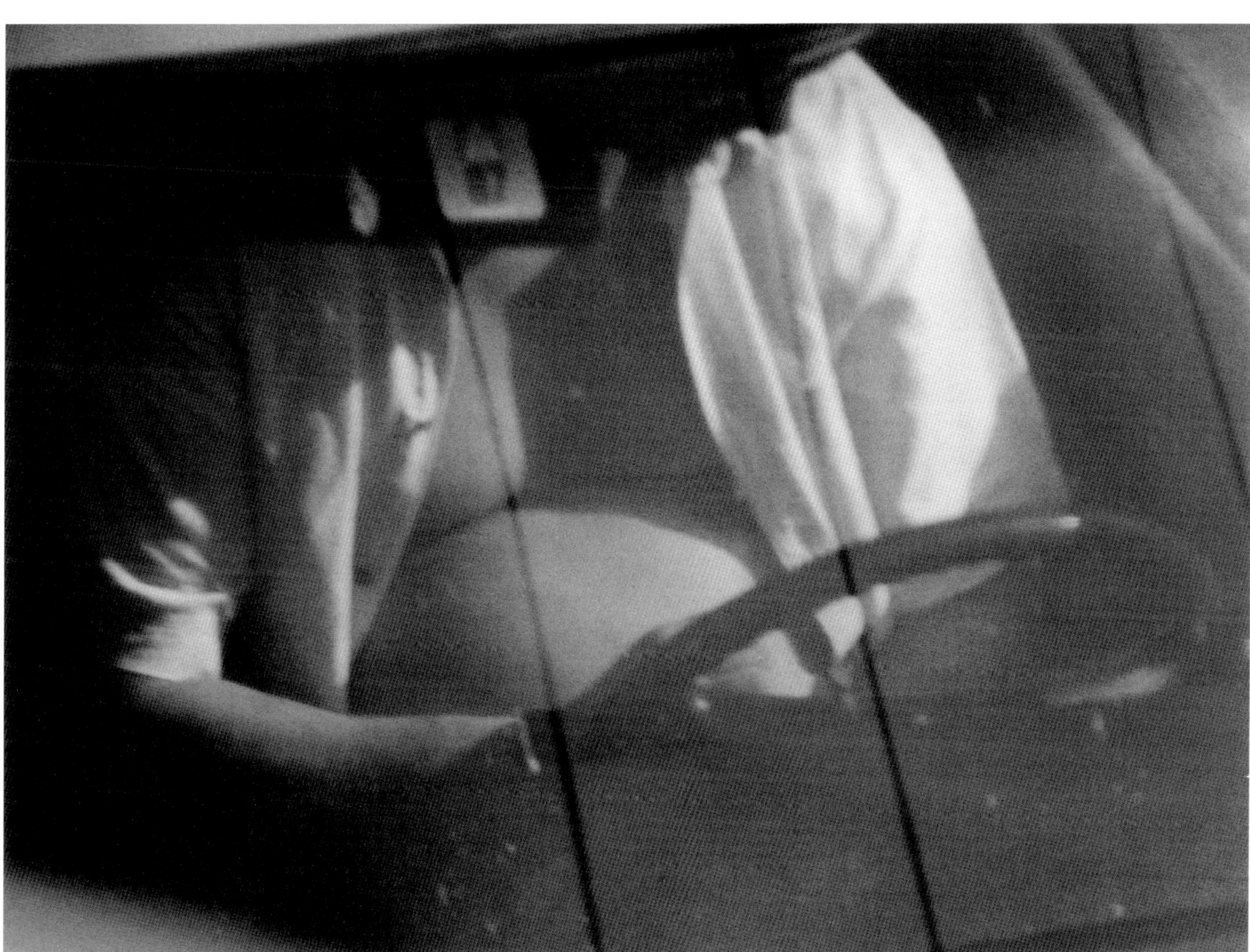

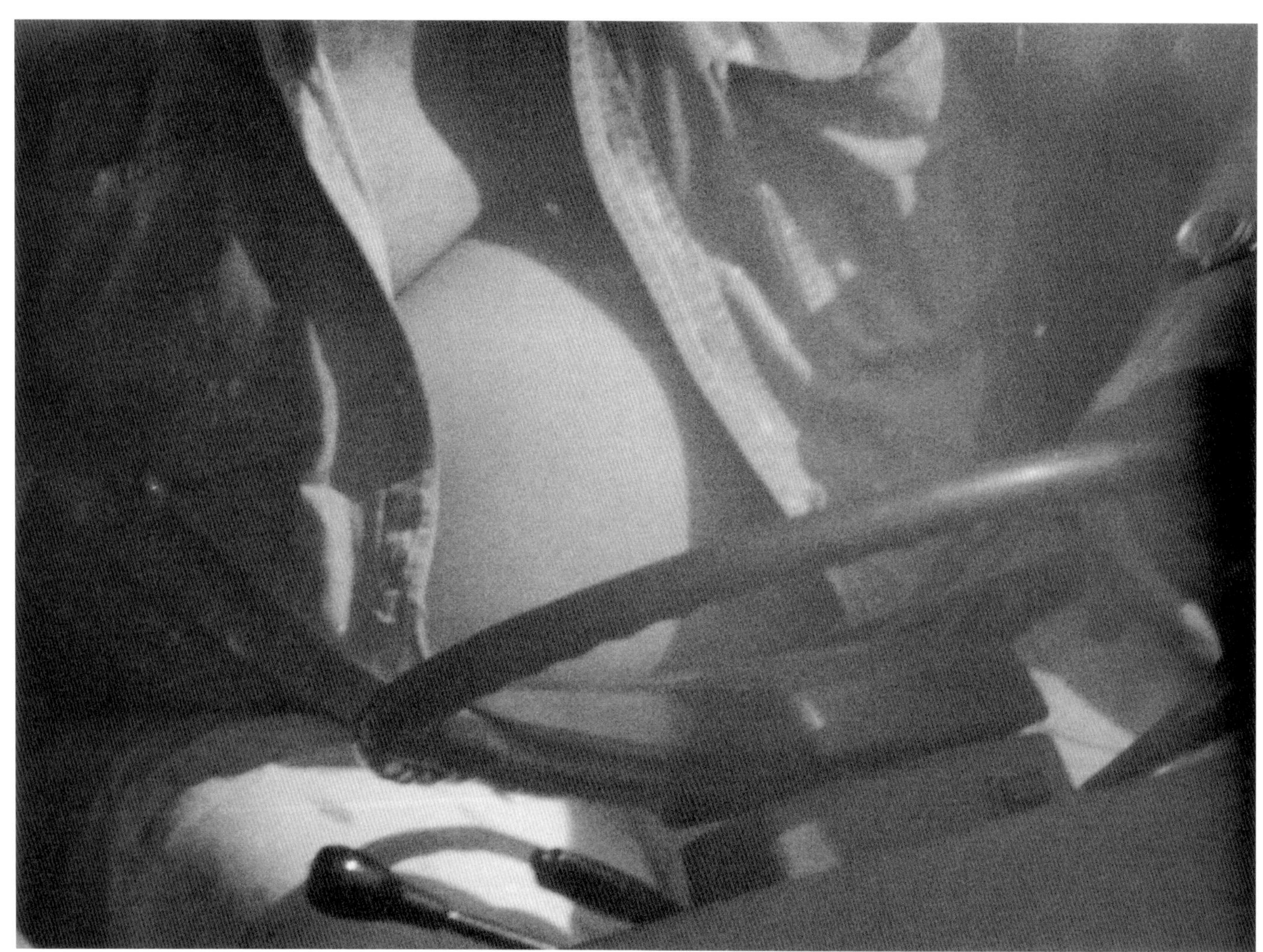

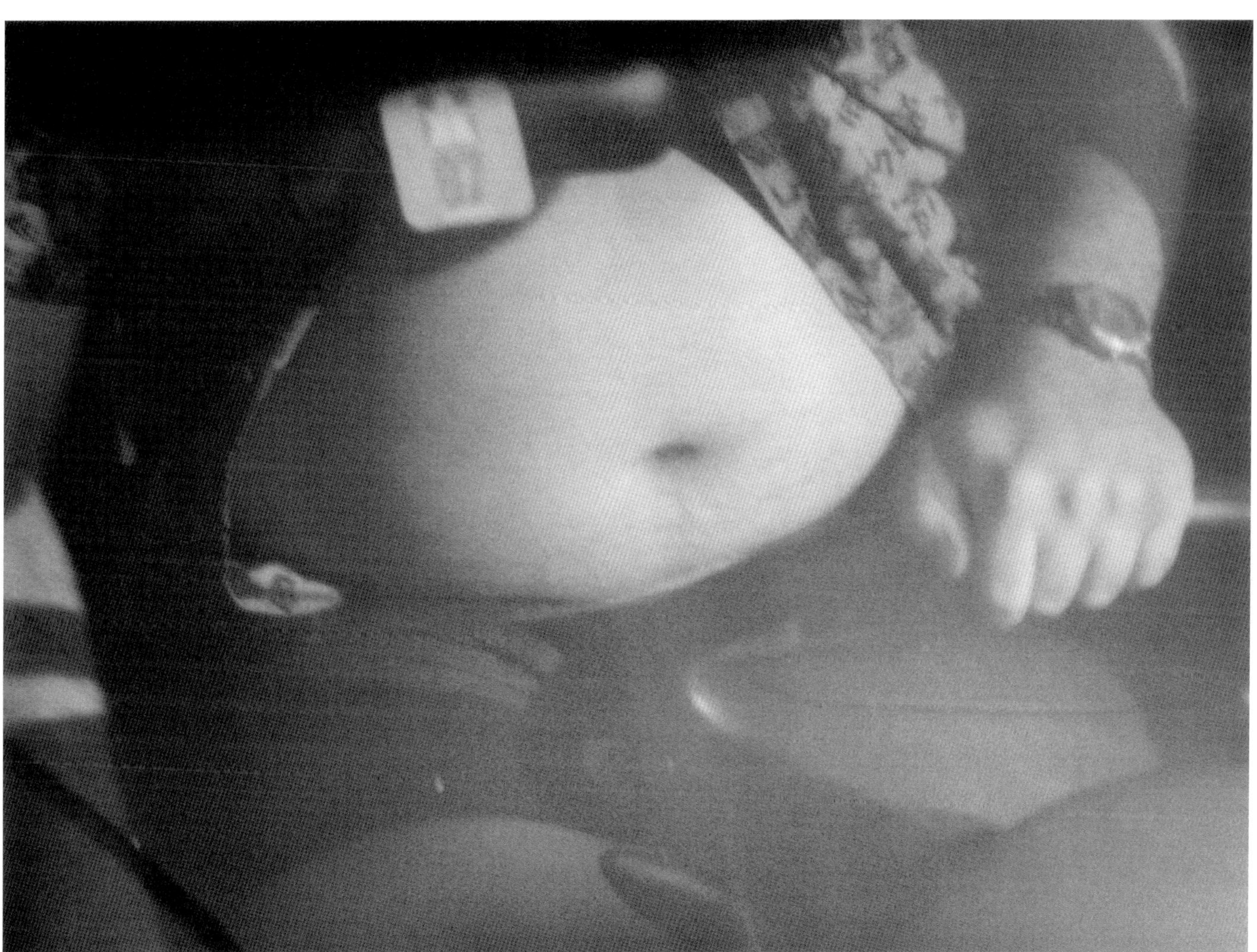

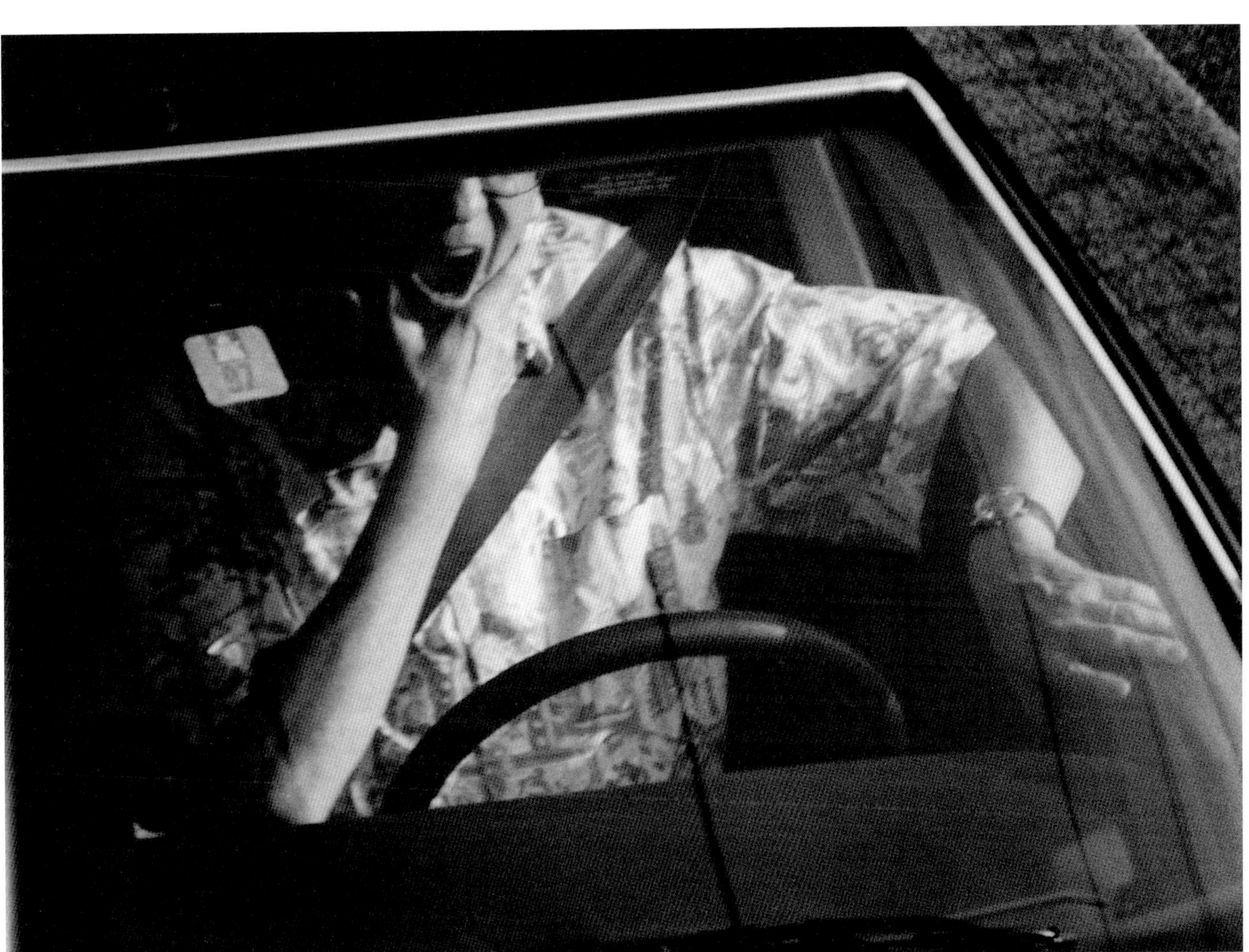

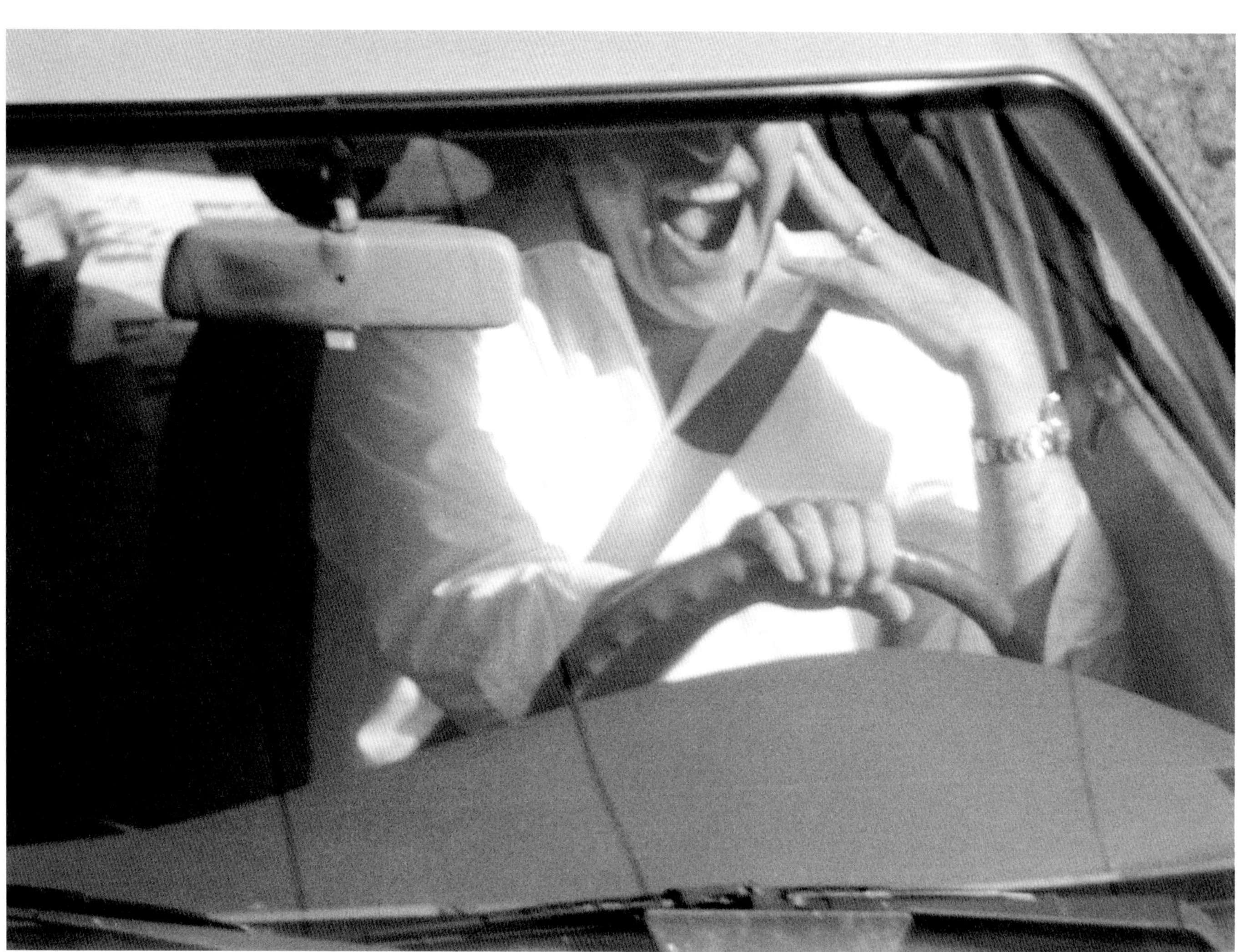

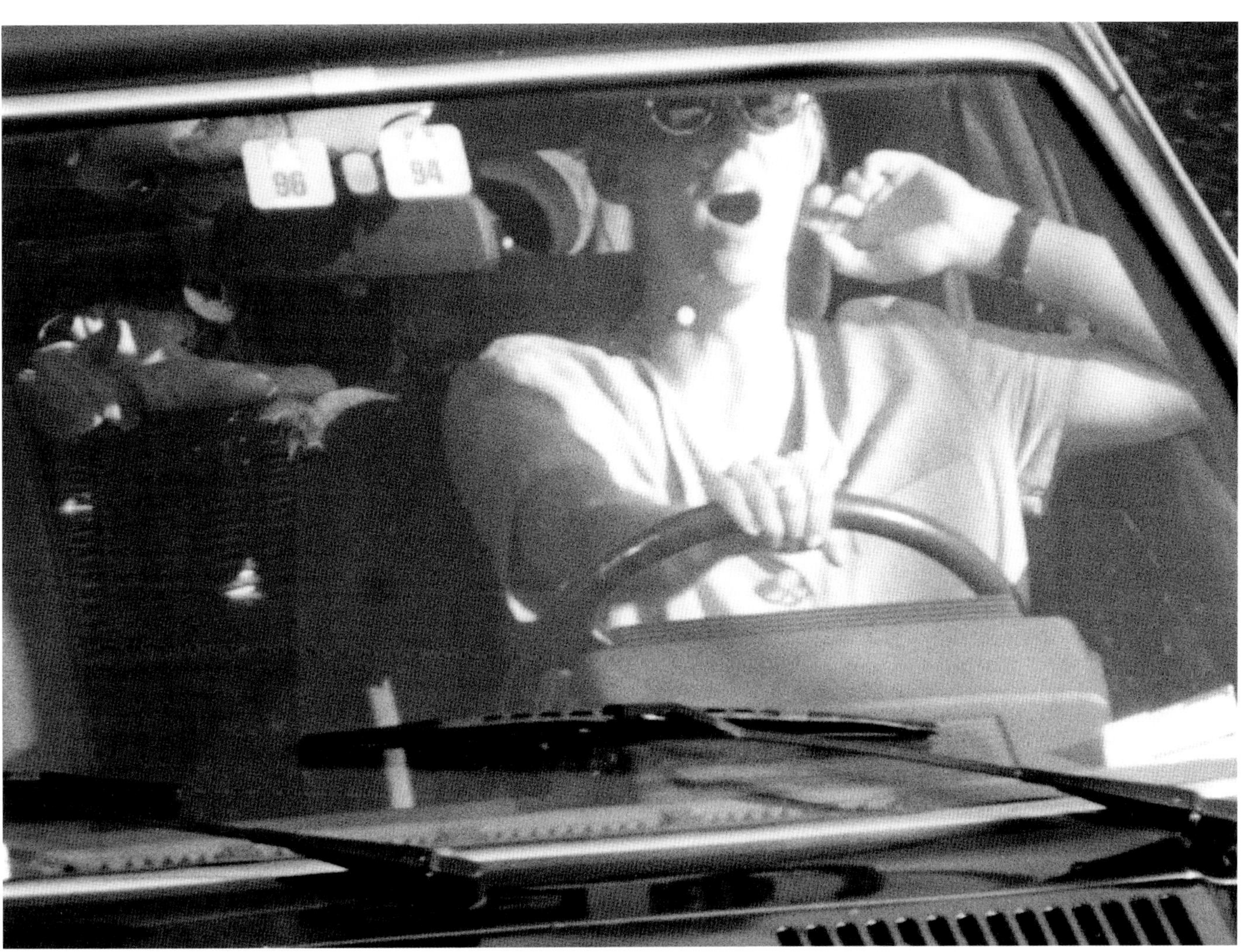

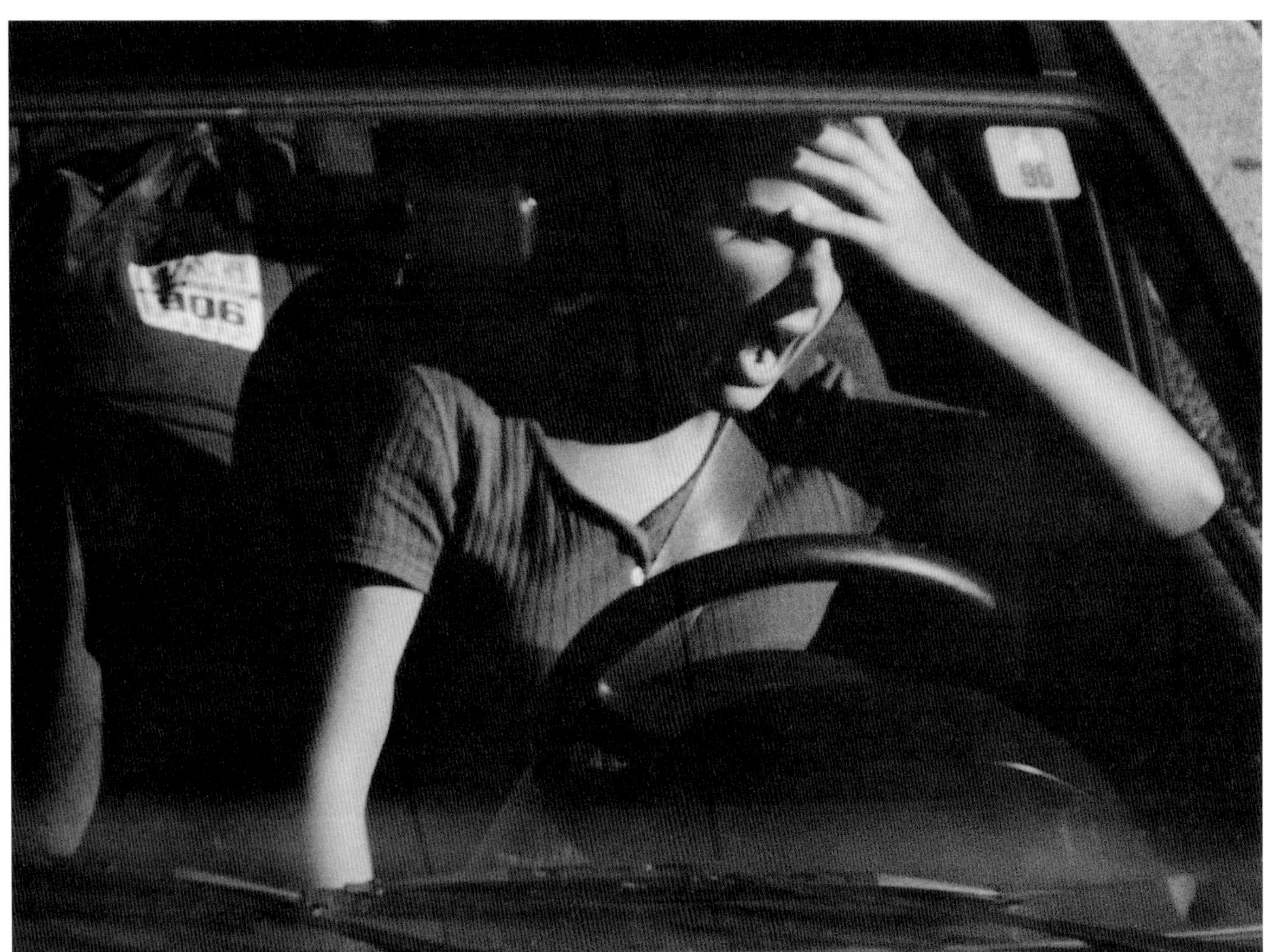

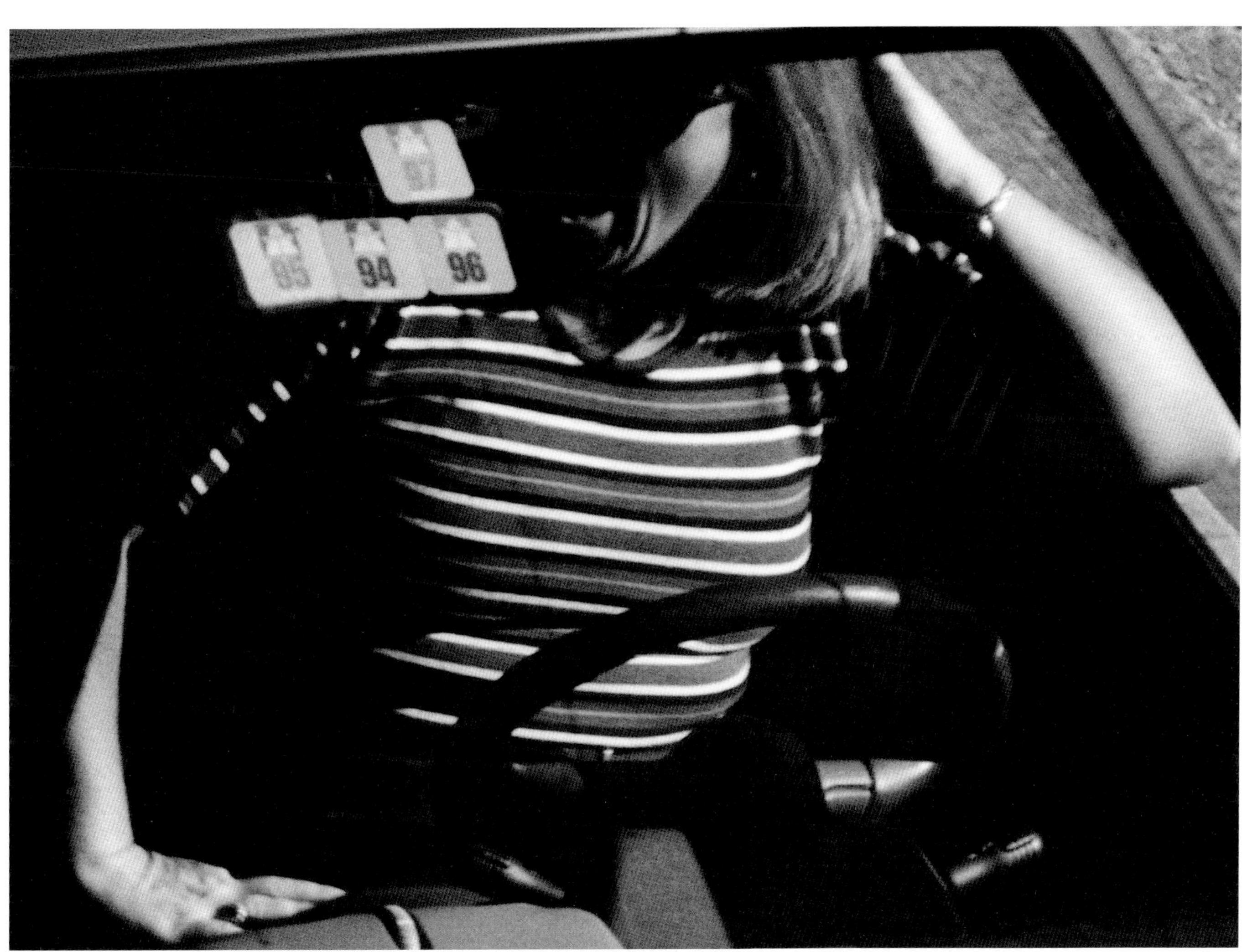

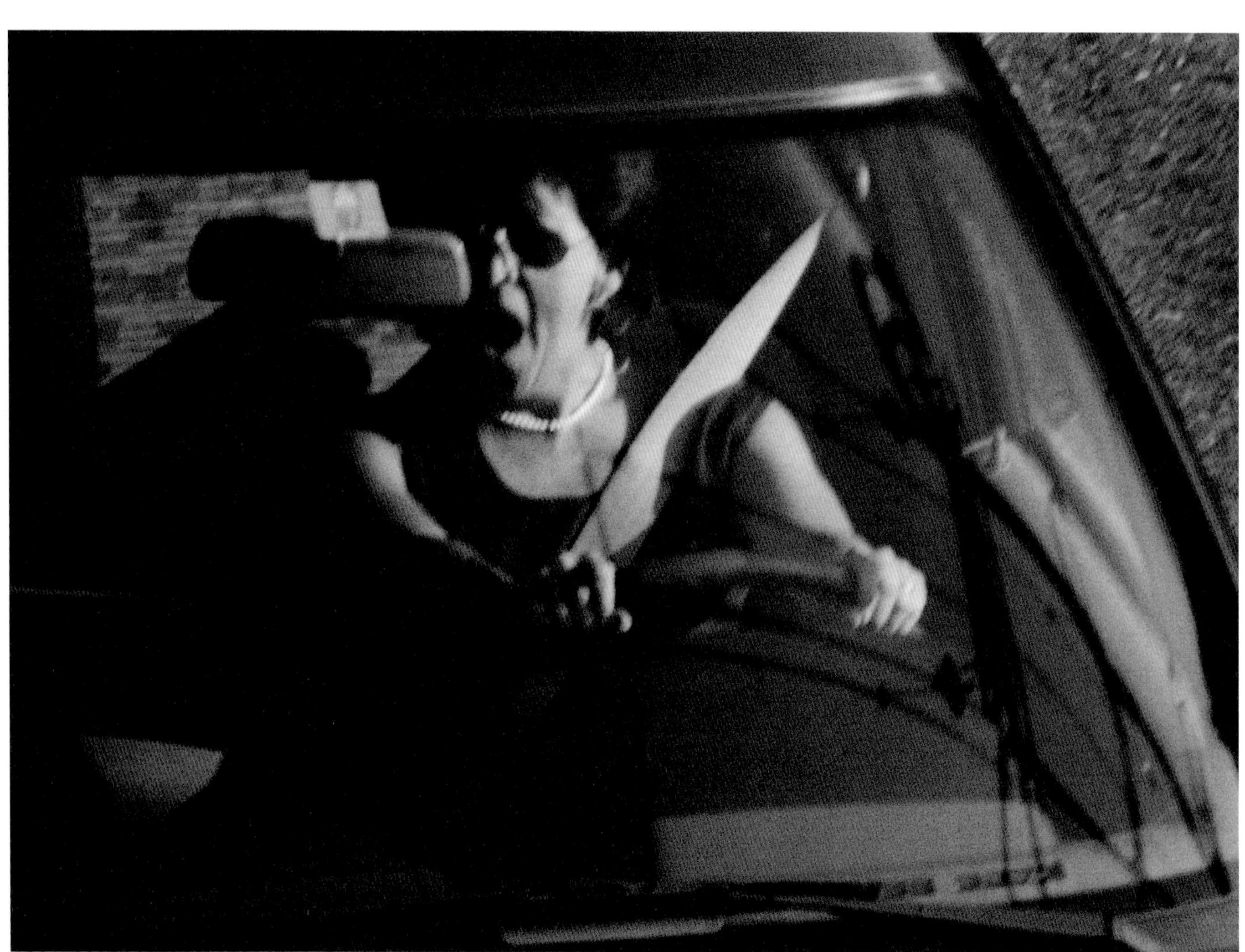

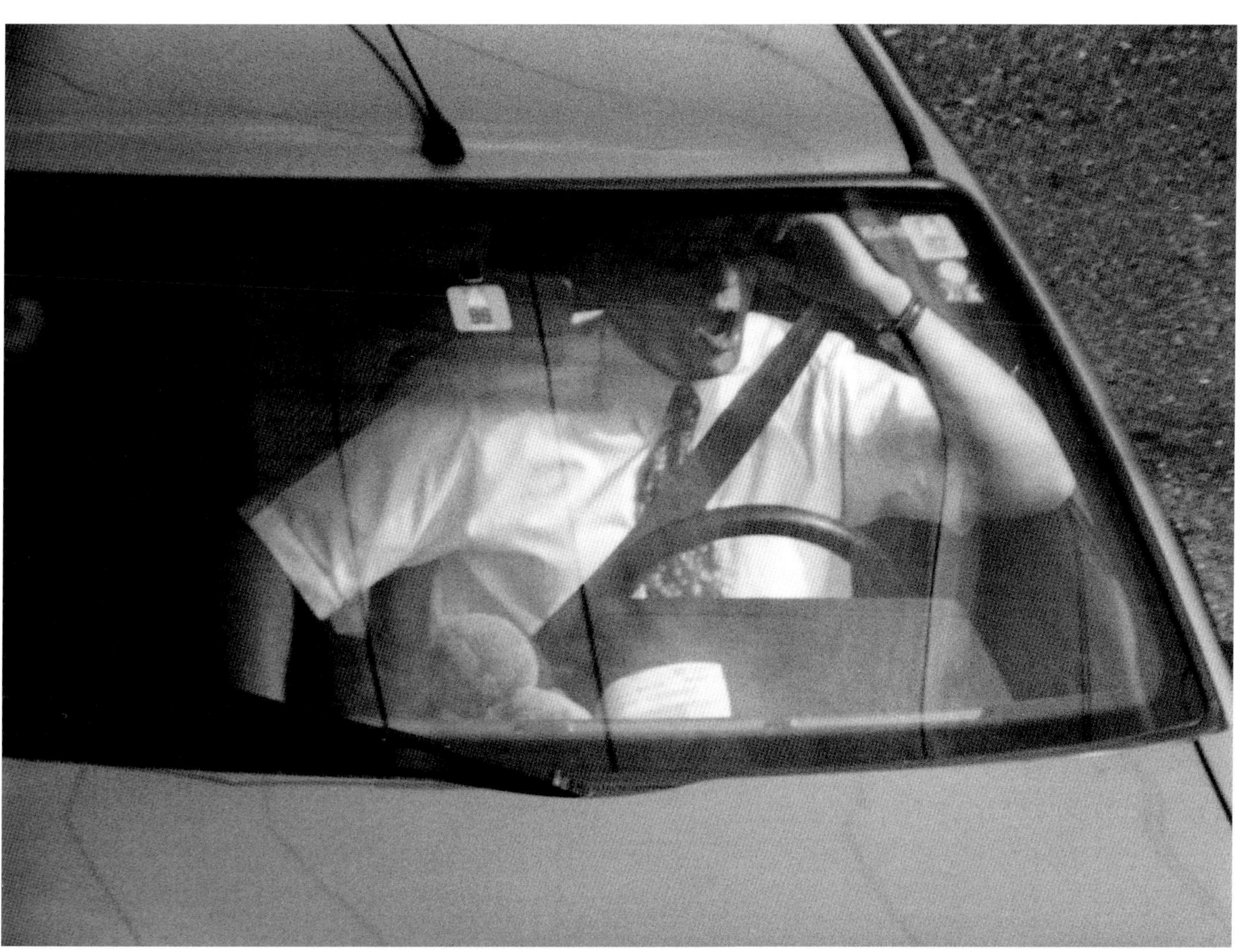

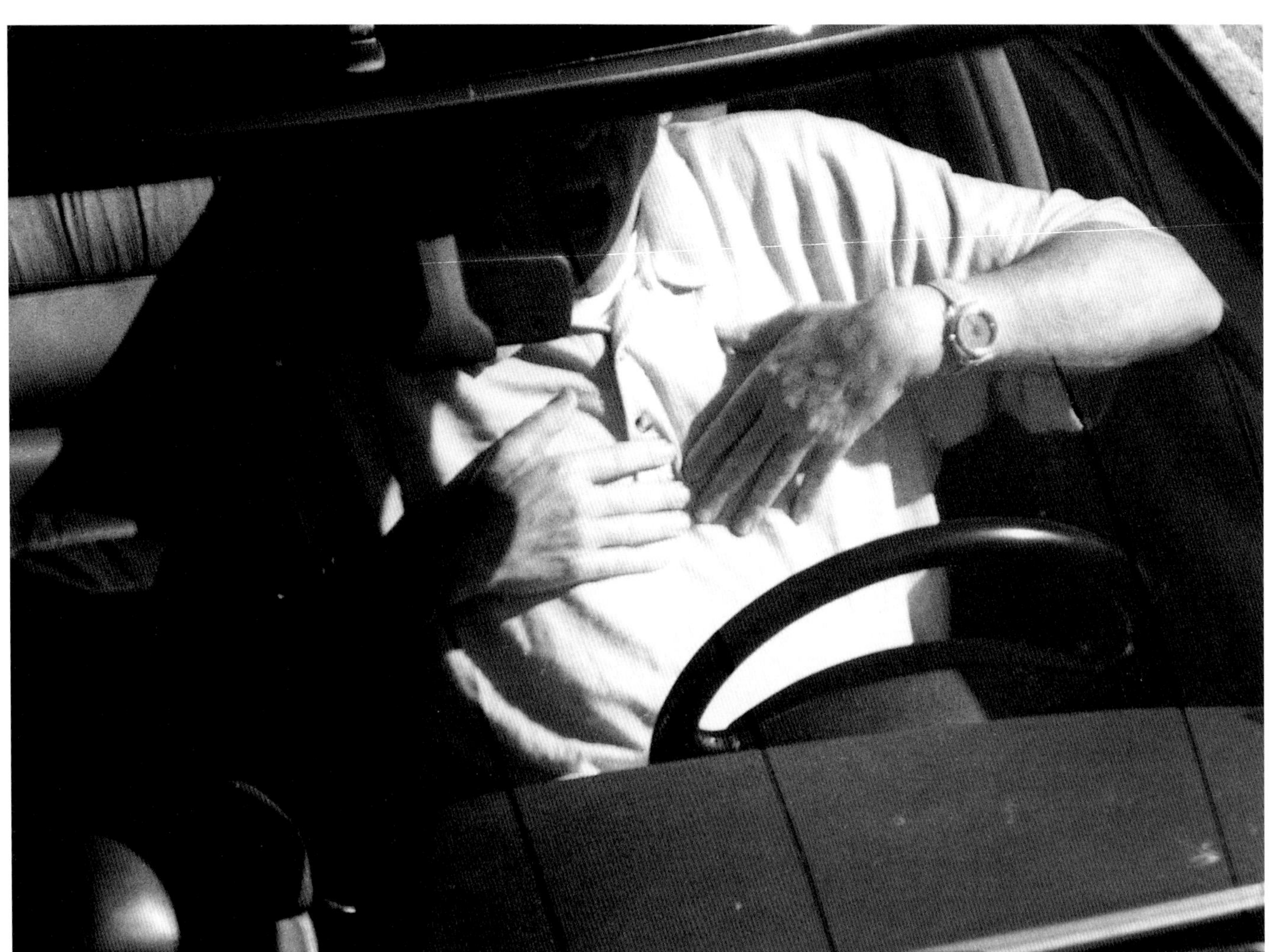

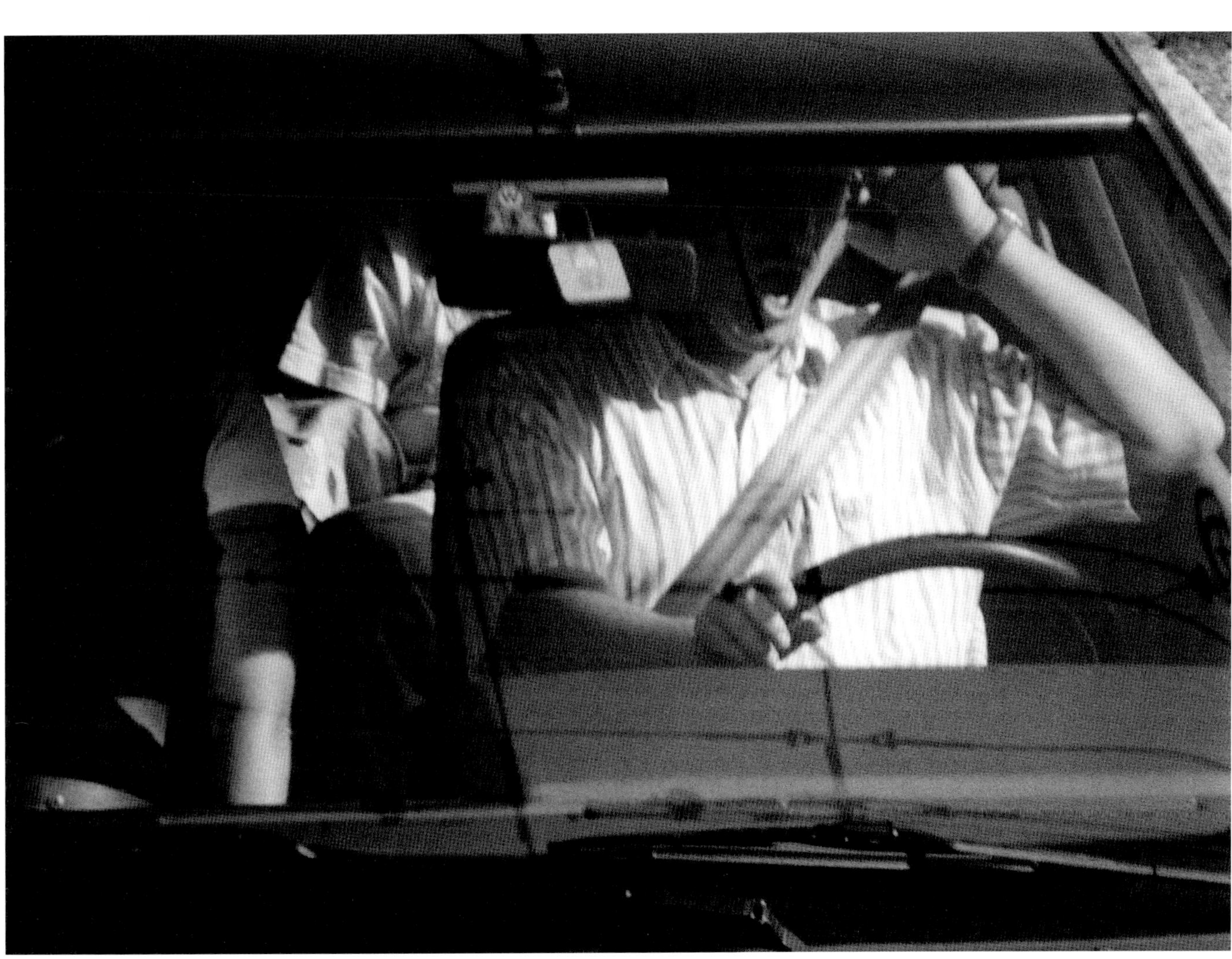

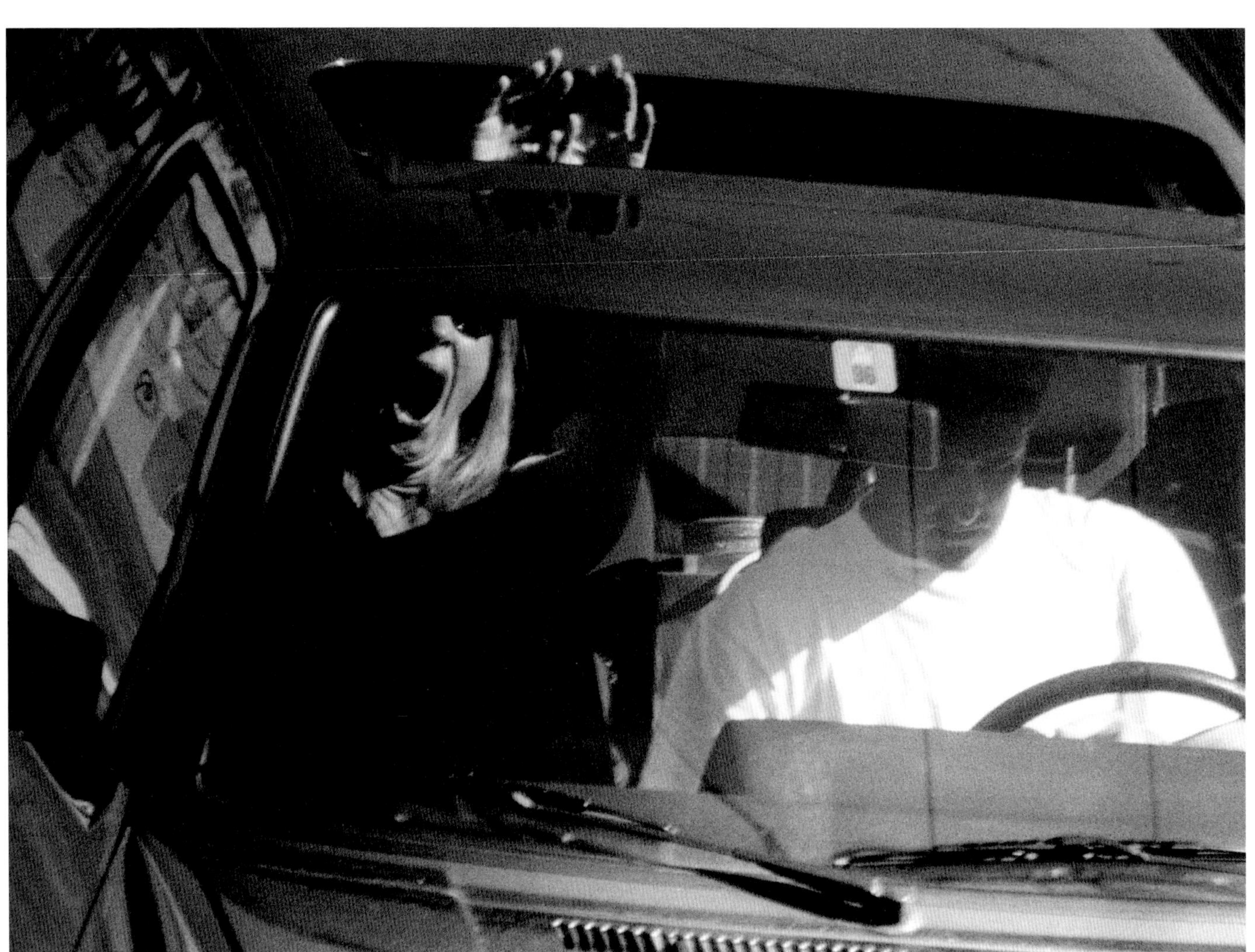

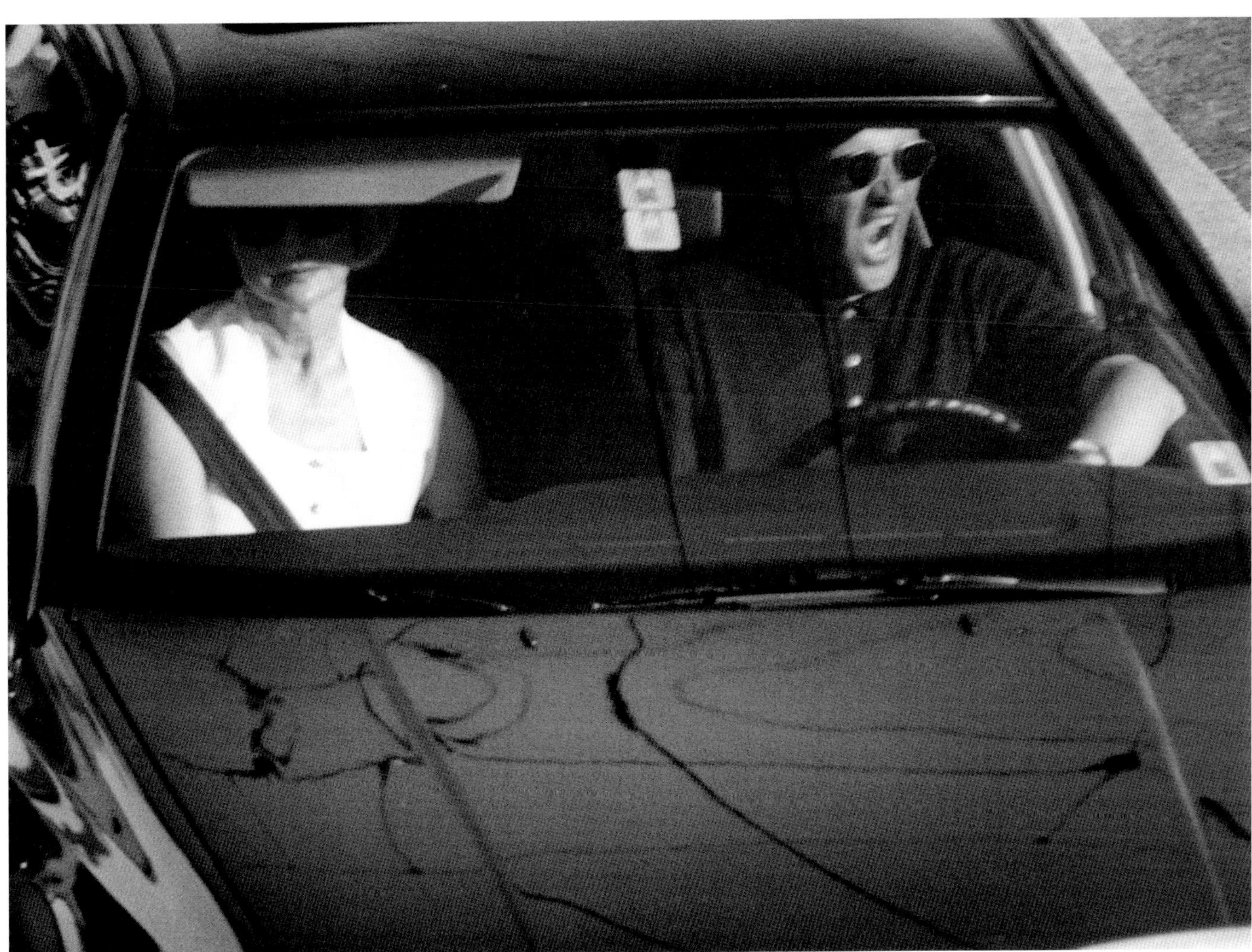

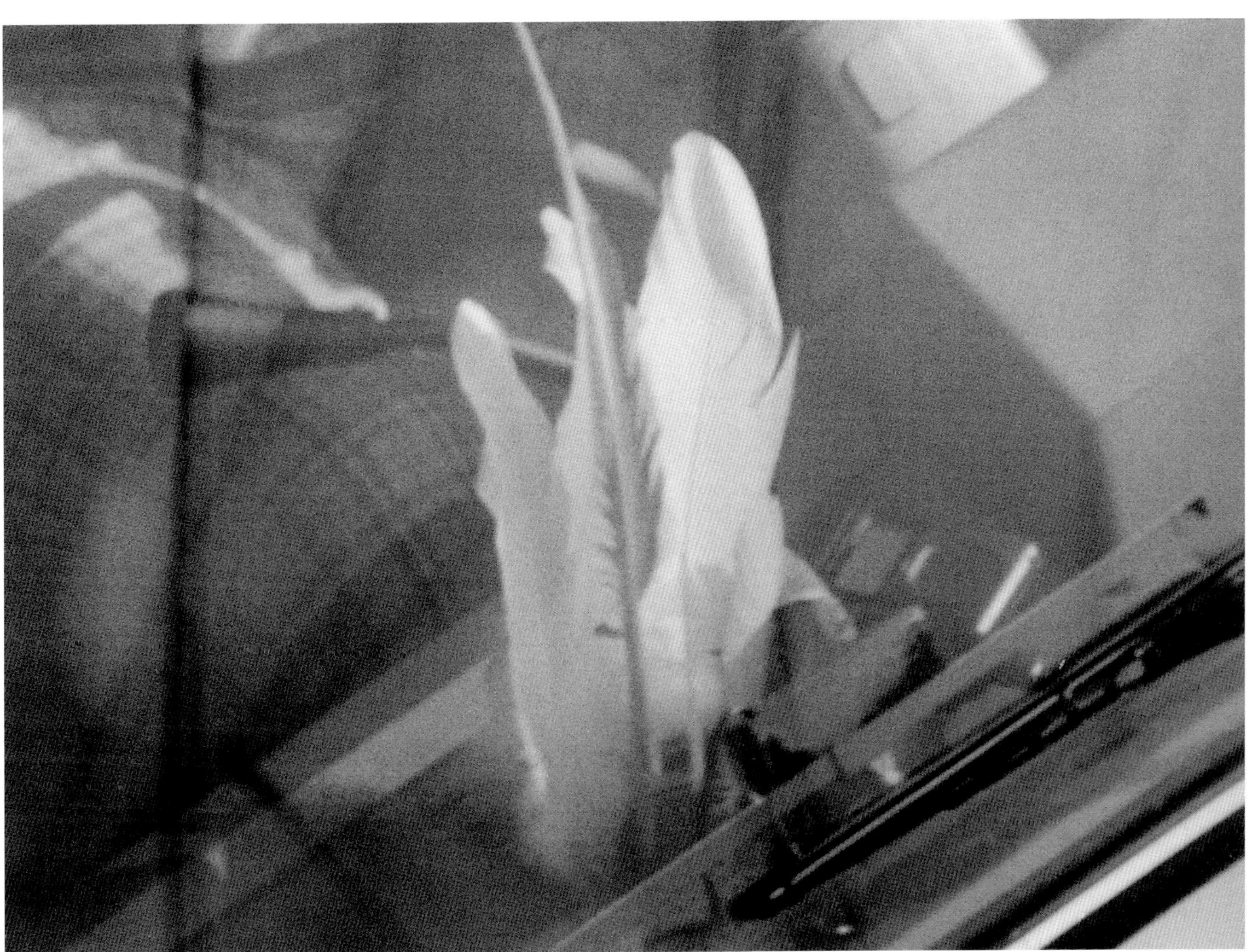

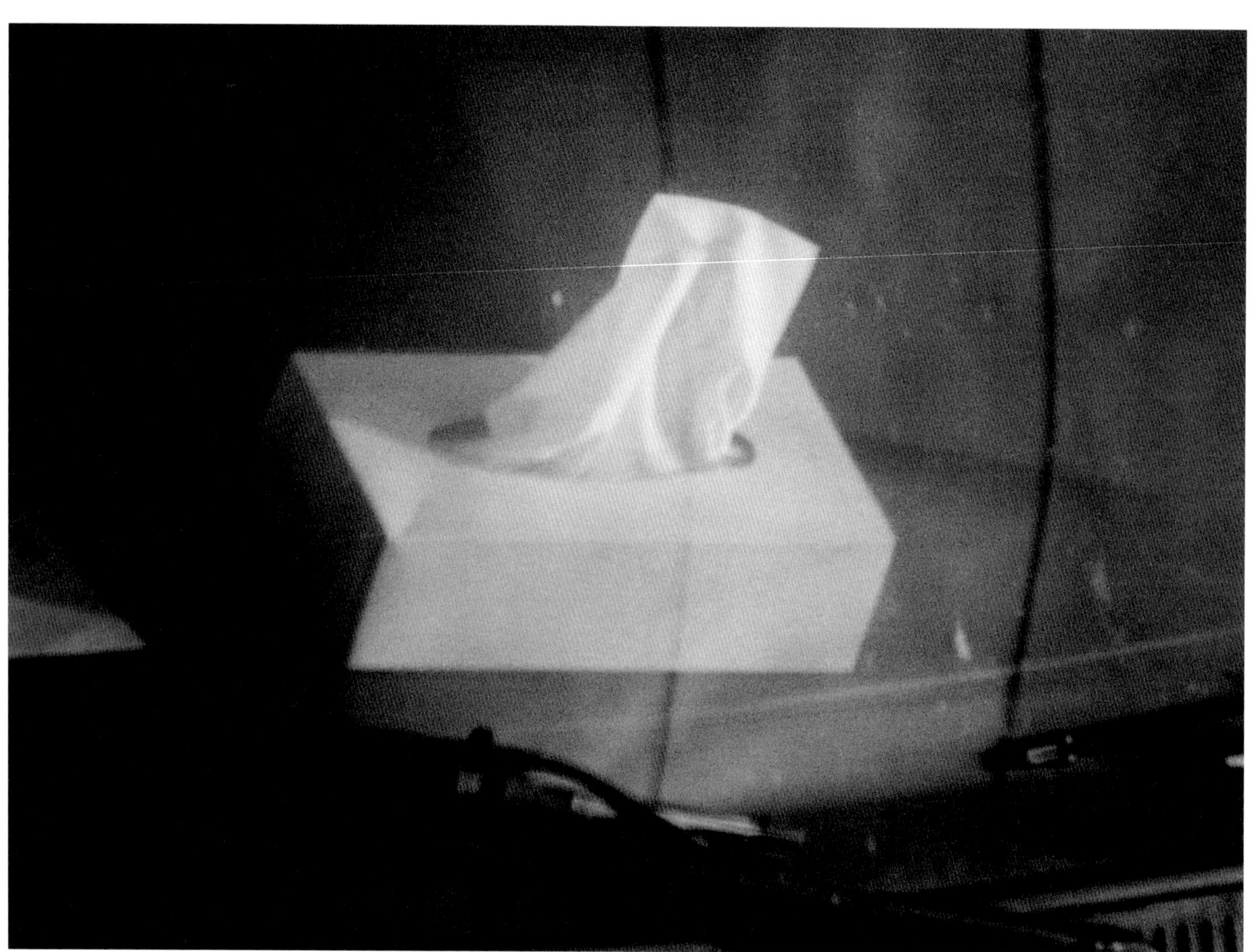

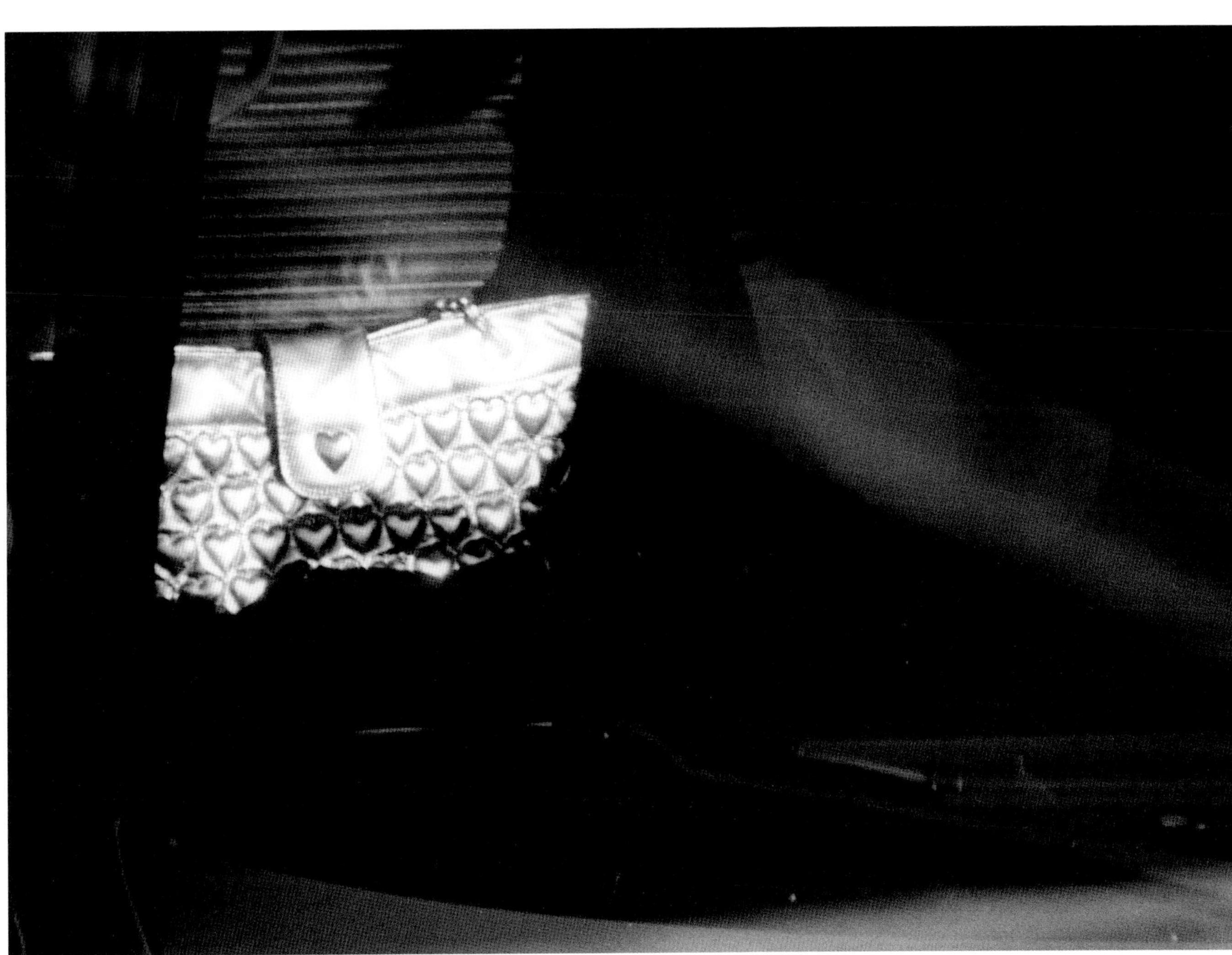

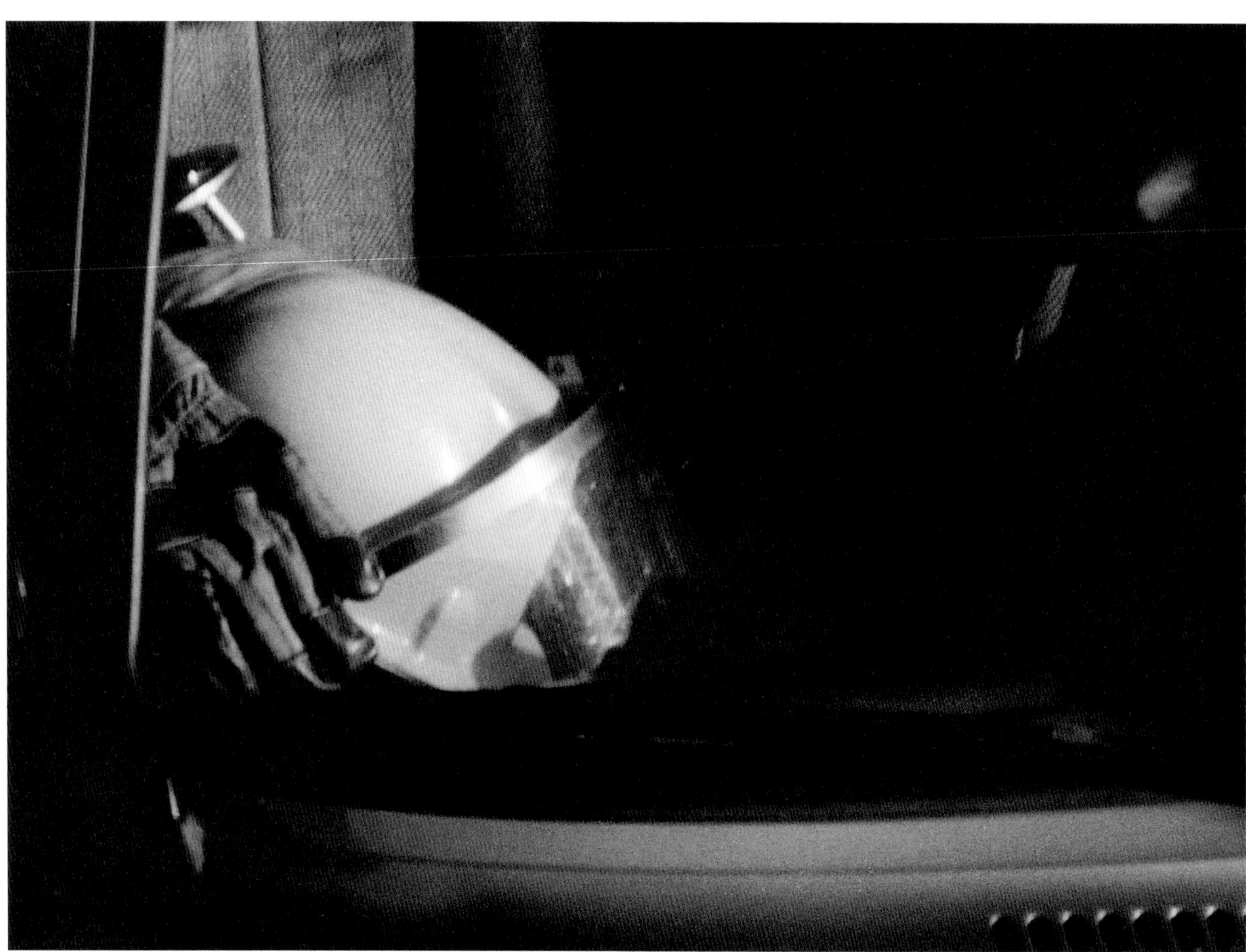

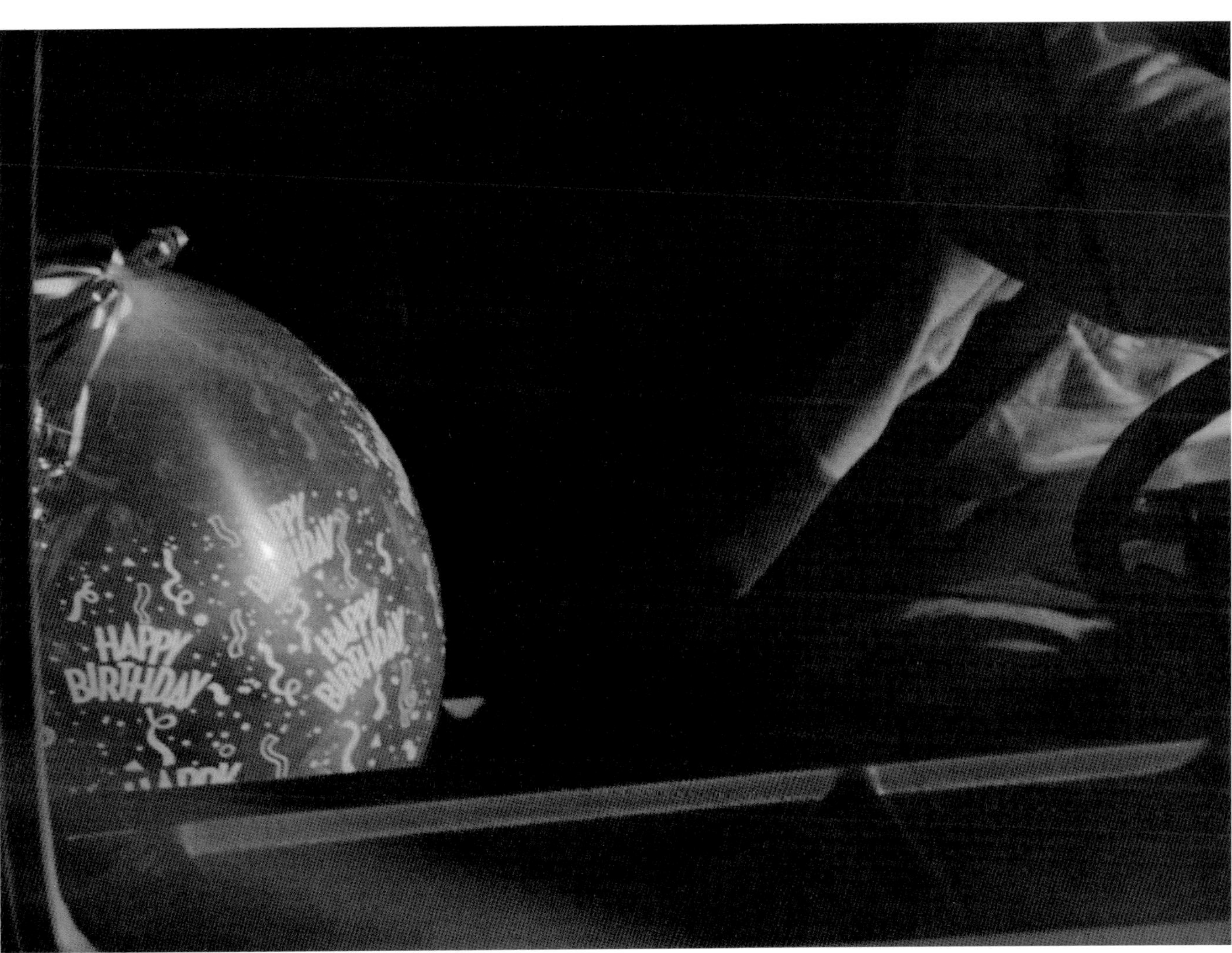

HAPPY BIRTHDAY
HAPPY BIRTHDAY

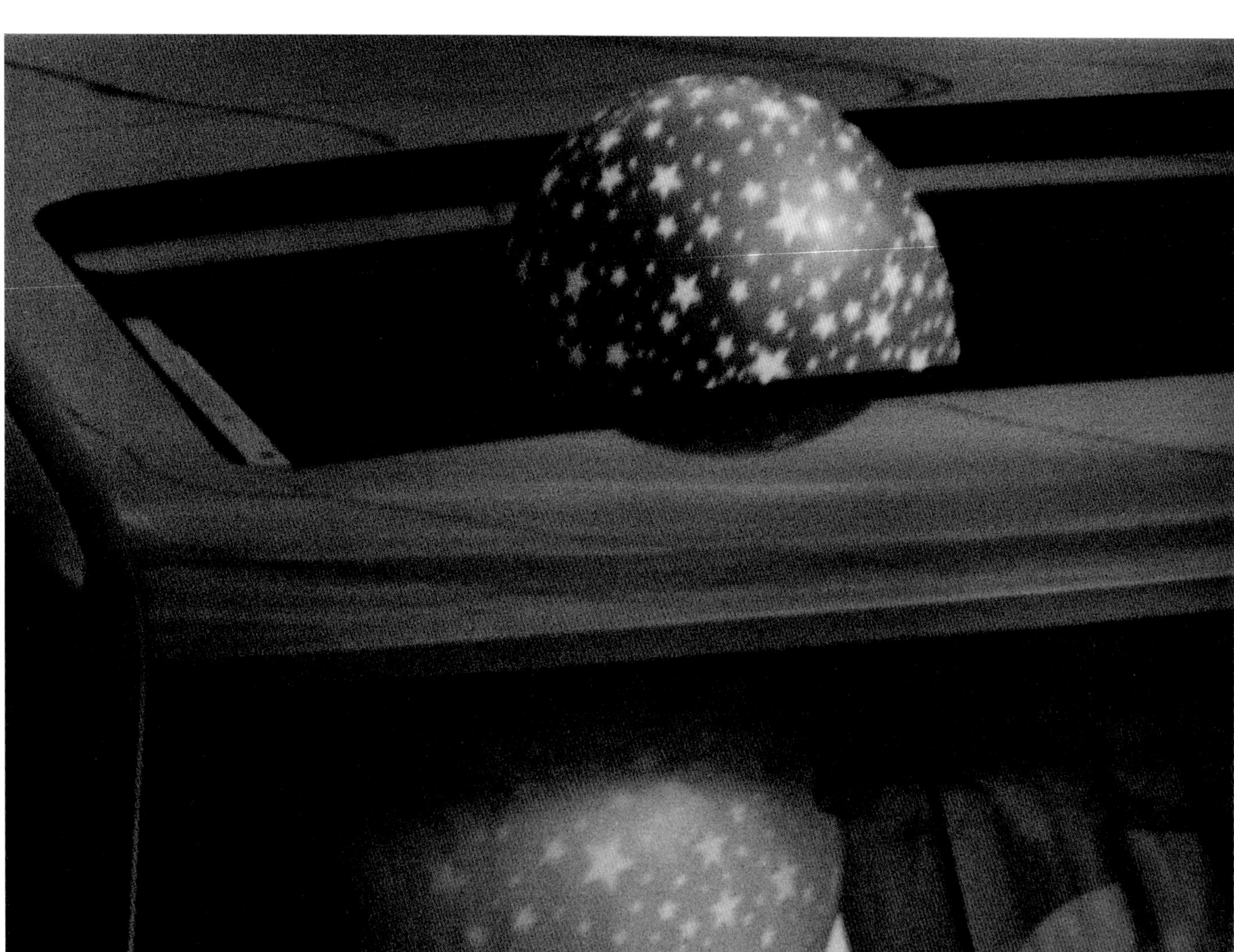

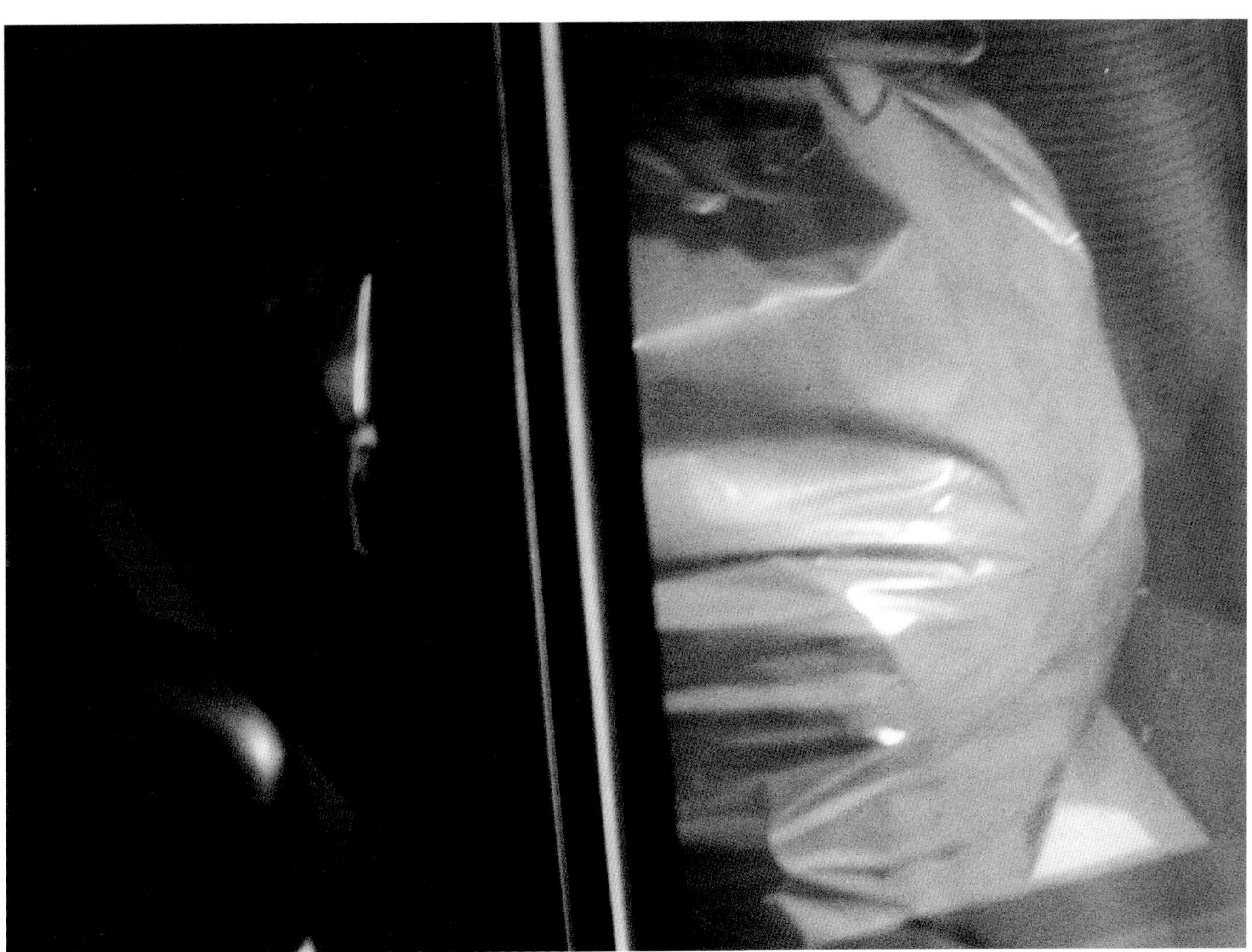

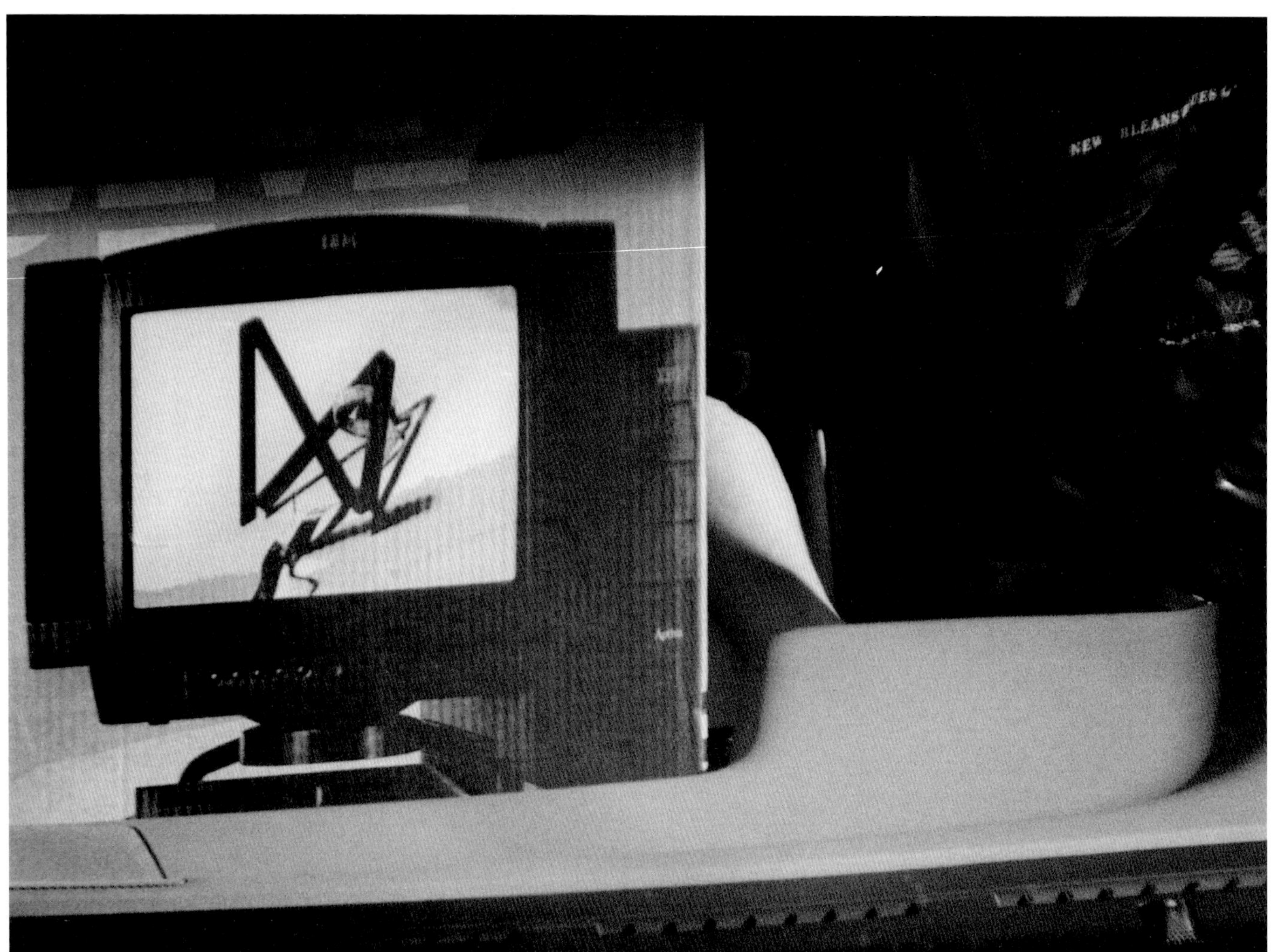

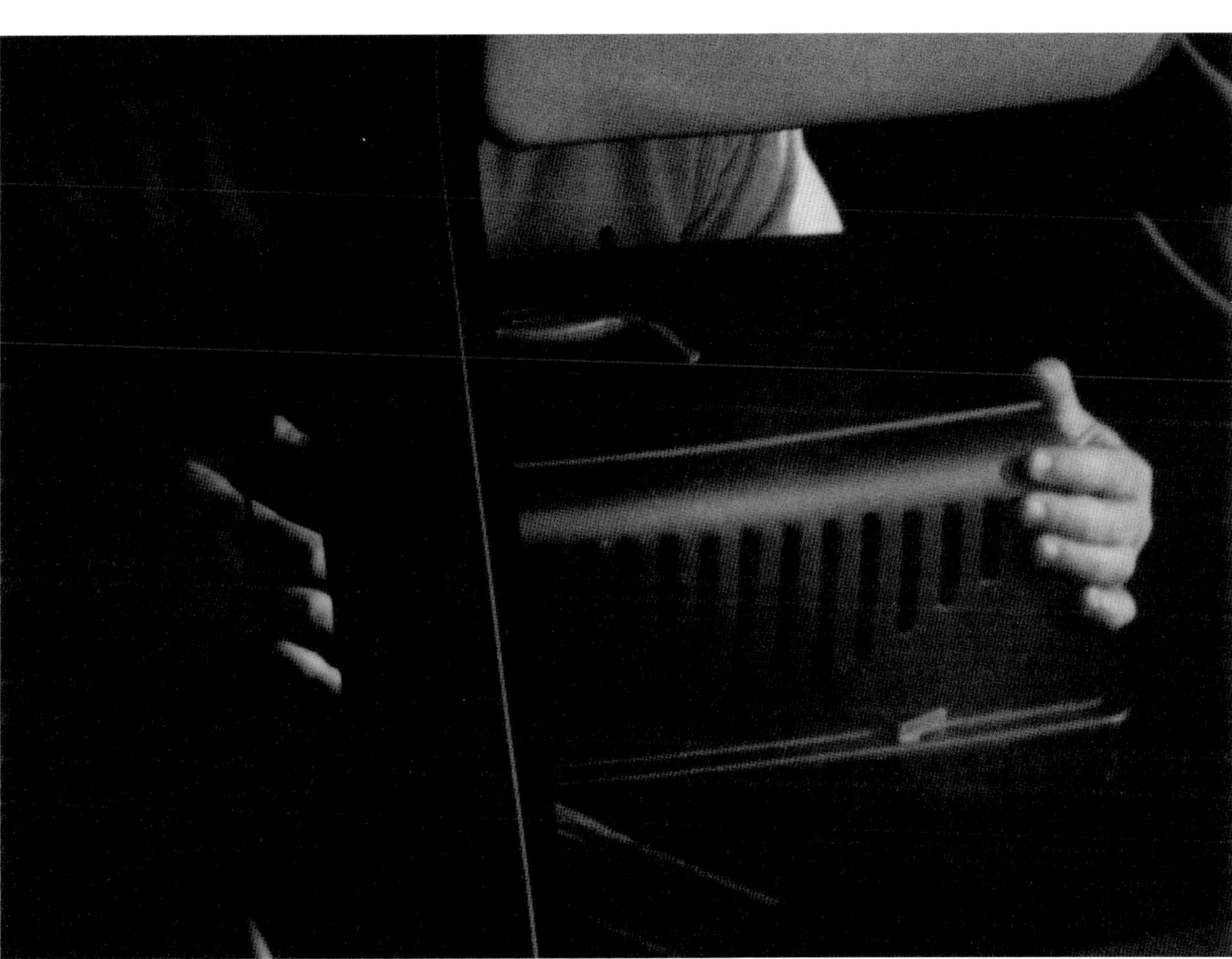

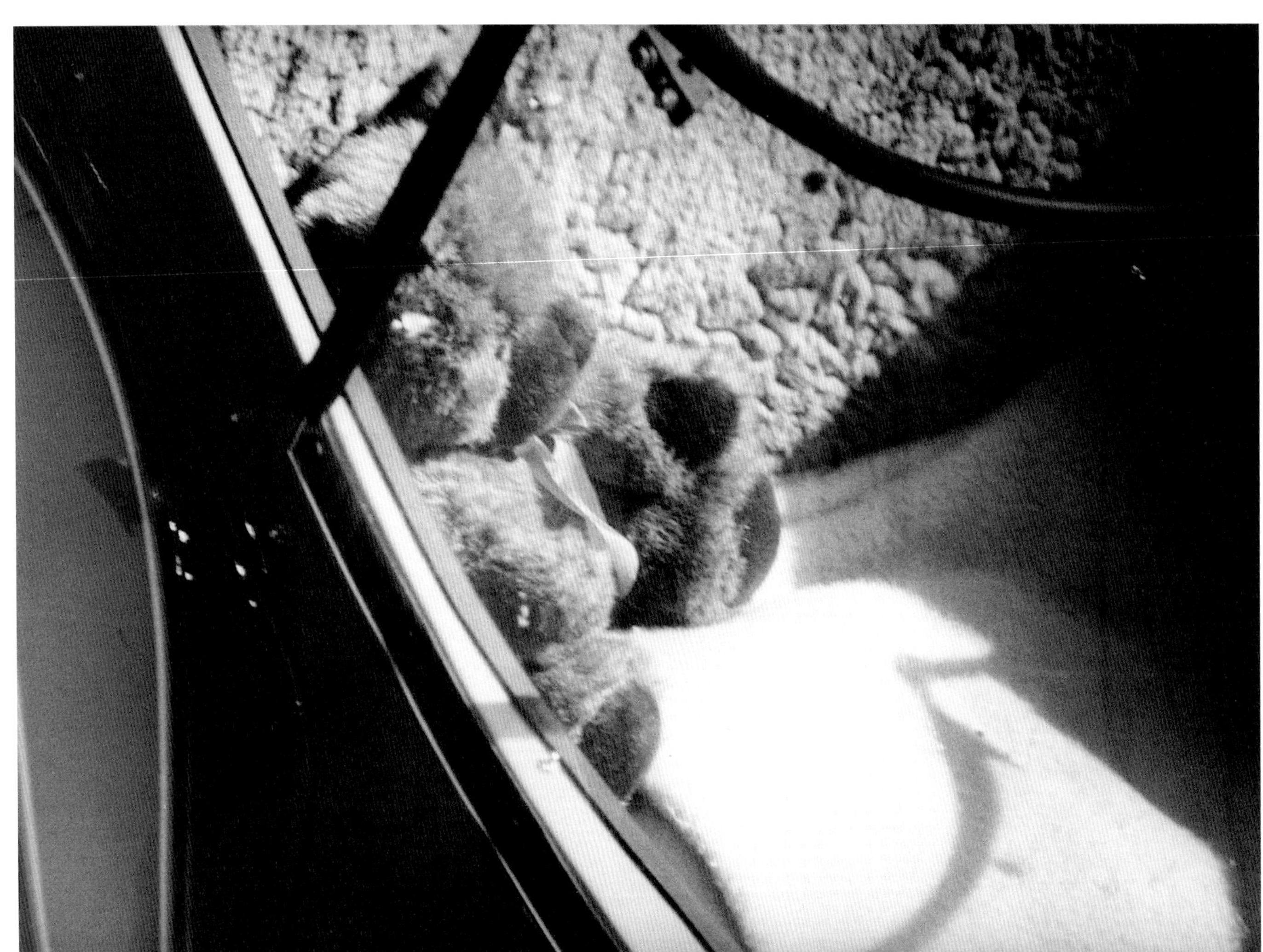

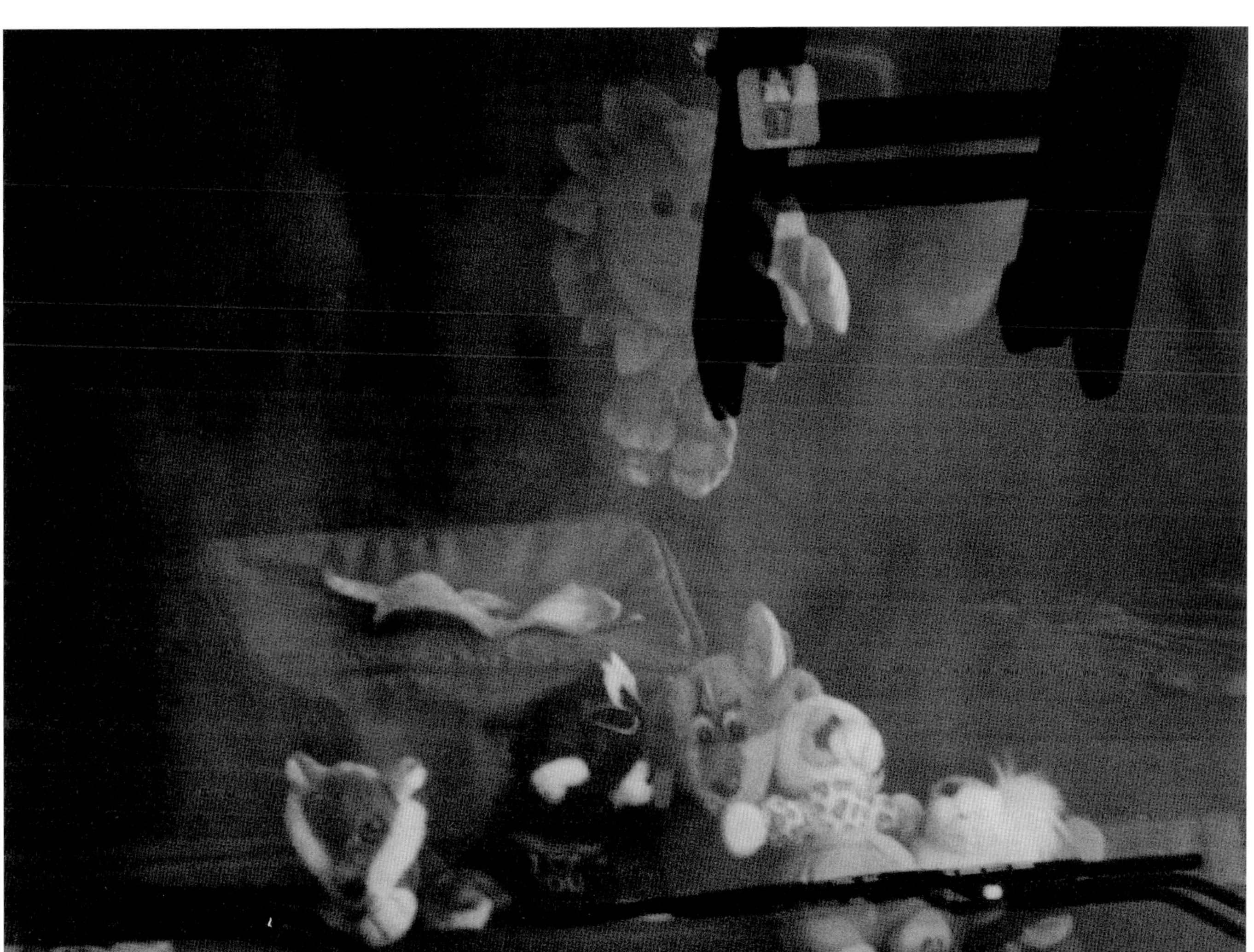

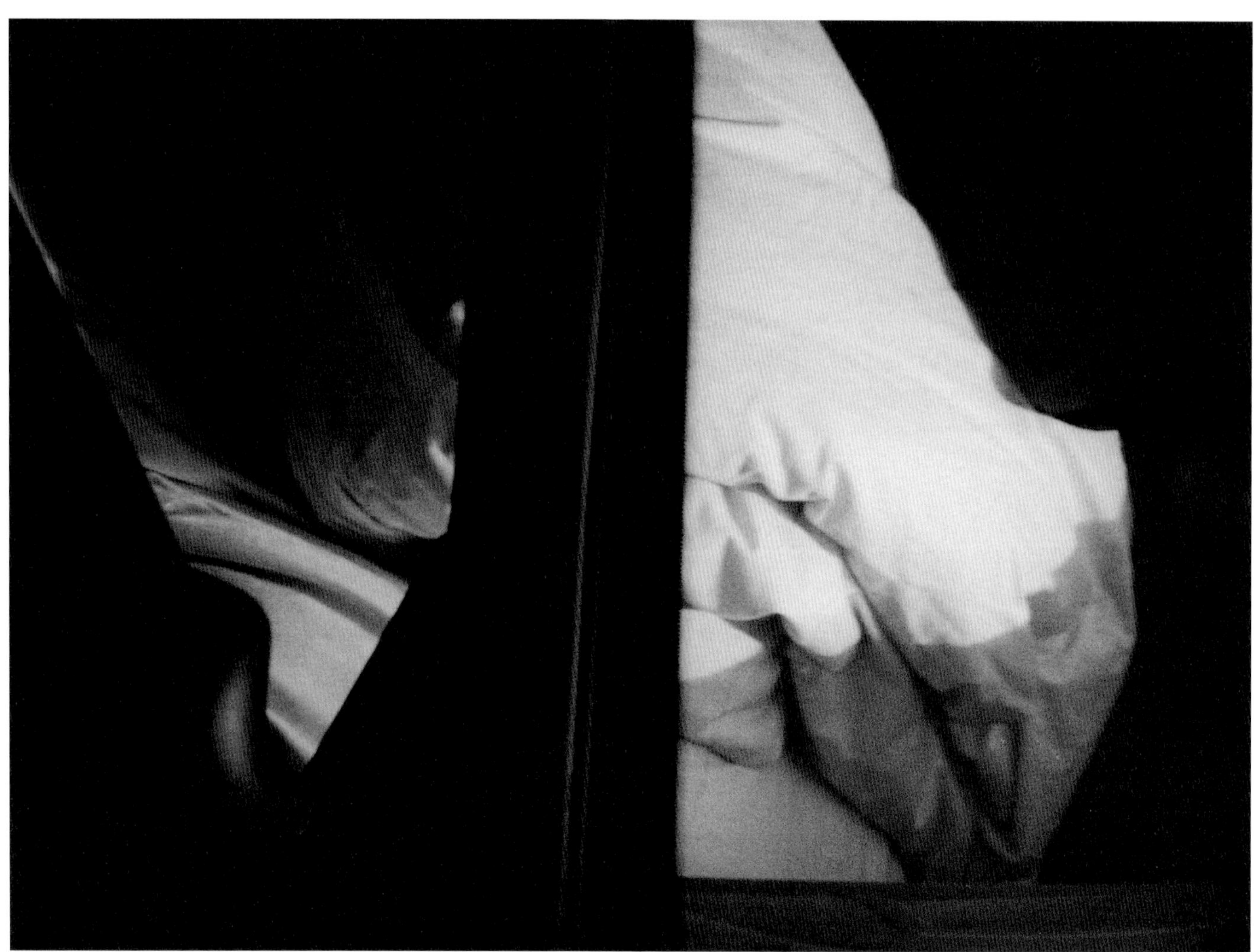

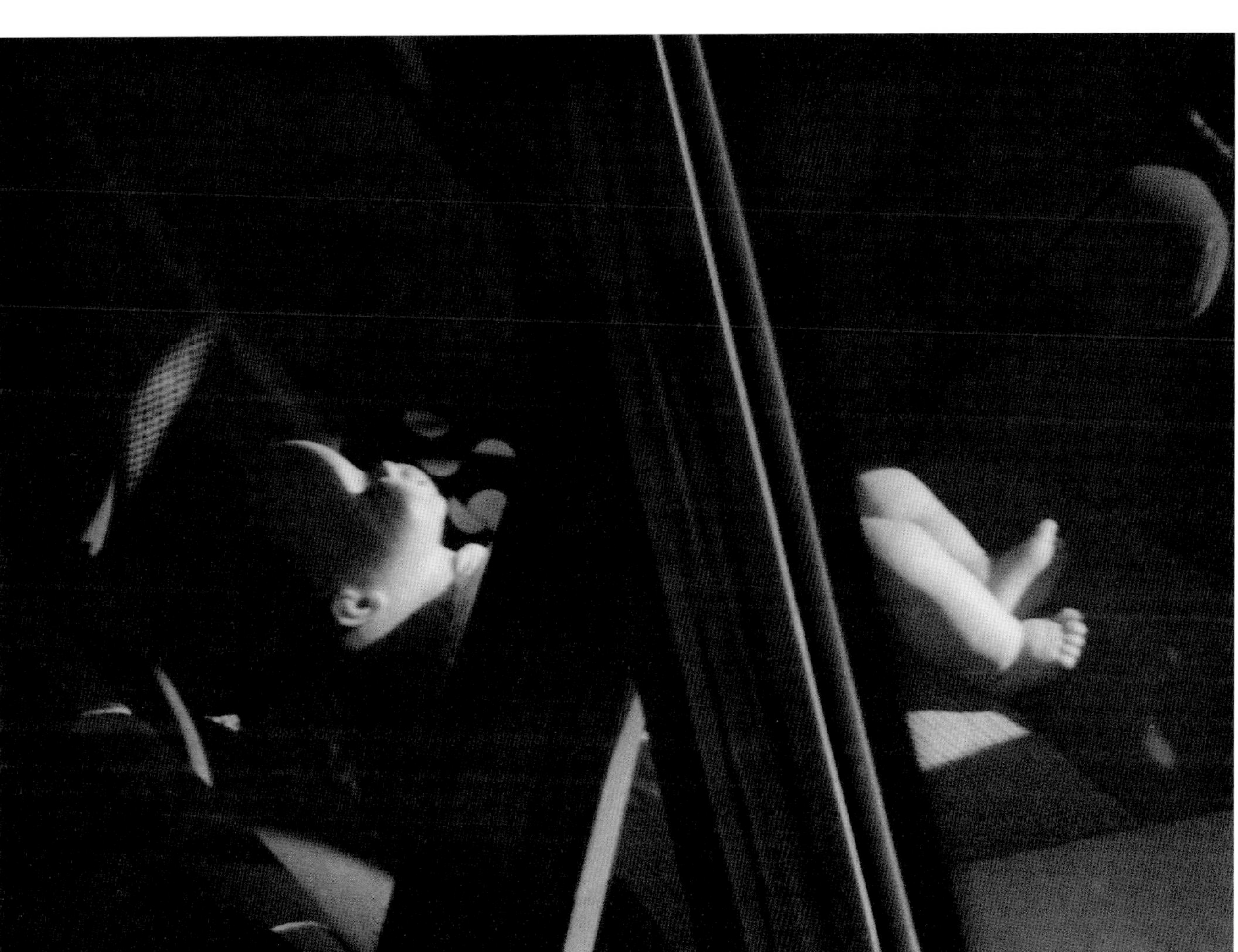

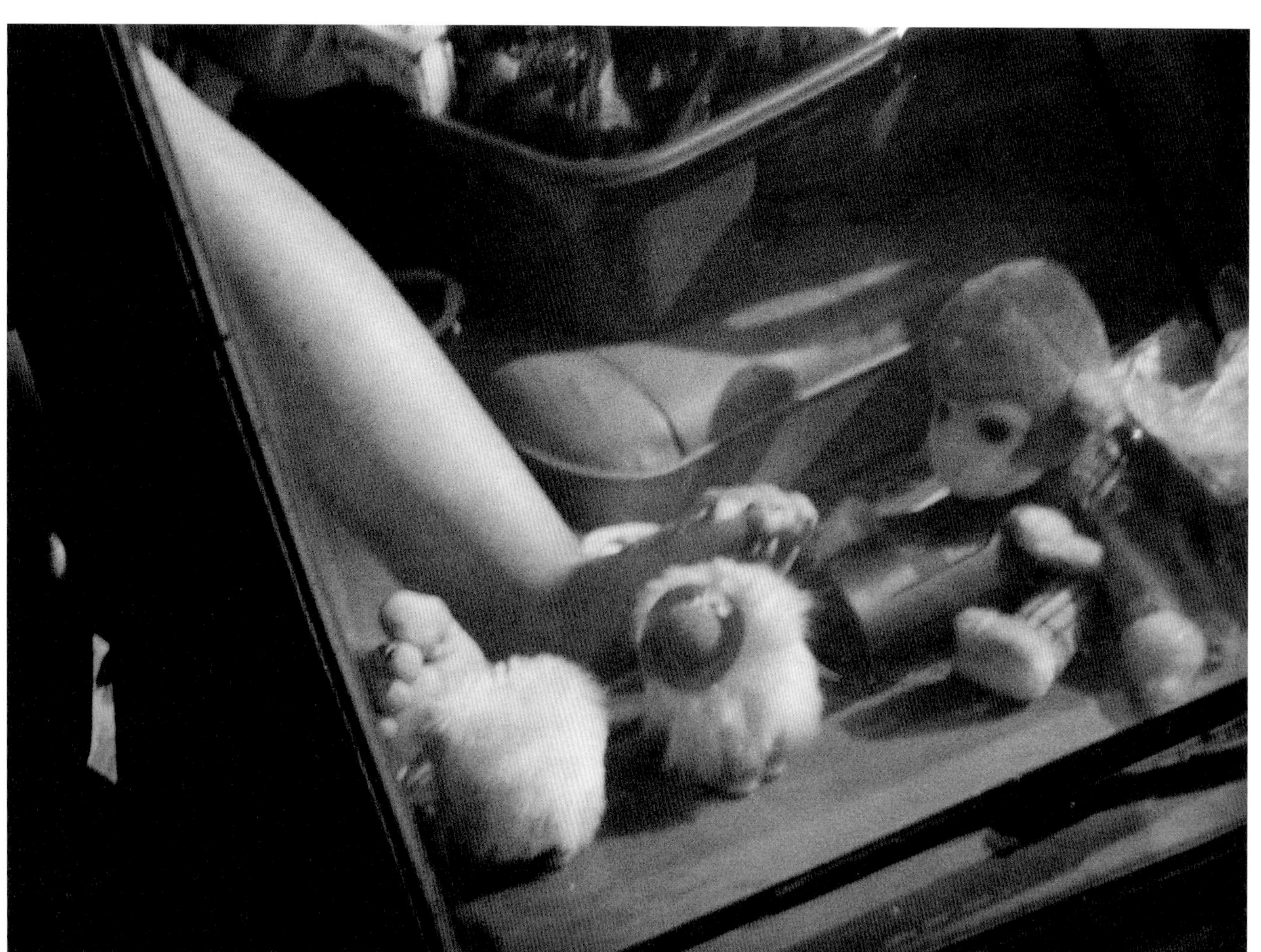

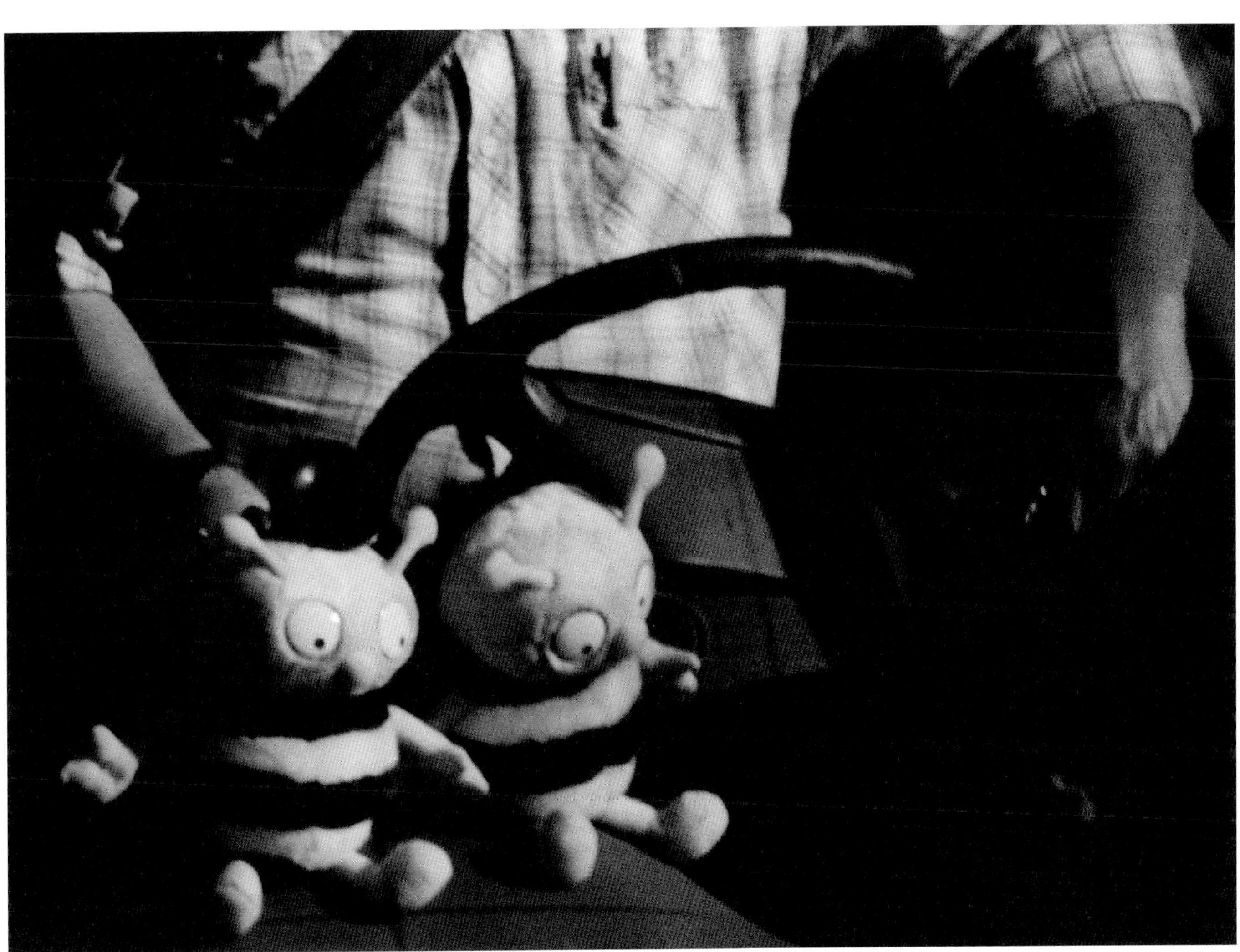

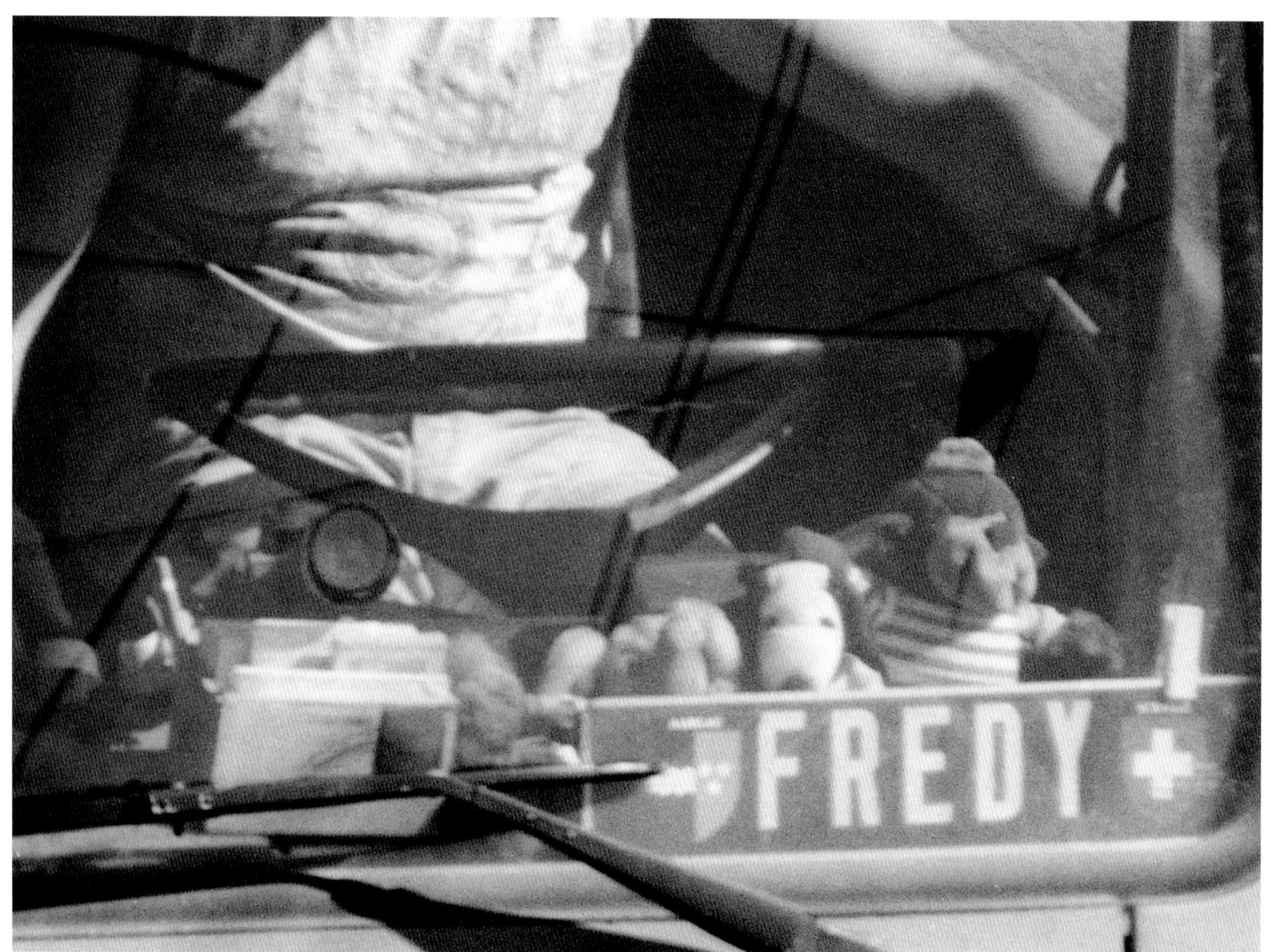
FREDY

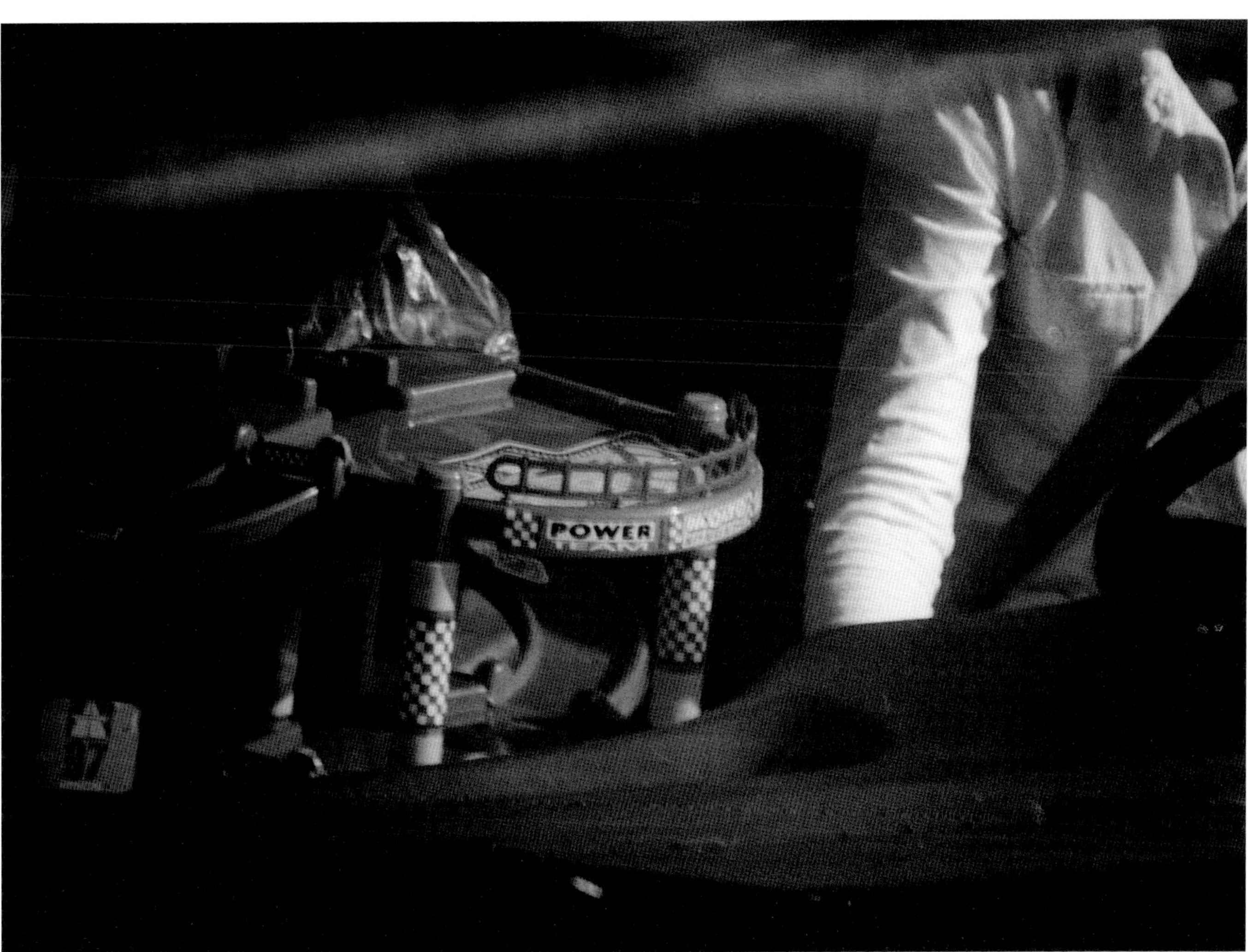
POWER

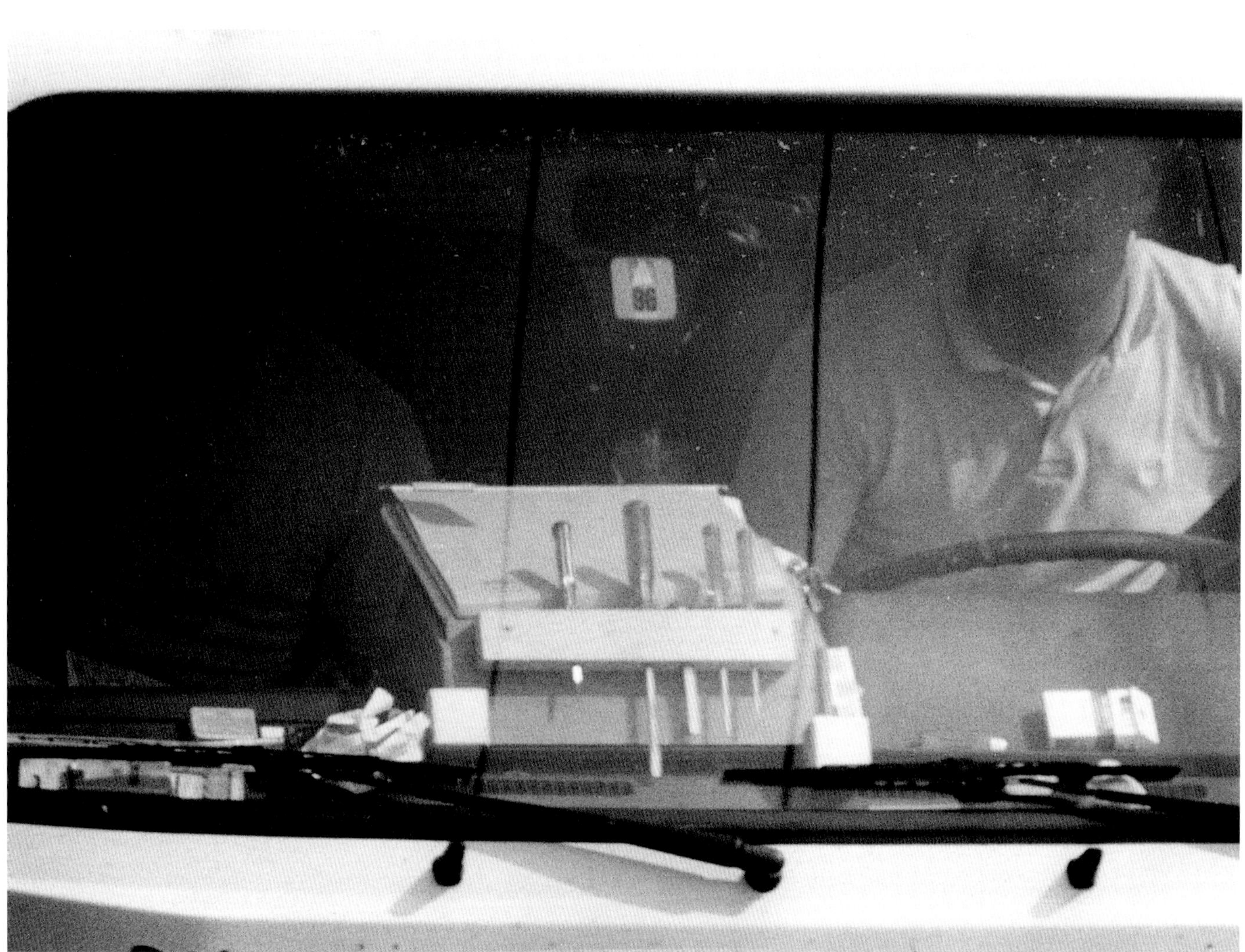

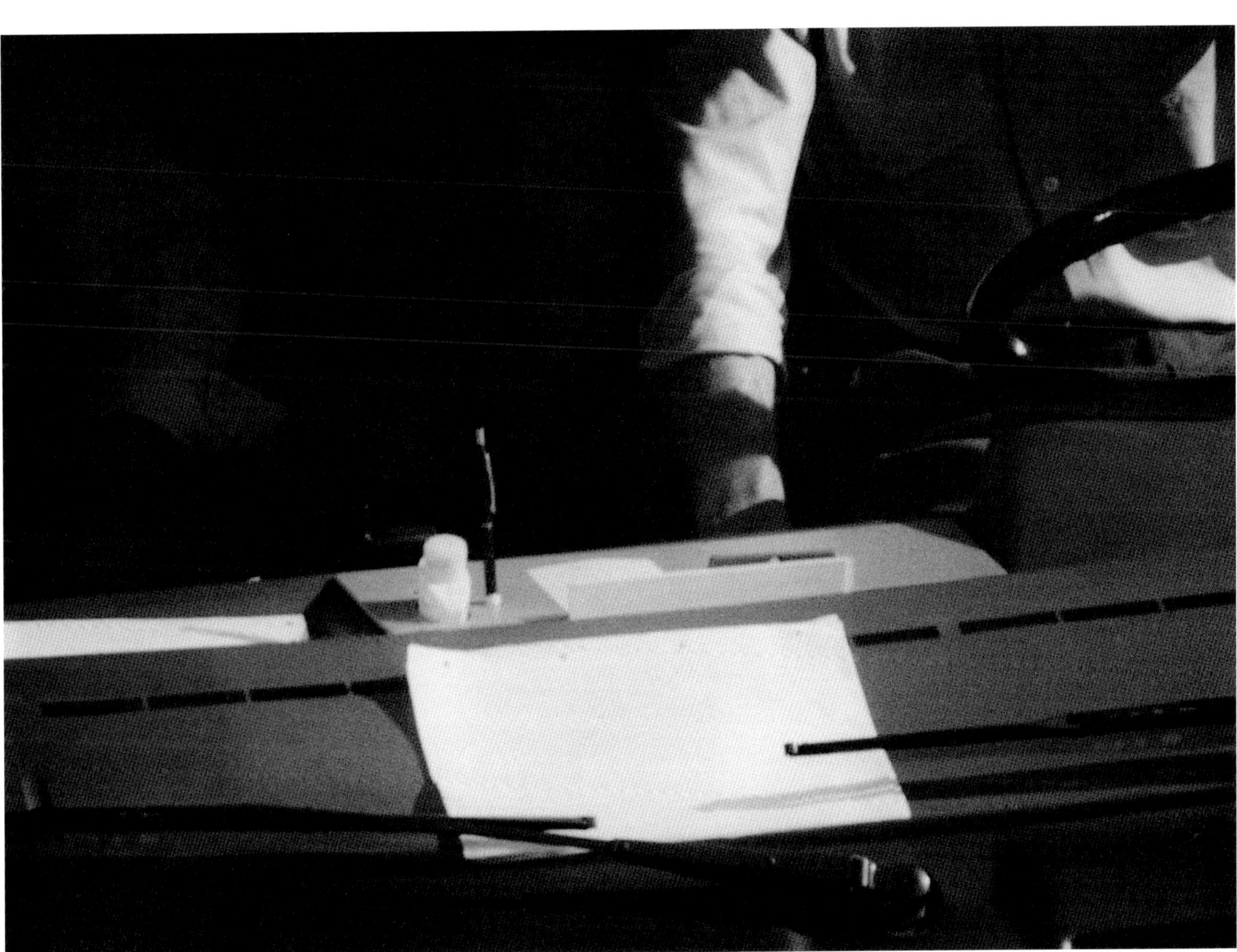

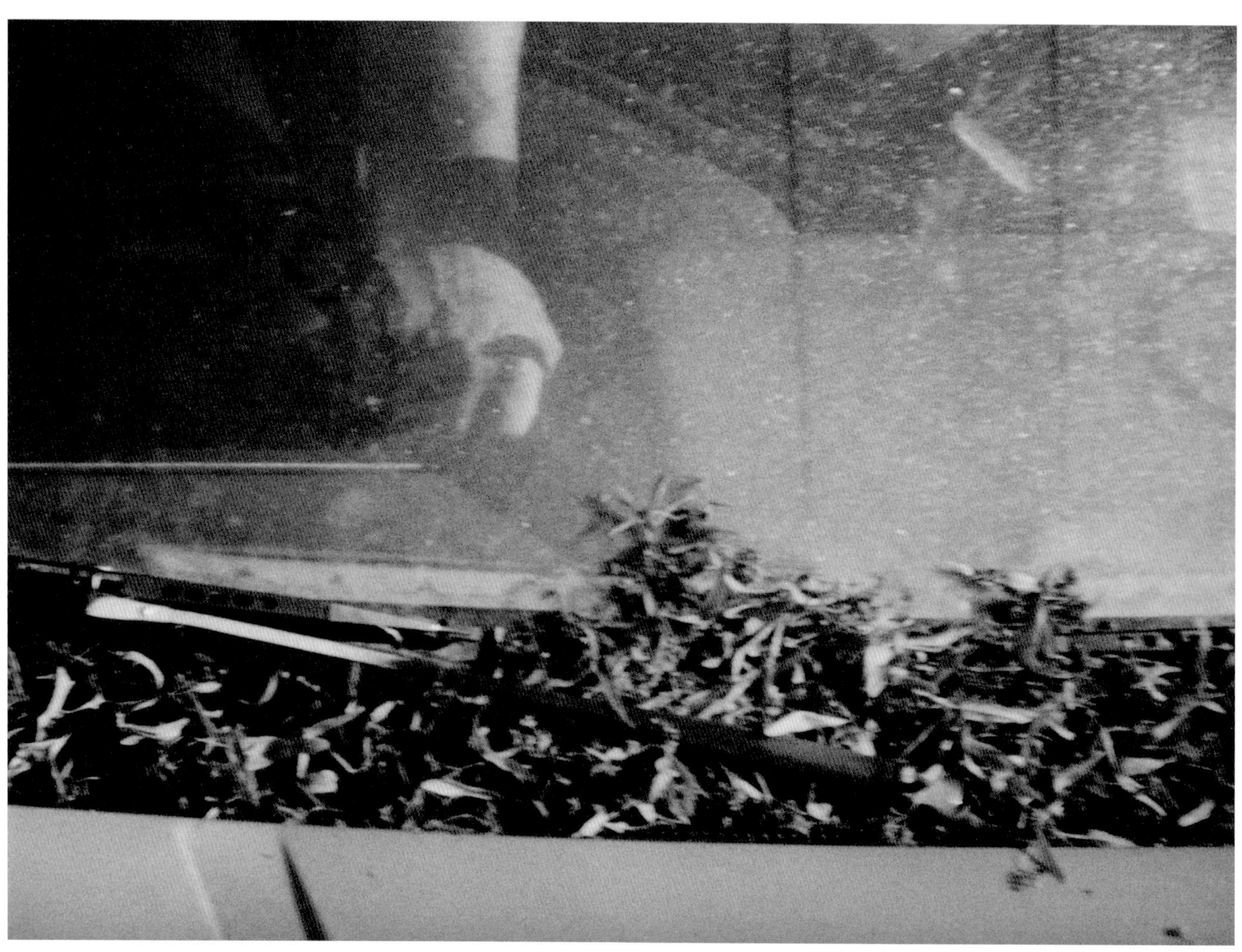

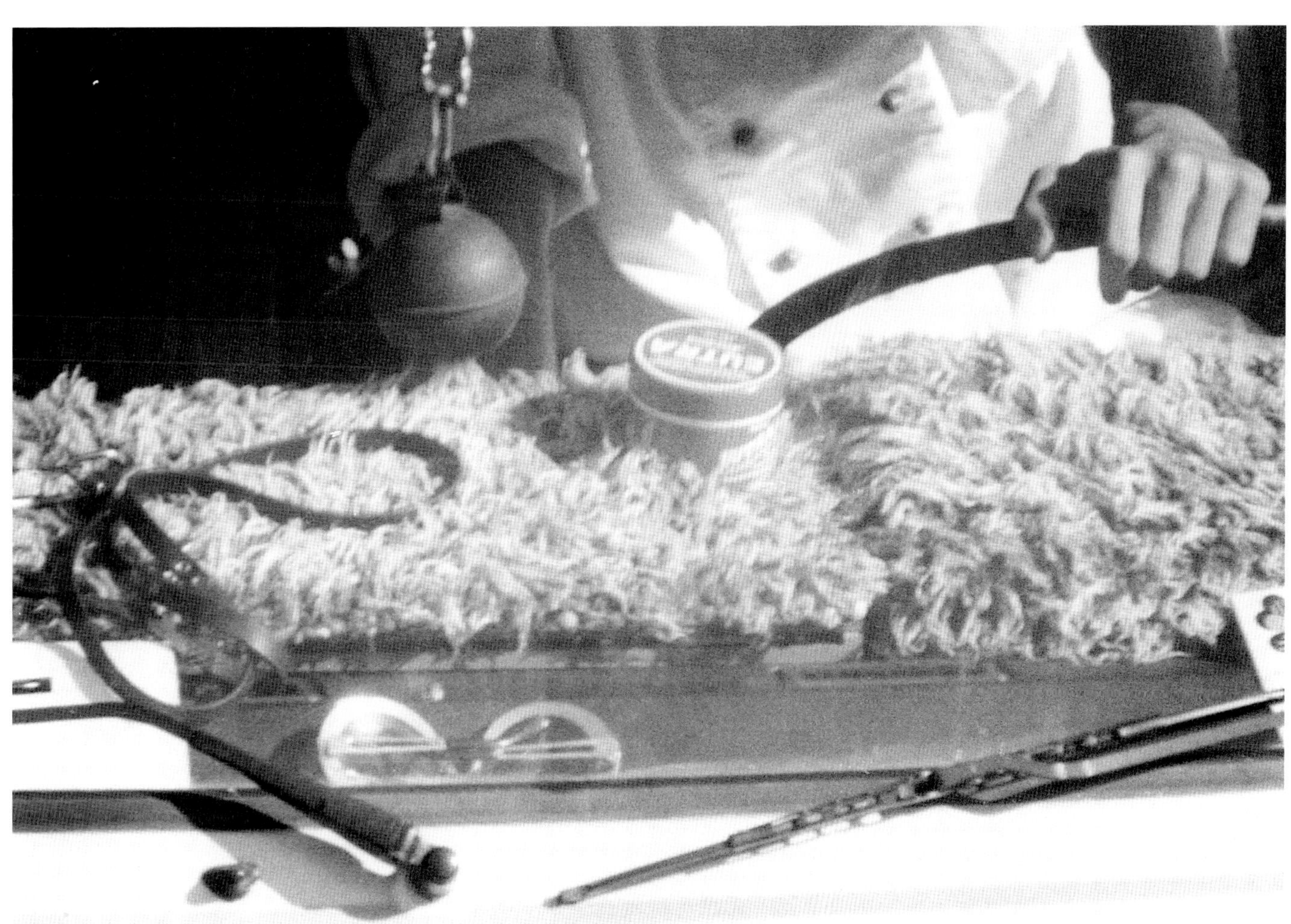

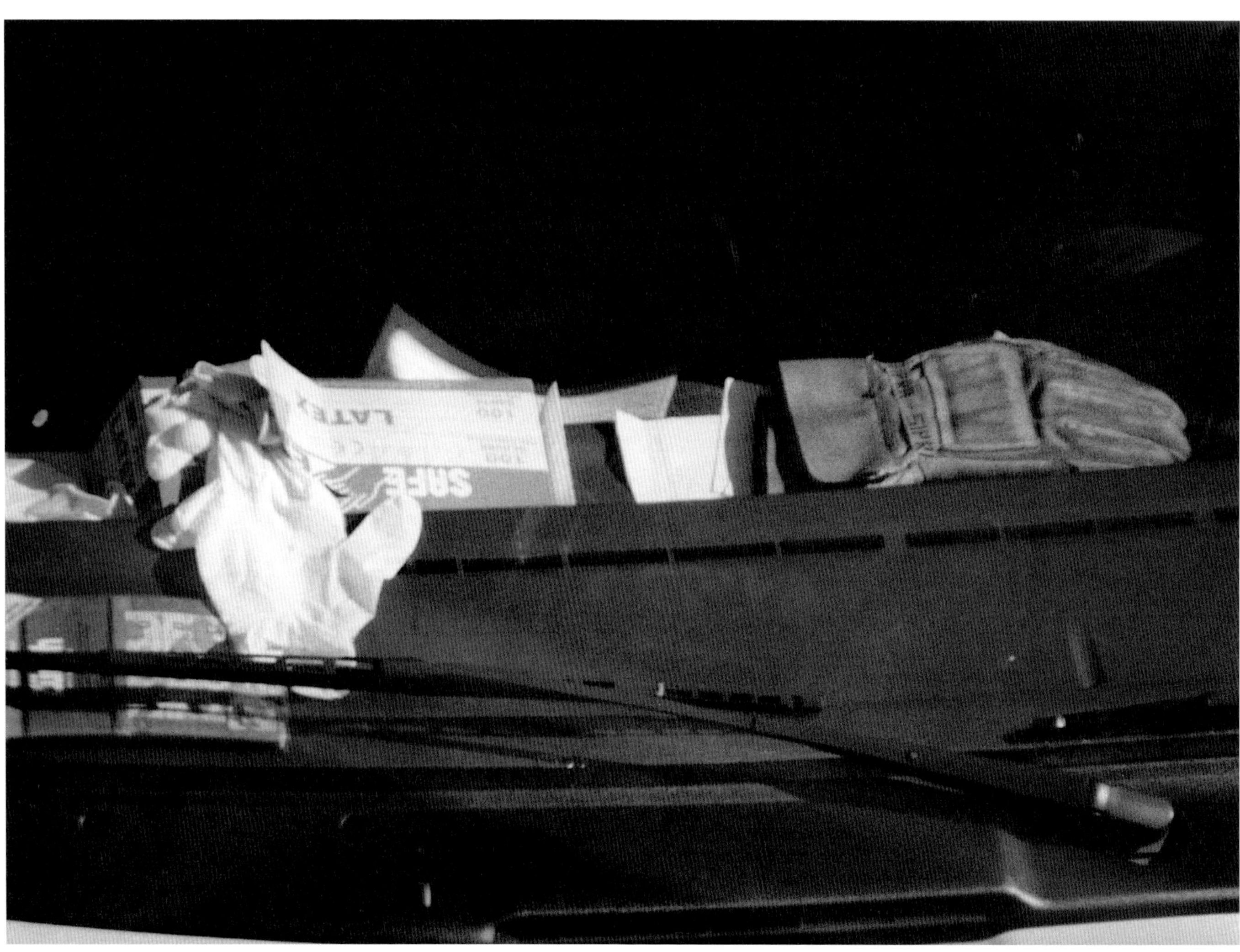

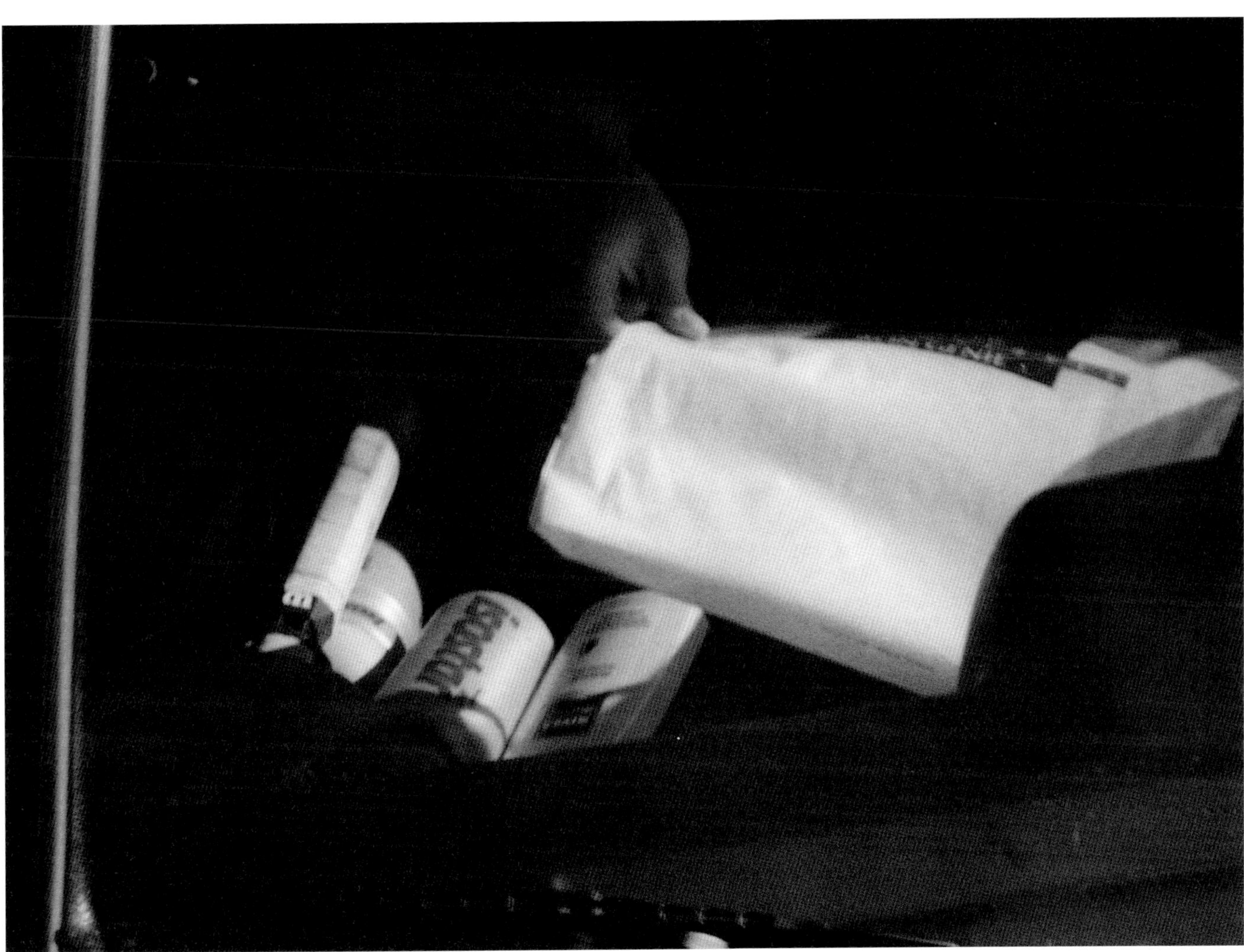

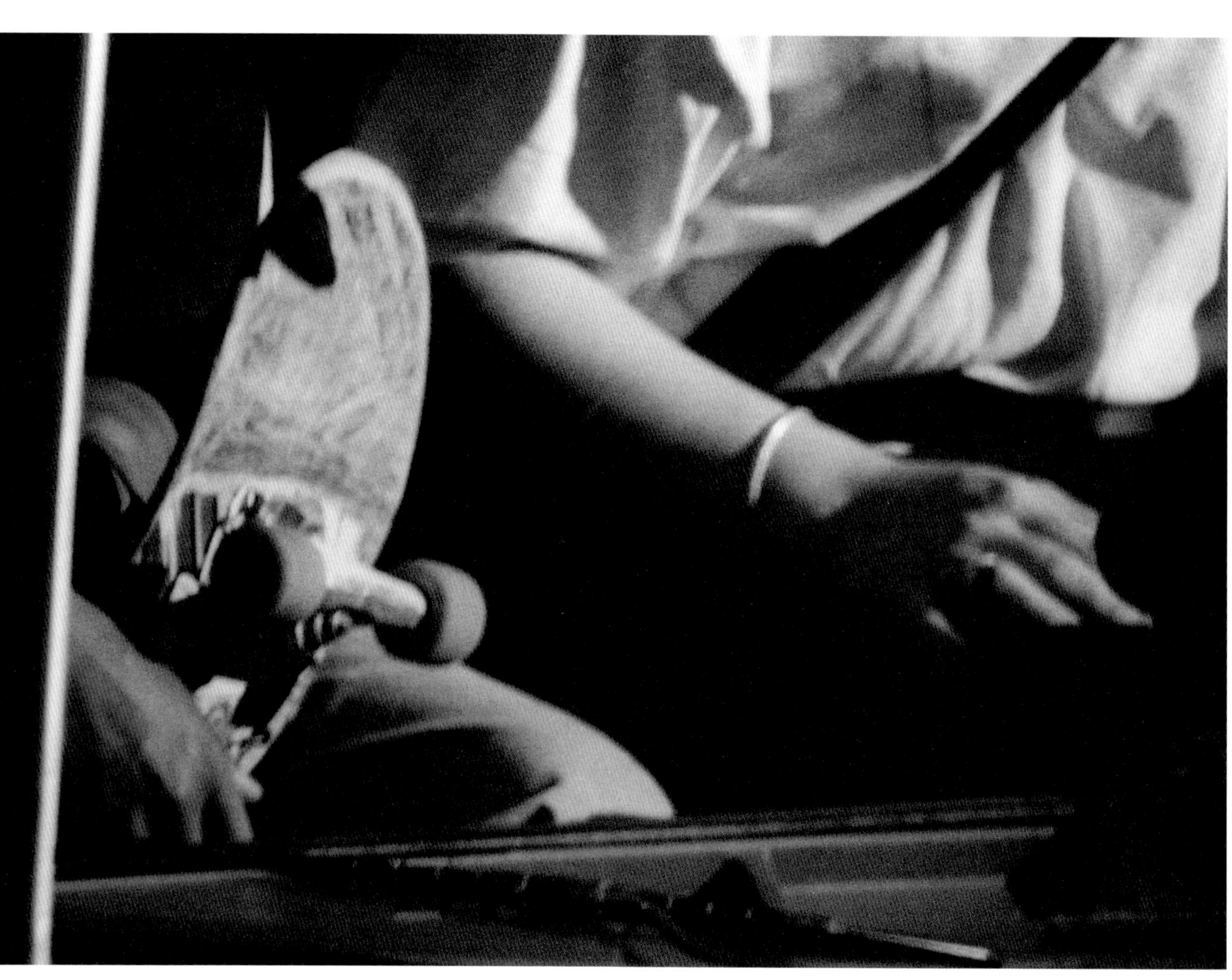

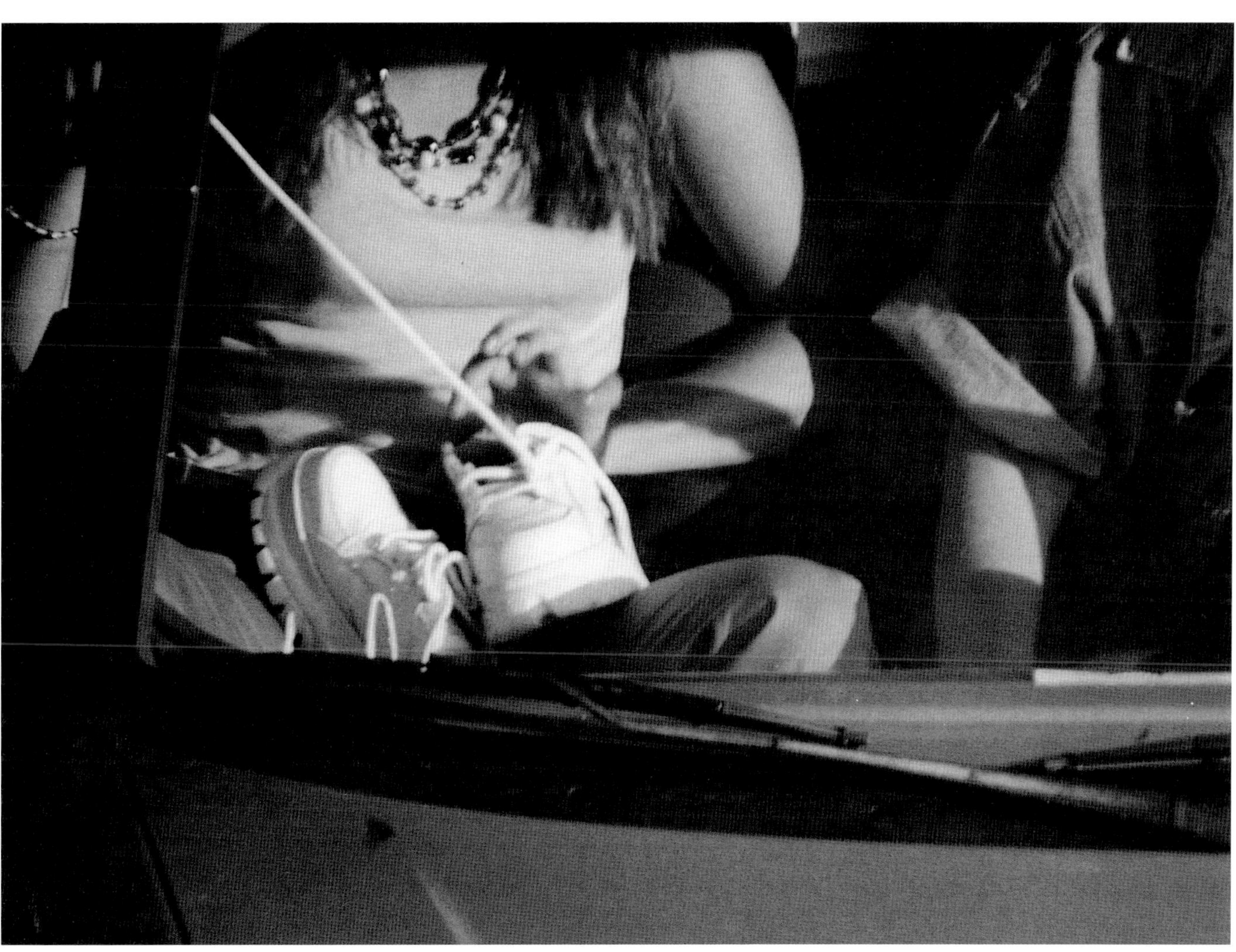

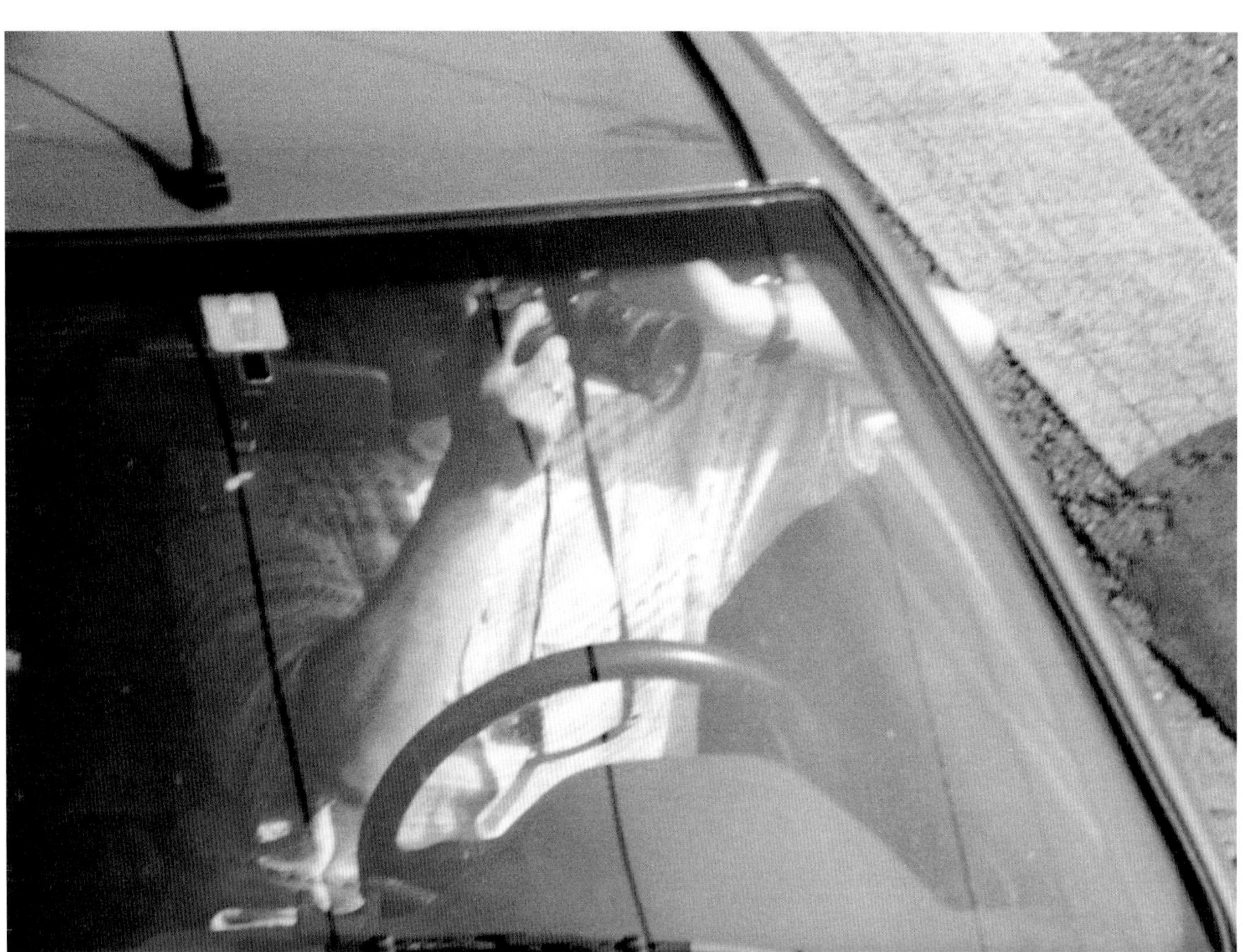

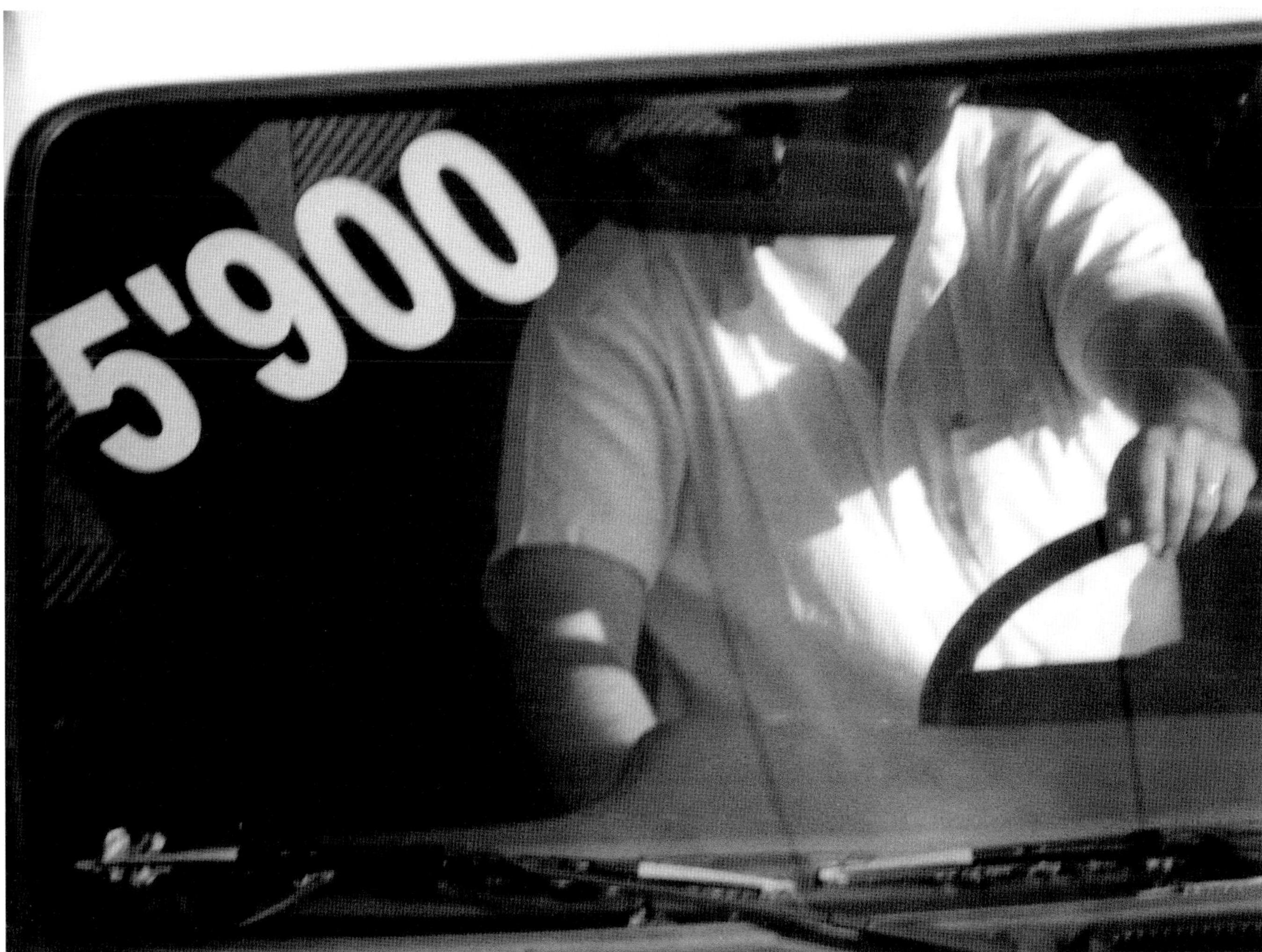
5'900

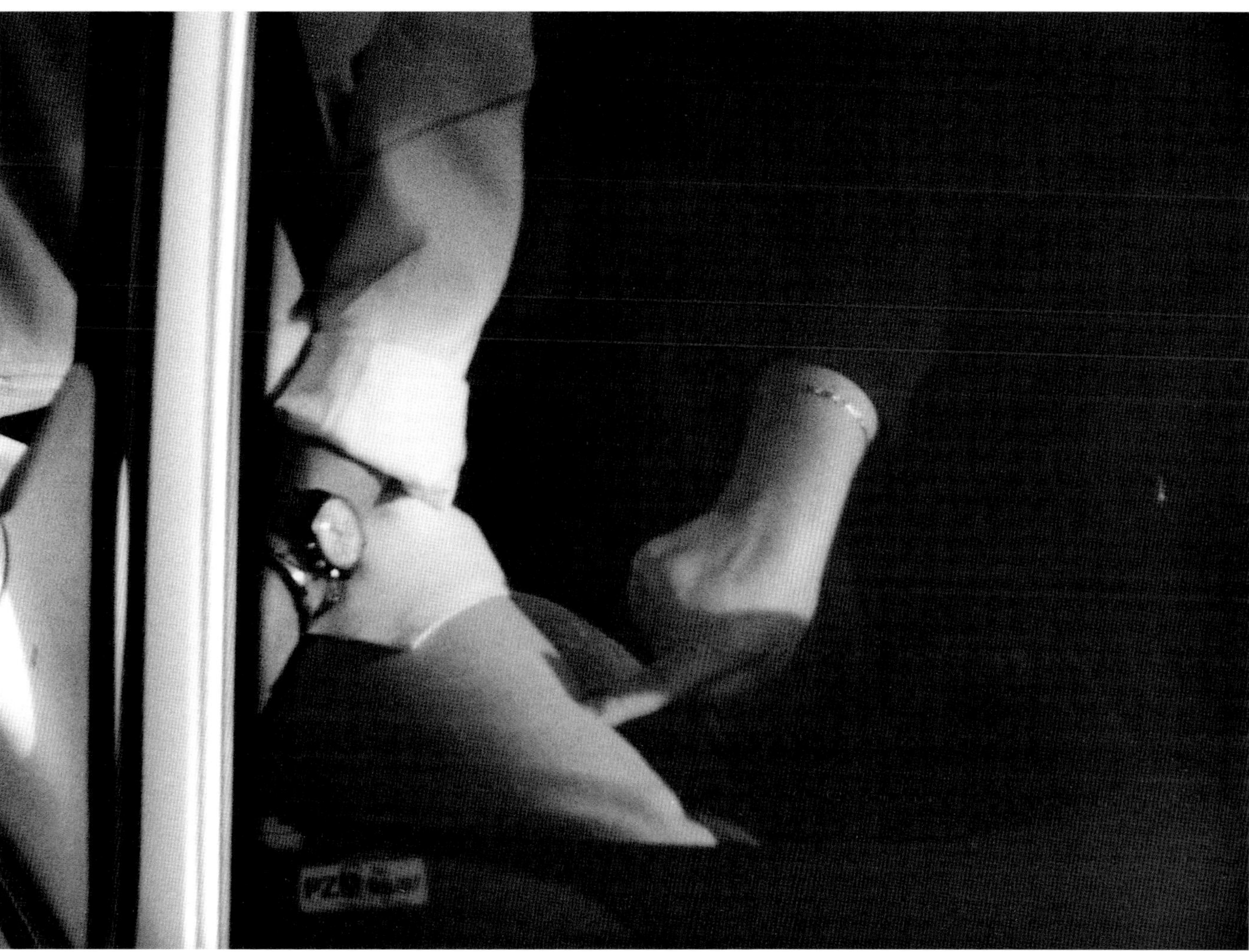

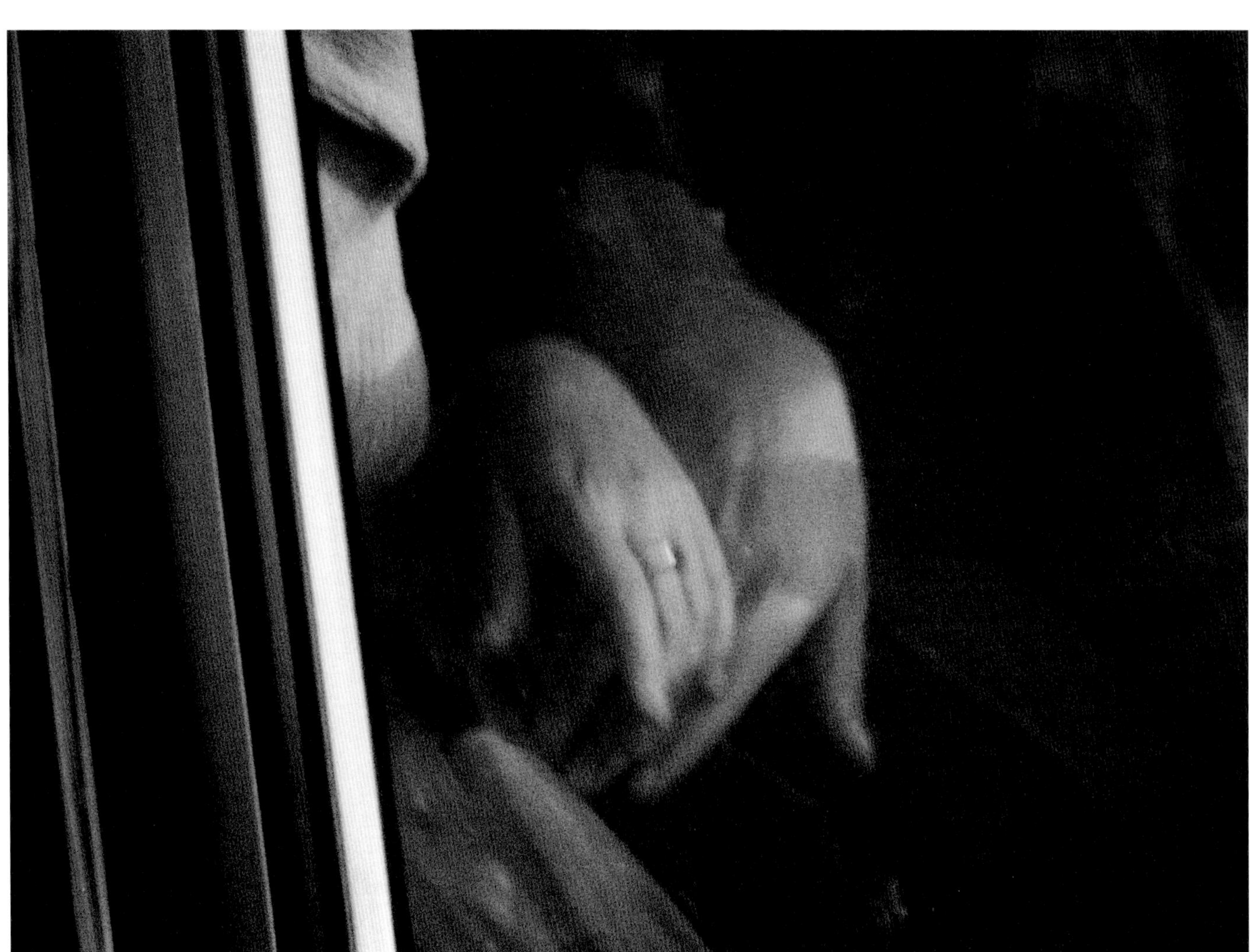

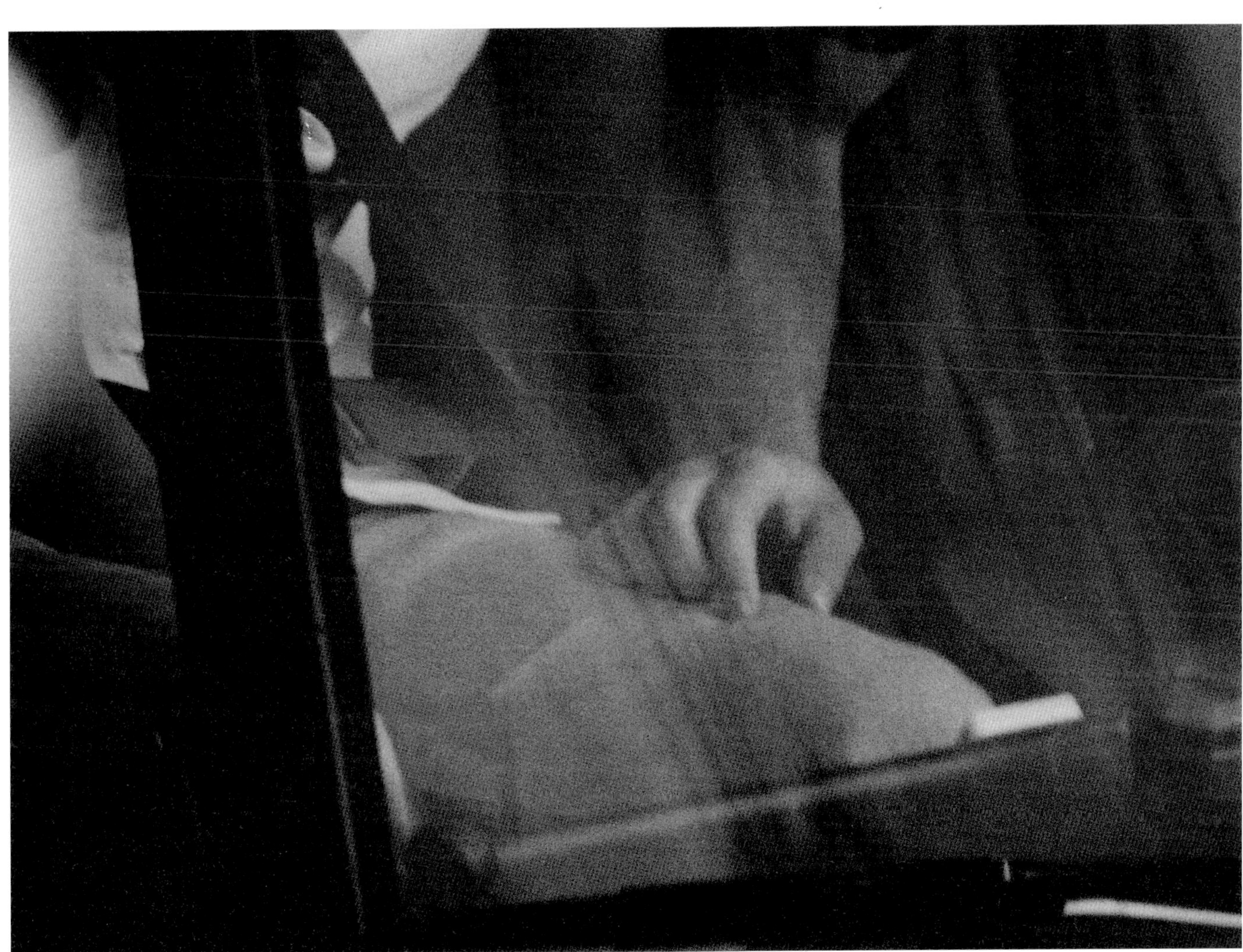

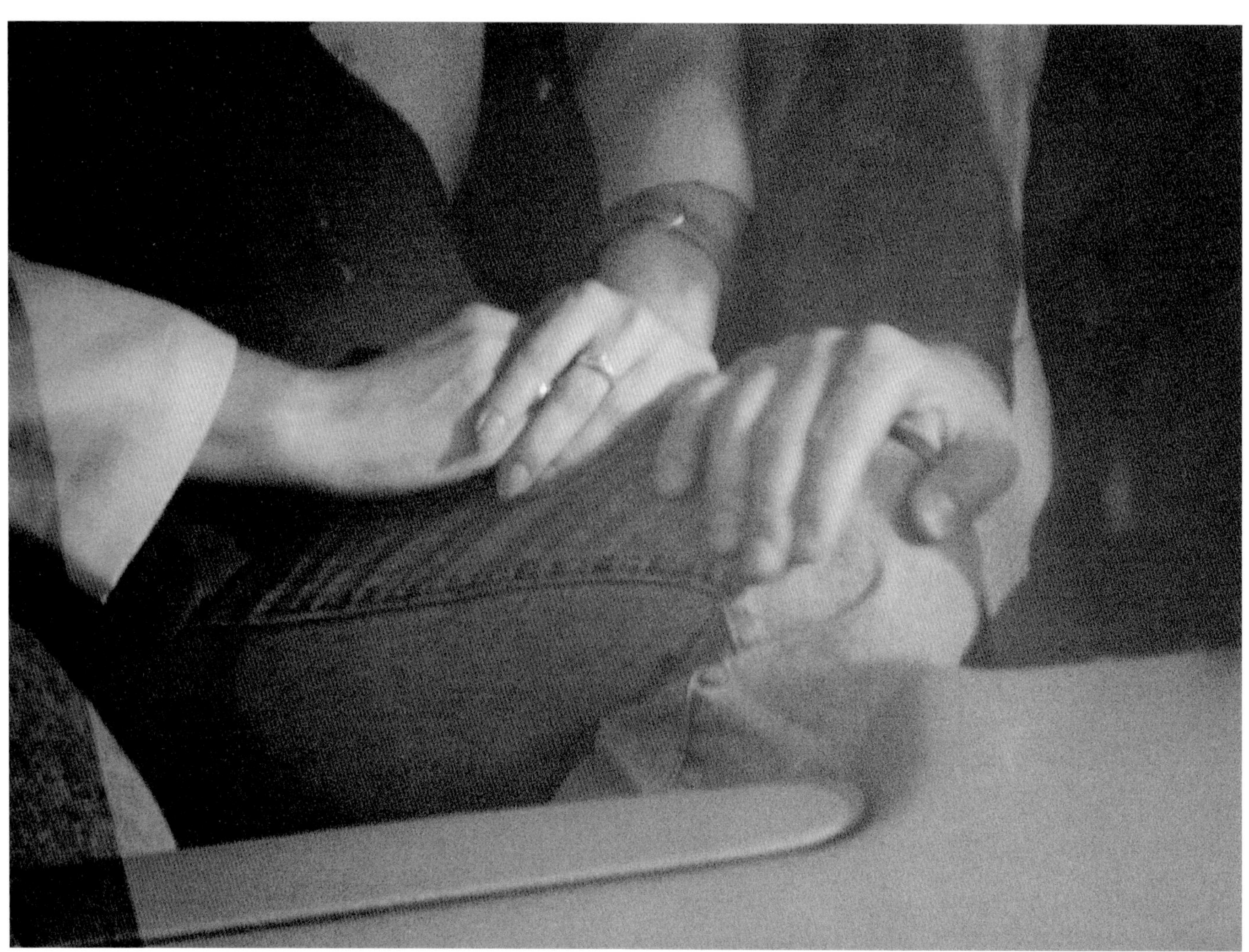

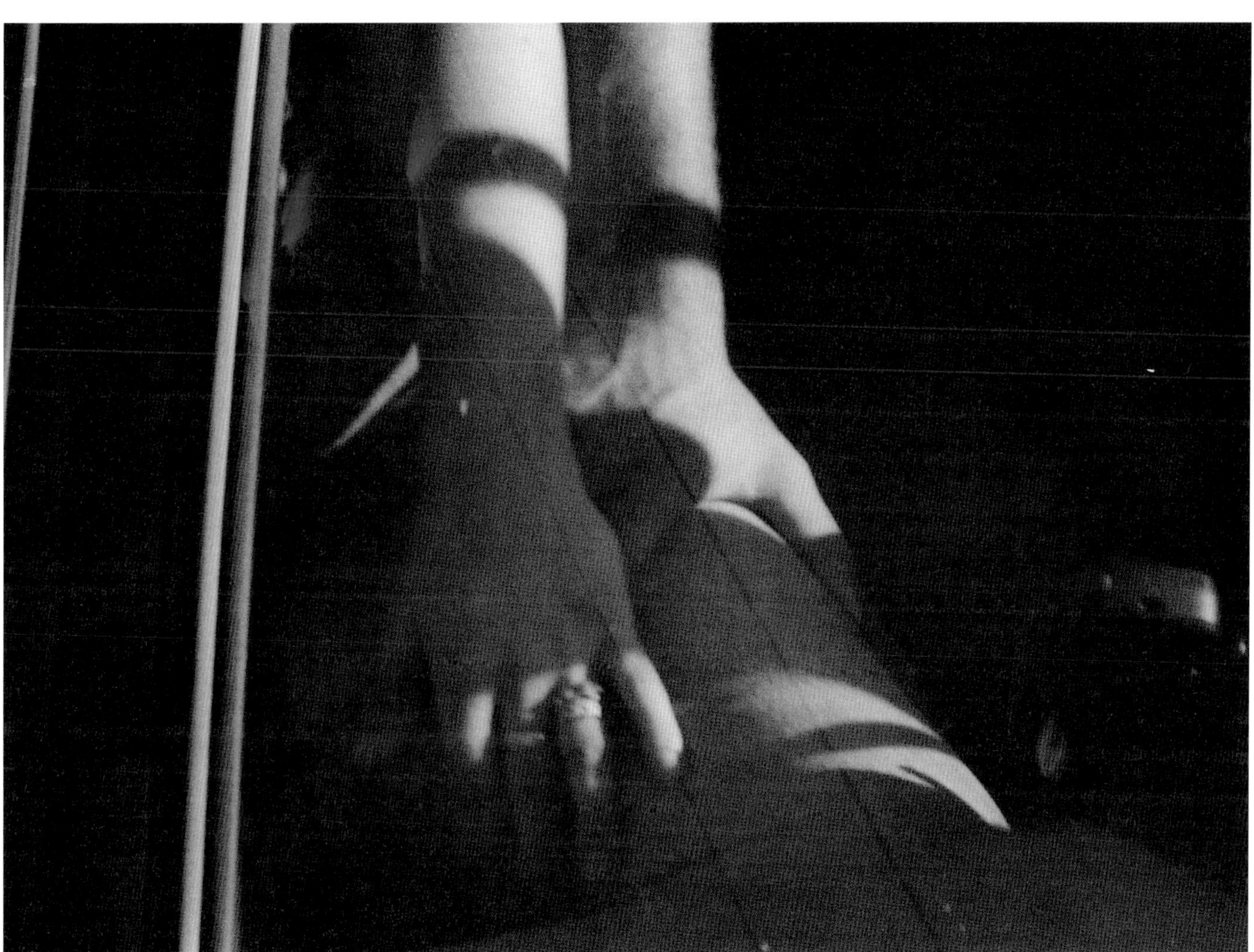

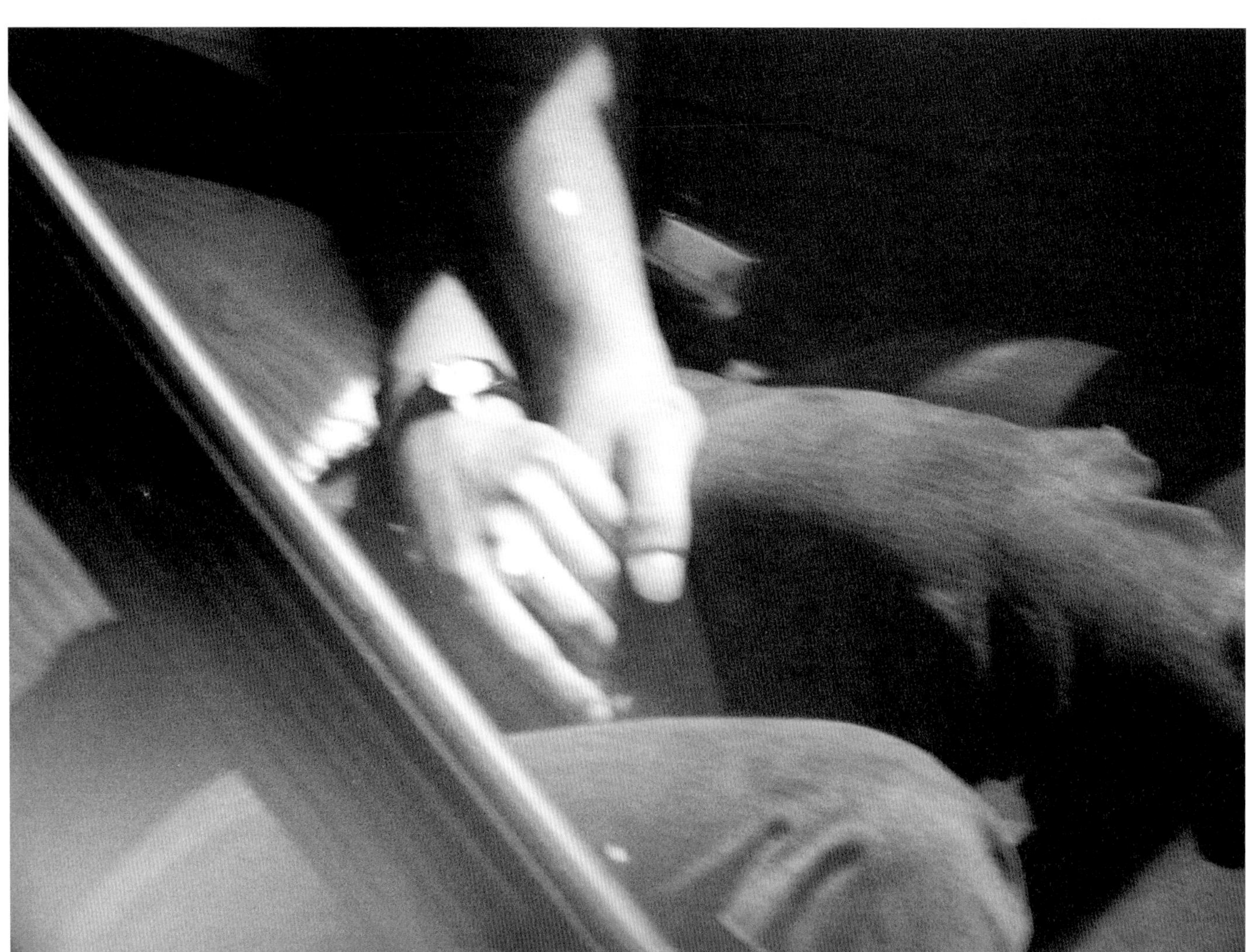

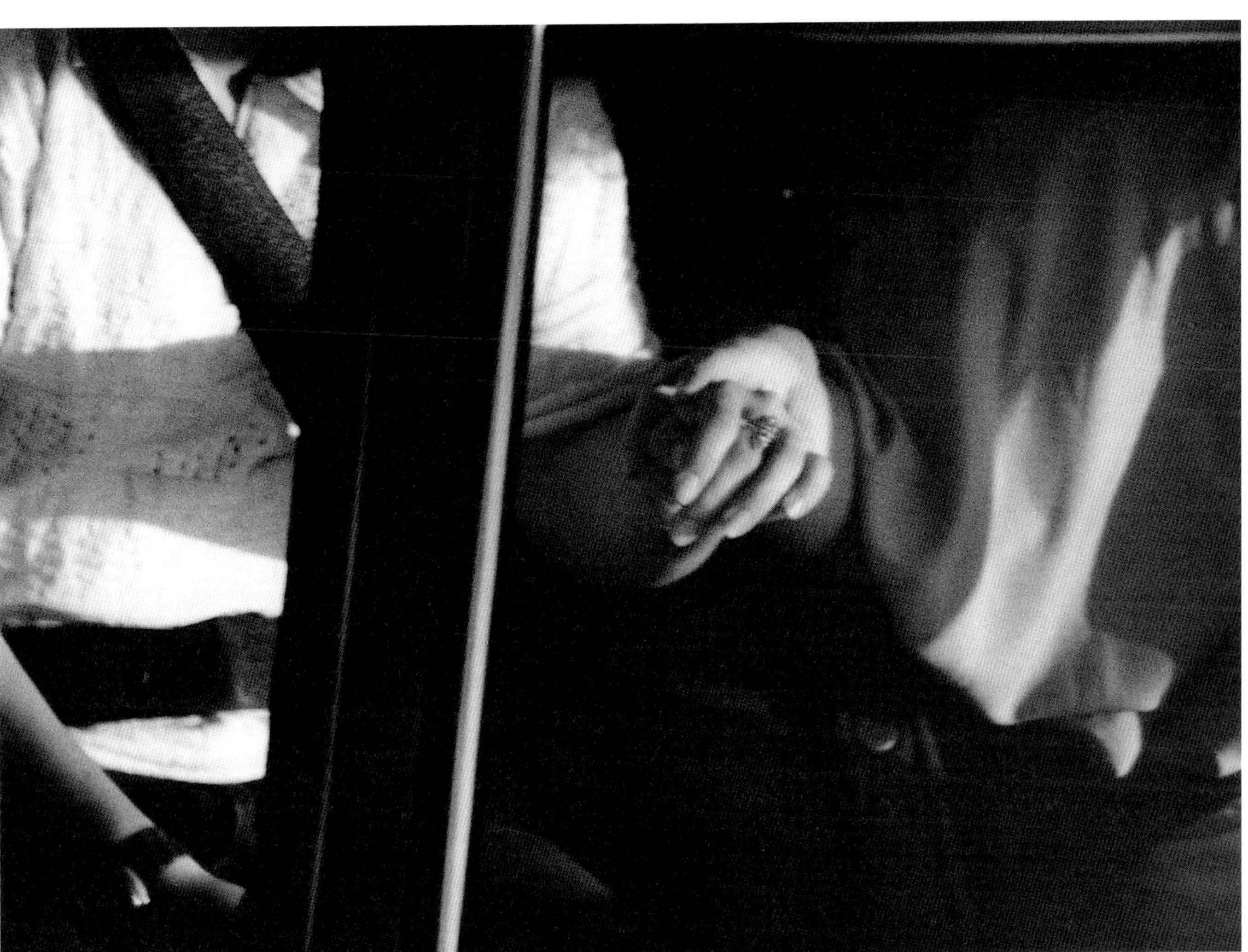

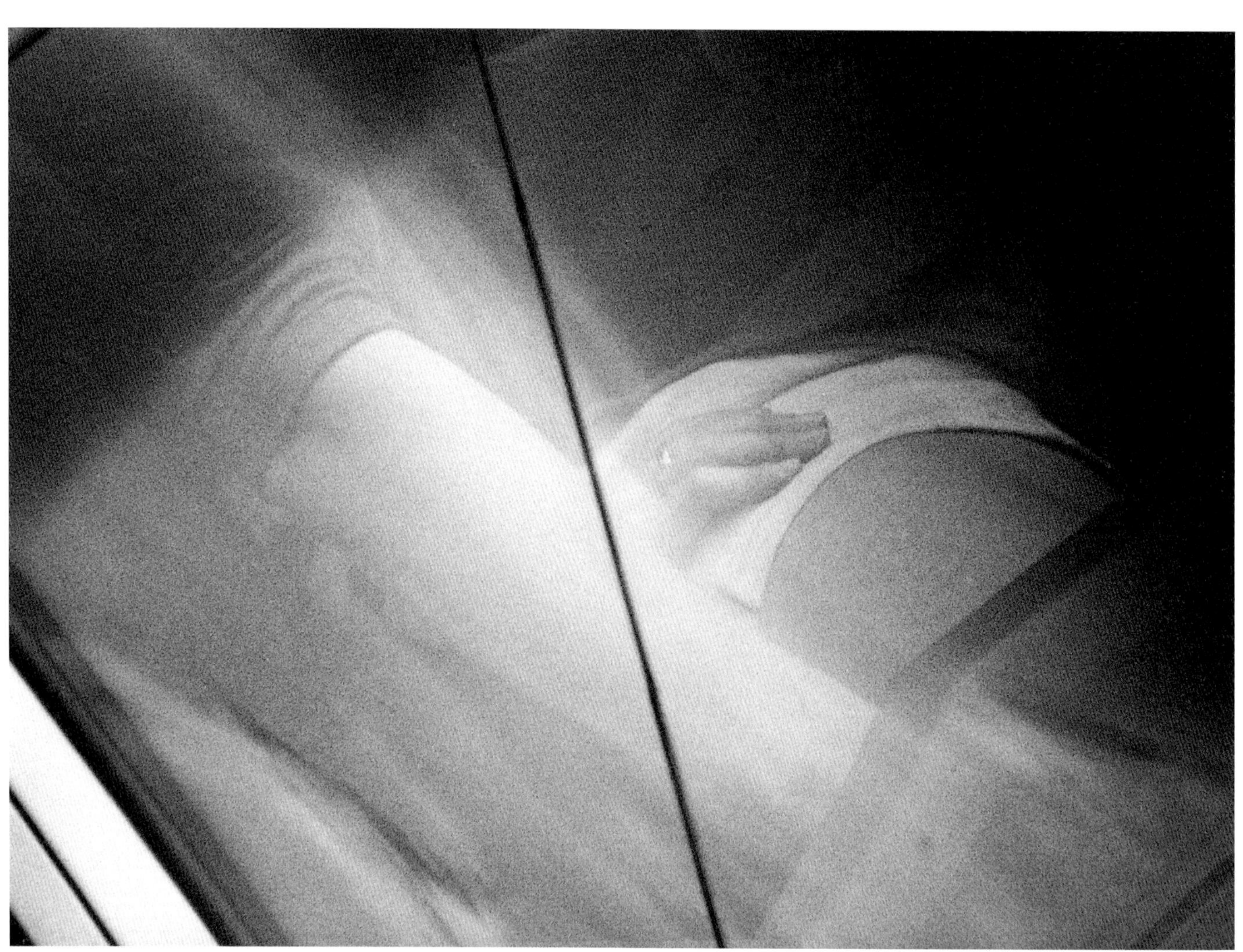

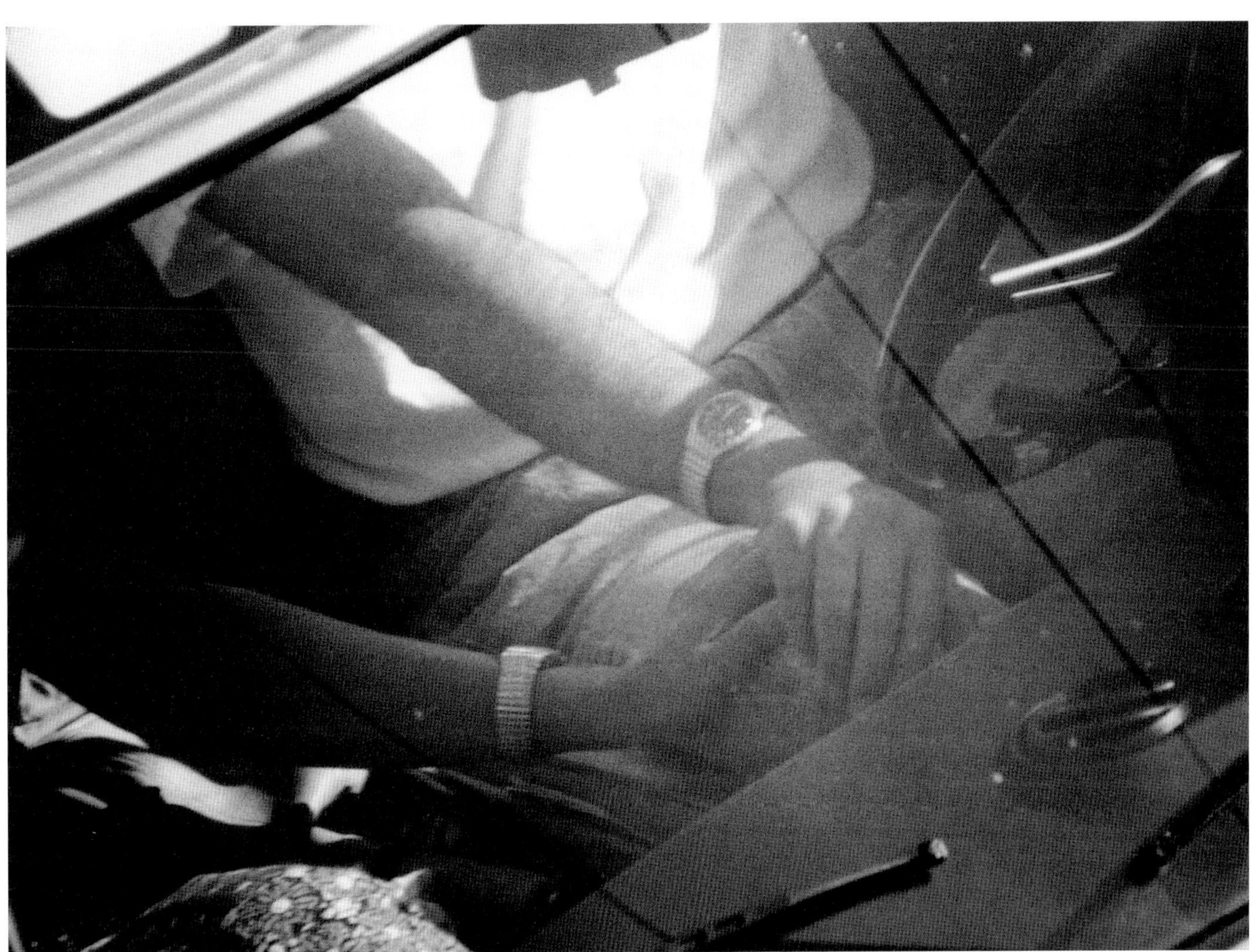

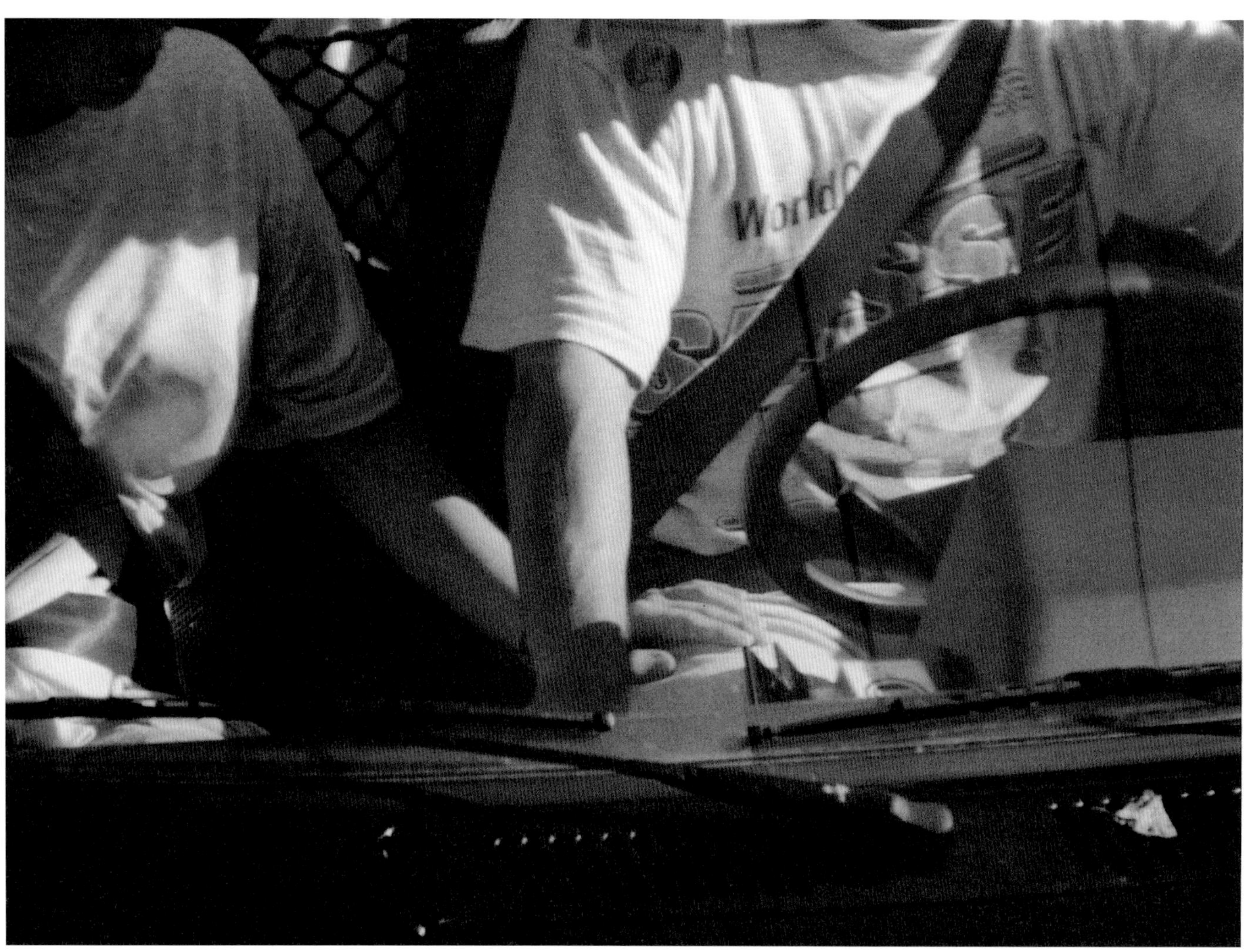

World C

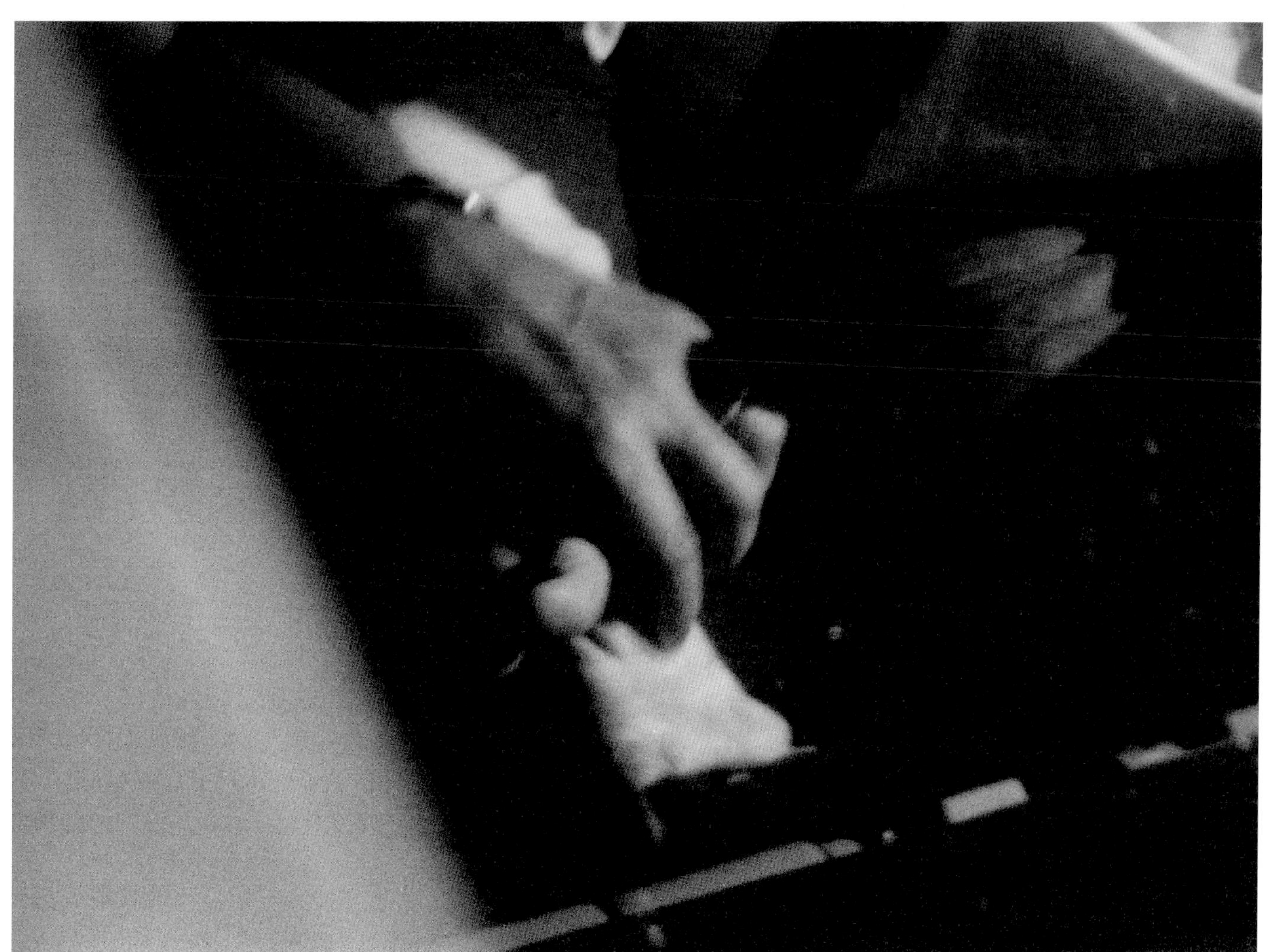

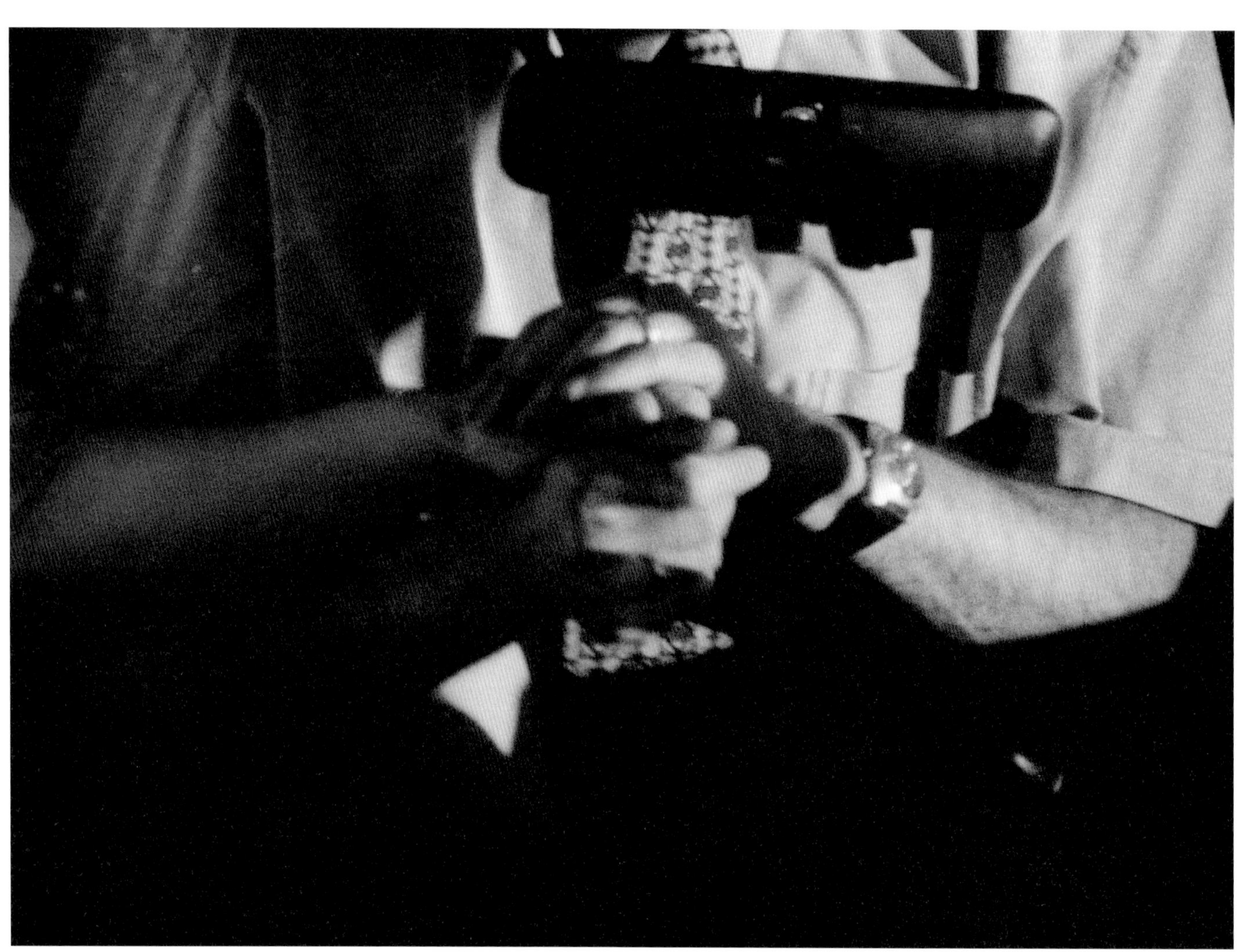

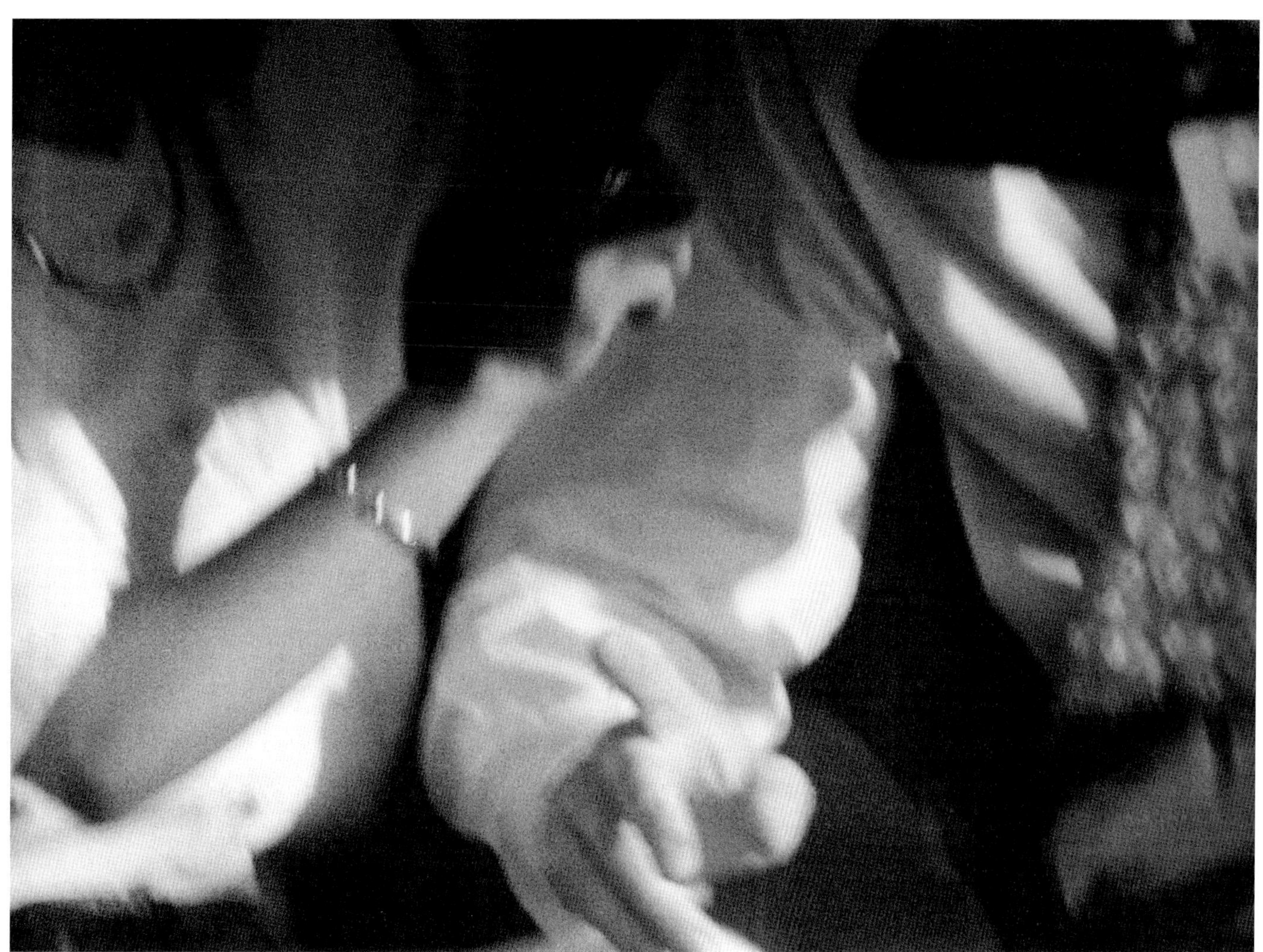

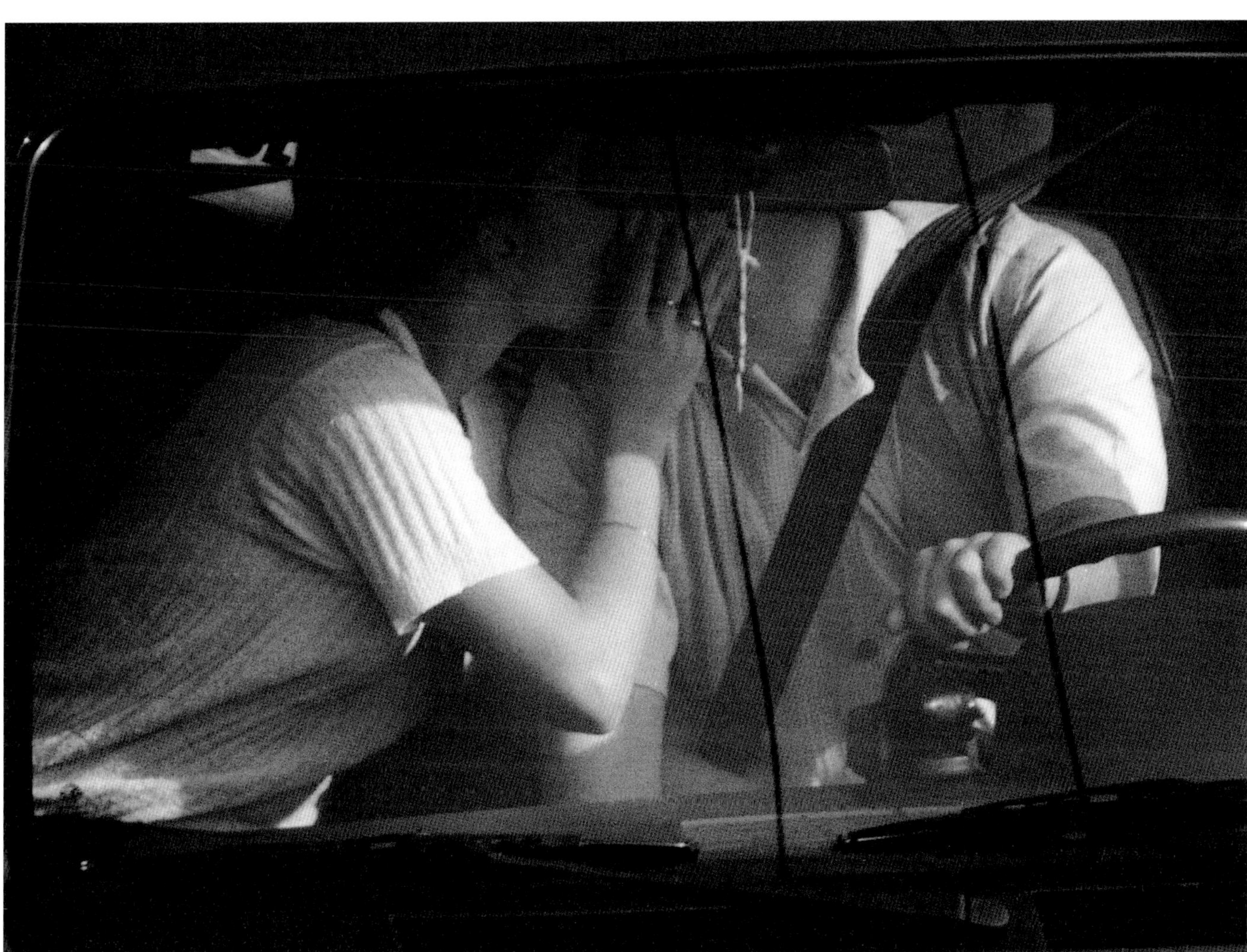

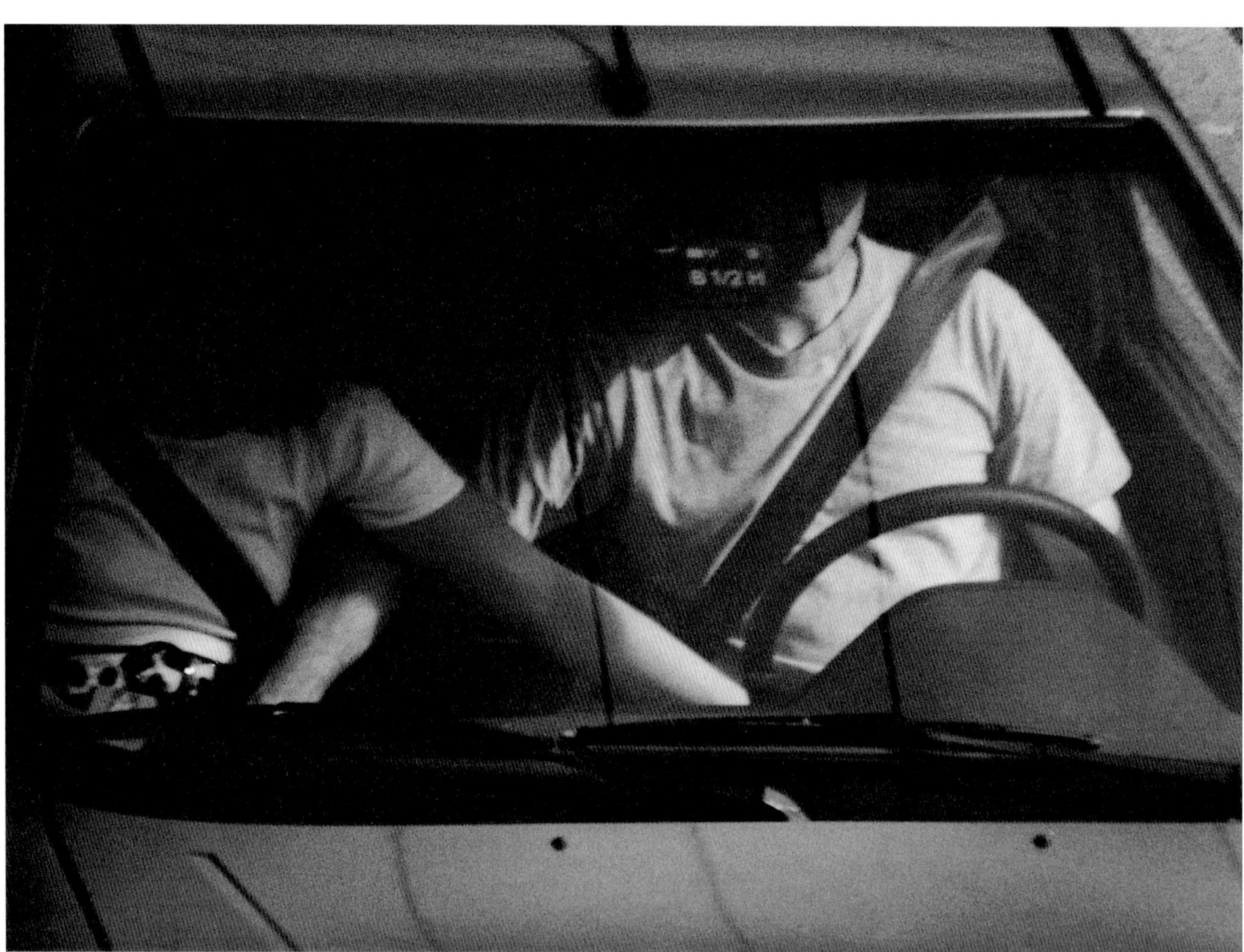

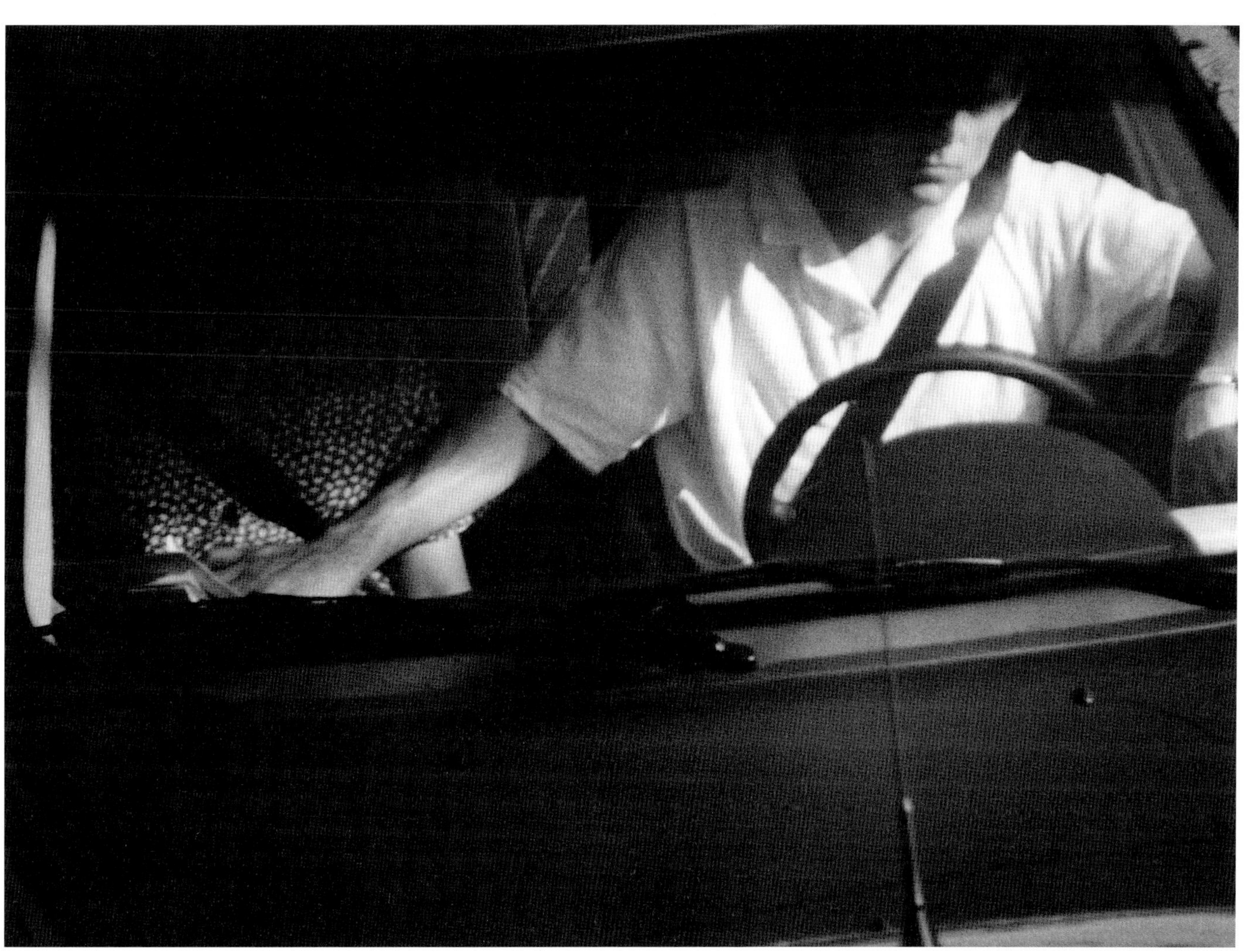

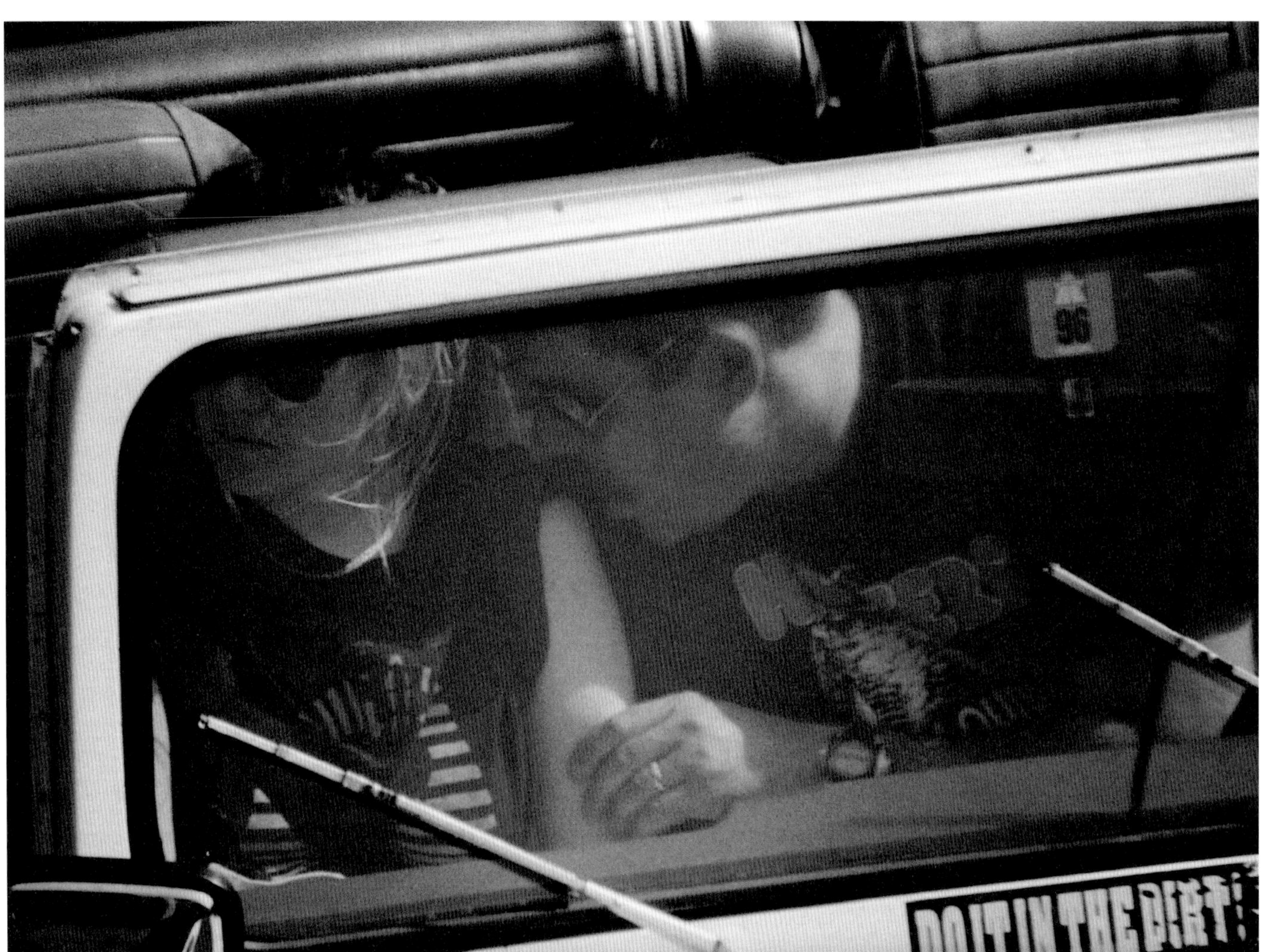

DO IT IN THE DIRT

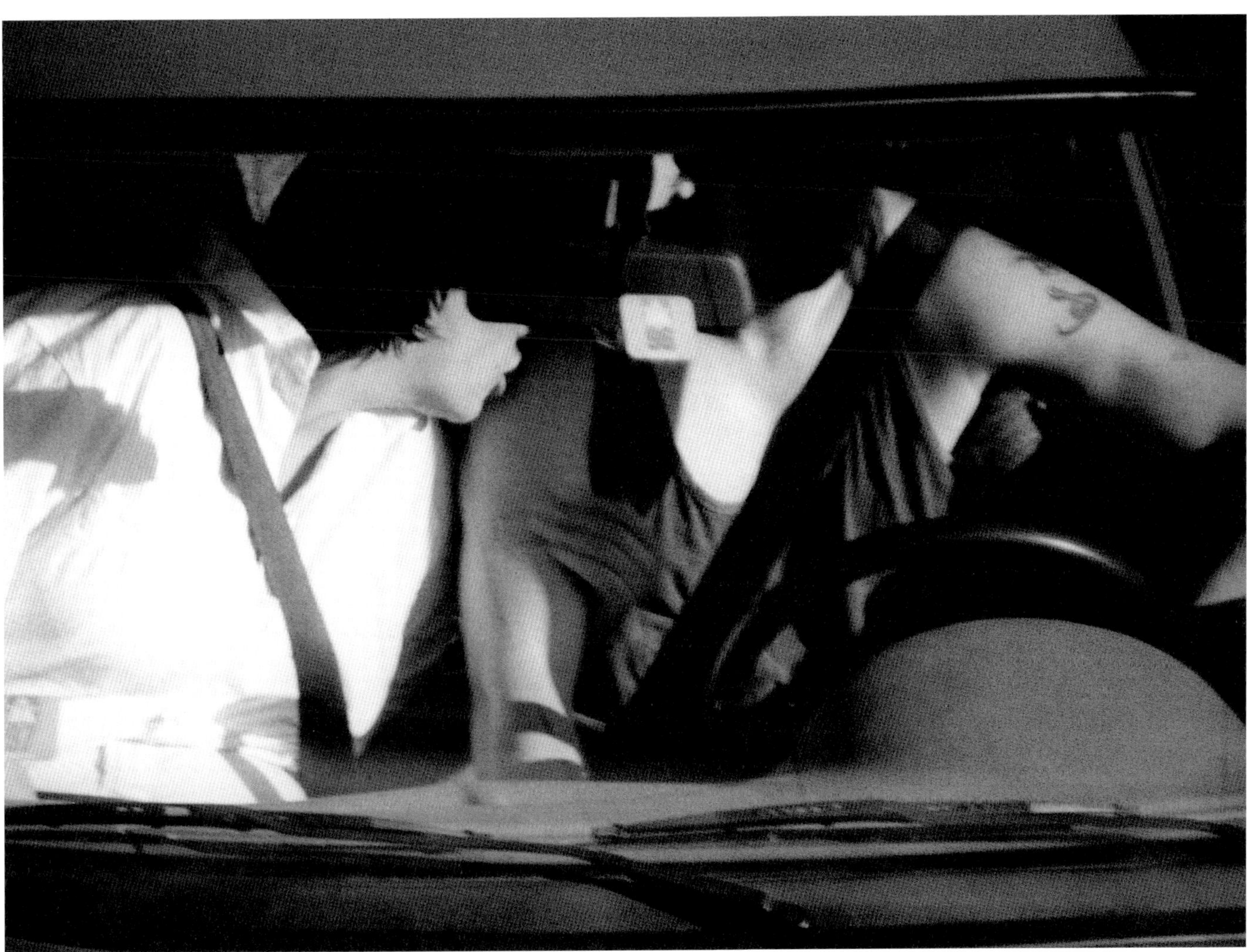

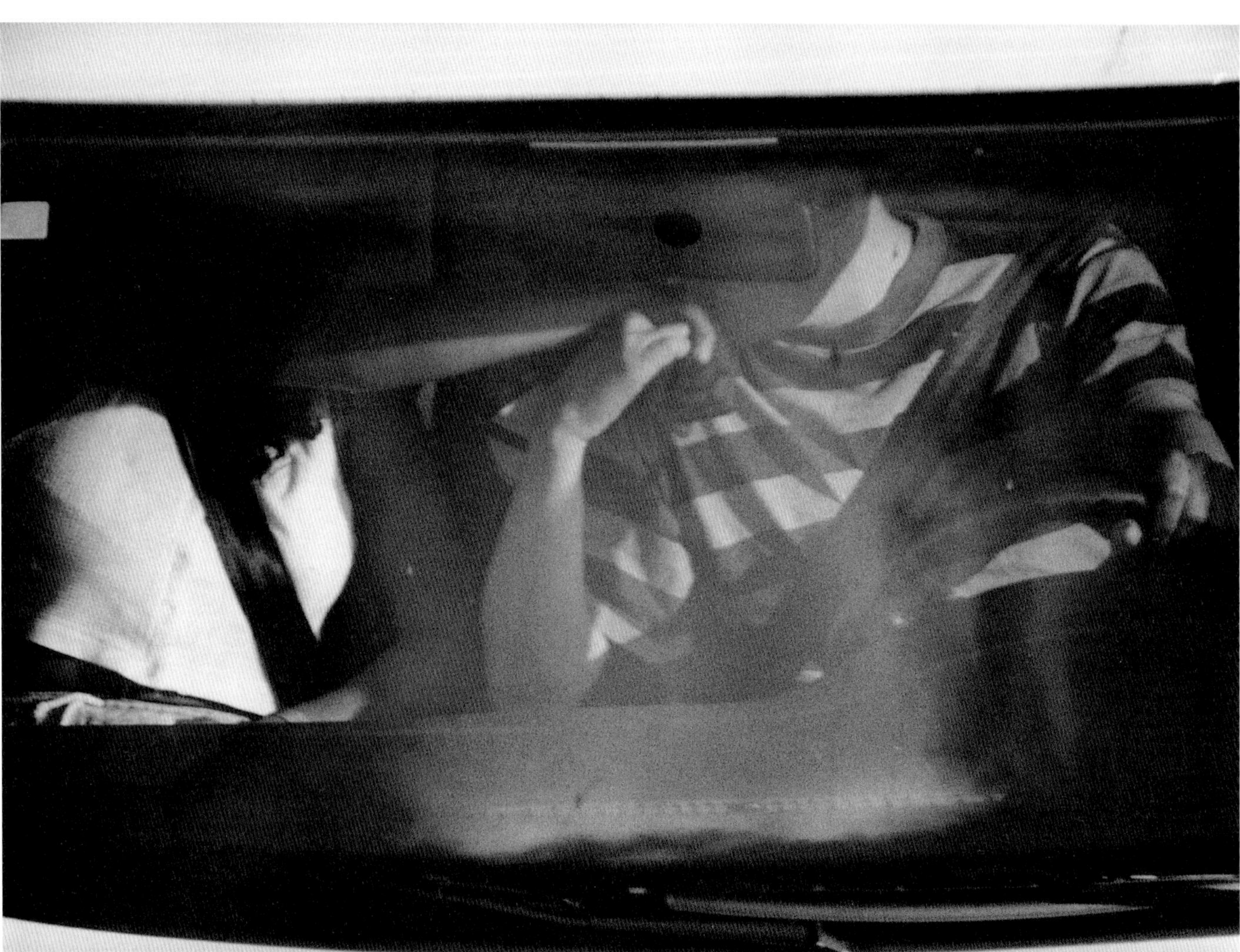

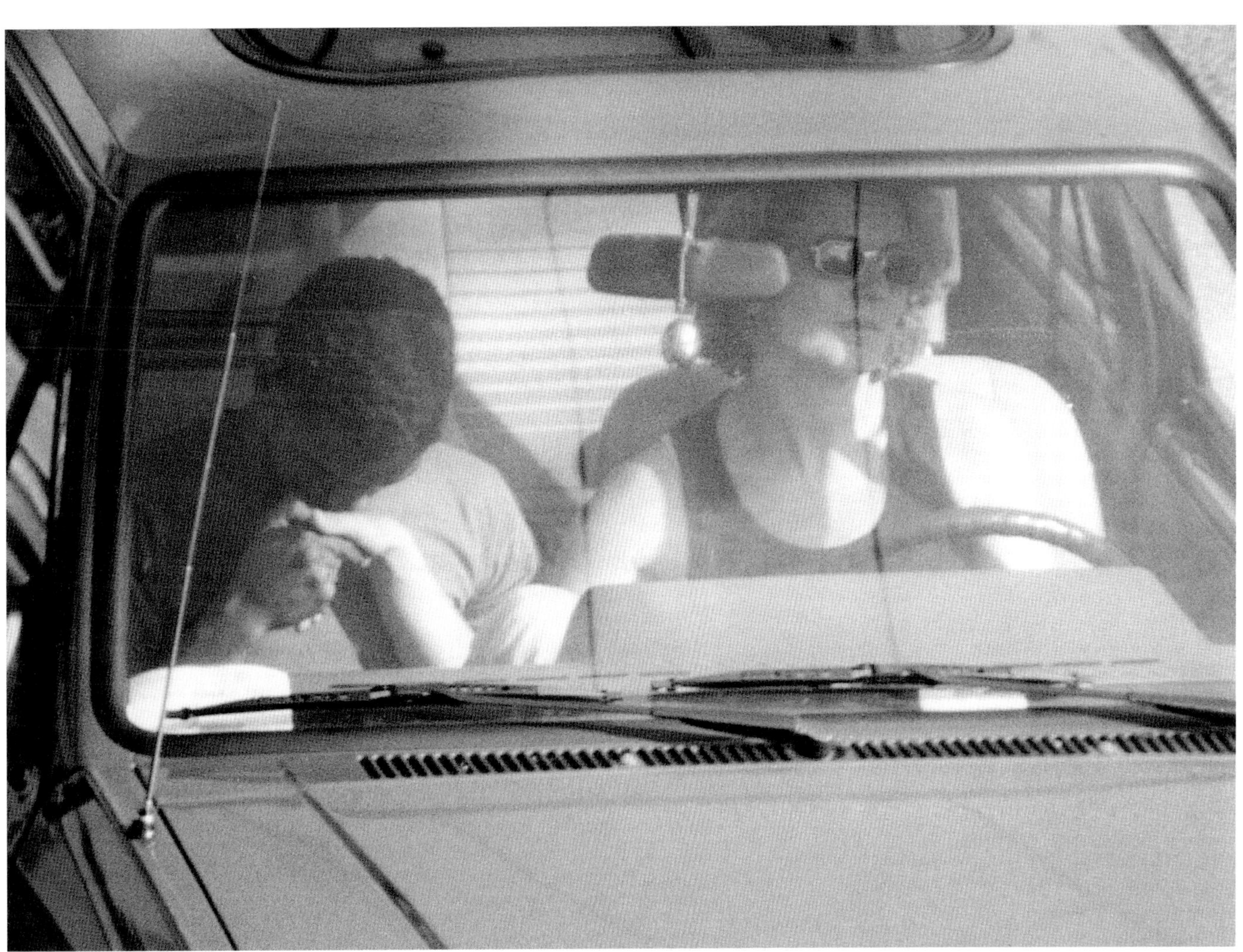

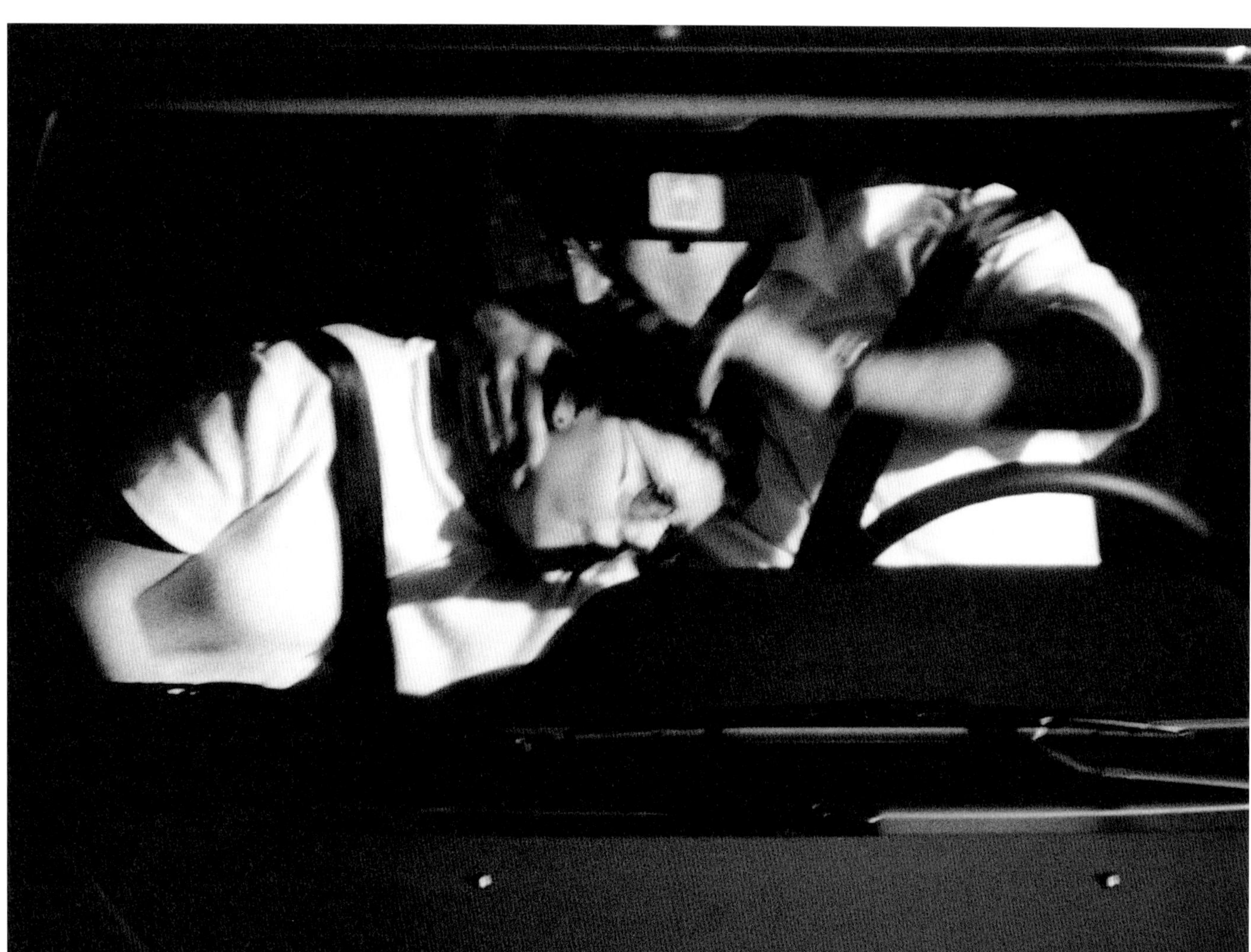

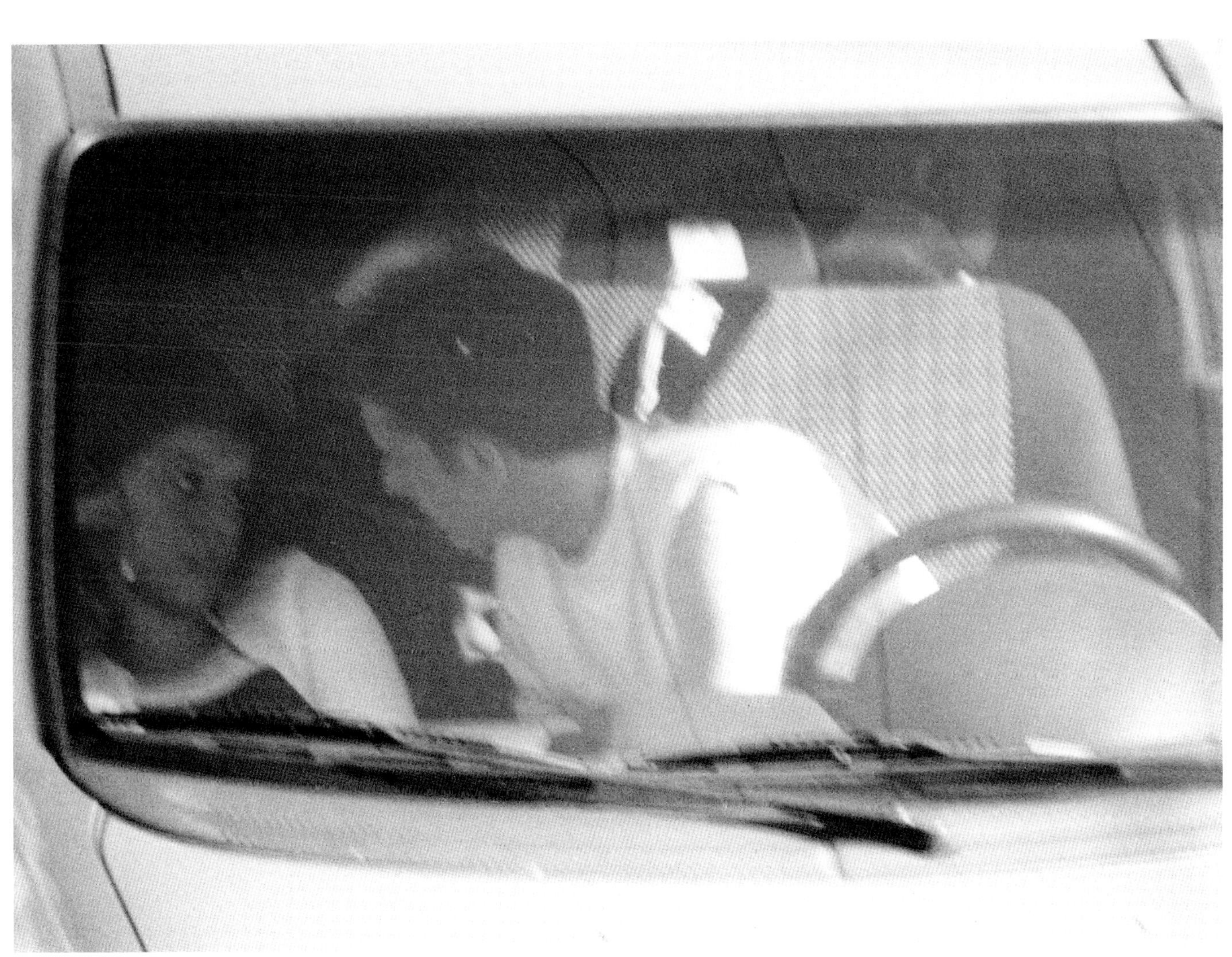

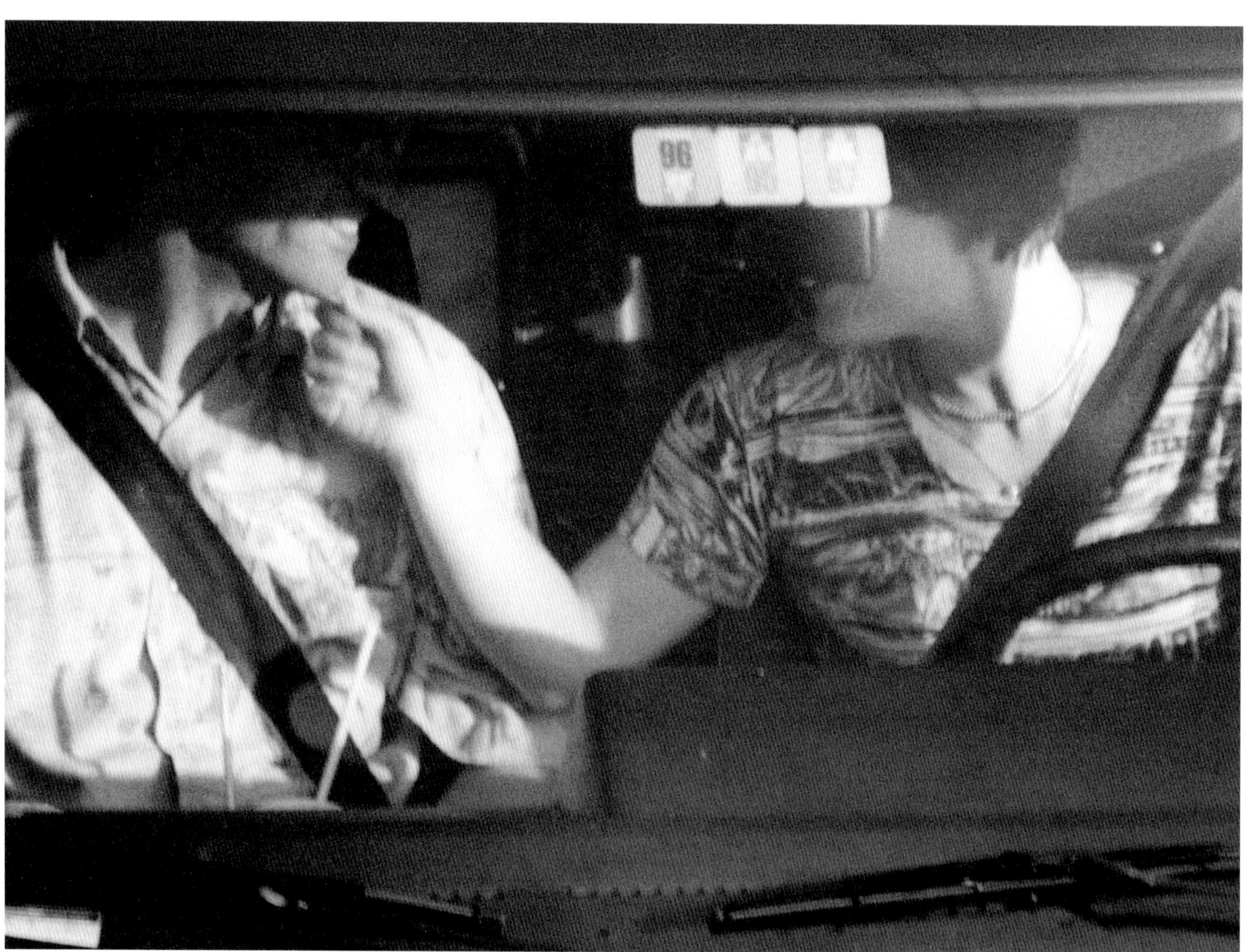

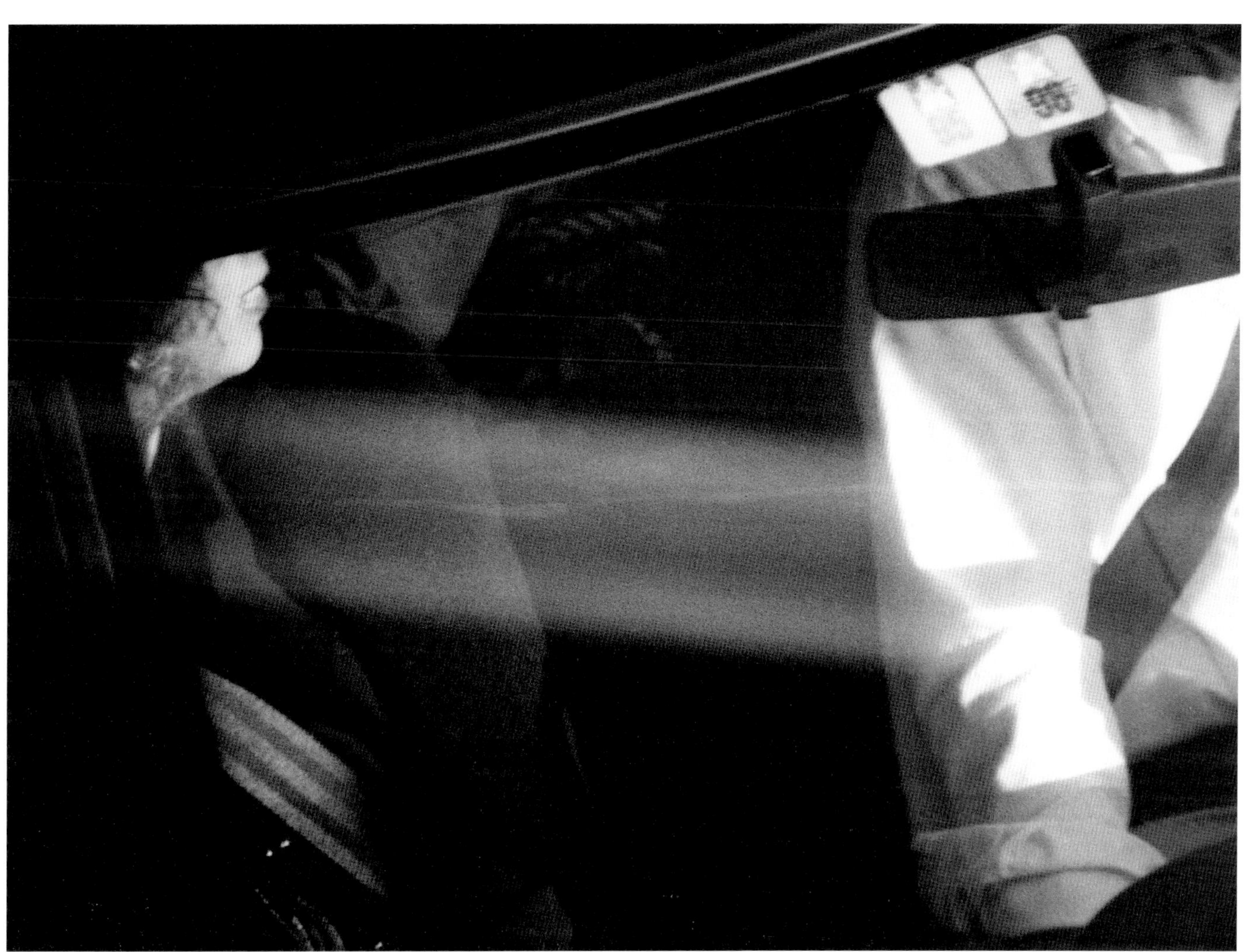

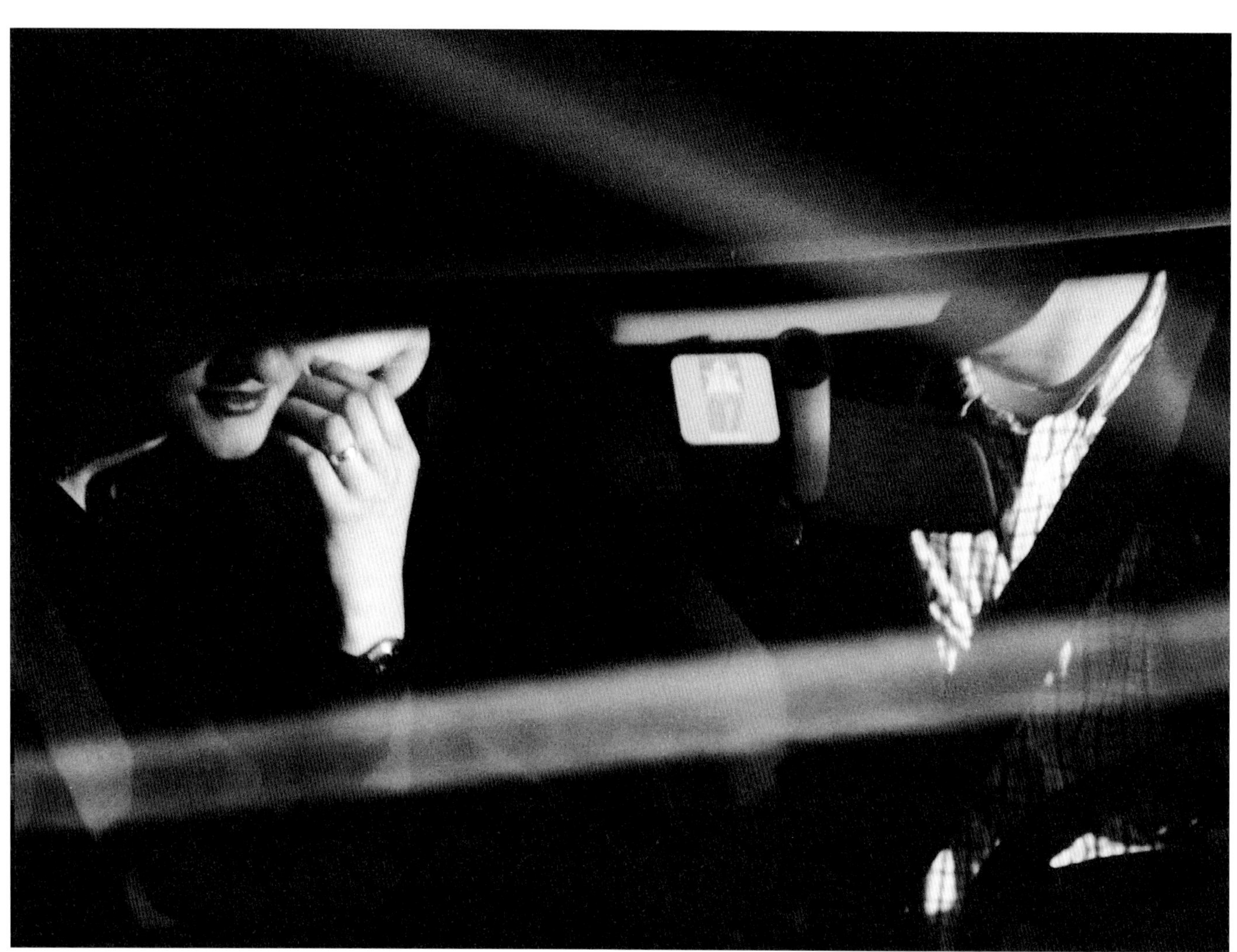

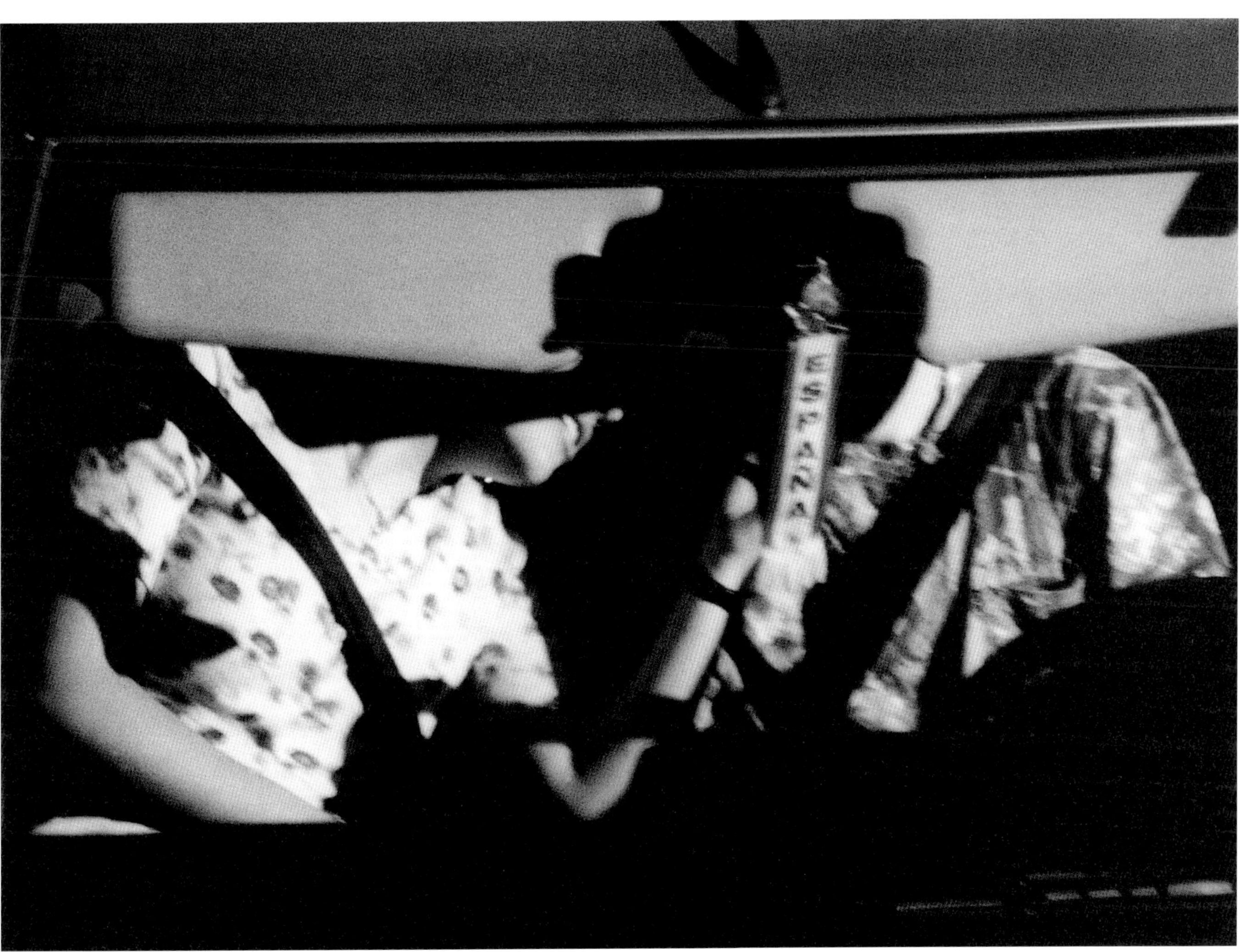

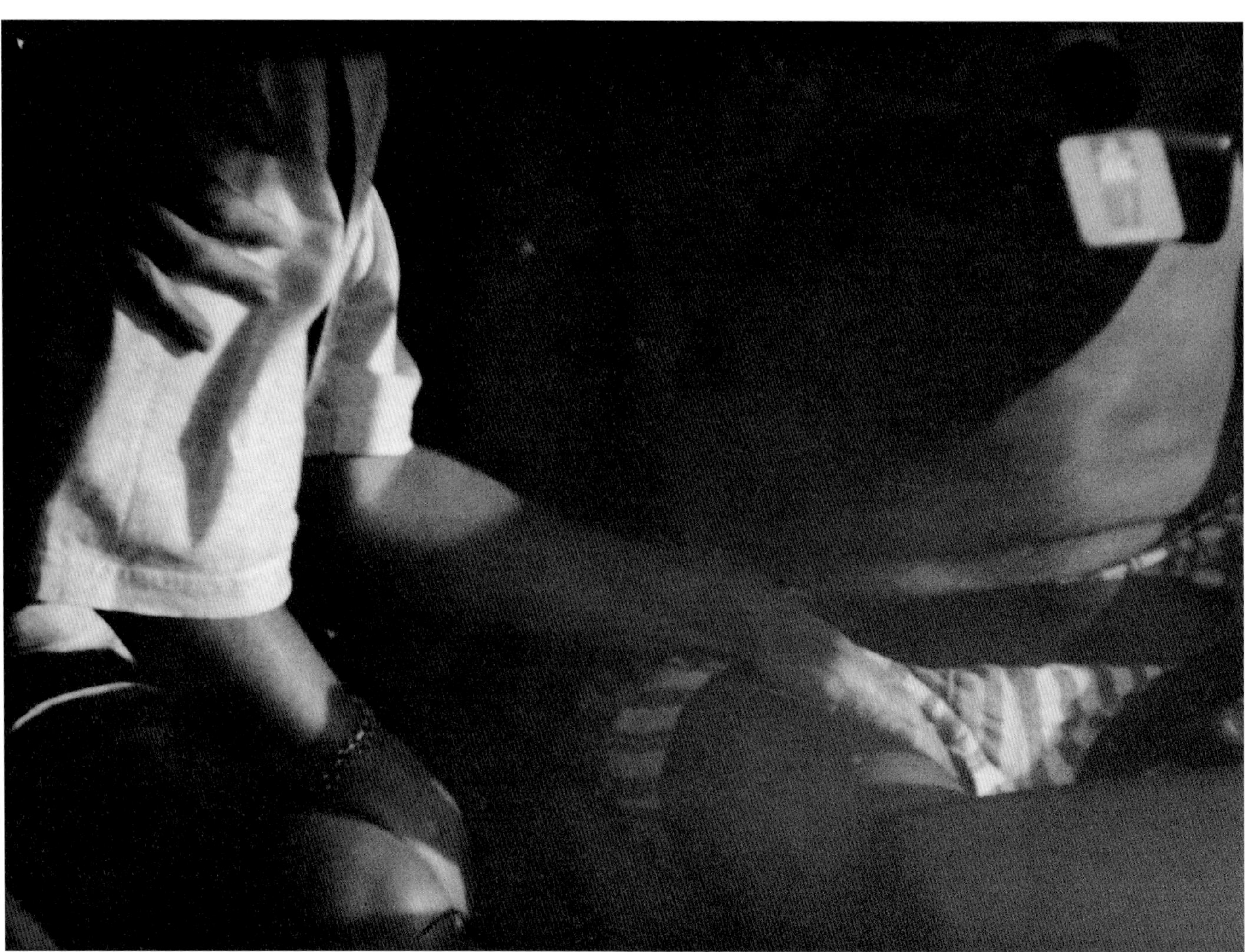

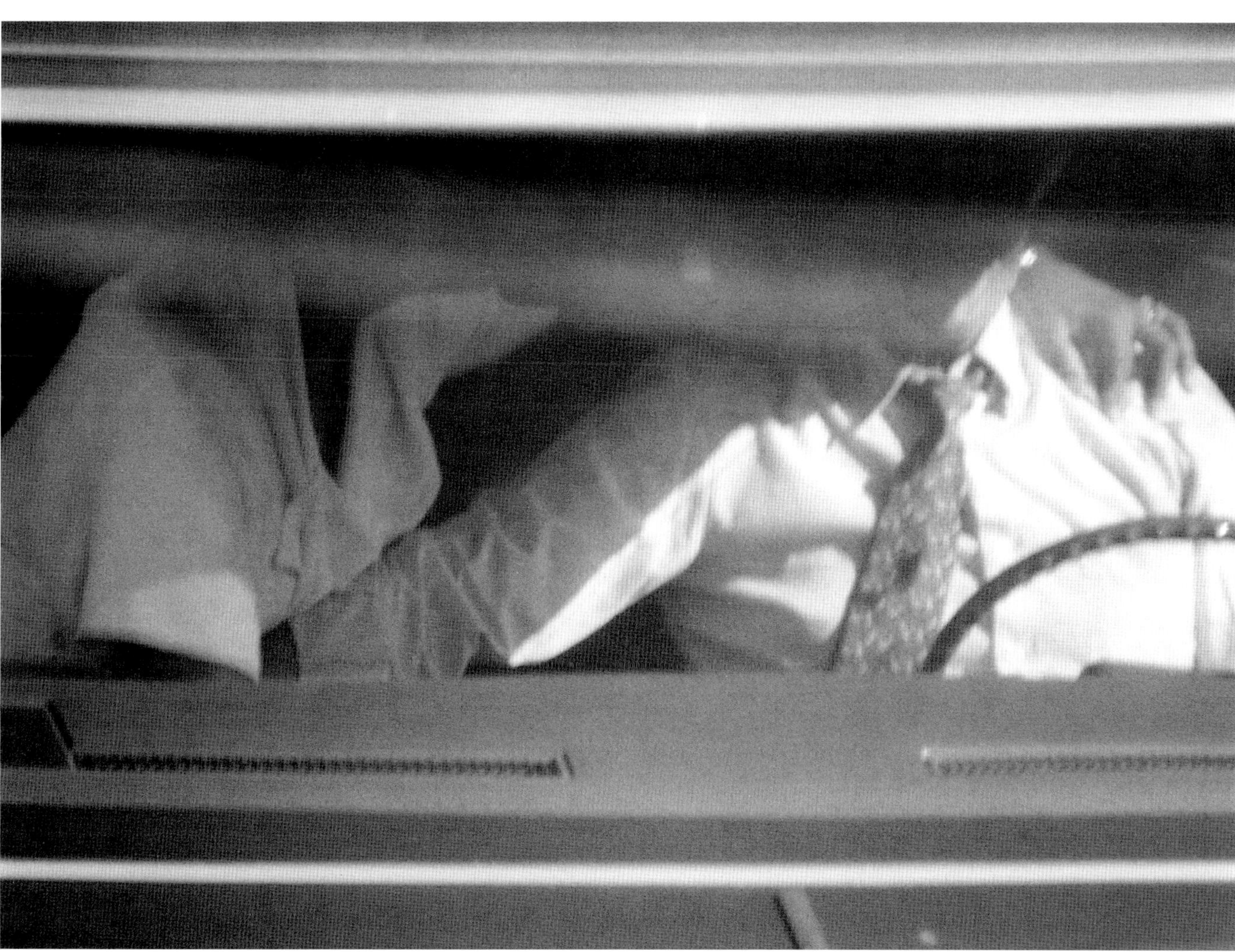

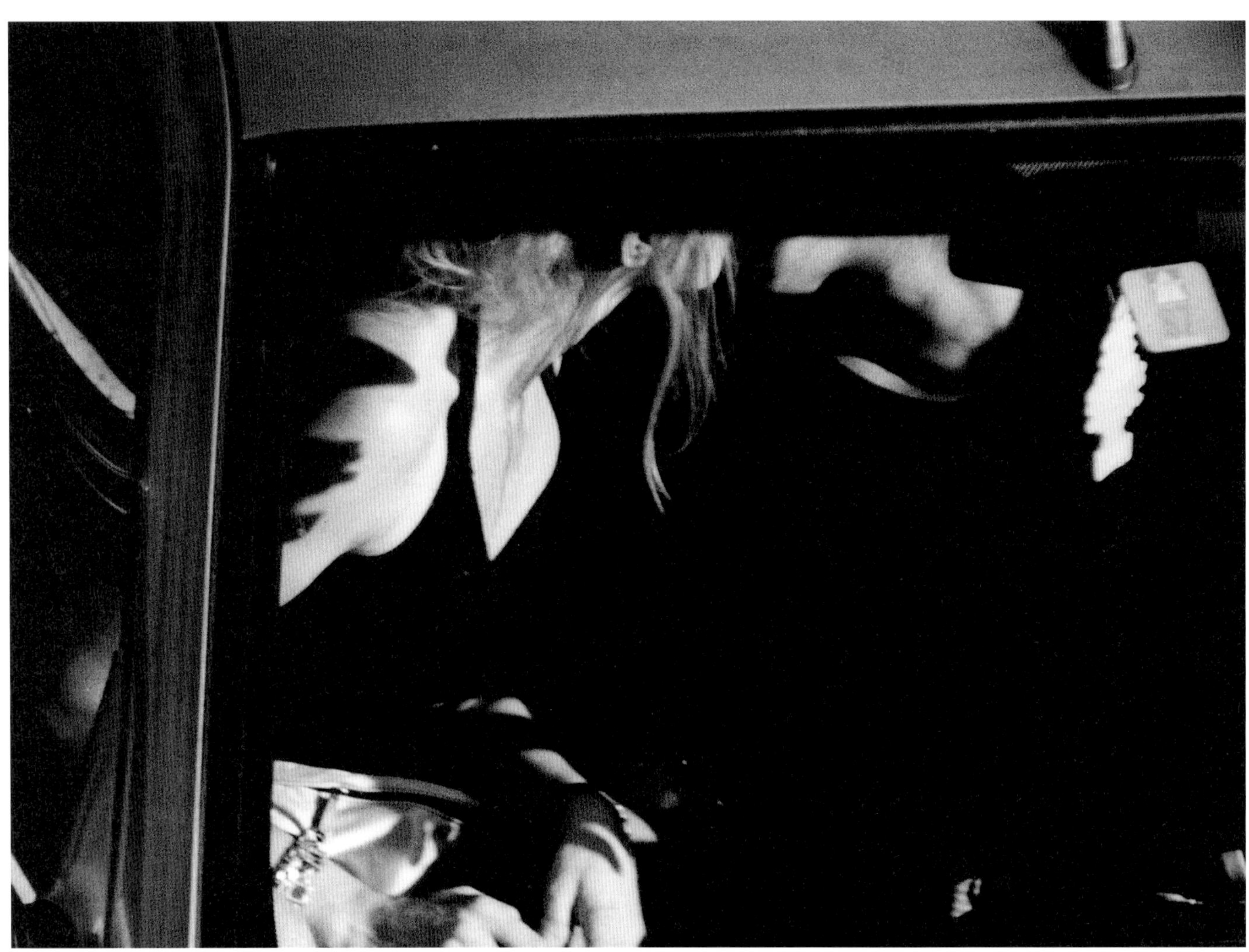

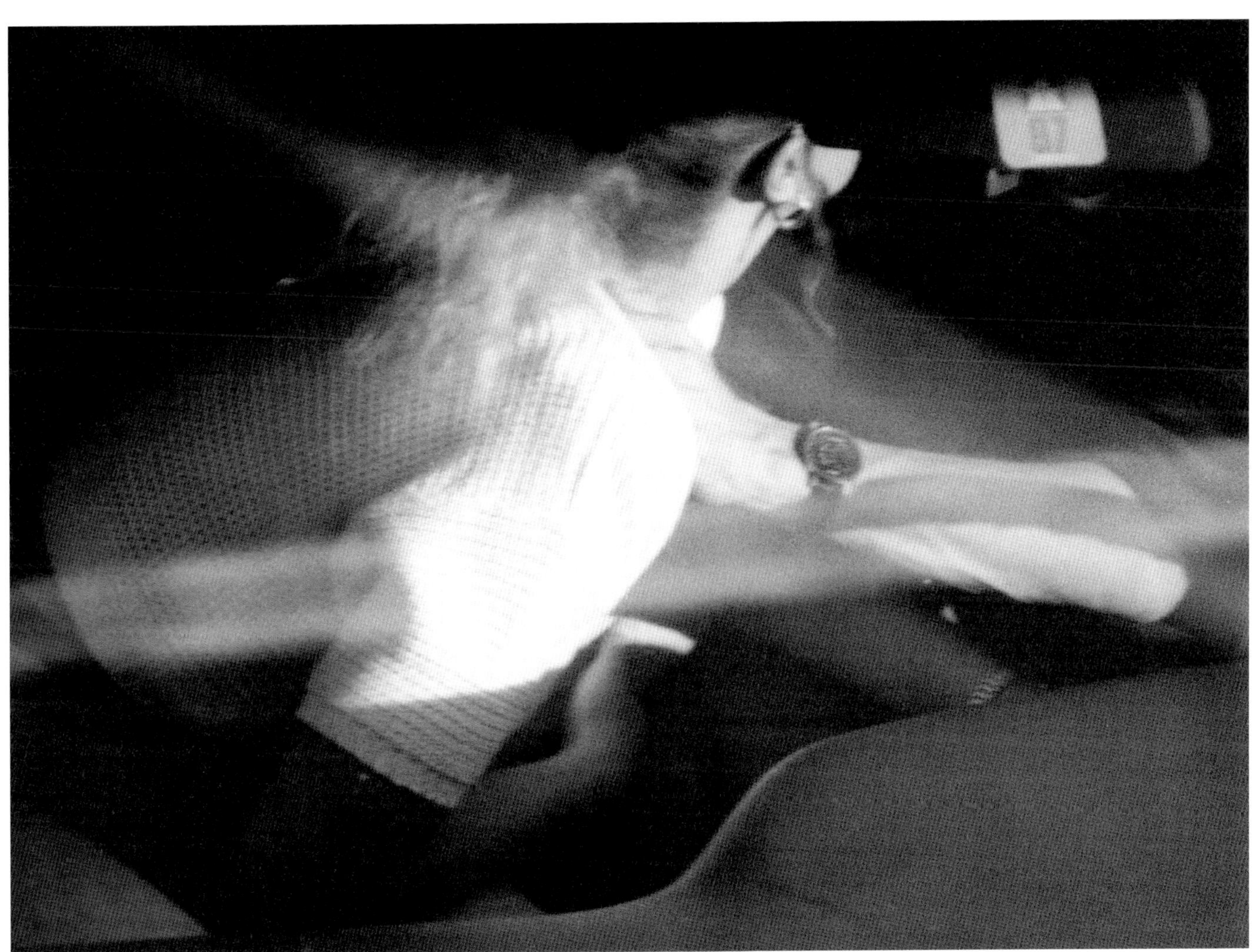

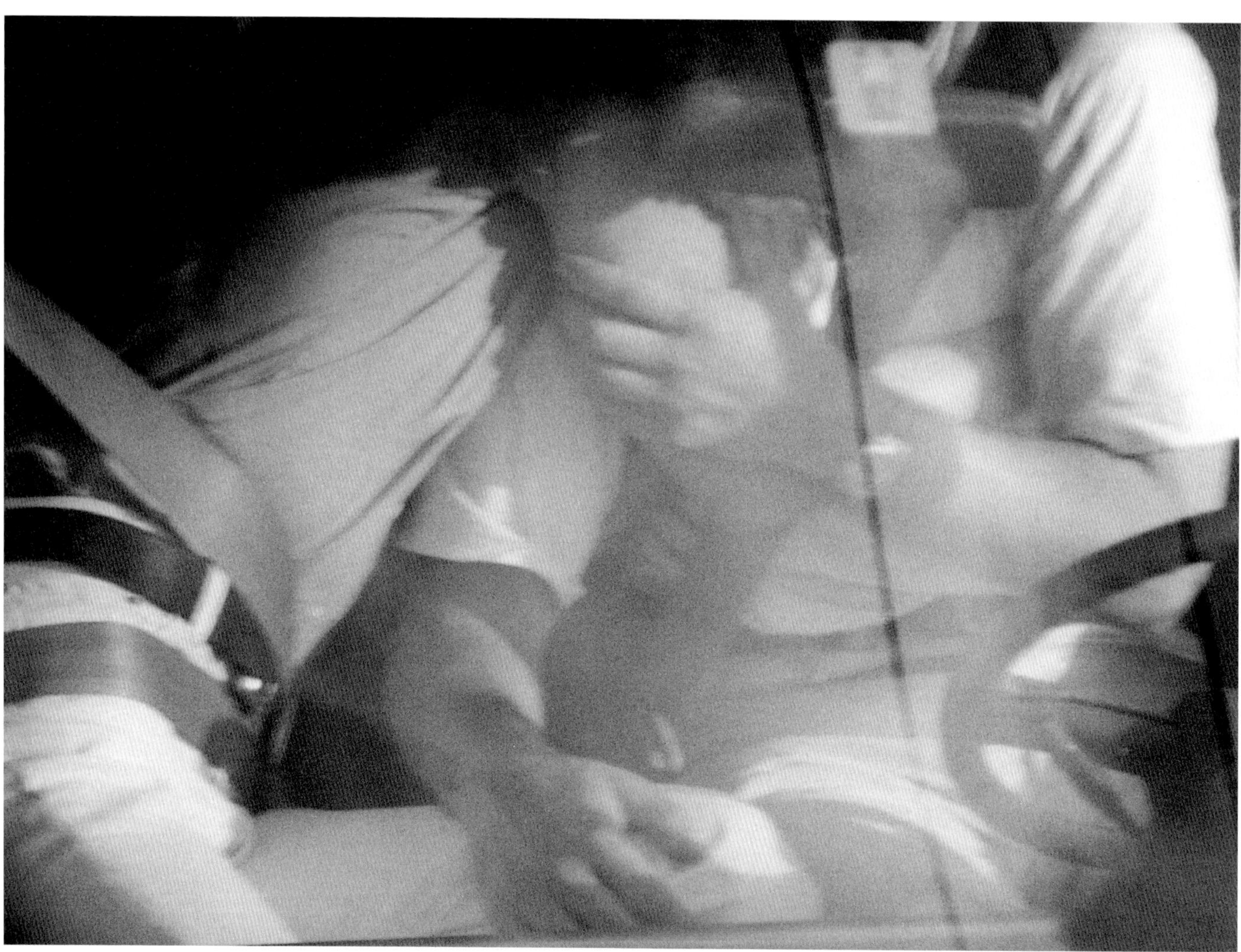

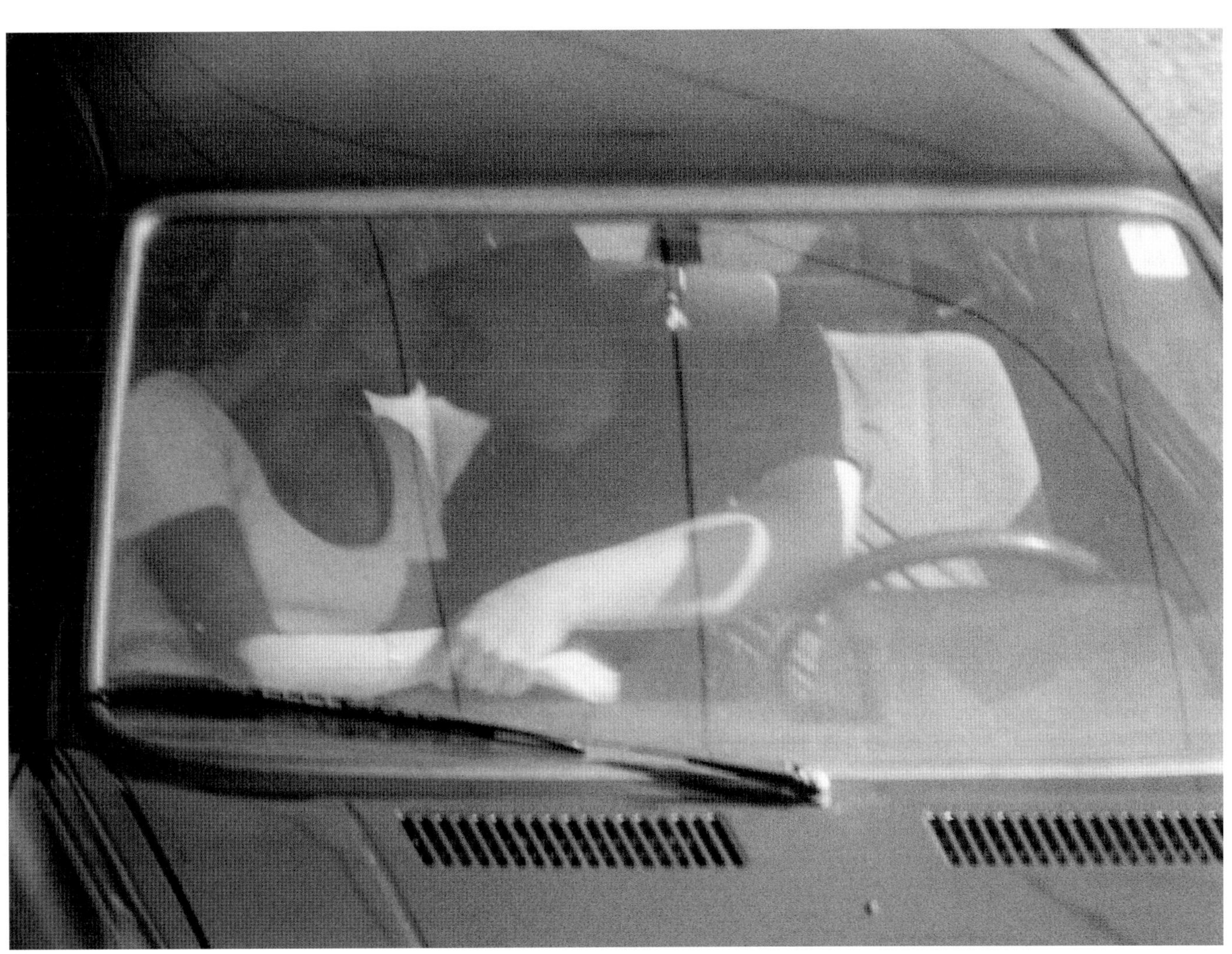

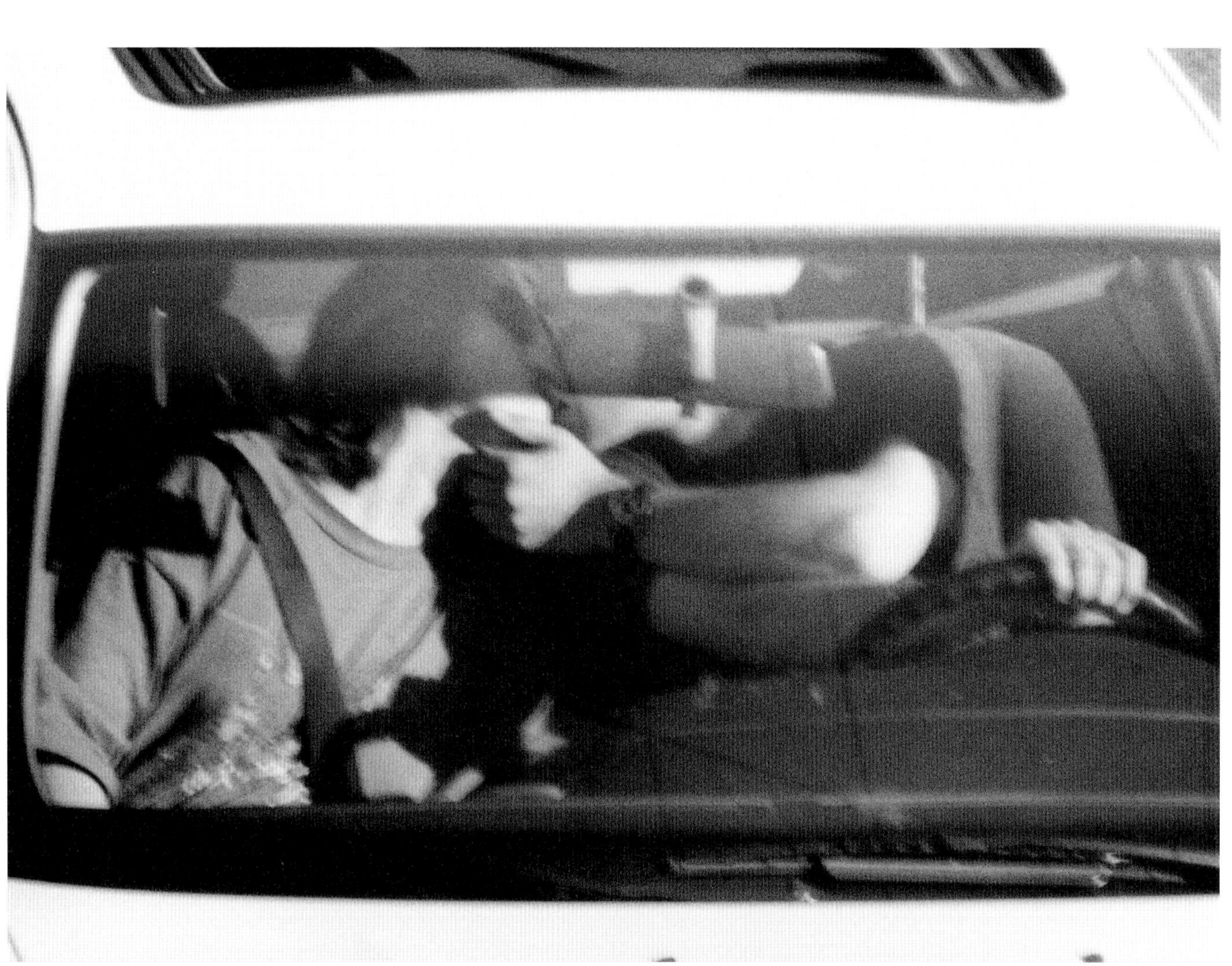

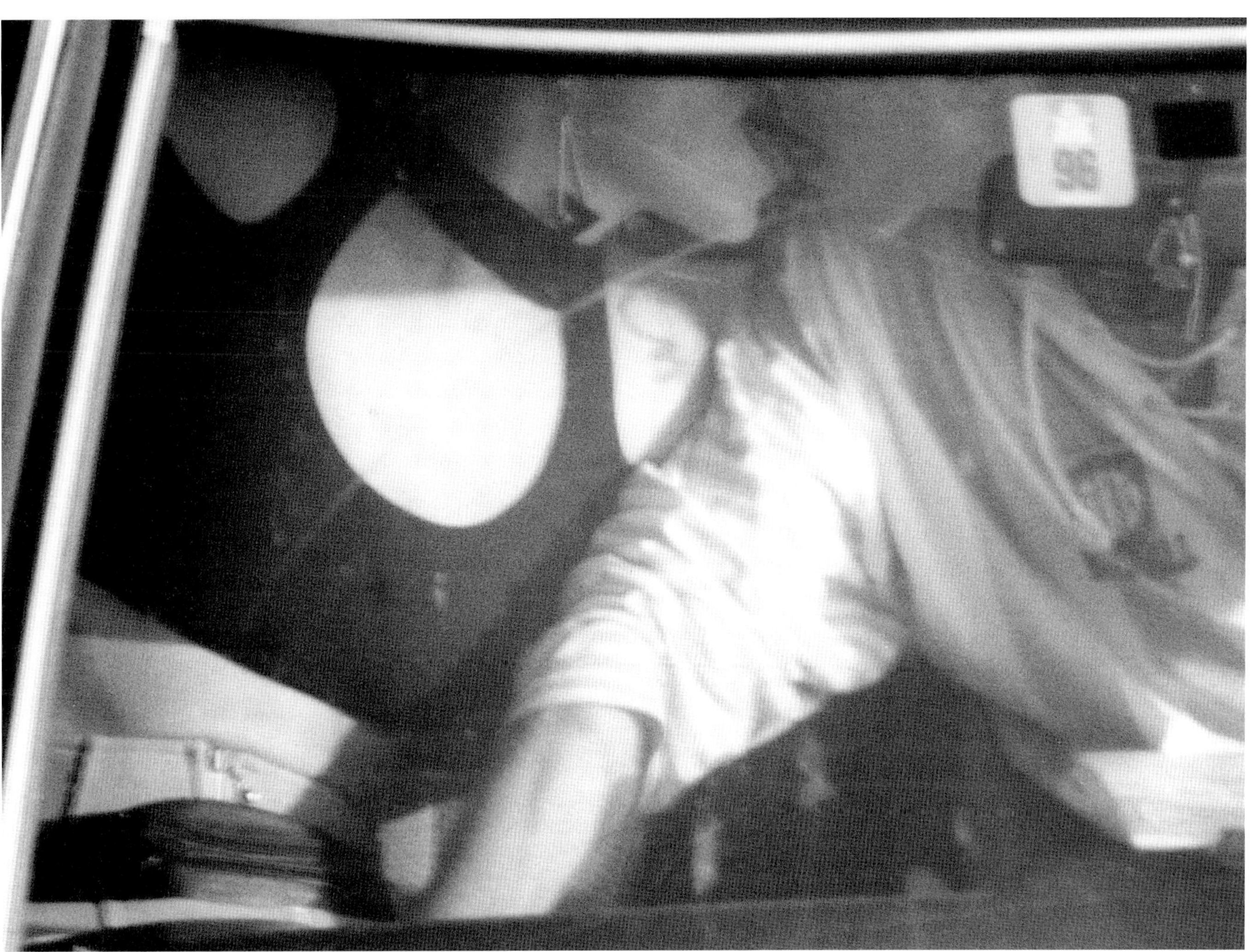

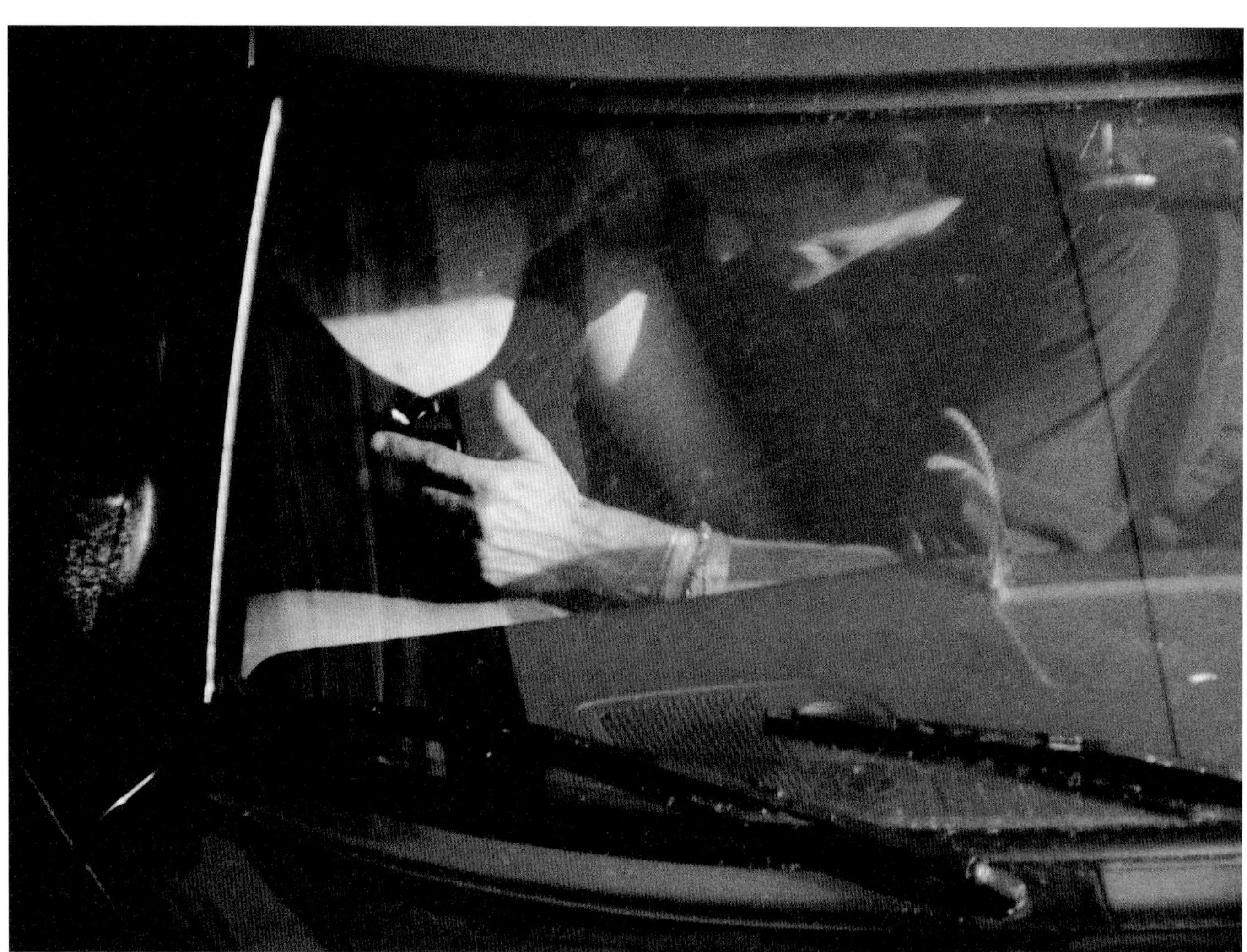

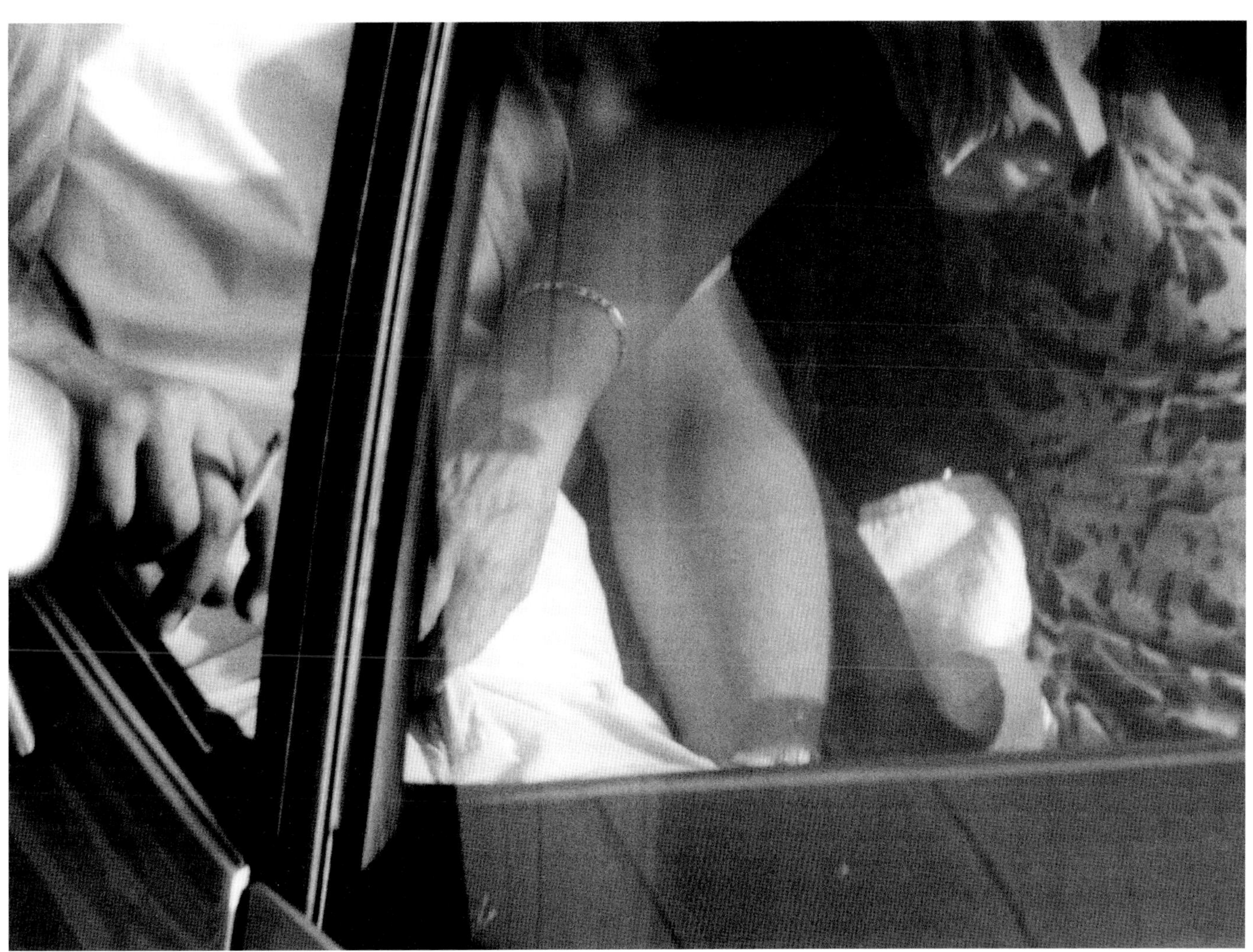

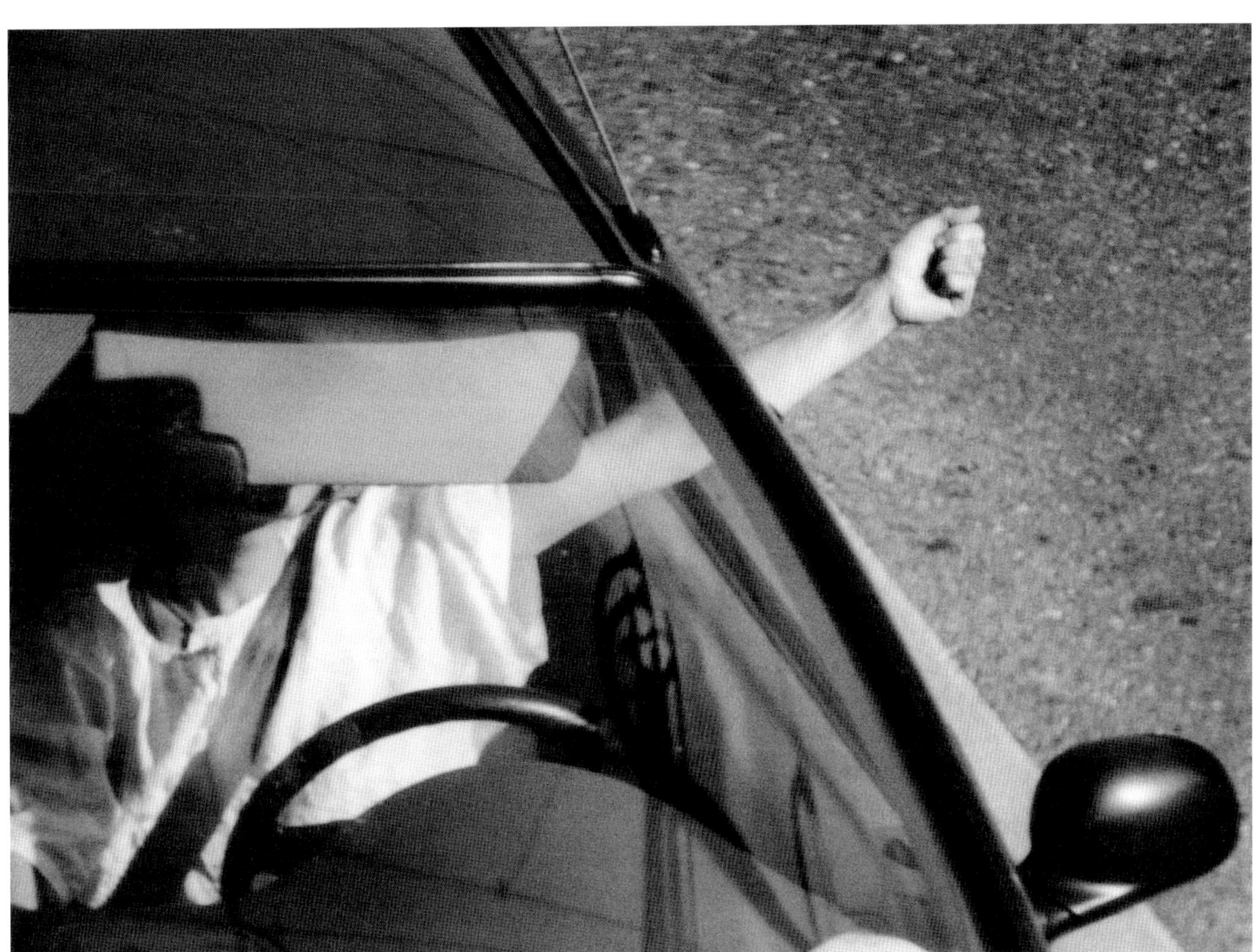

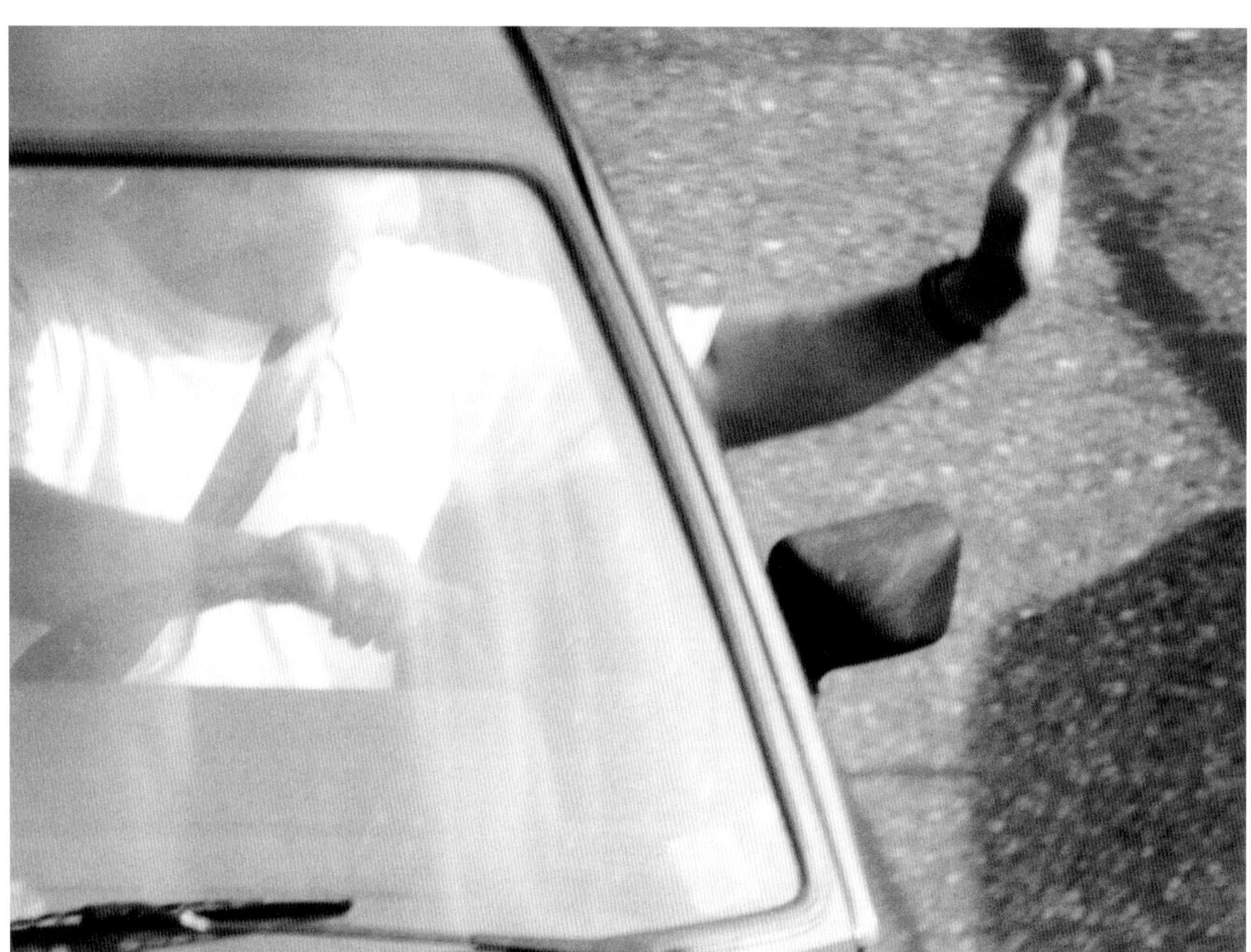

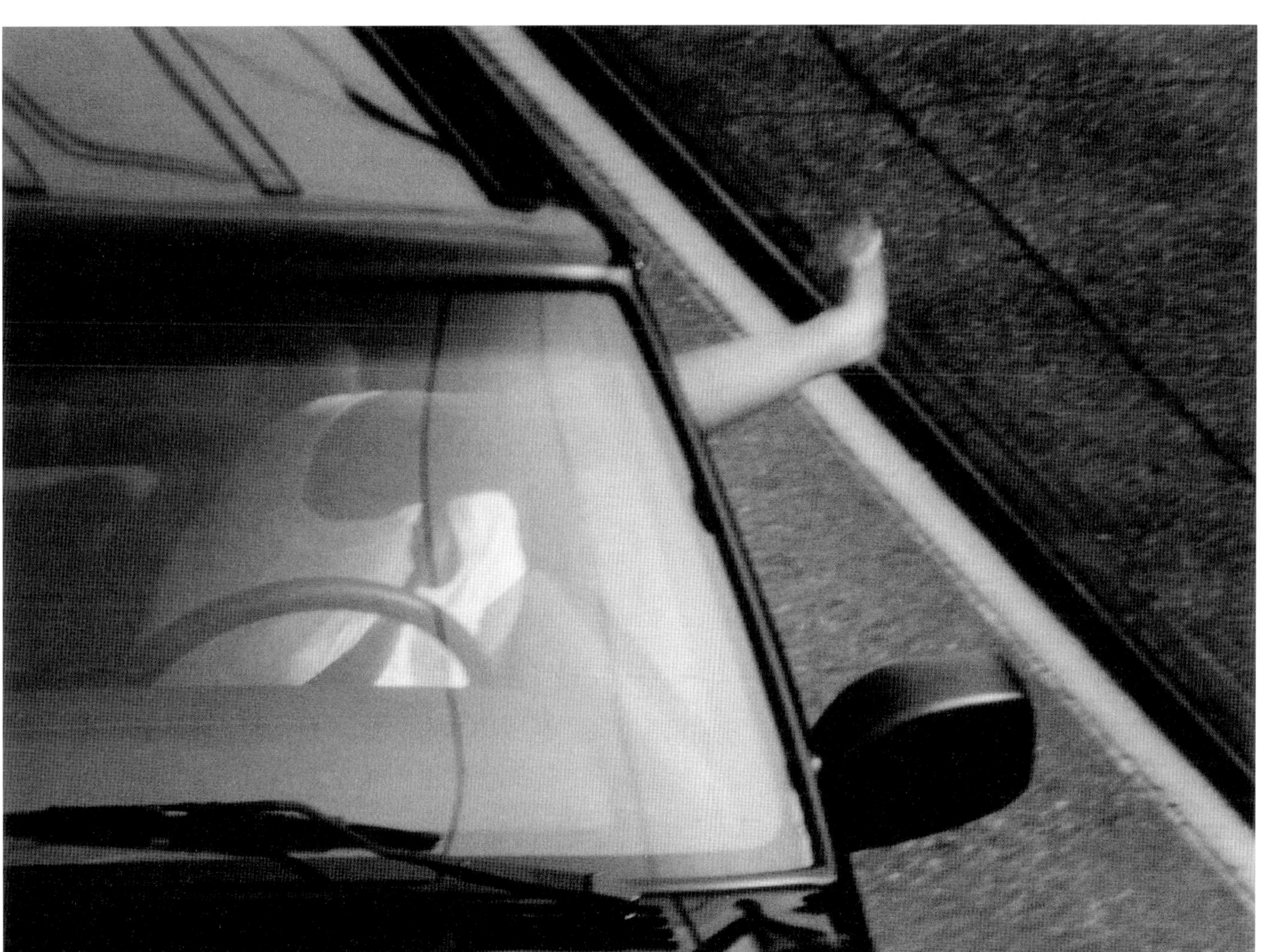

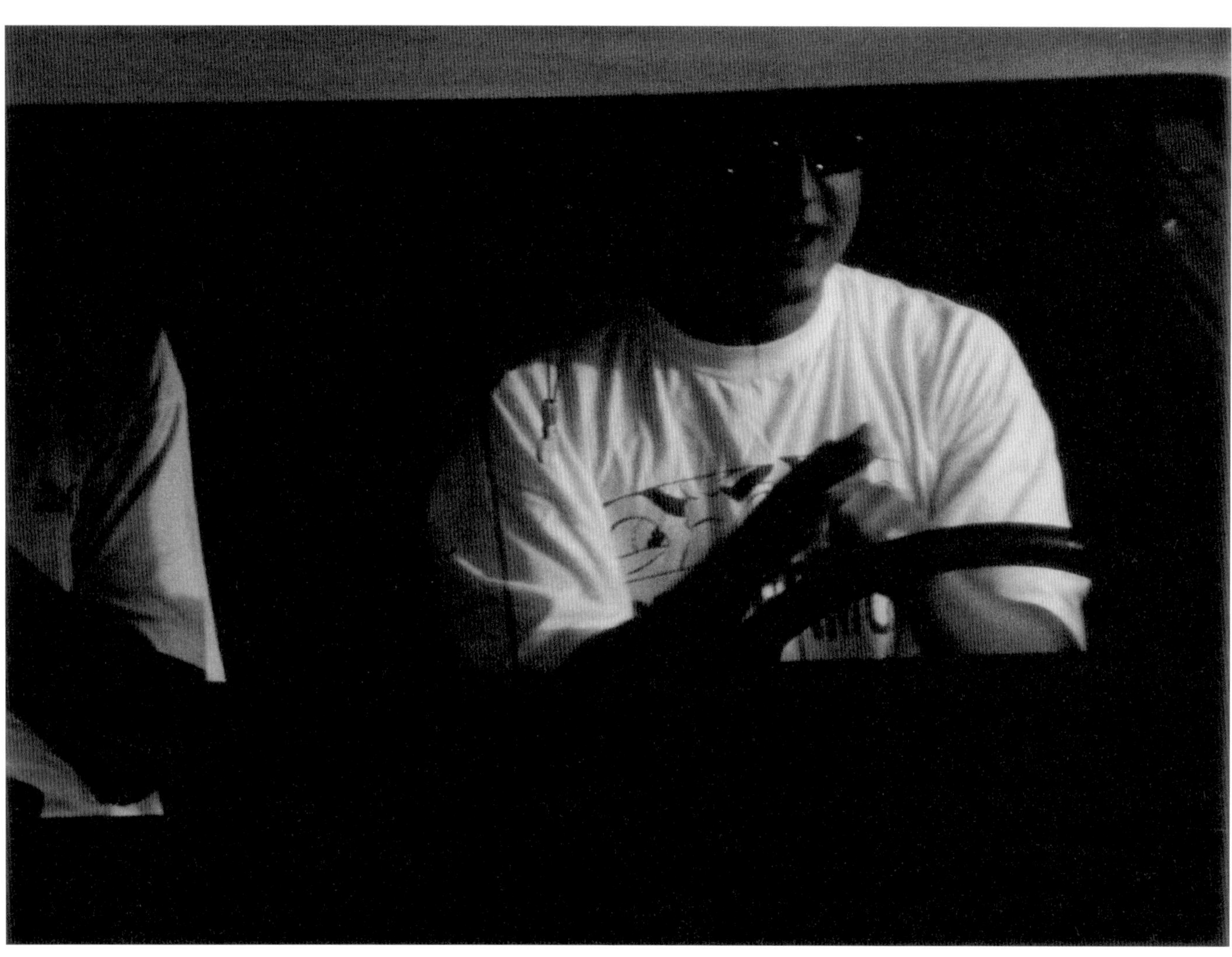

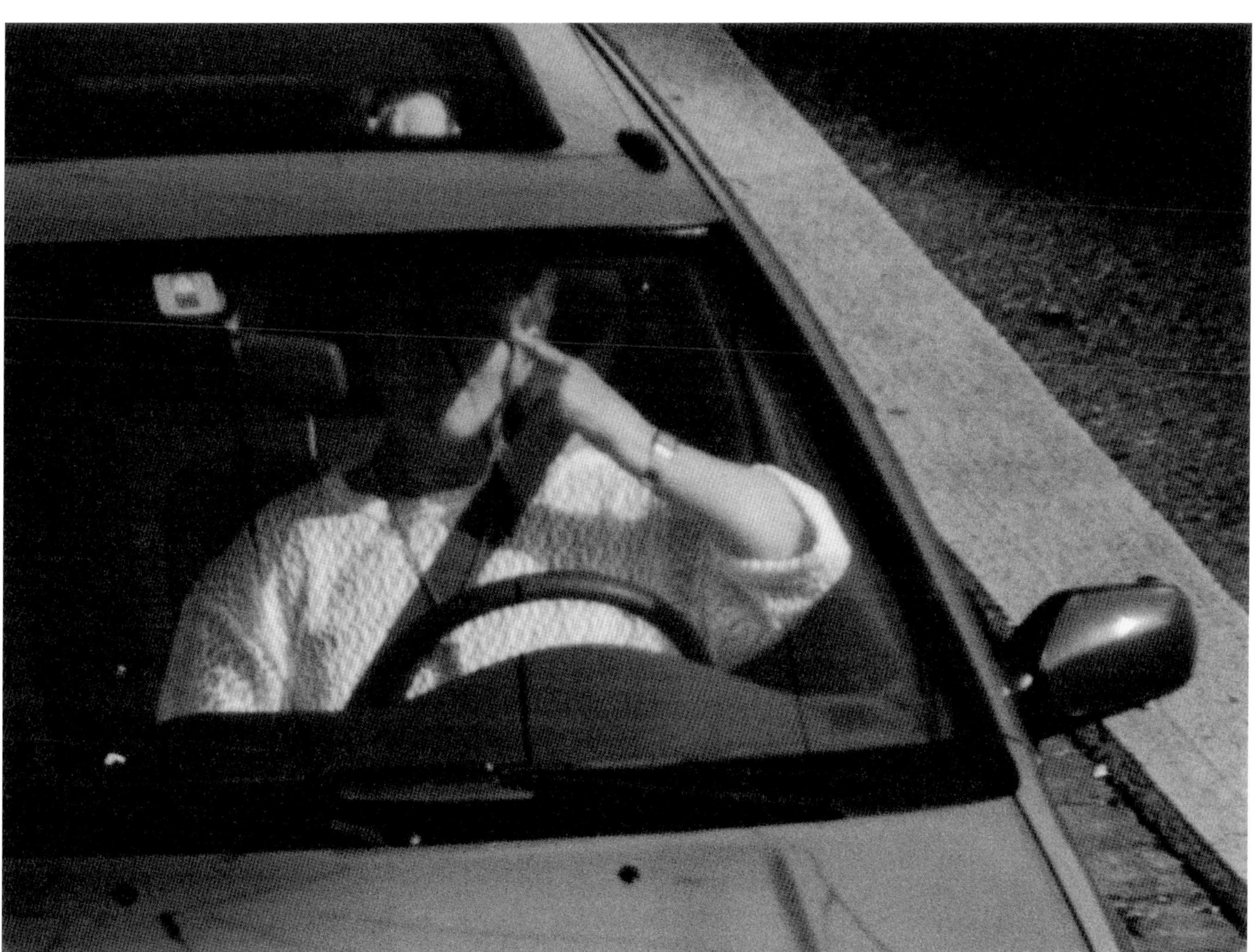

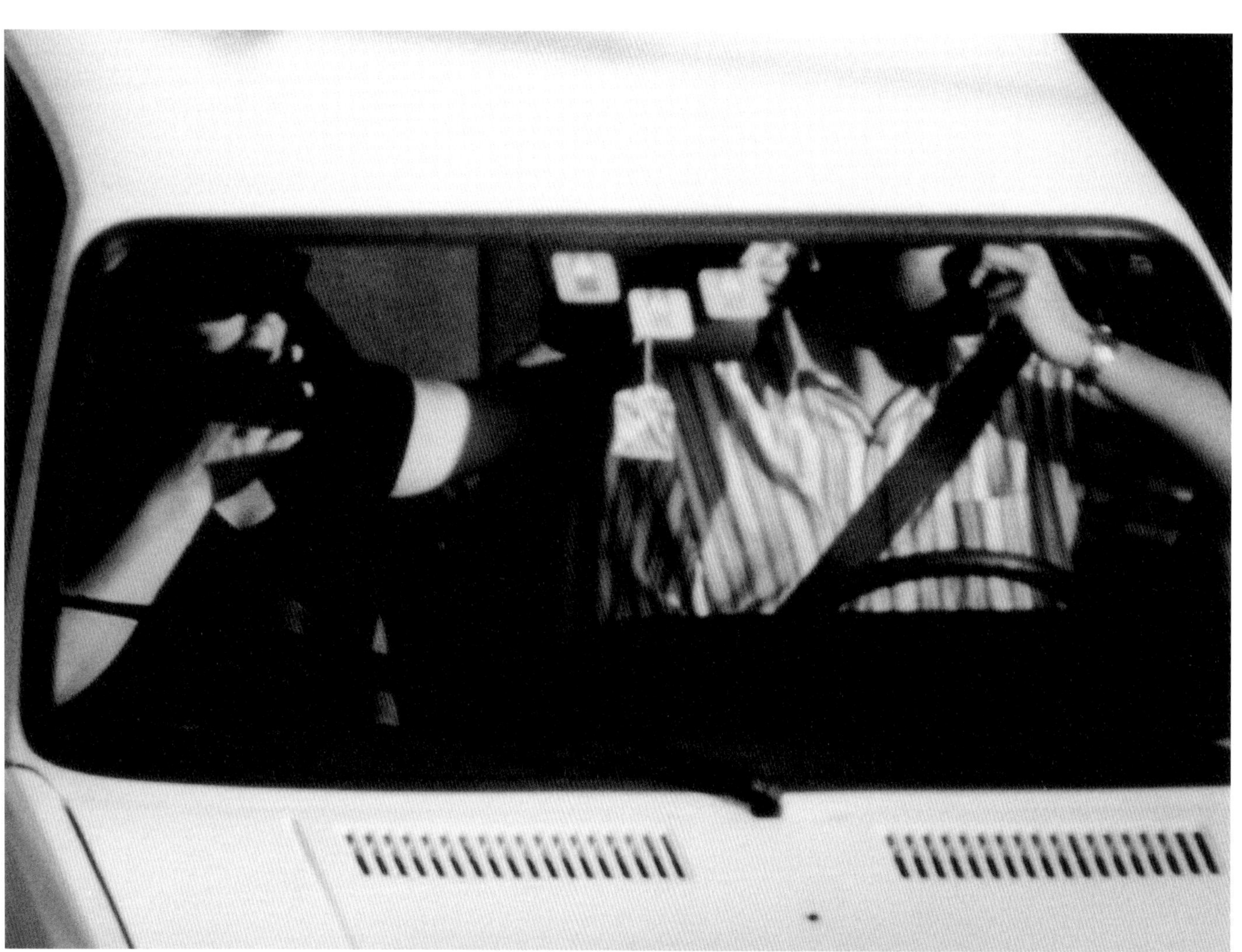

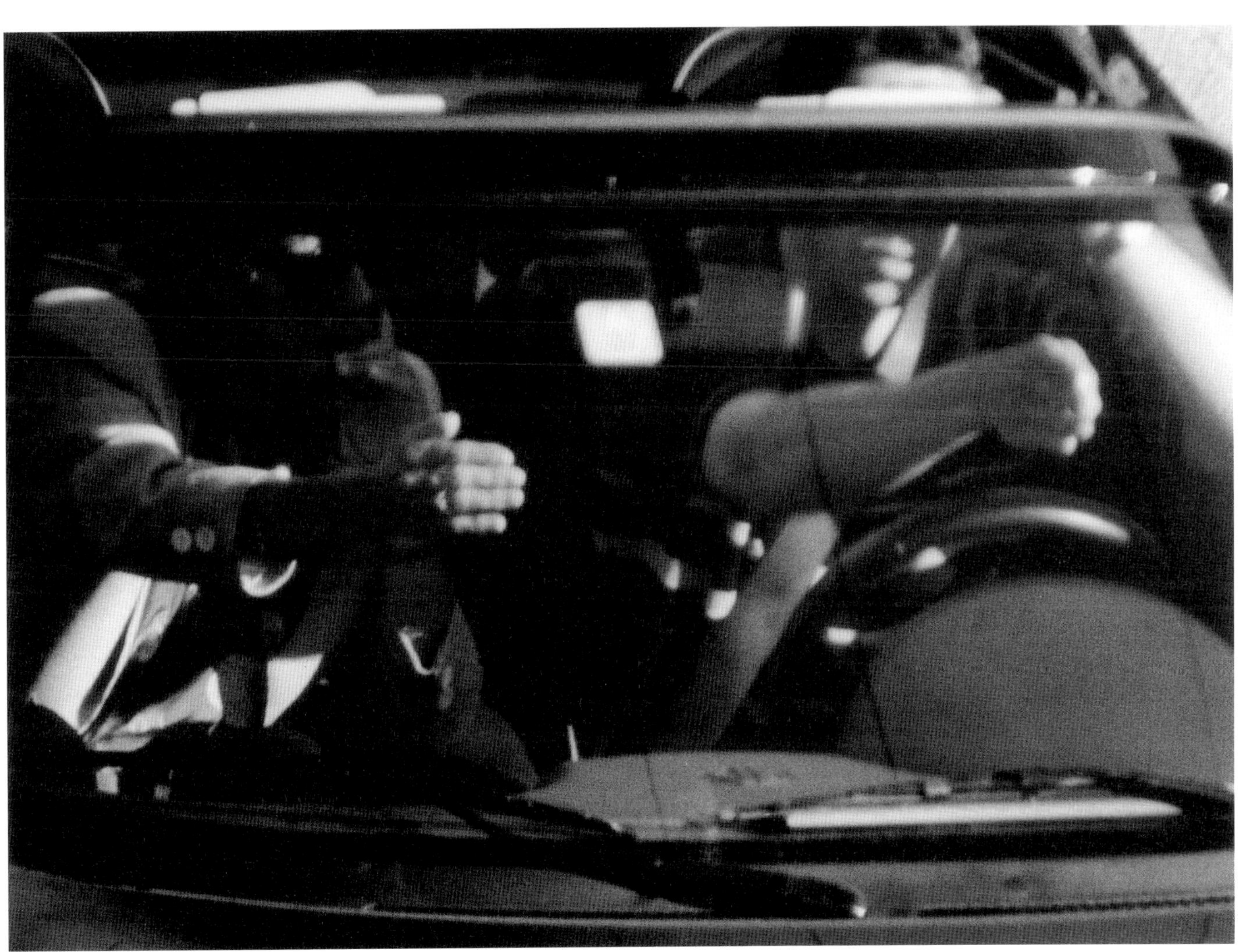

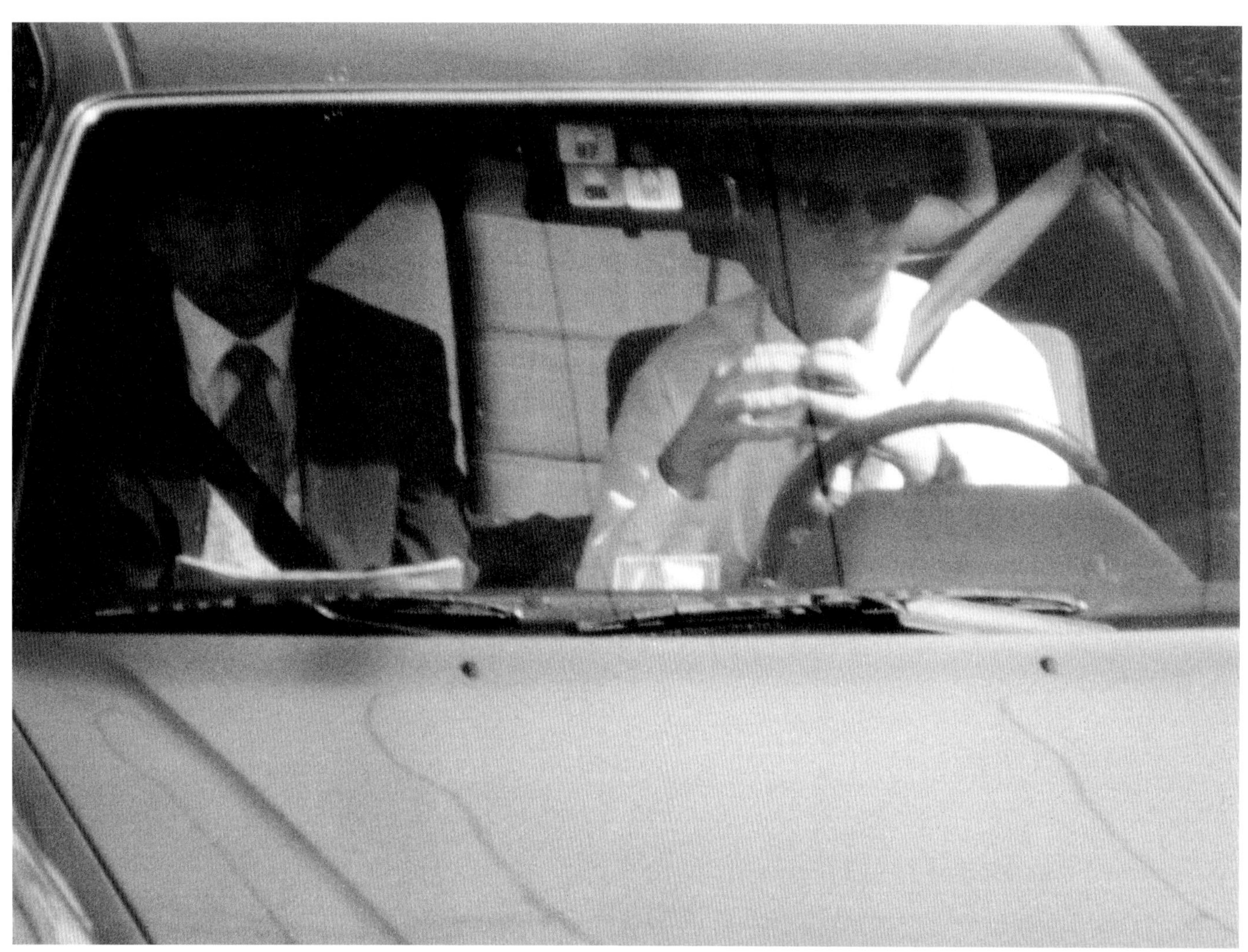

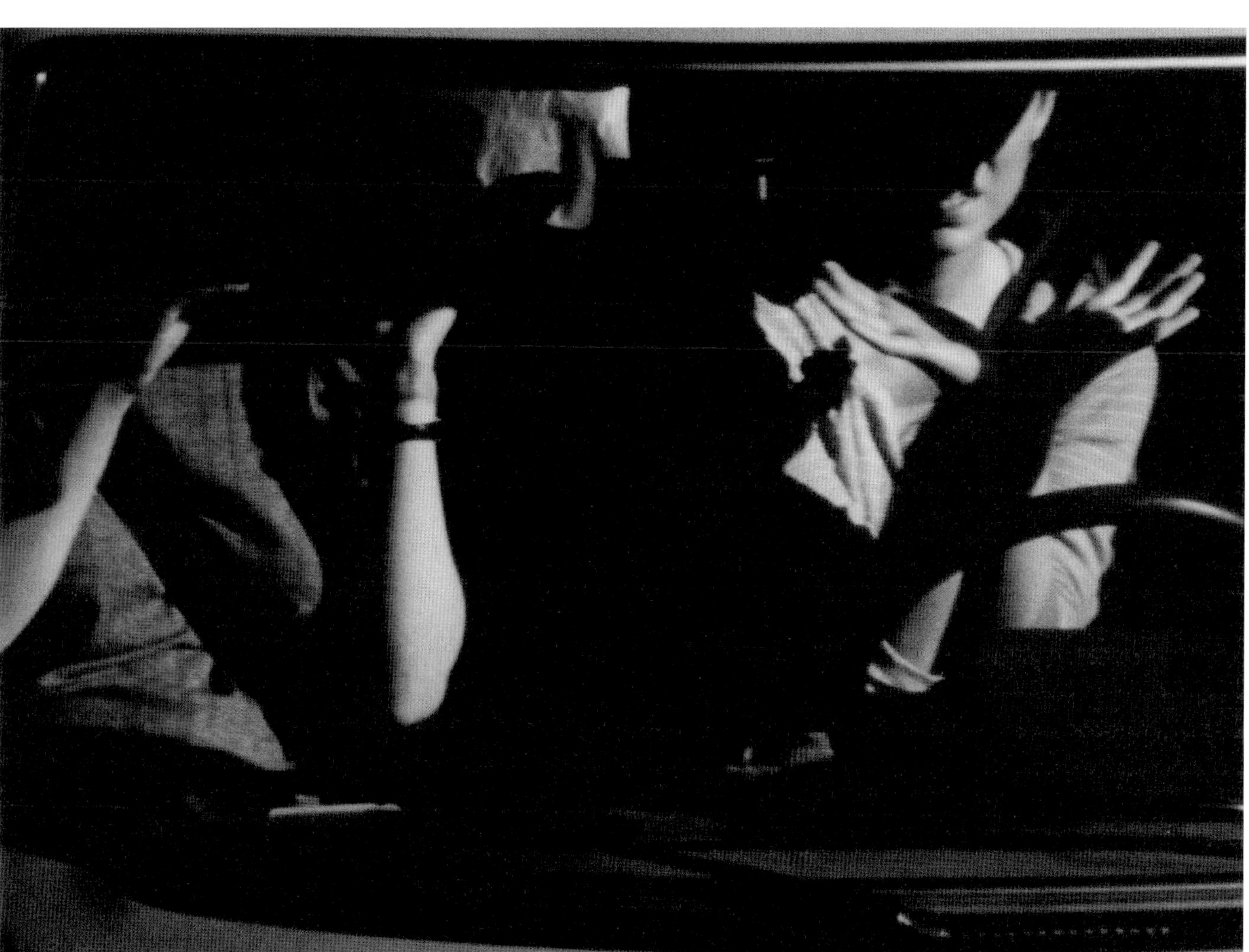

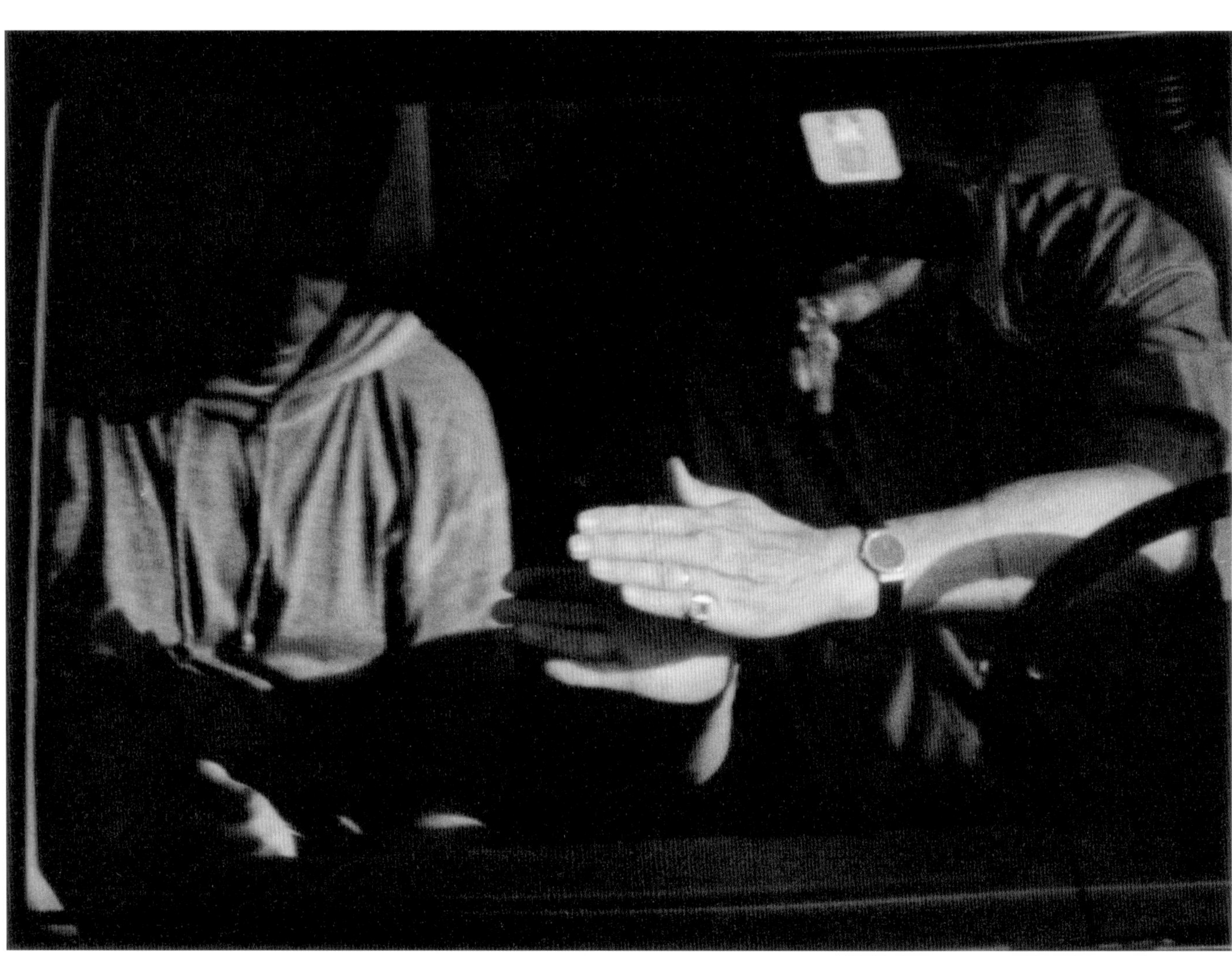

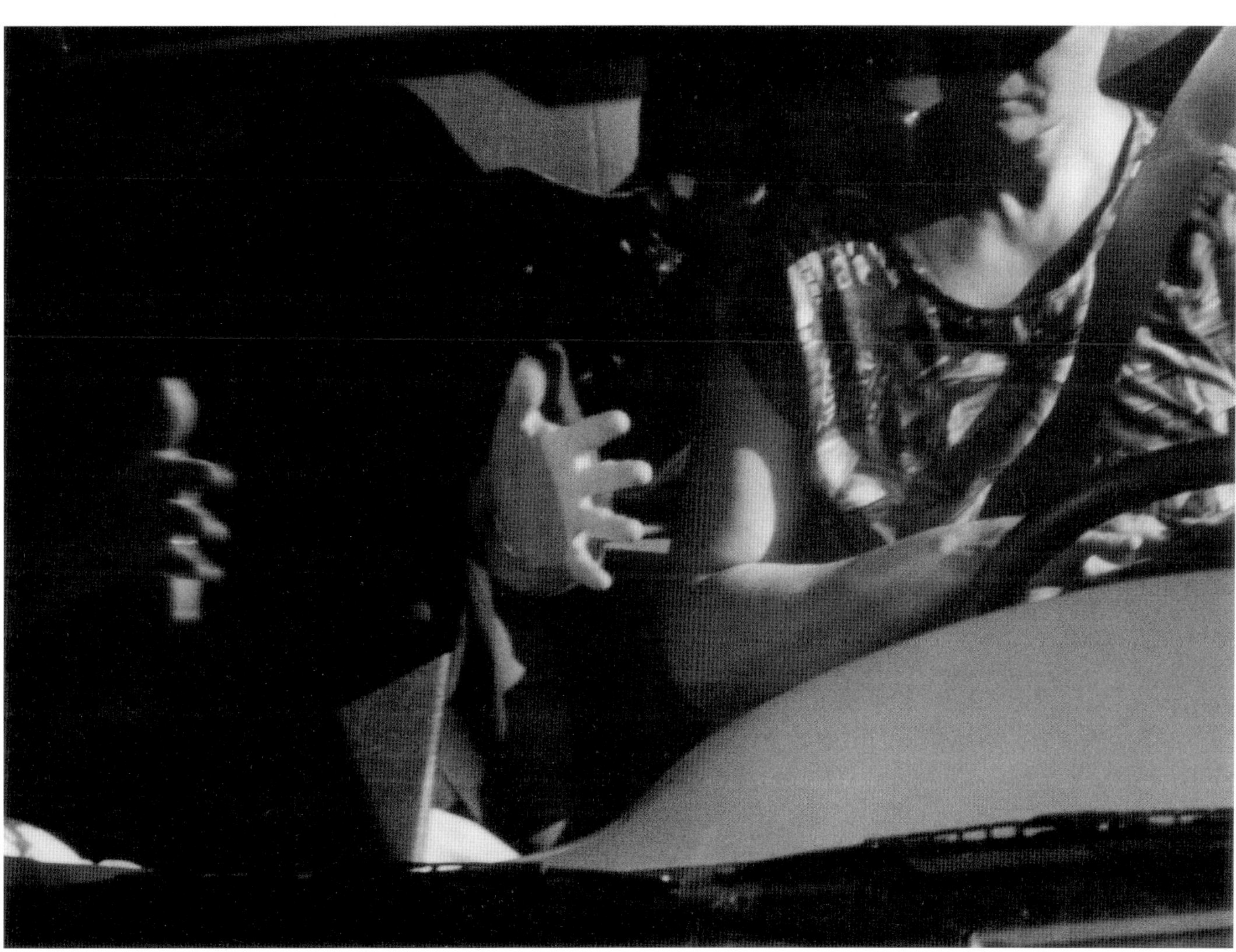

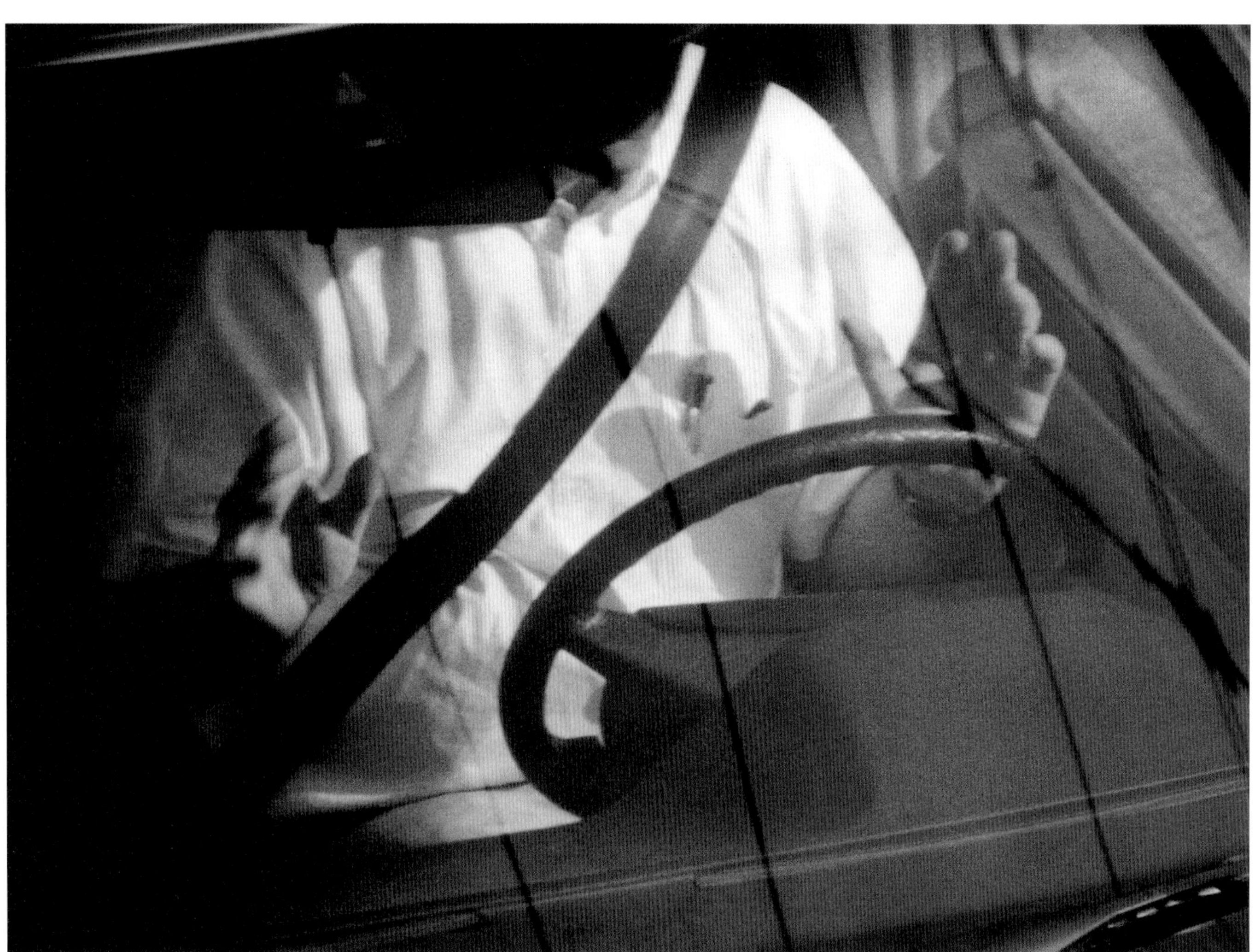

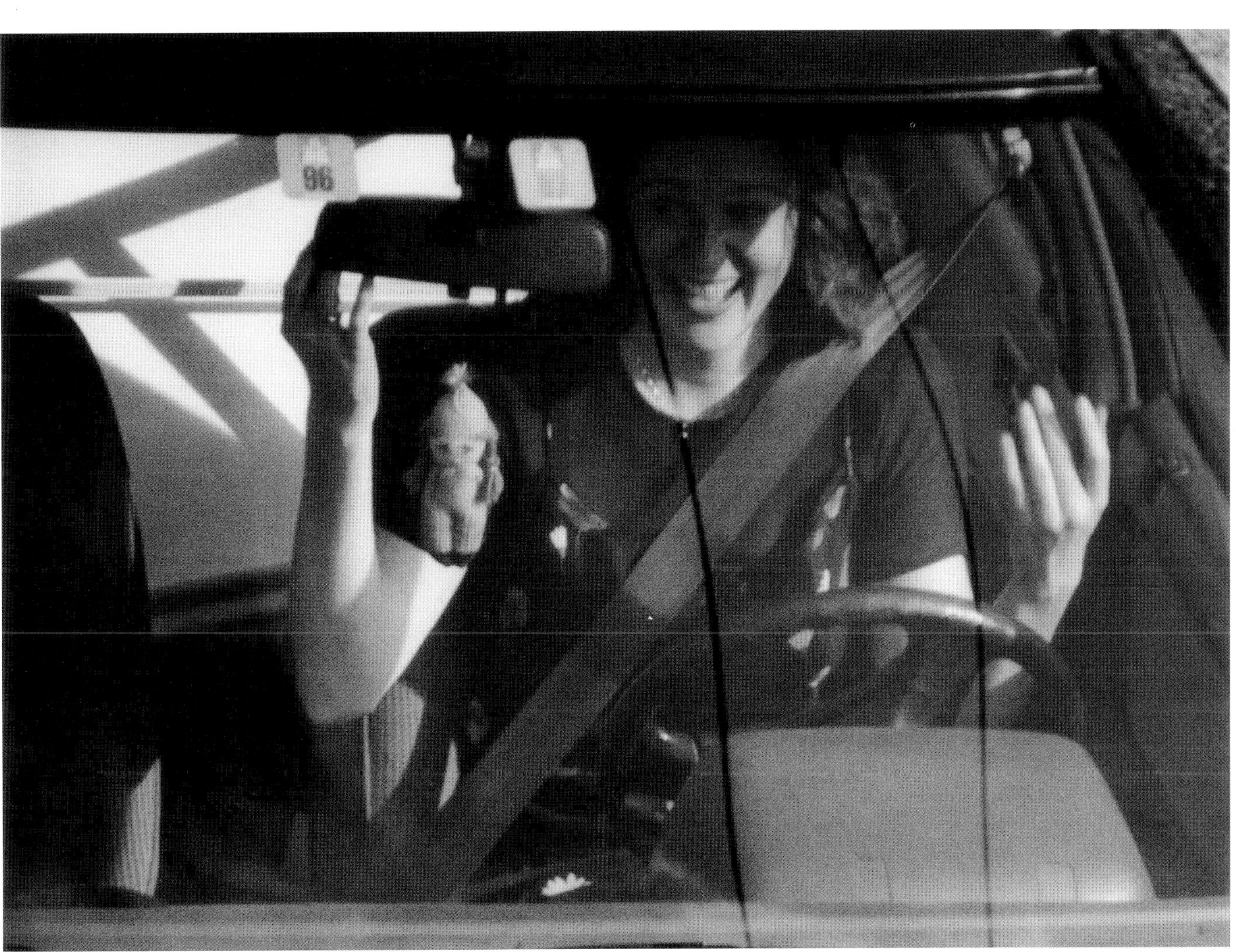

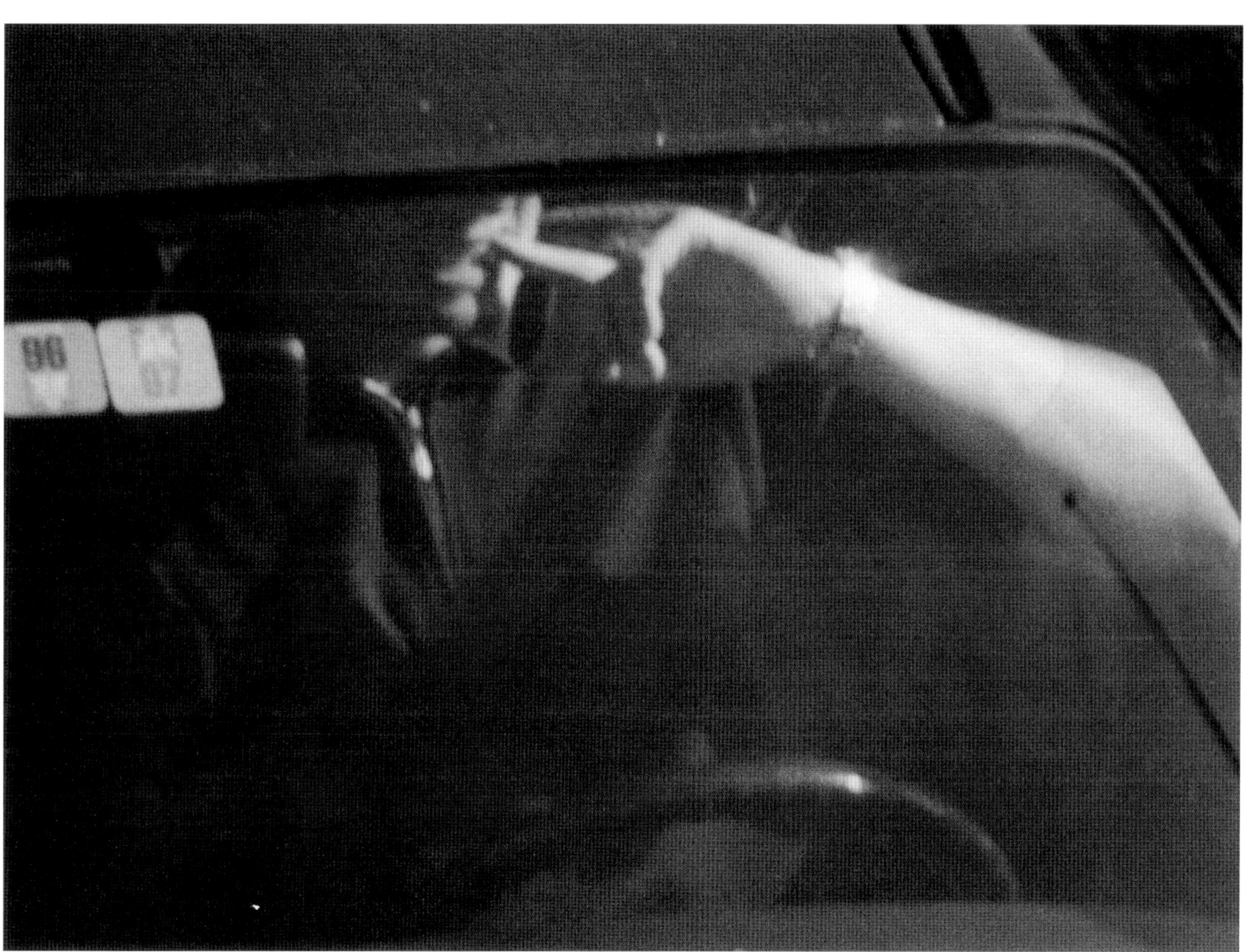

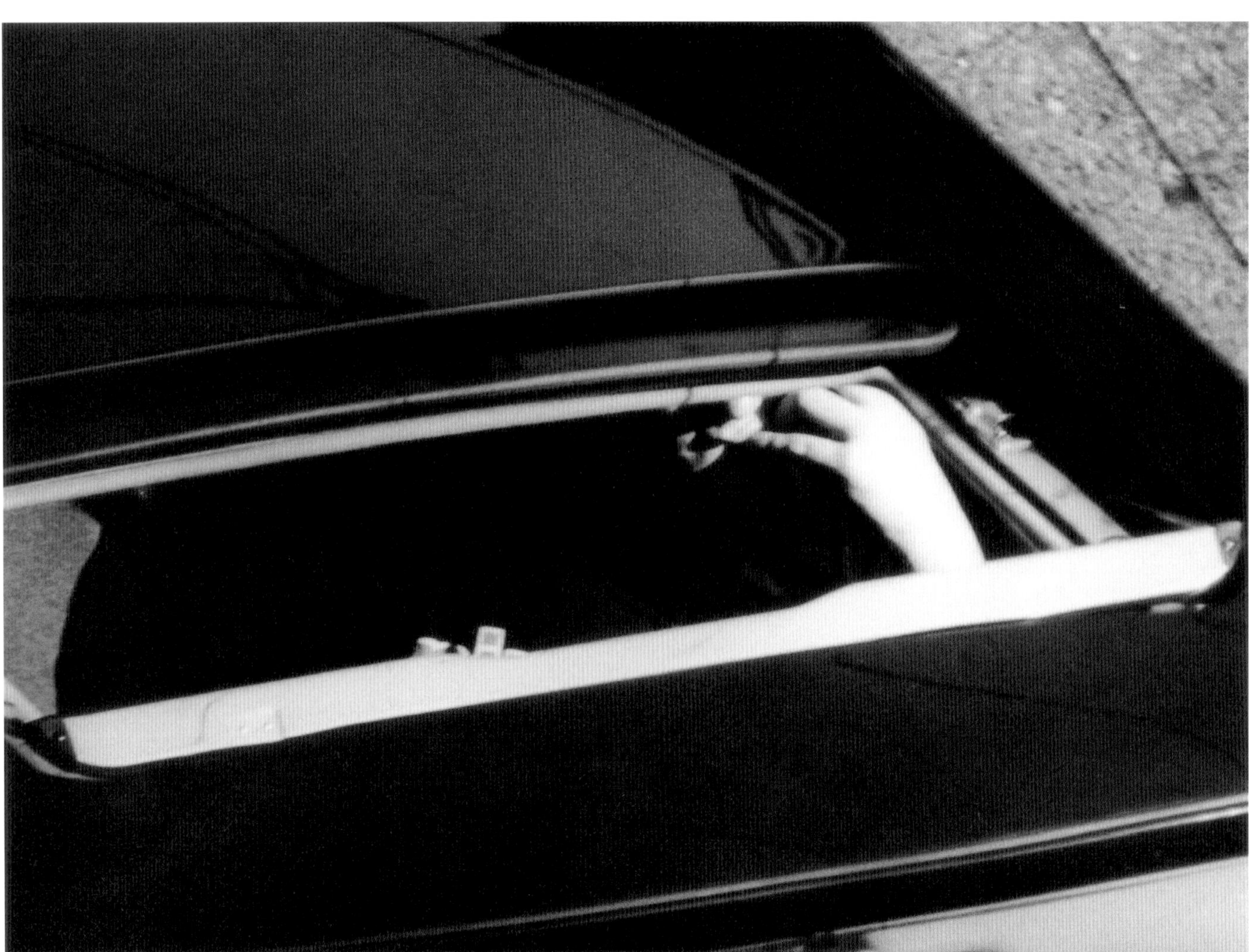

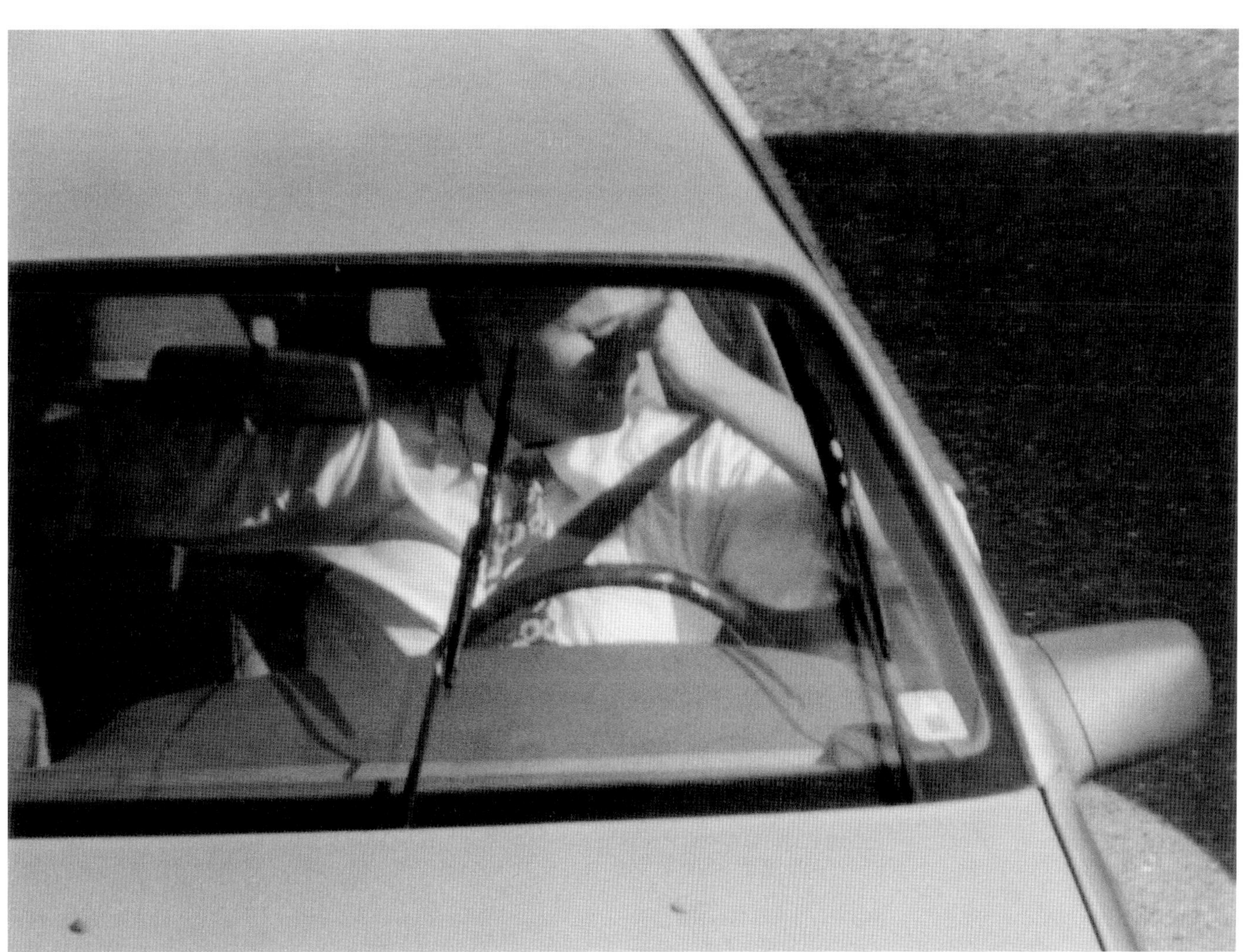

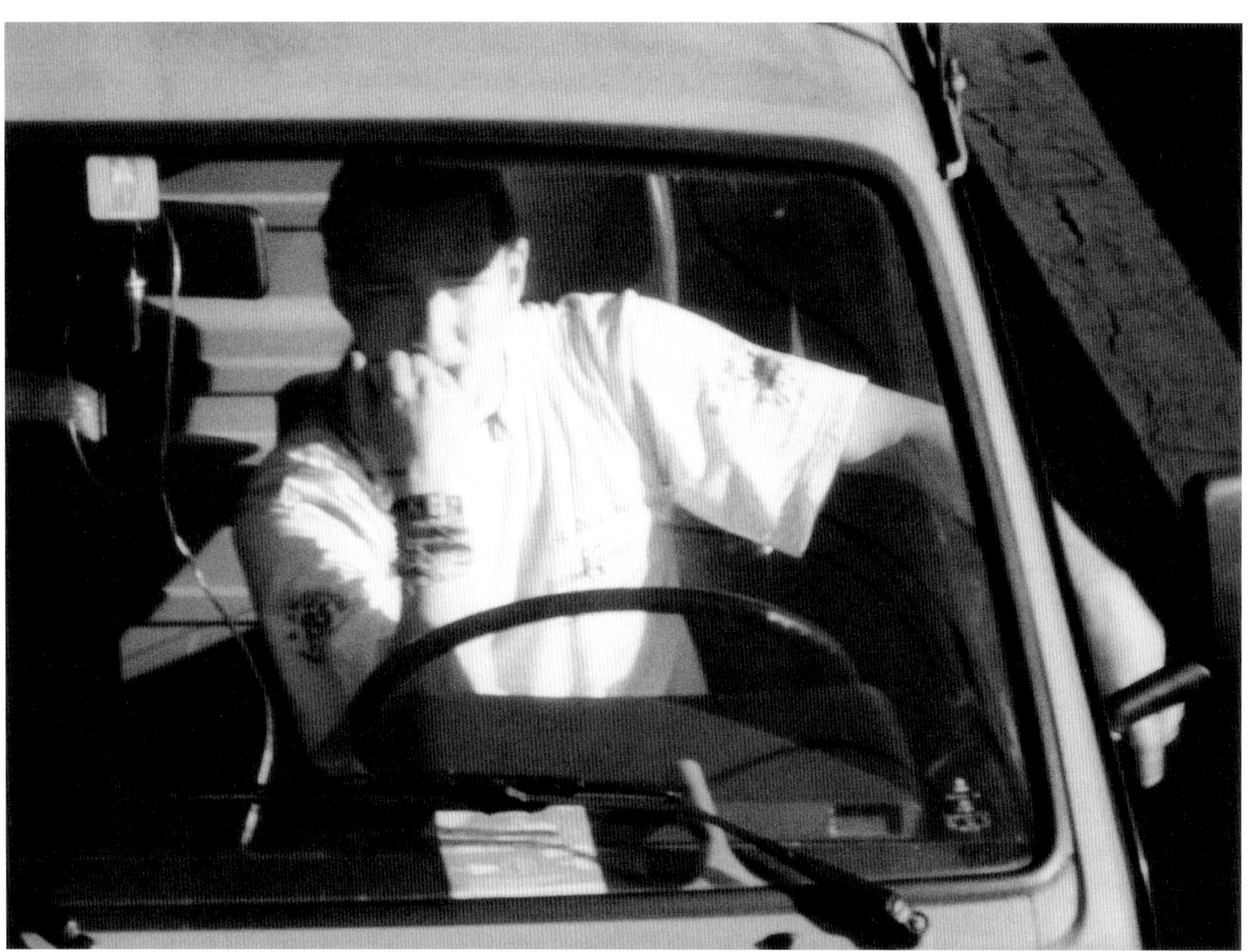

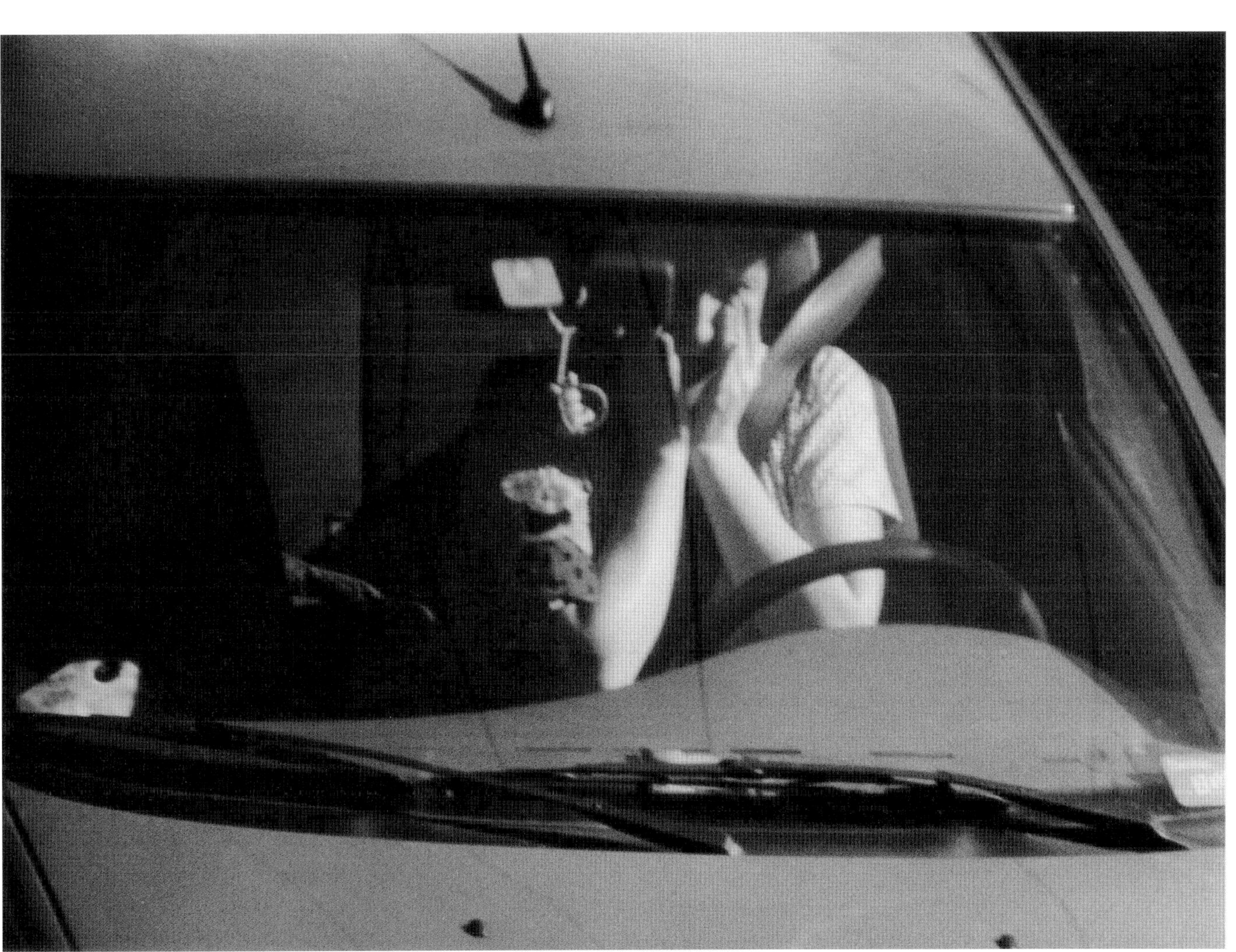

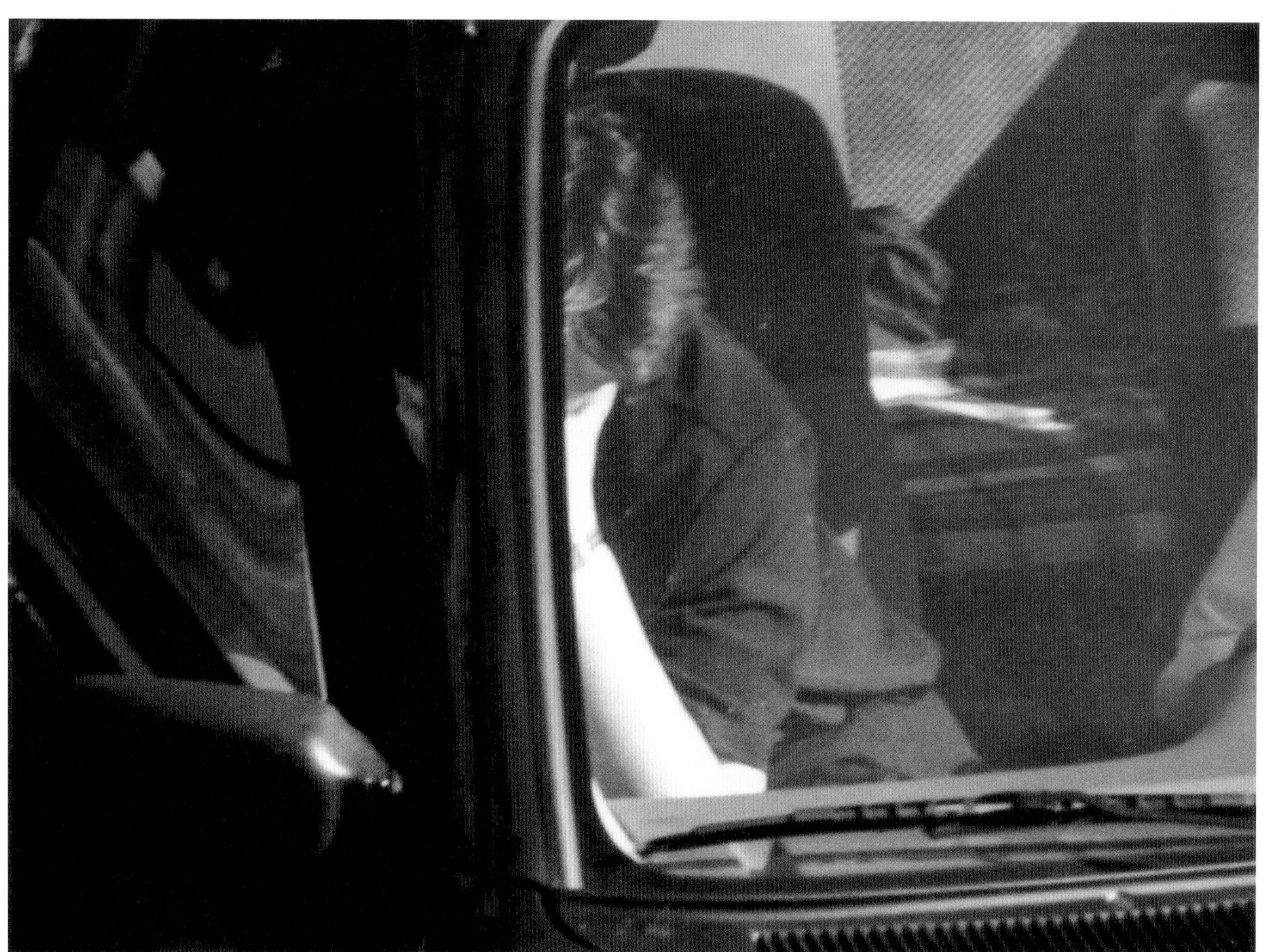

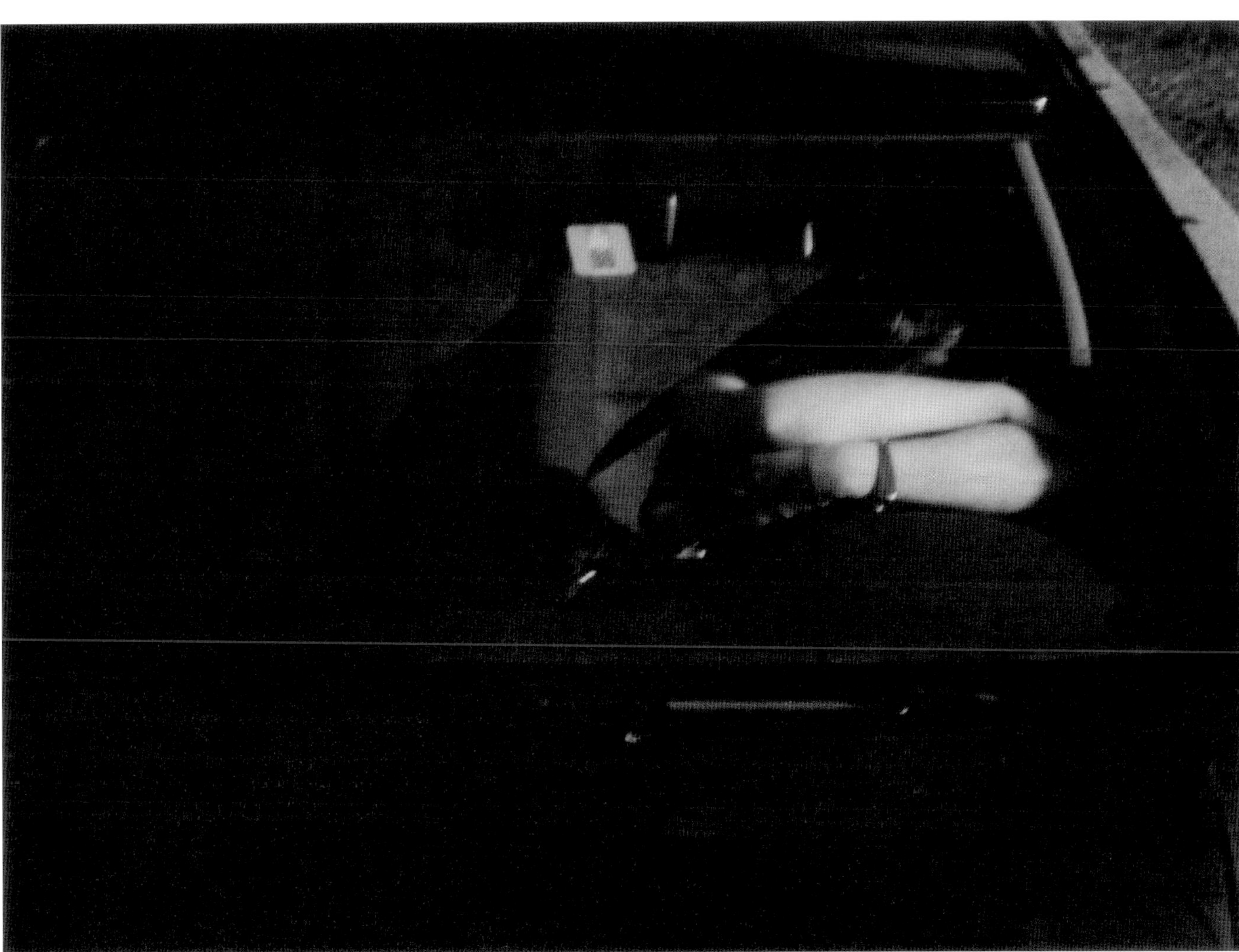

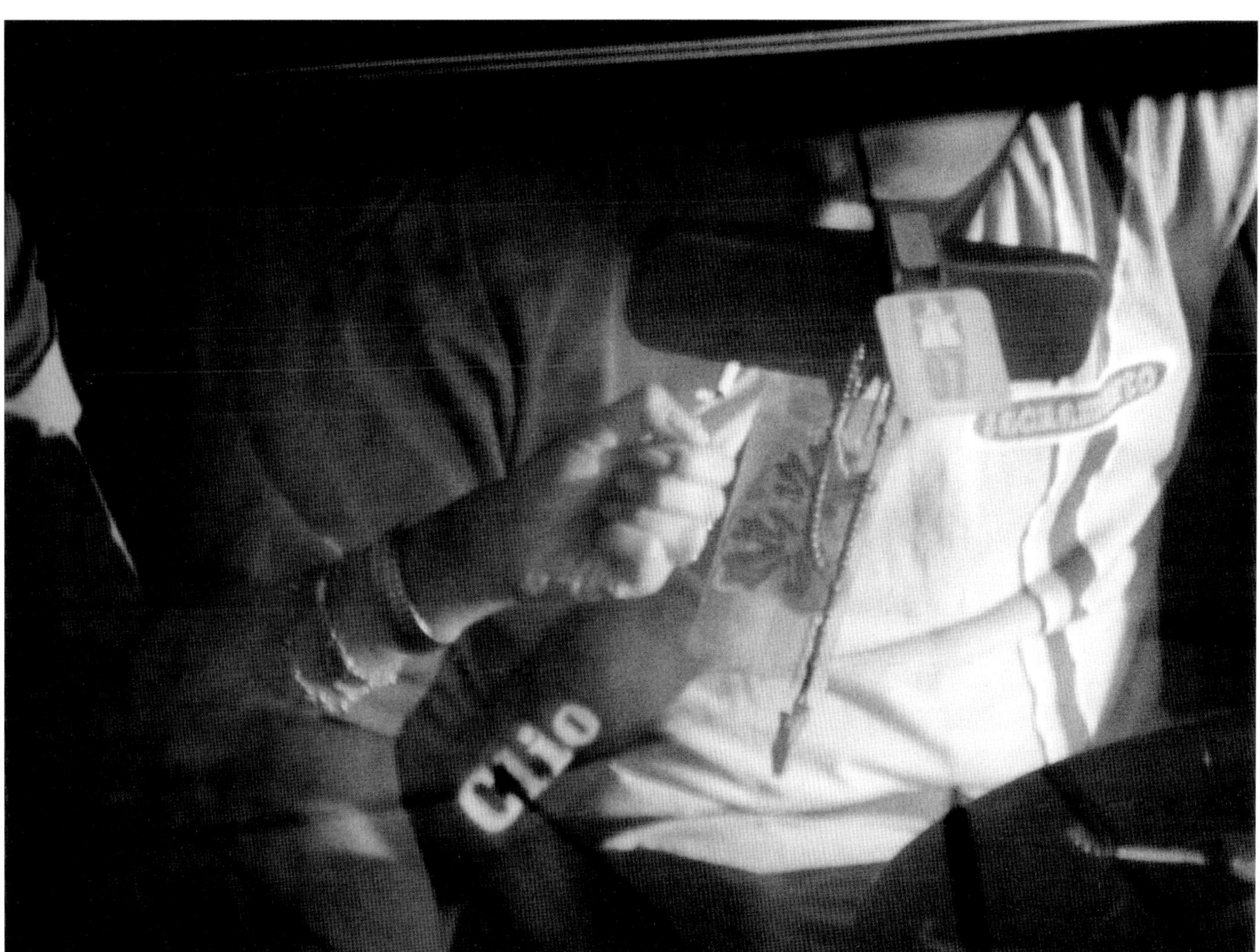

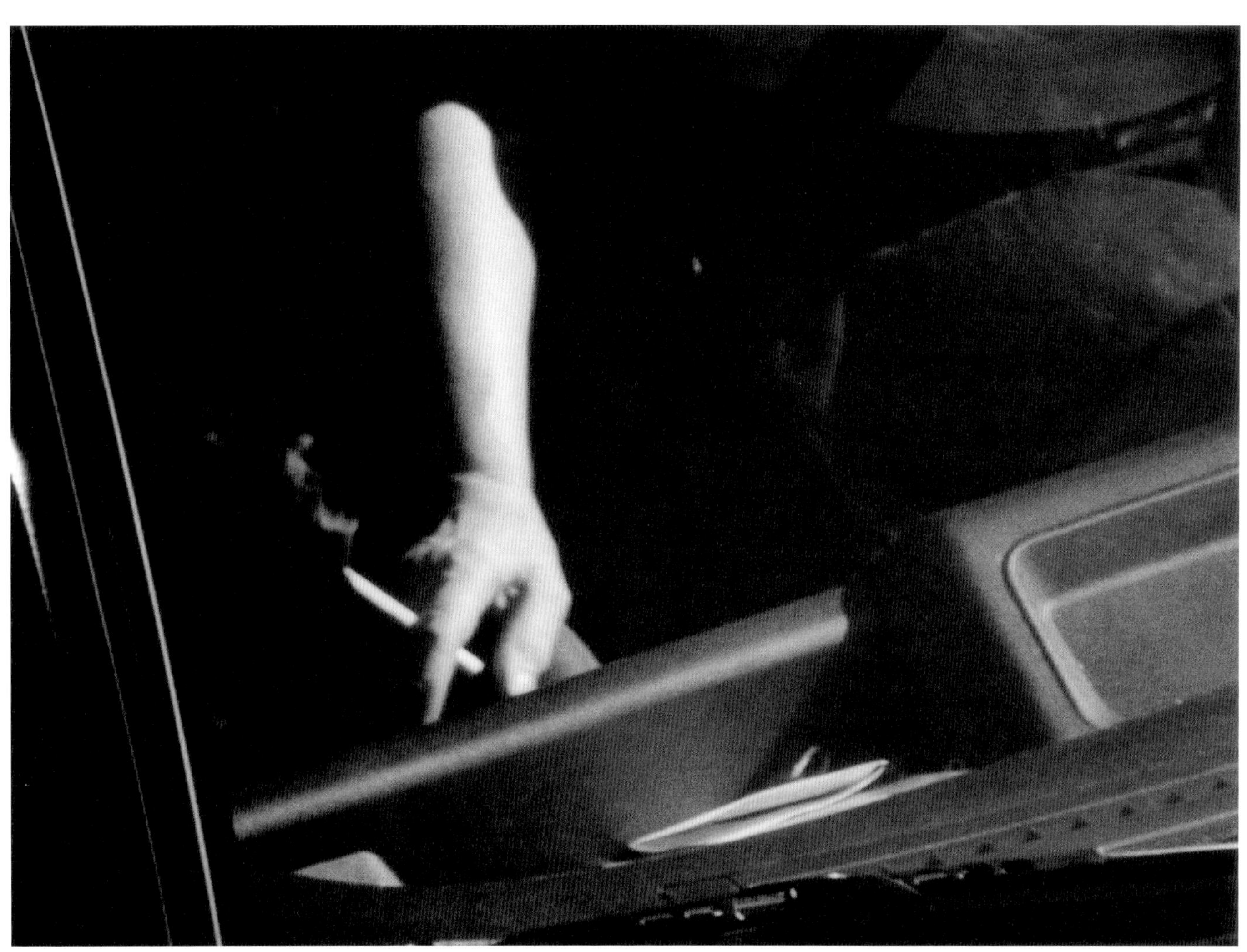

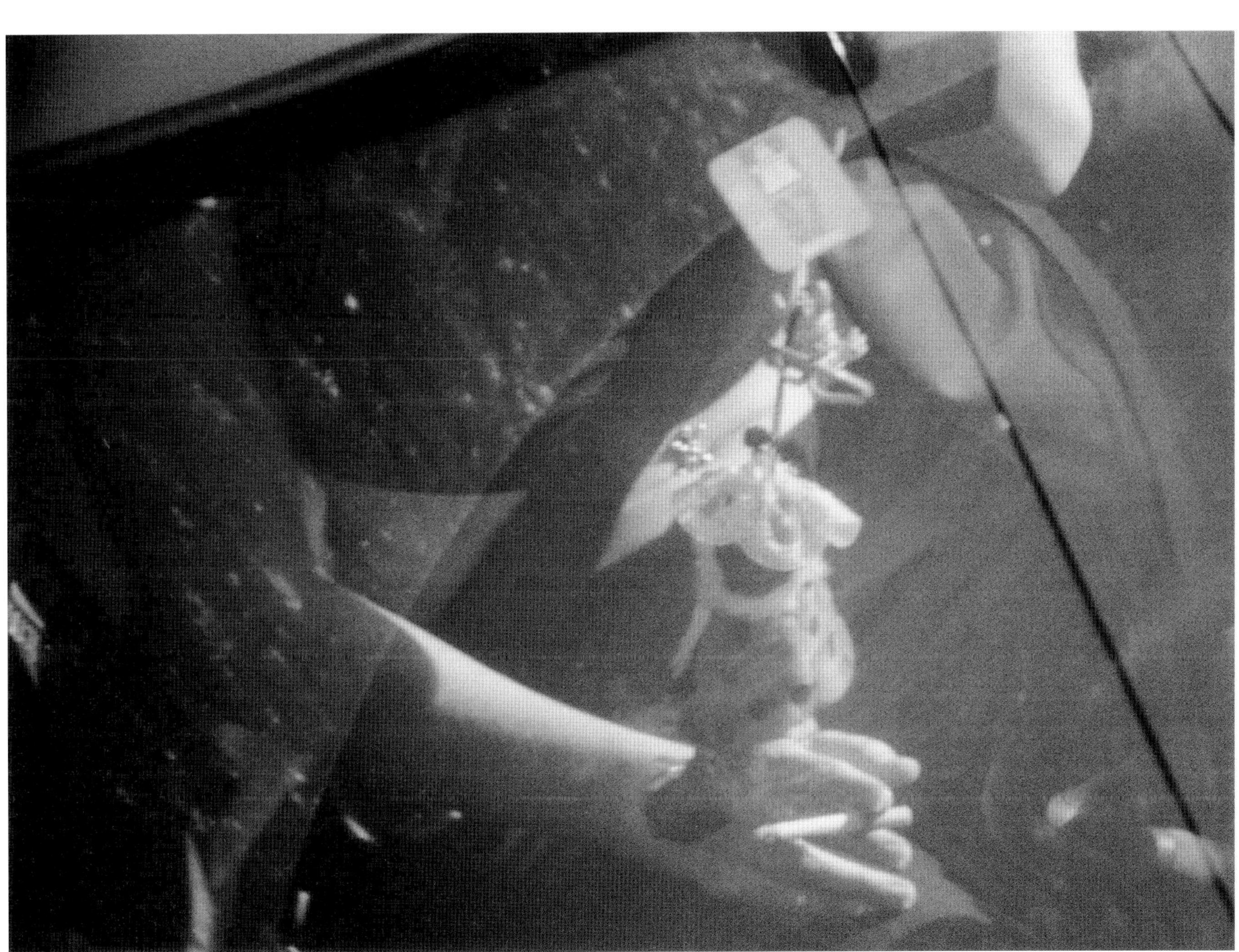

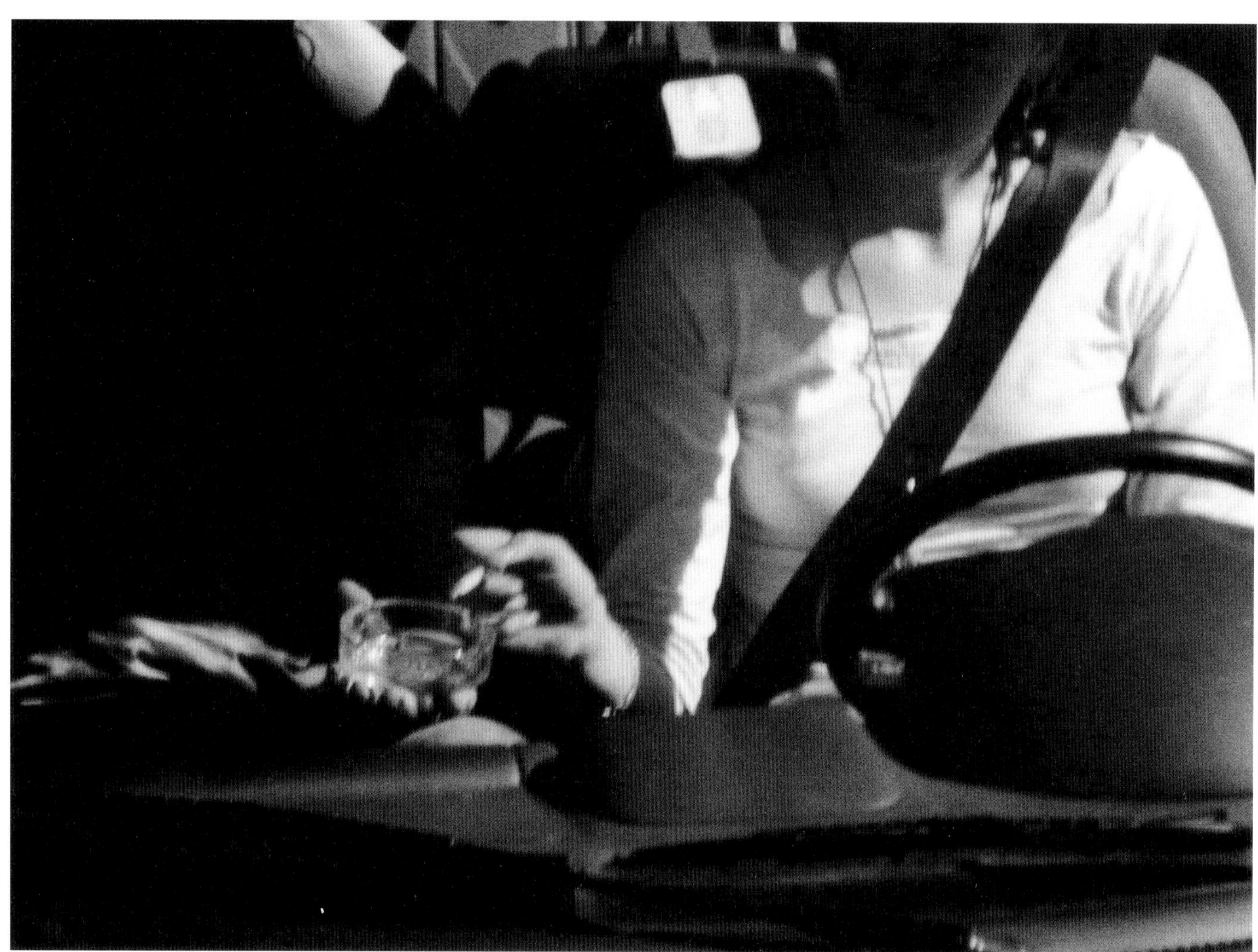

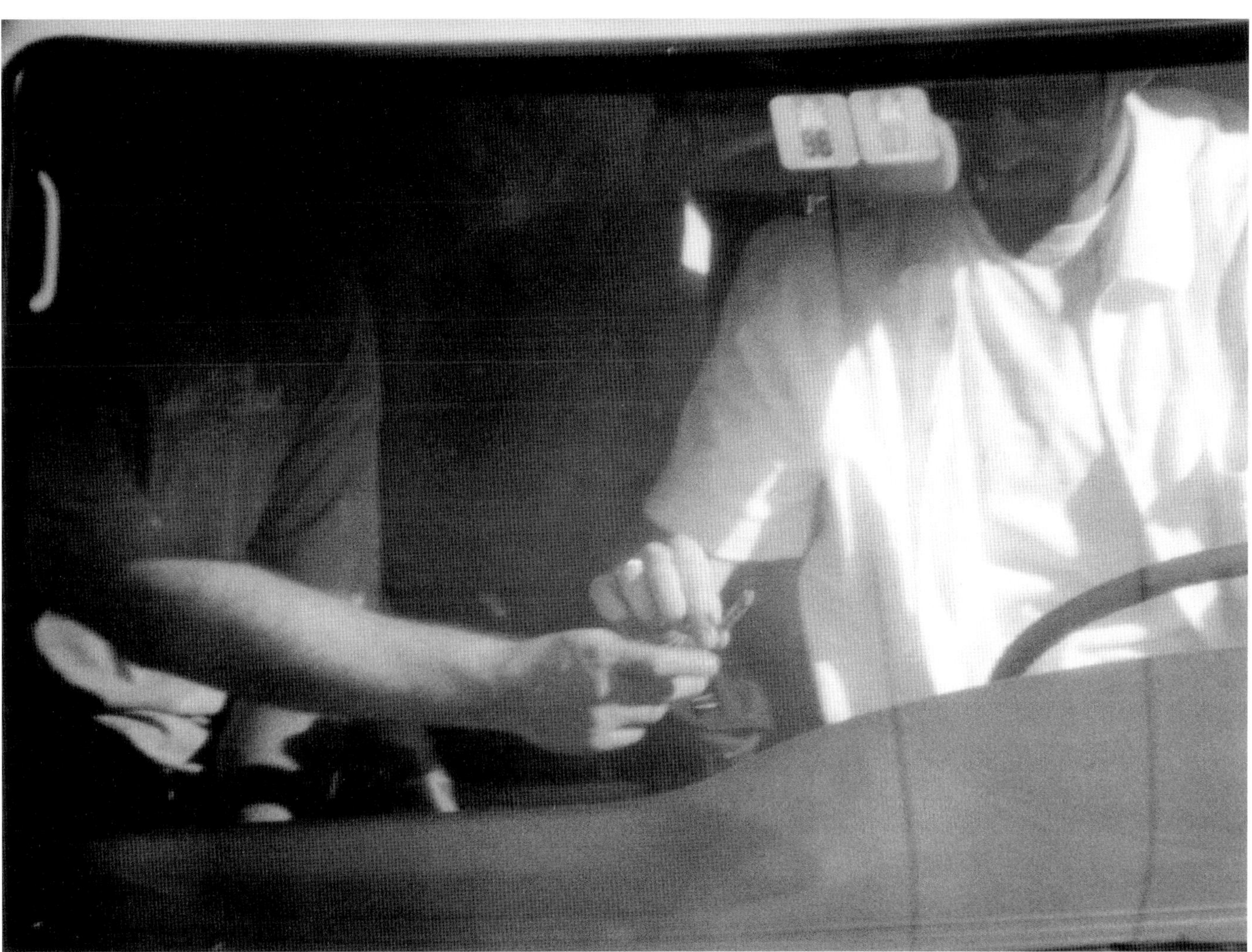

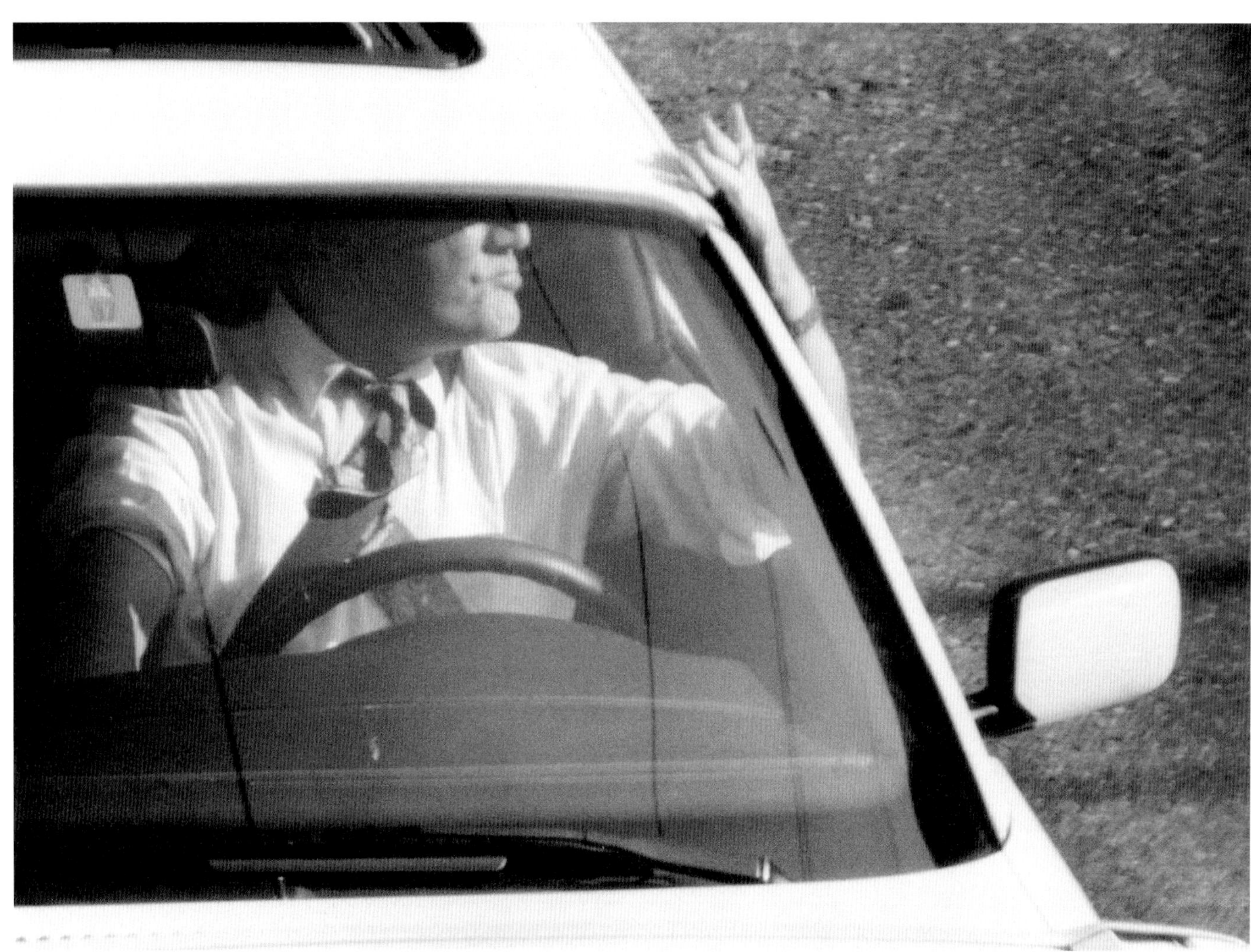

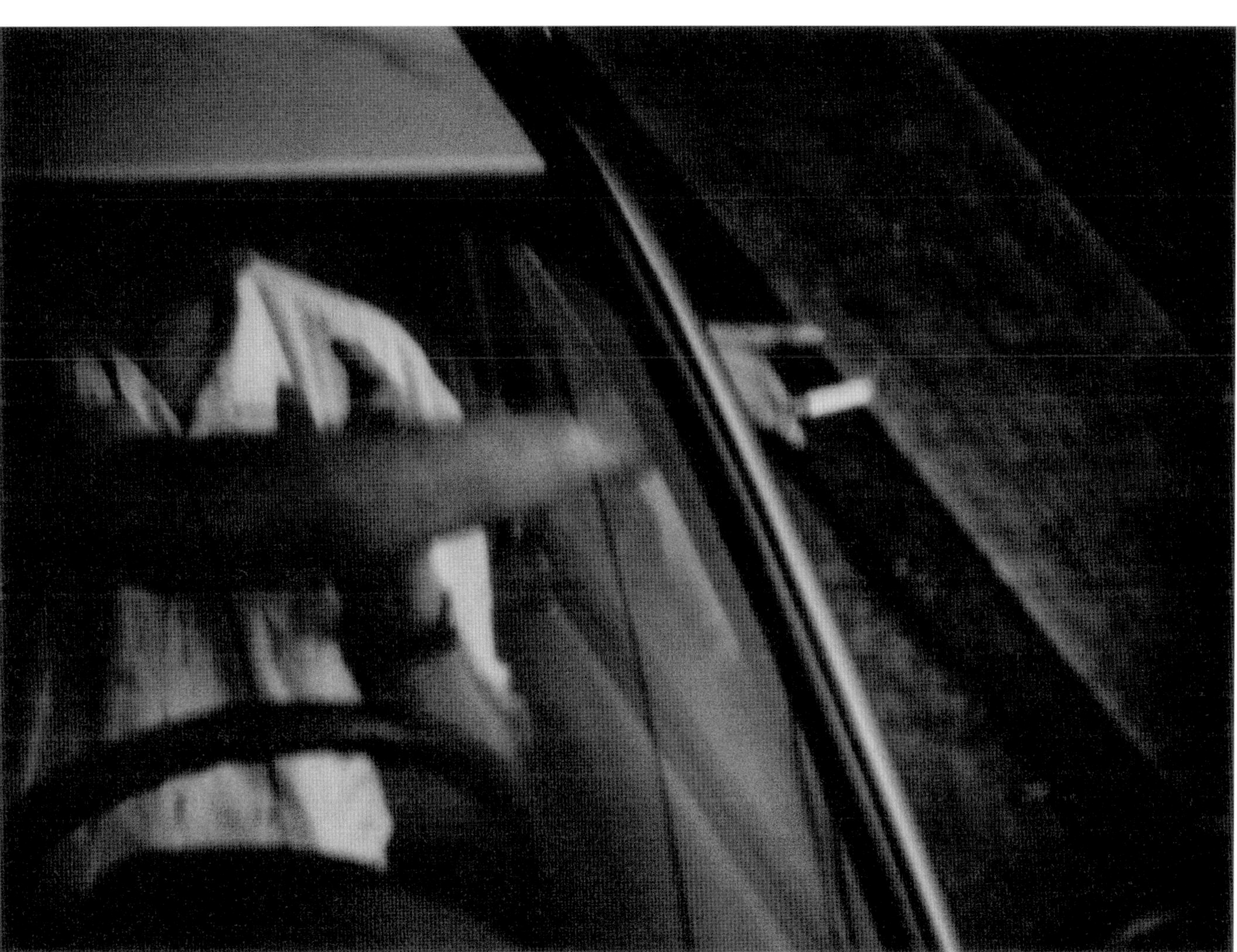

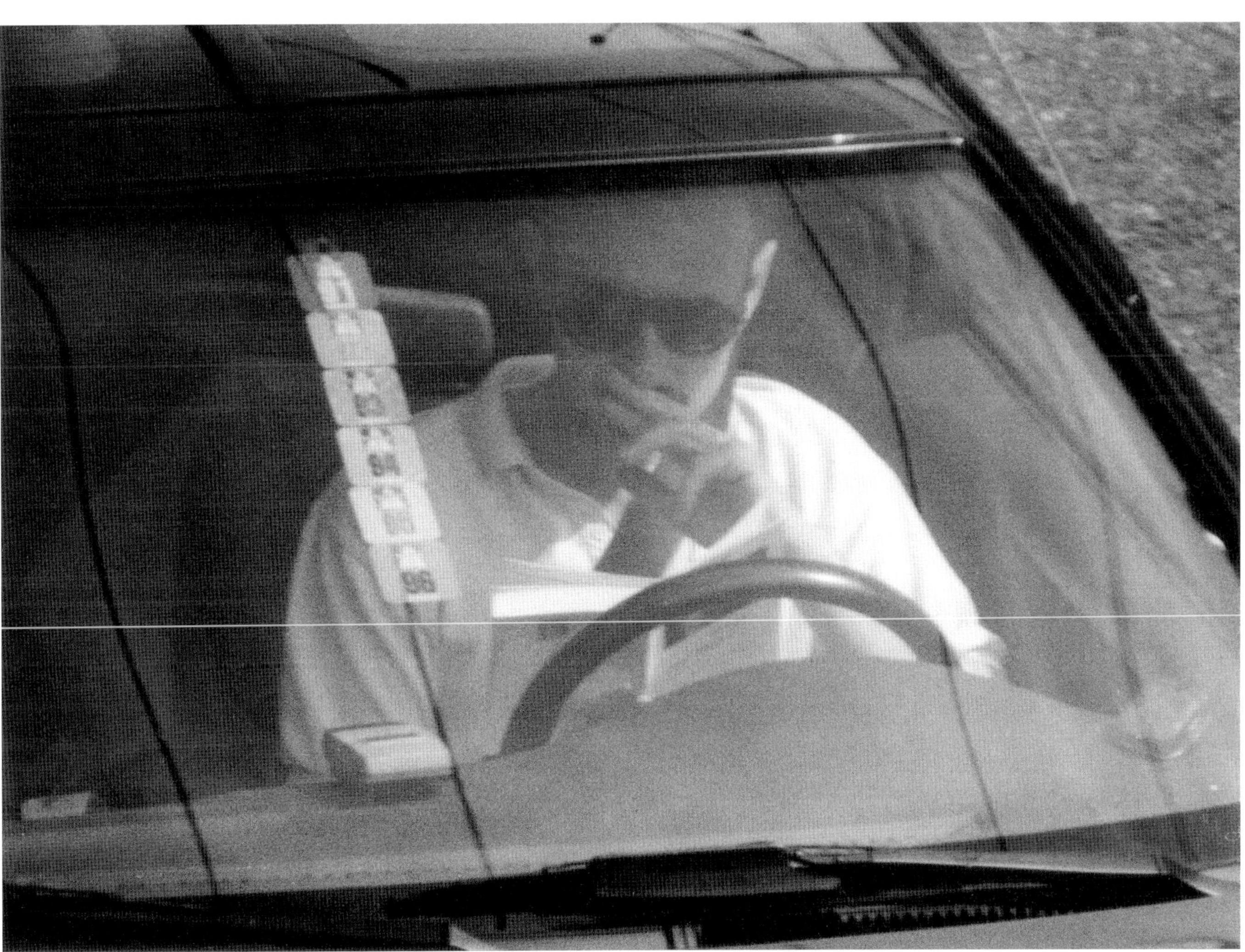

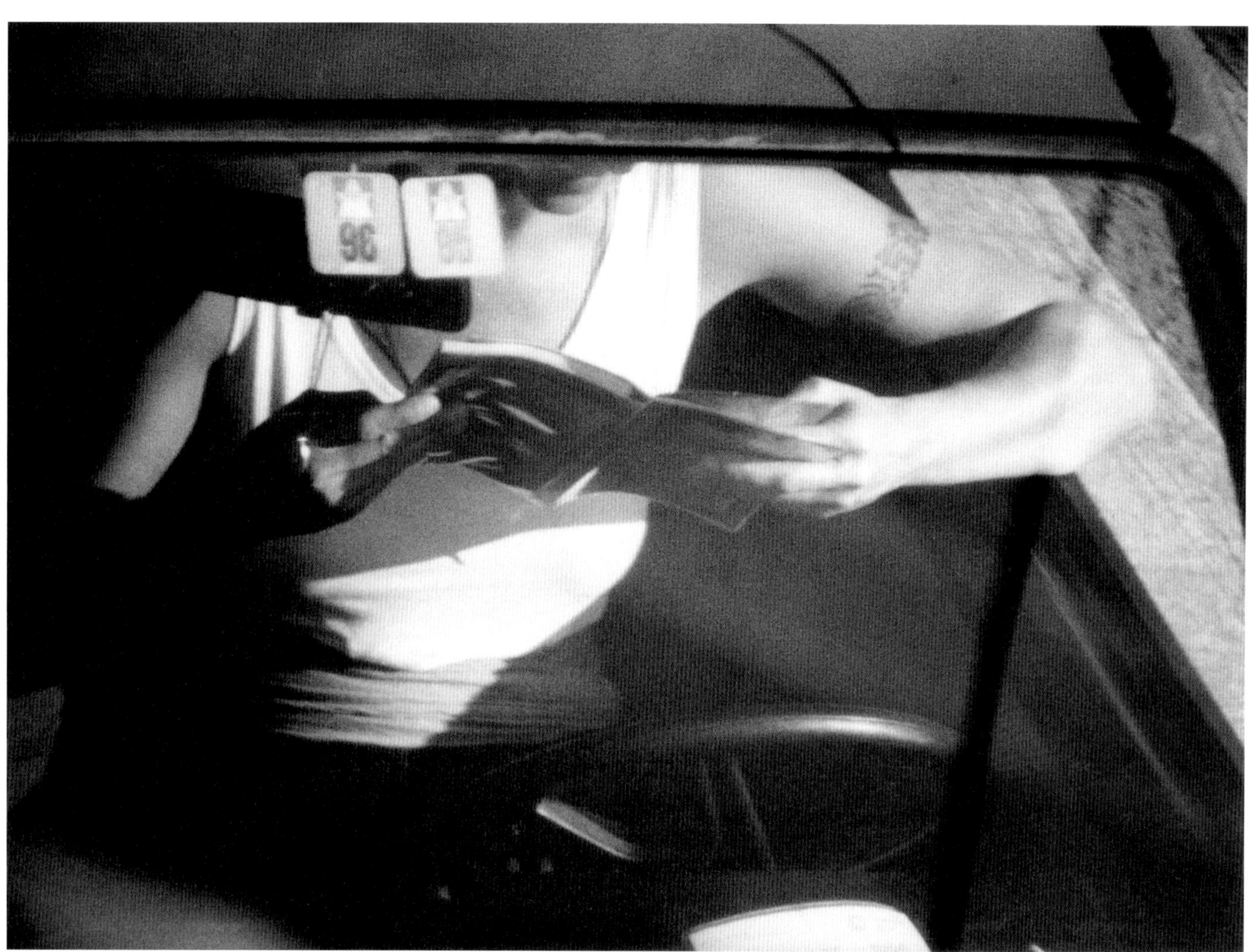

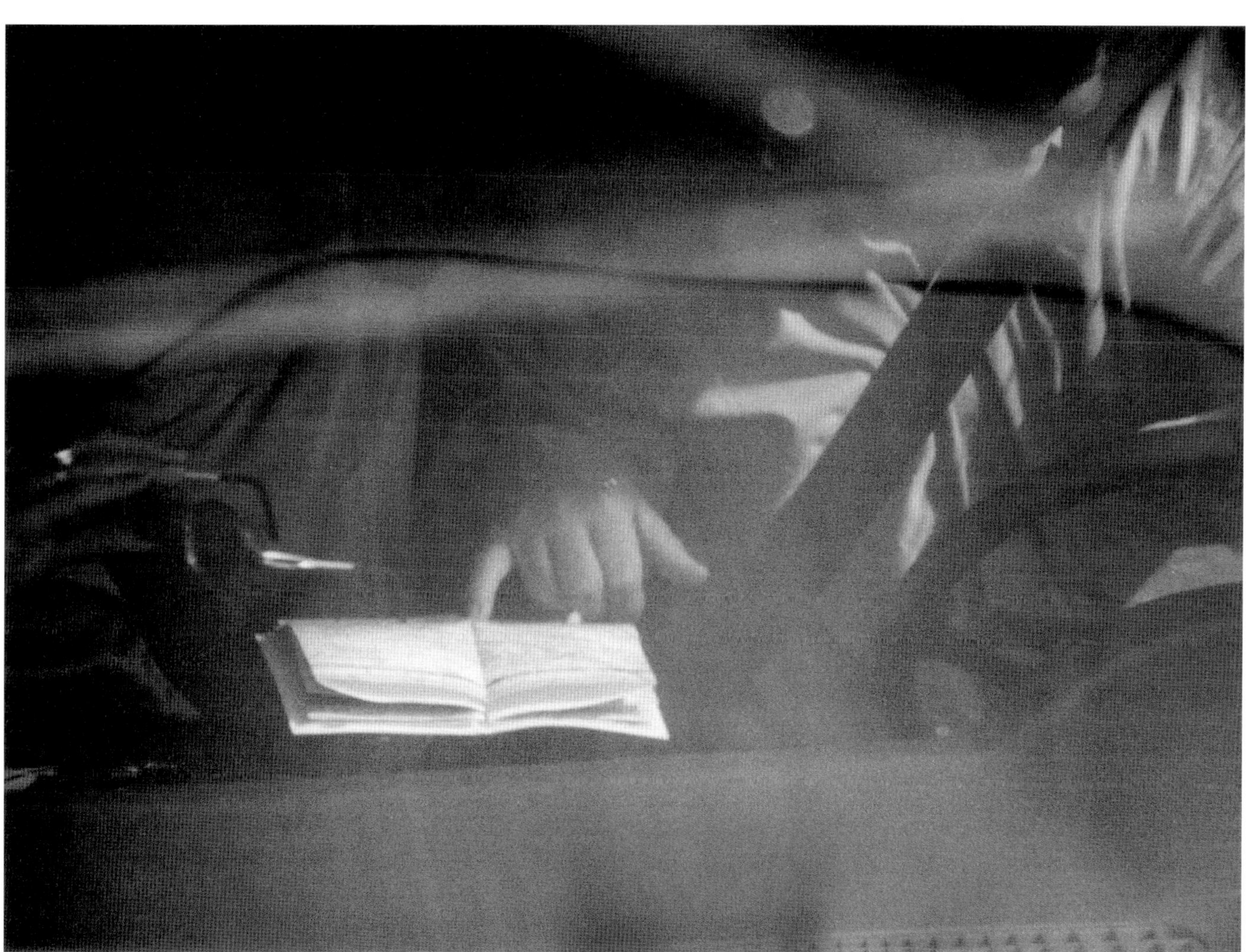

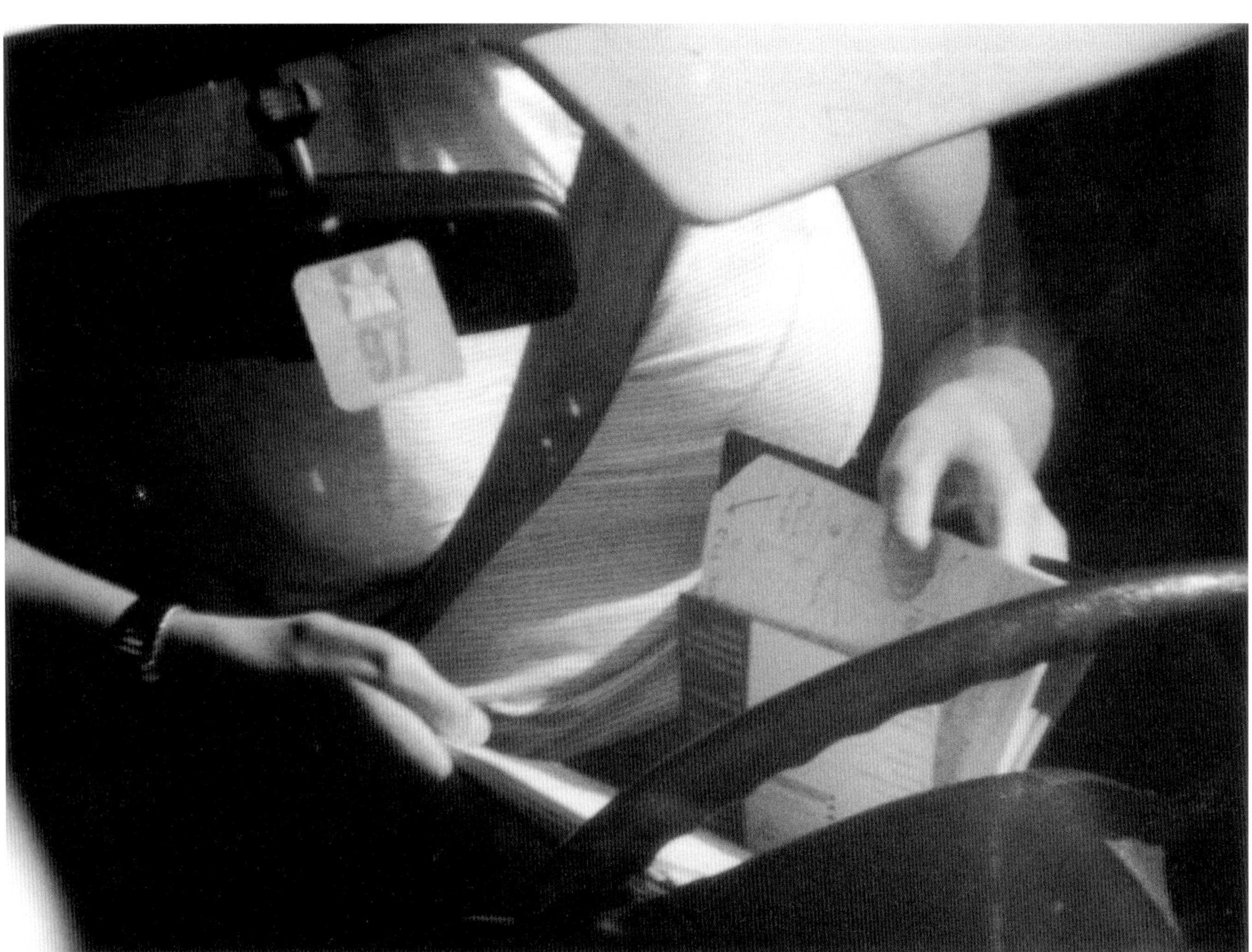

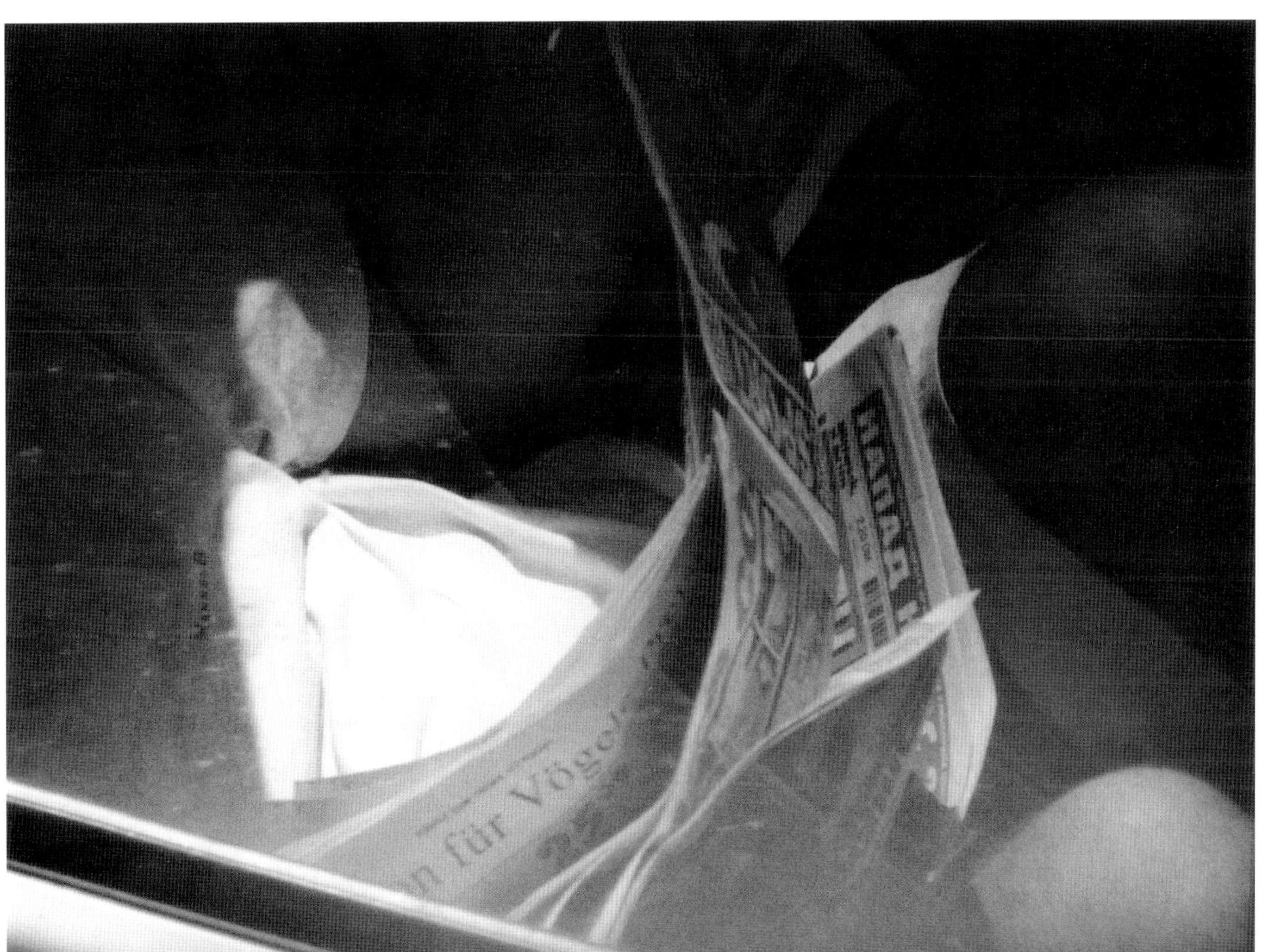
n für Vögel

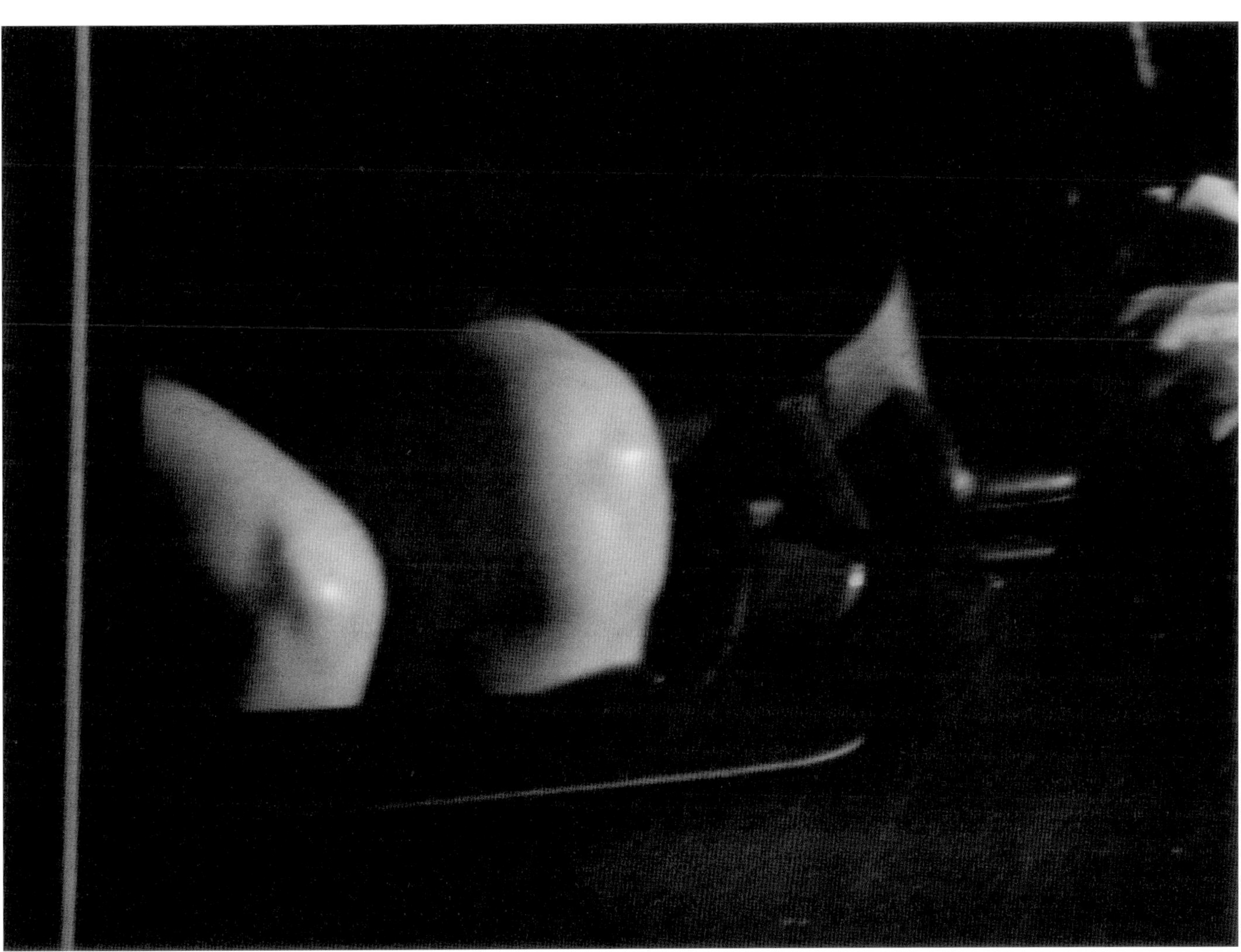

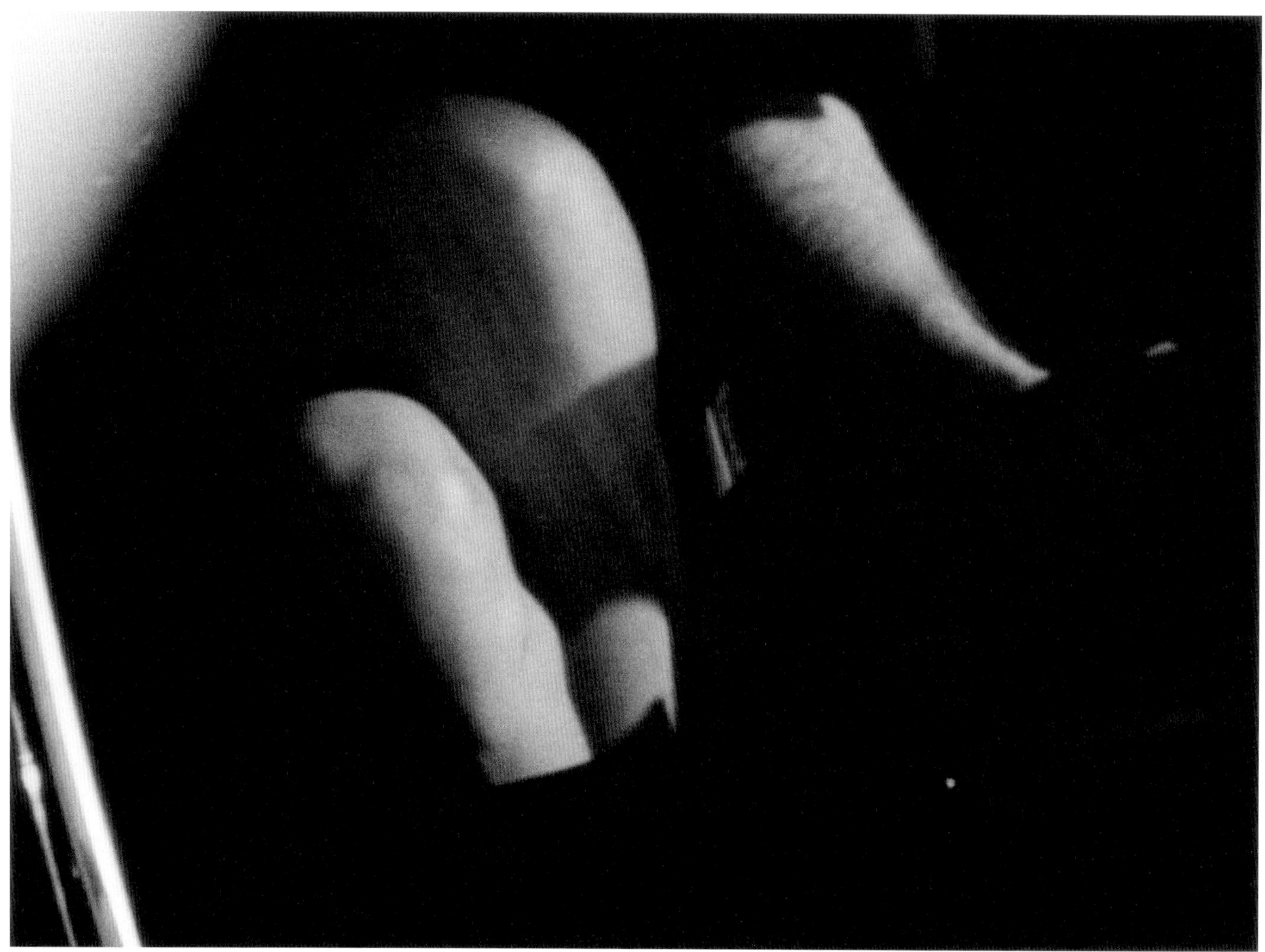

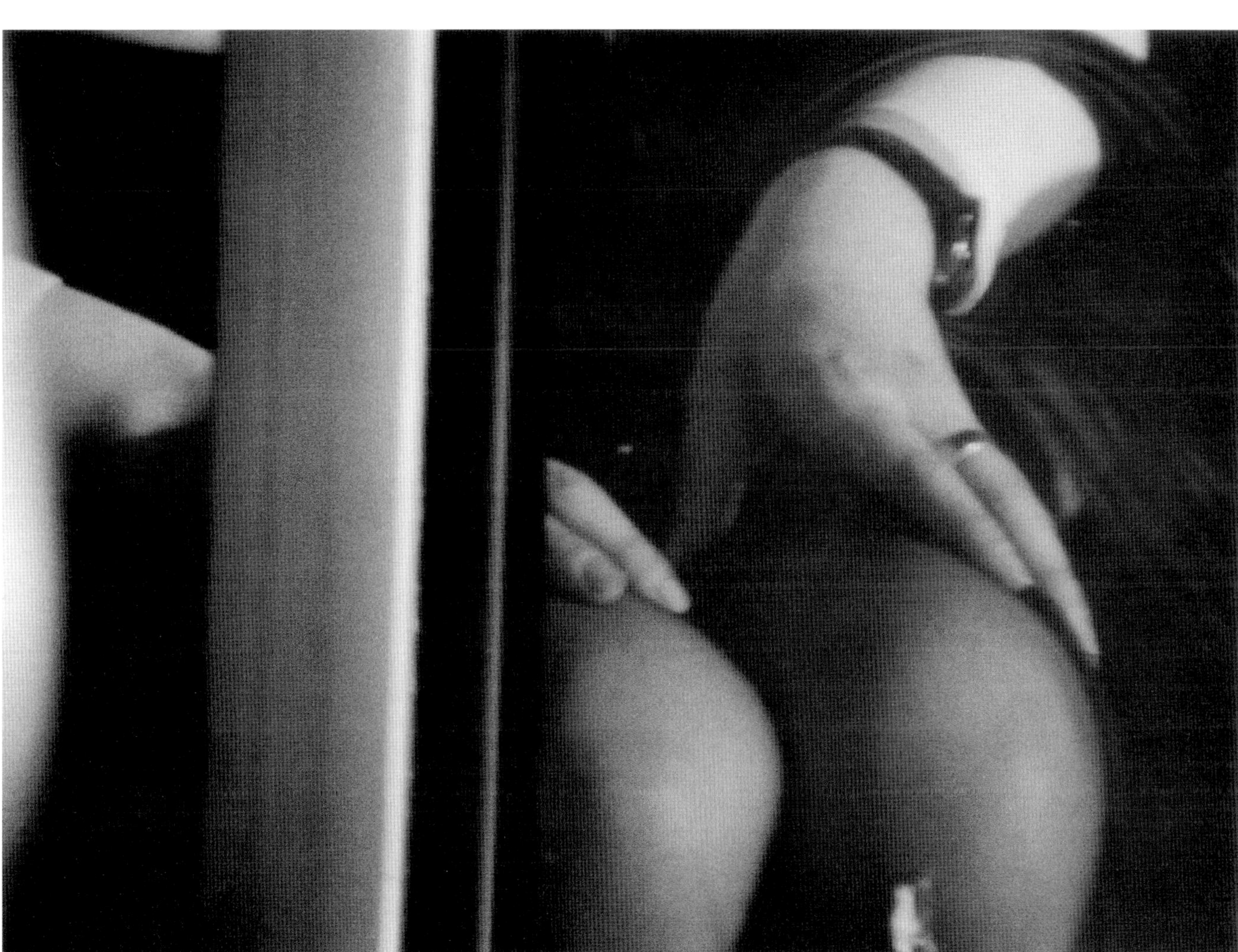

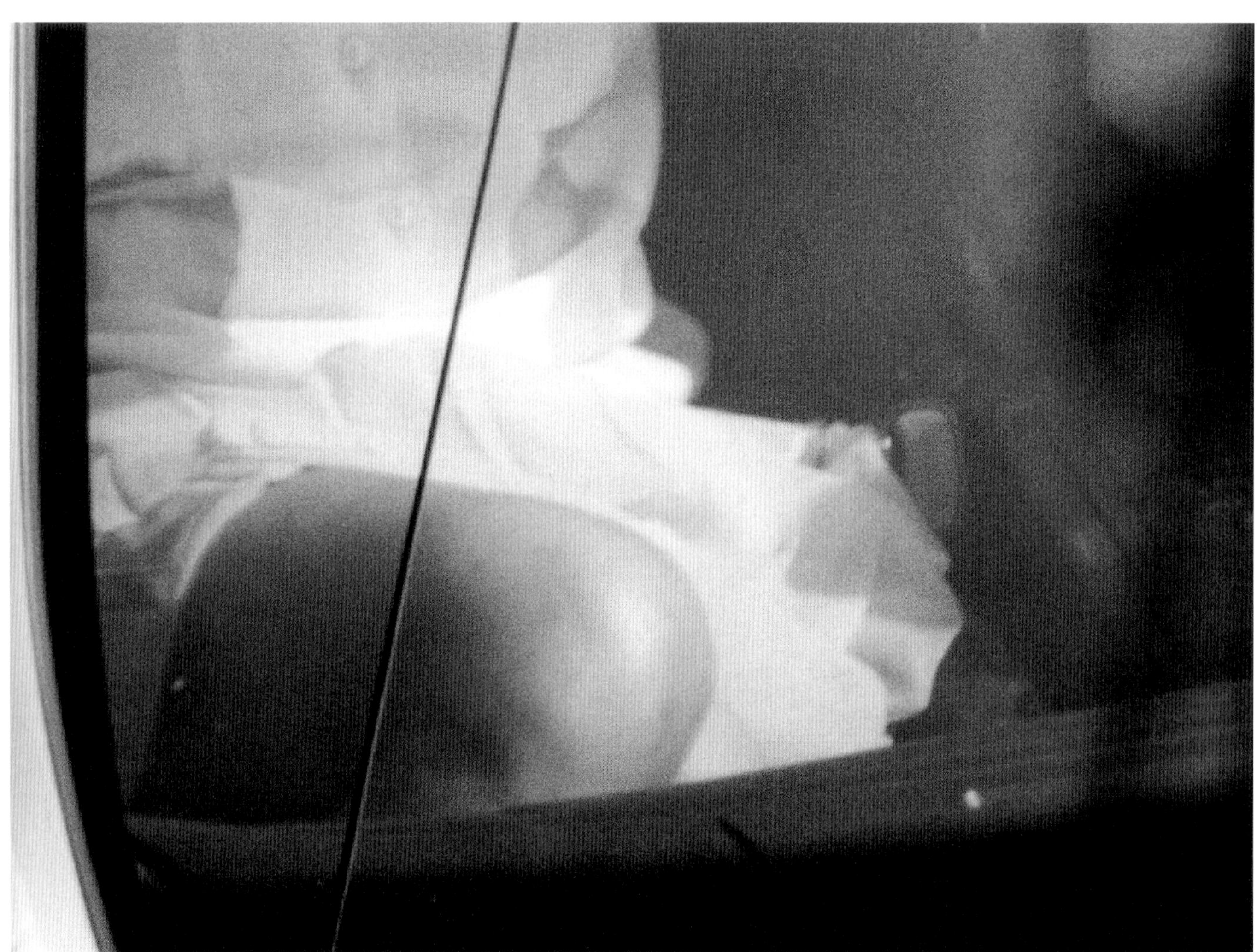

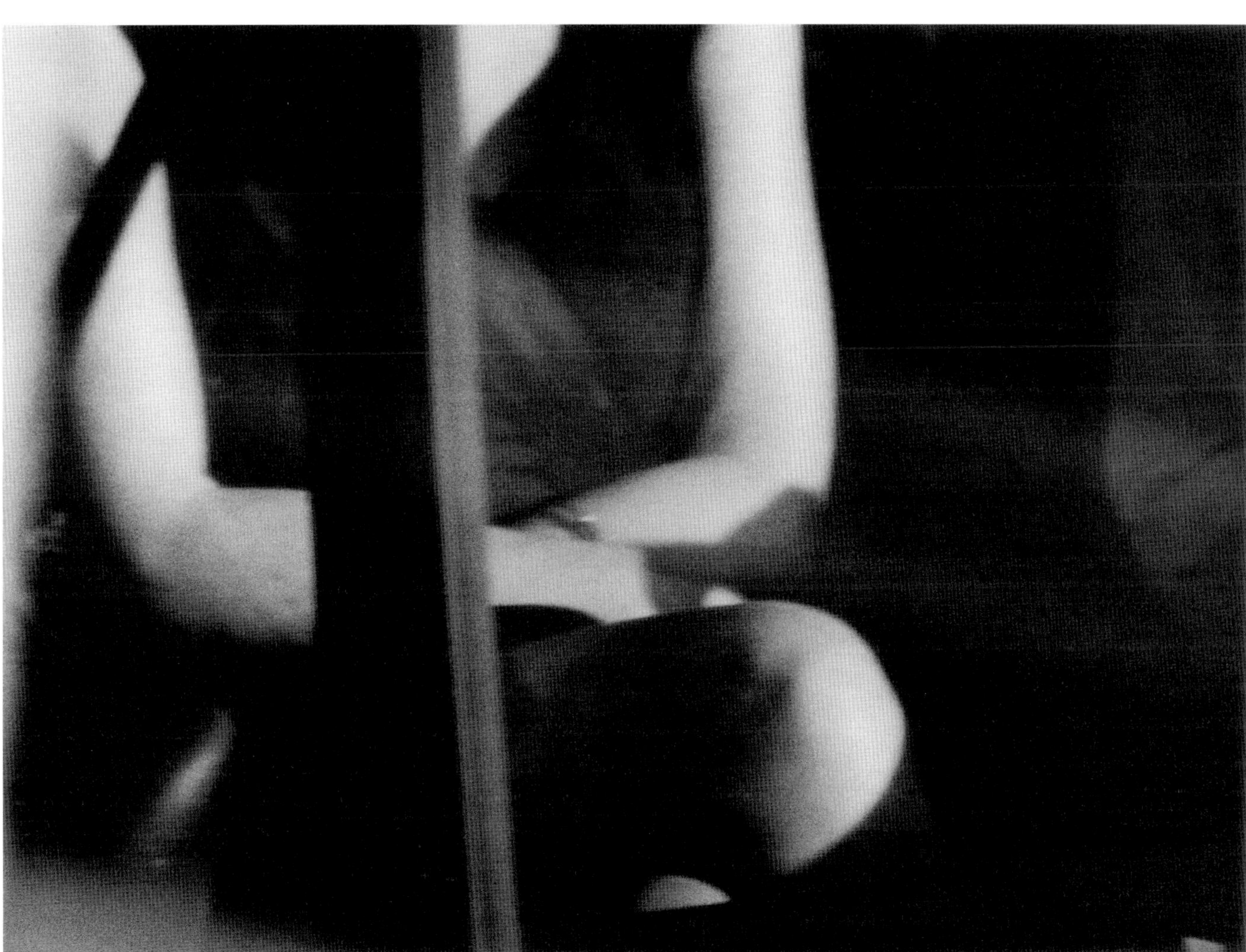

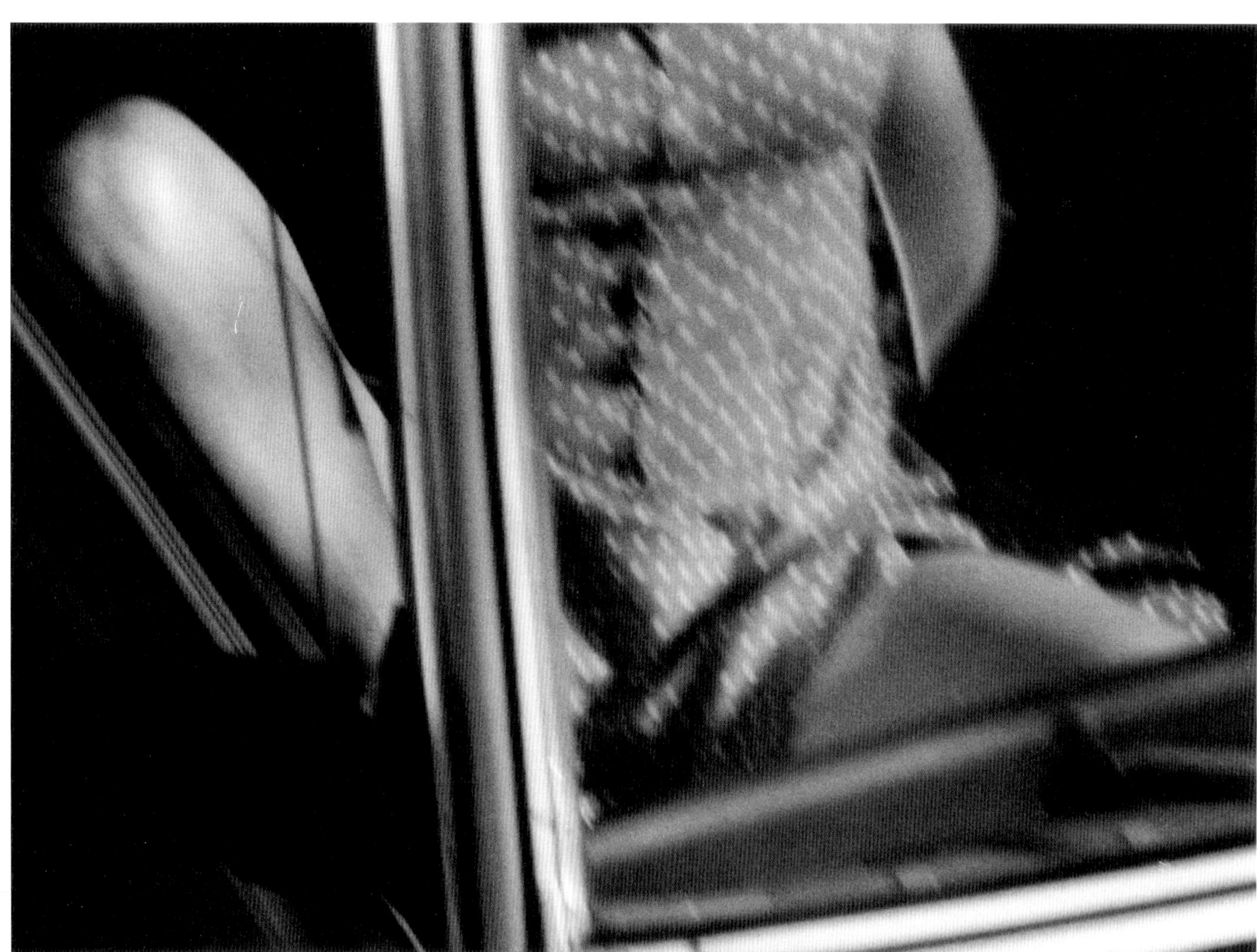

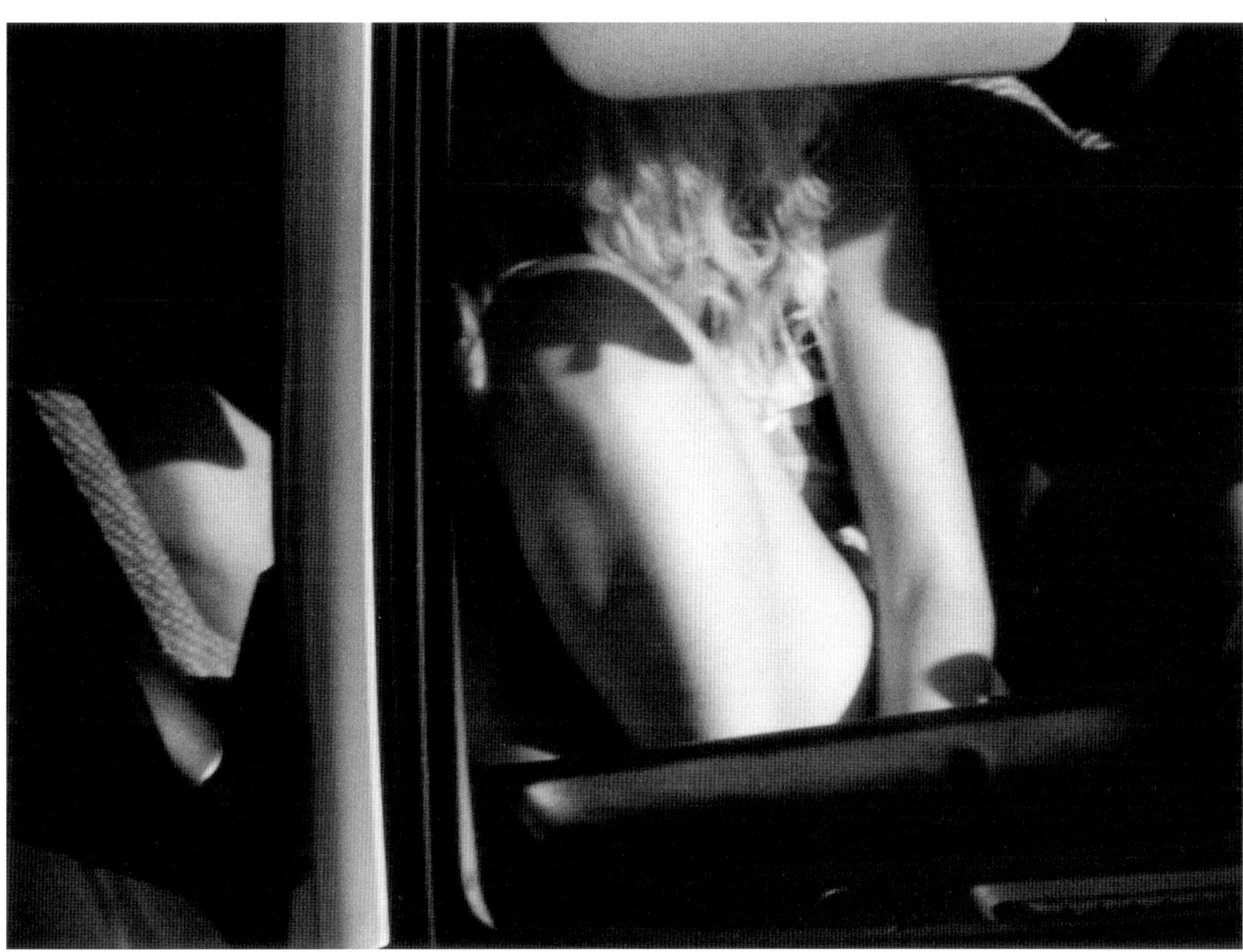

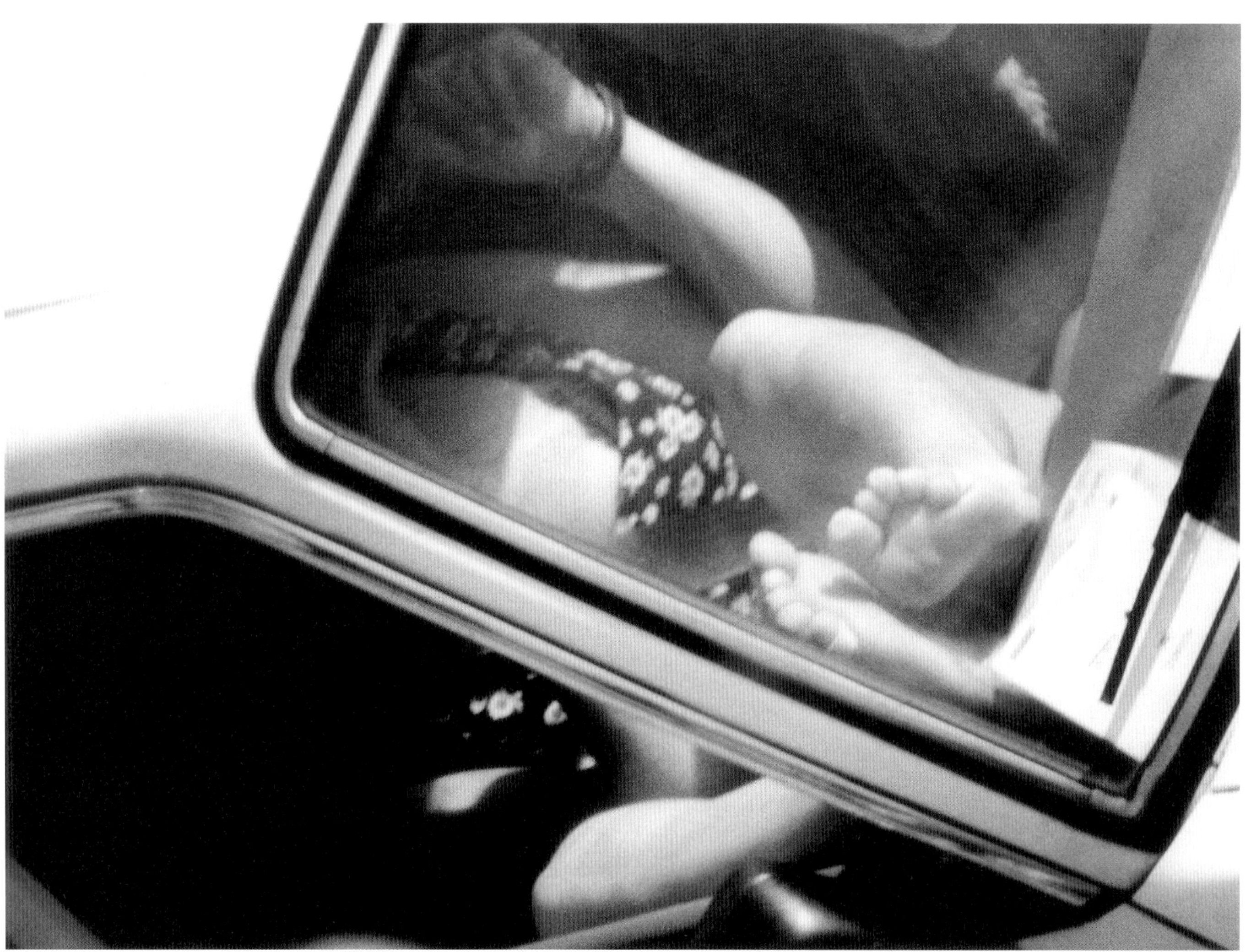

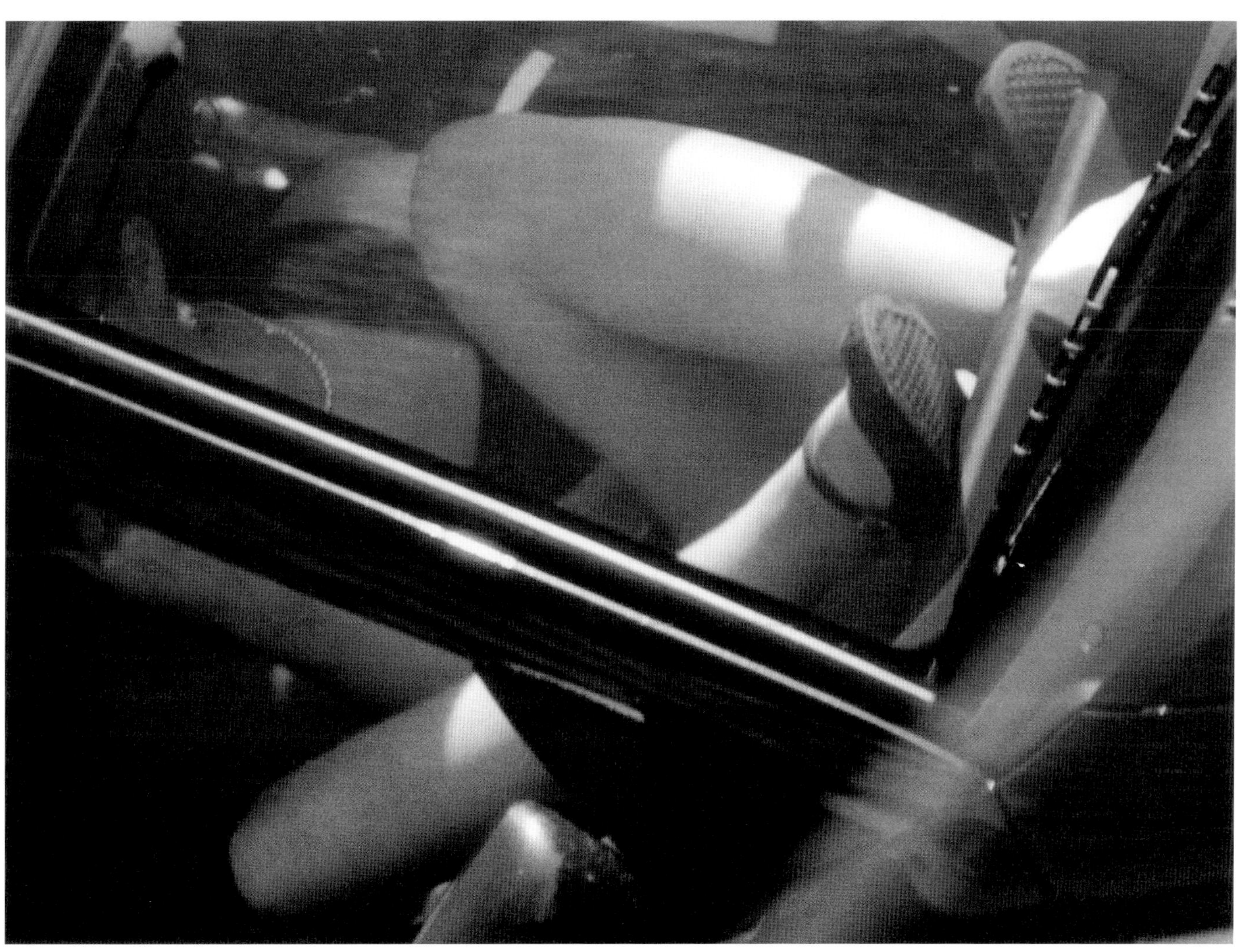

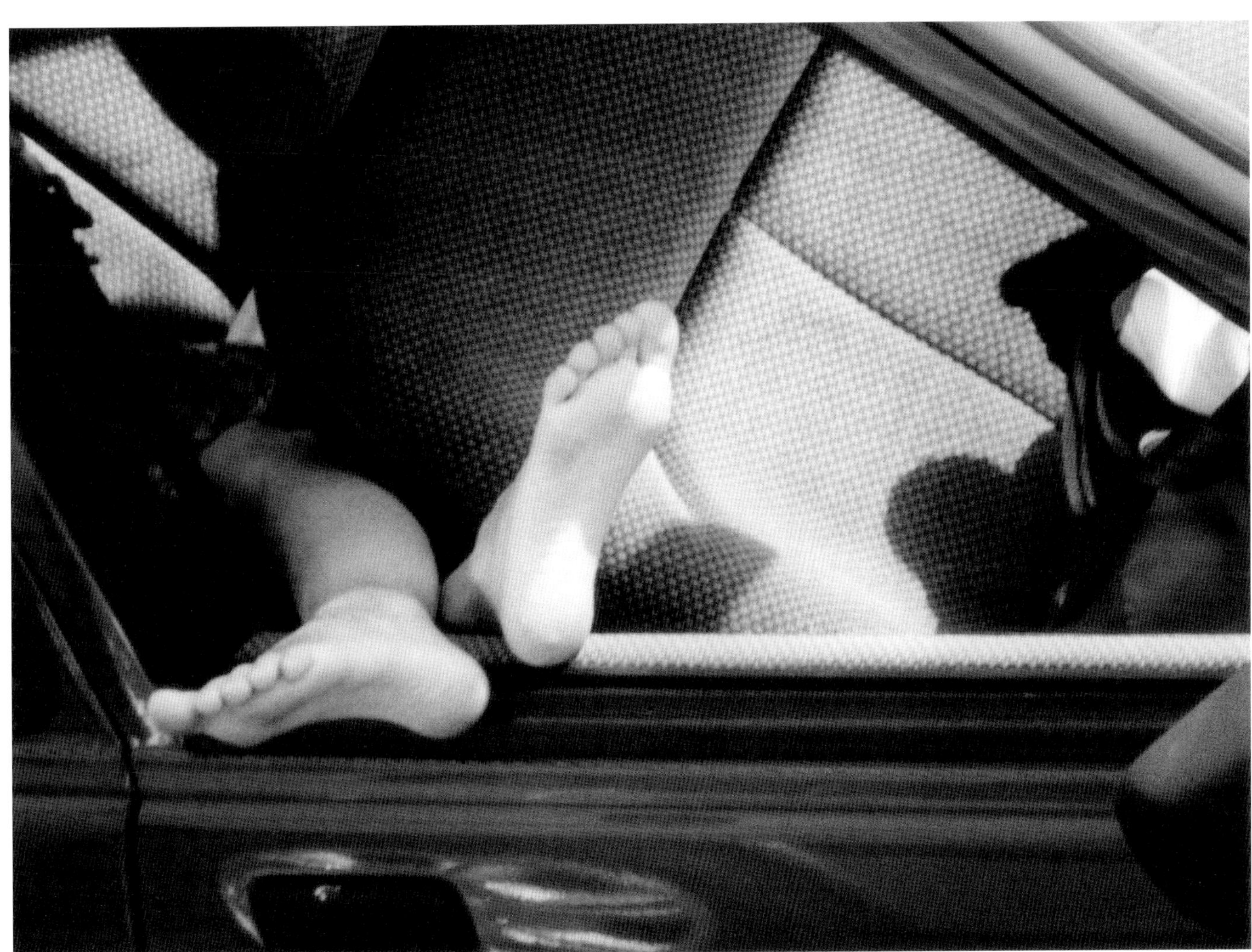

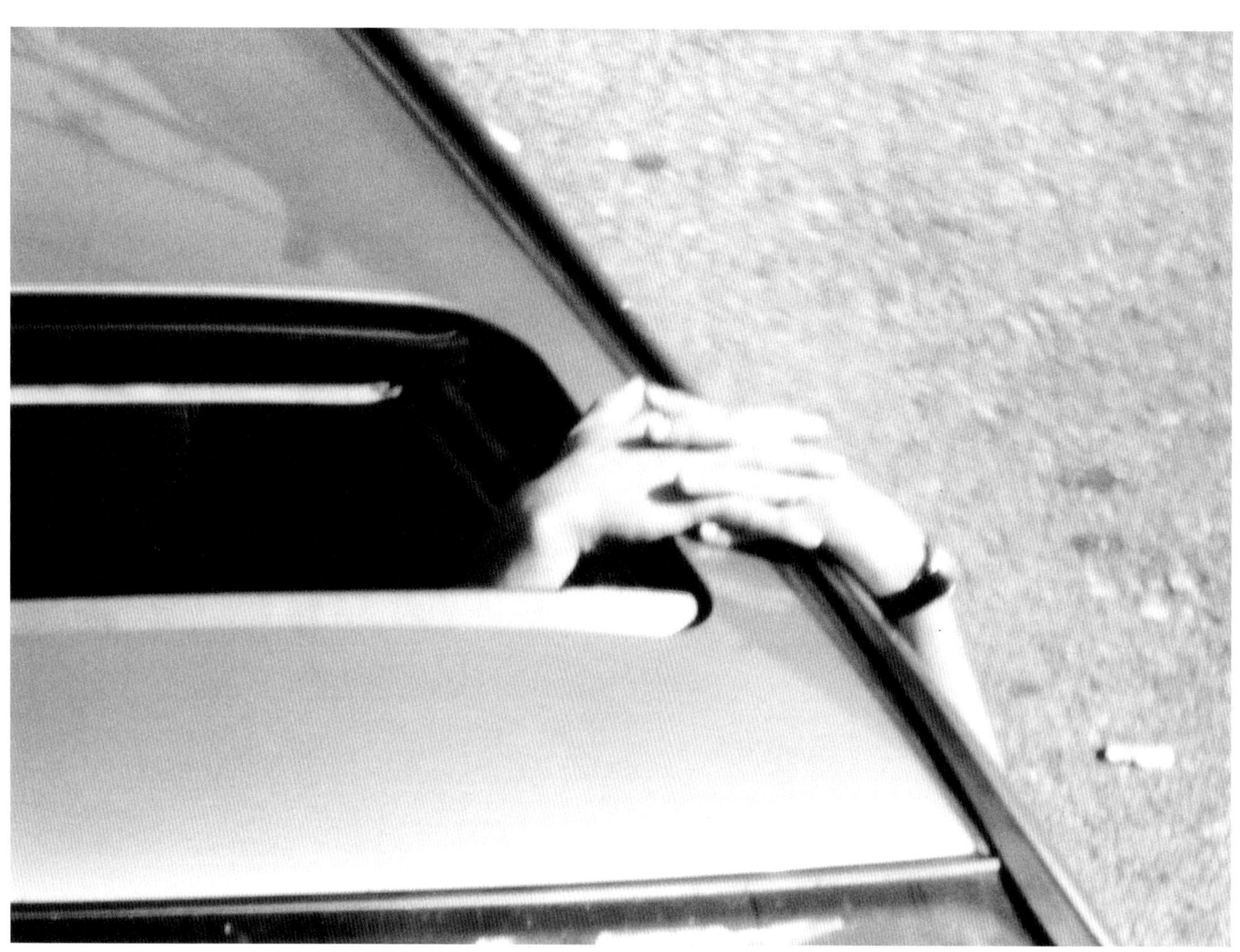

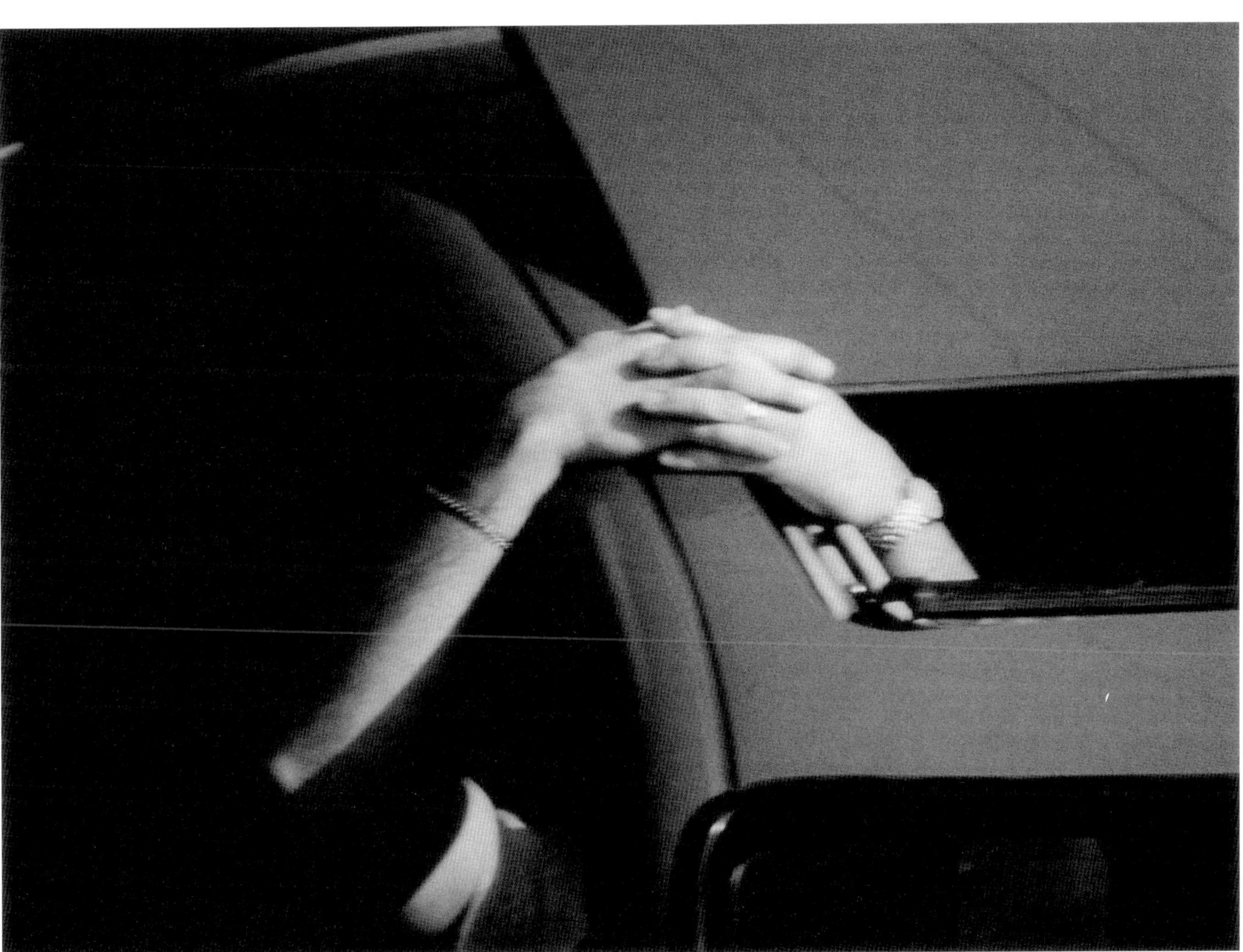

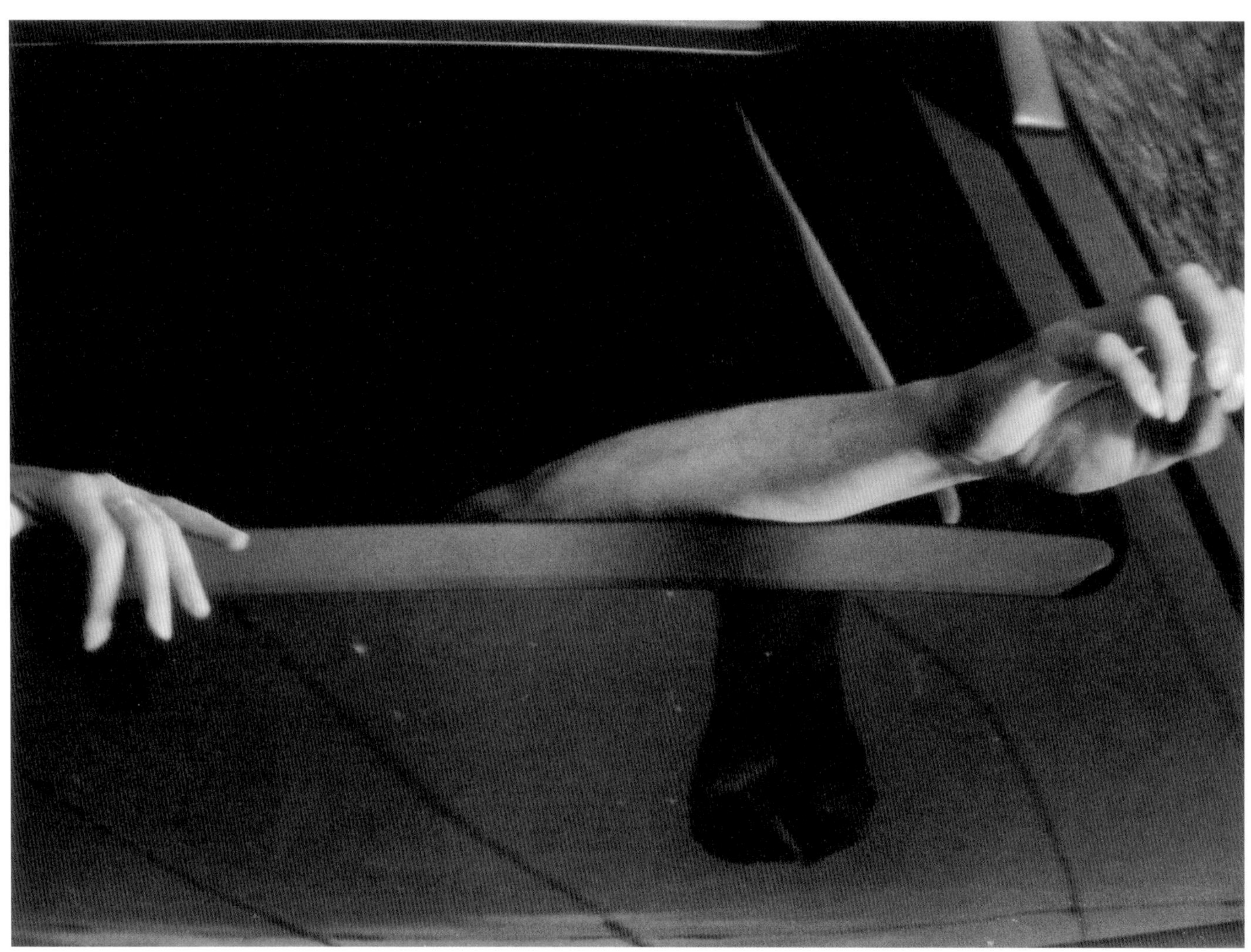

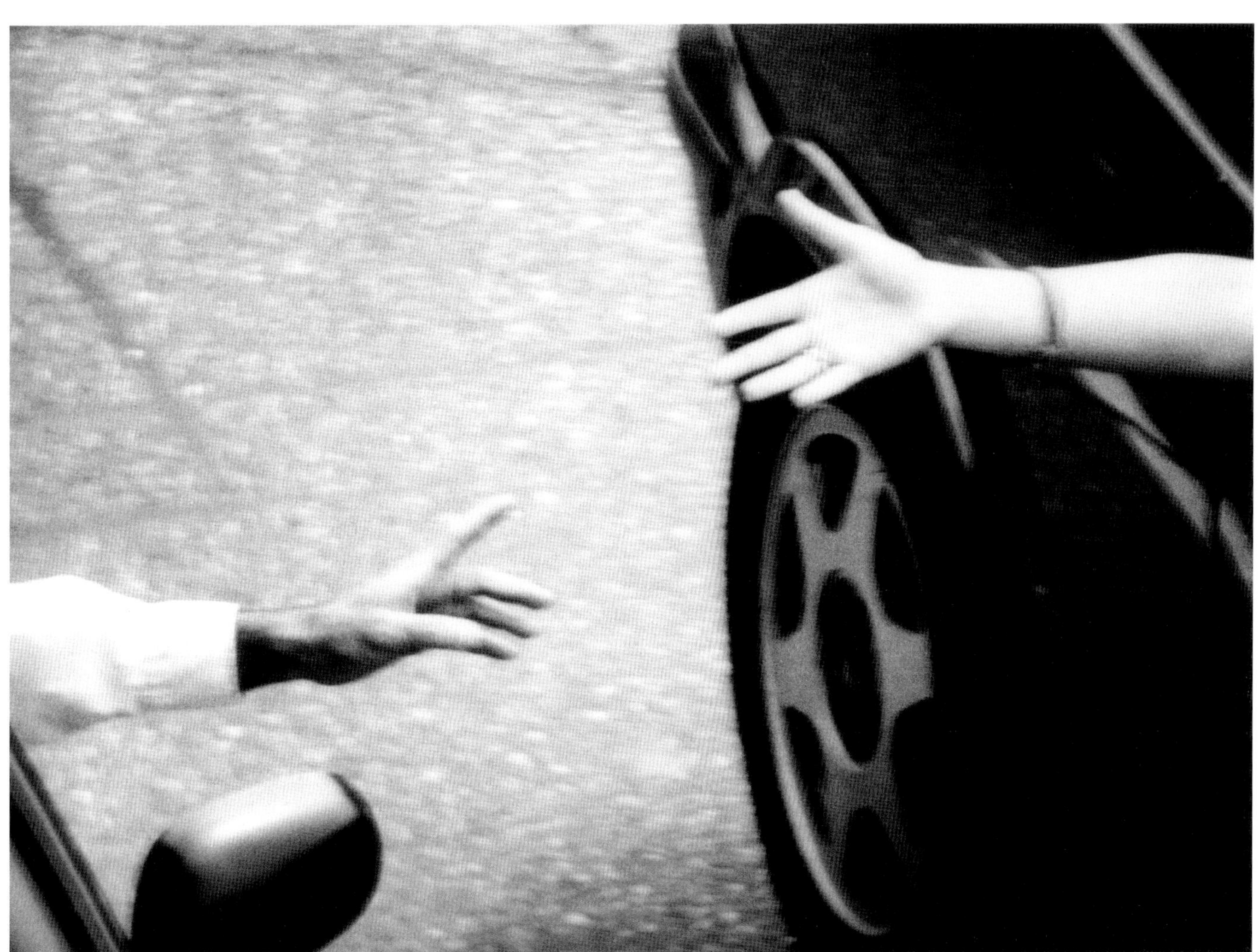

KURT CAVIEZEL RED LIGHT

DESIGN: Hanna Koller, Zürich
SCANS: Gert Schwab/Steidl, Schwab Scantechnik GbR, Göttingen
GESAMTHERSTELLUNG: Steidl, Göttingen

EDITION PATRICK FREY
c/o Scalo Zurich-Berlin-New York
Head Office: Weinbergstrasse 22a
CH-8001 Zürich
Tel. +41 1 261 09 10, Fax +41 1 261 92 62

© 1999 für die Fotos: KURT CAVIEZEL
© 1999 für diese Ausgabe: EDITION PATRICK FREY / KURT CAVIEZEL

Alle Rechte vorbehalten.

ISBN 3-905509-21-0